Learning to Teach Number

A handbook for students and teachers in the primary school

LEN FROBISHER, JOHN MONAGHAN,
ANTHONY ORTON, JEAN ORTON,
TOM ROPER, JOHN THRELFALL

Nelson Thornes

First published in 1999 by:
Stanley Thornes (Publishers) Ltd

Reprinted in 2002 by:
Nelson Thornes Ltd
Delta Place
27 Bath Road
CHELTENHAM
GL53 7TH
United Kingdom

09 10 11 12 / 10 9

A catalogue record for this book is available from the British Library

ISBN 978 0 7487 3515 0

Page make-up by Northern Phototypesetting Co. Ltd

Printed in China

Contents

Acknowledgements

This book is the outcome of many years of working with children, teachers and students. The creativeness, enterprise and originality of children in their individual ways of thinking and working mathematically never ceases to surprise, and it is to them that we owe our most grateful thanks: it is children who have taught us so much, and revealed how little we know.

To the many primary teachers from all over the world with whom we have worked, we offer our appreciation. The book would not have been possible without the encouragement, patience, goodwill and constructive comments of so many teachers.

Students embarking on a career in primary teaching face a daunting yet challenging task. We hope that we have in some small way been able to communicate to our many students our pleasure in the delights of mathematics and that they are now imparting enthusiasm for the learning of mathematics to every child they teach. The teaching of mathematics to young children is a most rewarding adventure, particularly to those students who found the subject difficult when they were at school. May your teaching of mathematics for ever prosper.

A final thanks is due to our families who have noted our eccentricities with patience and forbearance, and provided the encouragement and reassurance that the effort of being authors has its own reward.

About the book

Who is the book for?

This book is aimed at all those who are involved in many different ways in raising standards of attainment and improving the quality of teaching and learning of number in the primary years. These include:

- students who are preparing to teach in primary schools, whether on first degree courses or postgraduate studies
- lecturers who are involved in the preparation of future primary teachers
- advisory and support teachers in local primary centres and advisers who organise valuable in-service work with teachers
- schools and their teachers who wish to evaluate their practice of teaching mathematics, or are looking to rewrite their syllabus
- those who are constantly inspecting schools to monitor standards
- teachers who are working towards a further qualification.

How is the book organised?

The book is organised as independent modules. Module 1 explores early number ideas. It differs in style and content from the subsequent 20 modules as it reviews the number experience of the pre-school child in a variety of settings, and provides the reader with information about the informal knowledge children may have when they enter their first year of formal schooling.

The remaining modules are grouped into three major sections, each with an introductory module giving an overview of the major issues to come:

- Modules 2–10 look at the teaching of number concepts and number systems
- Modules 11–15 consider issues in teaching the four number operations
- Modules 16–21 examine the developing area of pre-algebra.

Structure of the modules

The modules, apart from Module 1, have the following structure:

- Introduction
- National curricula and the number topic
- Key terms
- Key issues in the number topic
- Children and the number topic
- Some ideas for teaching the number topic

- Test your own knowledge
- Review of key issues

How should the book be used?

There are a variety of ways of using the book depending on who you are and your particular objectives.

Students on Initial Teacher Training (ITT) courses

For such students the book can be used as a course book:

- supporting lectures, which, because of time constraints, cannot cover every number topic to the depth necessary
- providing background knowledge and direction for writing course essays
- discussing the essential knowledge of number that all primary teachers should have and issues associated with children learning number, both of which contribute to making lesson planning easier and better informed
- using the 'test your own knowledge' sections to audit your own knowledge, skills and understanding.

Lecturers on ITT primary mathematics courses

Because of the independent nature of the modules it is possible for lecturers to:

- organise their course using the same structure as the book, in which case the book can act as a course textbook
- select modules for the basis of lectures
- recommend modules, or parts of modules, as reading for follow-up work
- use sections of the modules to audit students' knowledge, skills and understanding of teaching and learning, and the 'Test your own knowledge' sections to assess students' mathematical knowledge and understanding.

Advisory and support teachers, and advisers who organise and run in-service courses

In-service courses on the teaching of number or numeracy can be structured around any module or modules. There are reflection points in each module which are appropriate for teachers on such courses to discuss:

- the connection between different aspects of number as illustrated in the issues maps
- common experiences in teaching the topic
- errors and misconceptions their children have
- the relevance of the suggested teaching activities
- the level of their own number knowledge.

Schools and teachers

Although the book can be used as a reference for teachers when teaching a number topic it has more relevance when used by groups of teachers in a school wishing to improve their own knowledge and understanding of the teaching of number. School in-service sessions could:

- be centred around a module or part of a module considering some particular issue in number – such as how the school textbook series matches up to, or is informed by, what is described in the module
- consider the nature of progression in any number topic using the book as a starting point for discussions
- use the whole book to help develop a new school syllabus, programme of study or schemes of work.

Local and national inspectors

Both local and national inspectors of primary mathematics will find this book informative in the way that it brings together mathematical knowledge, the major issues in teaching primary mathematics and the problems children encounter when learning the subject.

Teachers studying for a further qualification

Each module provides direction for those studying for further qualifications which include aspects of primary mathematics, and will be a useful companion to other books with a complementary approach.

Introduction

No book is able to adequately cover every aspect of the complex task of teaching number in primary schools. *Learning to teach Number* concentrates on the teaching of those areas of number that are common to most national curricula.

Teachers need to be conscious that there are many more issues to teaching number than the content of a curriculum – for example, attracting and retaining children's interest in, and developing their excitement and passion for, number. We discuss some of these issues briefly here, and relate them, where appropriate, to particular modules.

What is mathematics?

What do you think mathematics is? How may your views of mathematics influence your teaching? Share your views with colleagues.

The Scottish Guidelines (SOED, 1991) claim that mathematics can be seen as:

- a body of collected knowledge and procedures for working with patterns and relationships in number and space
- a powerful, concise and unambiguous way of organising, manipulating and communicating information
- a means by which aspects of the physical and social world can be explained and predicted
- an activity involving processes such as discovering, discussing, ordering, classifying, generalising, drawing and measuring
- a source of challenge, satisfaction and pleasure.

You will find that not everyone would agree with this description. Although it is not possible to provide an agreed definition of what mathematics is, a distinction can be made between mathematics and school mathematics, the latter often being a distorted version of the former.

The listing of primary curricula content is frequently an incomplete description of what mathematics is, as the subject is also about a way of thinking and reasoning, involving pattern and structure which cannot be communicated in a contents list. It is also a collection of structured systems, which children encounter for the first time when they extend the whole number system to other systems such as rational numbers (see Module 2). Unfortunately, curricula tend to emphasise the utilitarian aspect of mathematics to the detriment of its aesthetic appeal and its logical method. A balanced primary curriculum in number is essential if children are to value its beauty, elegance and usefulness.

To think about

In what ways have recent lessons you have taught reflected one or more of these aspects of mathematics?

To do

Ask a class of children to write about what they think mathematics is.

What number should children learn and teachers teach?

The National Numeracy Strategy (1999) in its framework curriculum lists three strands which relate directly to number, with use and application of mathematics incorporated into each strand.

- Numbers and the number system
- Calculations
- Solving problems.

The structure of this book follows closely this categorisation and extends it by looking at the teaching of ideas in pre-algebra, thus covering those parts of the teaching of number that appear in most national primary mathematics curricula.

Children learning number

Learning is a social process. It is a sharing of experiences and knowledge; teachers interact with children and children with each other. There are many theories of how children learn number concepts, of knowledge, of skills and of the ability to apply them in problem situations, each having something to offer teachers in their efforts to make learning number enjoyable, challenging and satisfying. The major impediment confronting teachers, particularly those in early years, is bridging the gap that exists between children's learning of number in social contexts and the formality of number in the classroom (see Module 1).

Thinking and reasoning with number

A major aim of a primary mathematics curriculum should be to develop children's thinking and reasoning skills. When children practise known procedures in word problems little thinking is demanded of them. However, realistic problems, to which children are able to relate, cannot be solved without them reasoning about the relationships between:

- the context of the situation and its meaning
- the numbers in the situation
- the choice of operation
- the knowledge and skills which they can have available to find the answer.

Many children find realistic problems more challenging, meaningful, satisfying and rewarding than repeating what teacher has shown them how to do.

Children, whilst holding particular views, conjectures and uncertain conclusions about how to solve problems and the solutions, have common experiences to discuss. Encouraging children to discuss and justify their thinking, strategies and methods results in a depth of learning and an expansion of thinking and reasoning skills which cannot be achieved when children are merely passive listeners. This is an important message for teachers.

Being creative with number

Described in the book are examples of children's creative thinking,

To think about

In what ways have you recently encouraged children to share their experiences and knowledge of mathematics?

To think about

When you were a learner in primary and secondary school, how often did you have the opportunity to be creative in mathematics? Describe your experiences to colleagues.

particularly children's explanations of how they performed mental and written calculations. Given the opportunity and a suitable classroom environment, primary children readily display their creativity. Mathematics is a subject which provides untold opportunities for children to be creative and in doing so to enlarge their knowledge of number, its systems and structures, and to use such knowledge in appropriate situations. Creativity should be encouraged and fostered at all levels and ages in the primary school by teachers providing number activities and challenges that promote intuitive and imaginative reasoning, and actions. Children's learning in such activities can take place in leaps, with new relationships becoming established between apparently unrelated ideas, and new procedures developing without direct teaching. Reasoned guessing, intuition, inductive thinking and conjecturing are all processes which support creative thinking.

Understanding number

The claim that 'I teach mathematics for understanding' is a commonly heard phrase used by teachers. What is your 'understanding' of numbers (see Module 2)? The word 'understanding' is also used frequently in national mathematics curricula without clarification of its meaning. Understanding is an ever-changing state of knowledge in mathematics, growing and unfolding as new experiences require children to evaluate their existing concepts and knowledge in the light of new evidence. When designing learning activities, teachers should be conscious of children's level and nature of understanding, and how they wish to deepen or extend it. The purpose of number activities and tasks is to enable children to overcome any cognitive barriers, thus moving to a higher level of understanding.

Skemp (1976) describes two types of understanding in mathematics: instrumental and relational. Children who know how to 'carry' when adding multi-digit numbers, but do not know why or what the carry is for, have *instrumental* understanding. Within its limitations instrumental understanding is initially relatively easy to learn and the extrinsic reward, a tick, readily achieved. Later, as more and more has to be learnt, such understanding becomes increasingly difficult. Children who know that the carry when adding is the outcome of grouping the previous units into tens have *relational* understanding.

To do

Read more about Skemp's ideas of instrumental and relational understanding. Discuss your views with colleagues.

Some mathematics educators advocate that children are taught for instrumental understanding, claiming that at a future date they will, in an unspecified way, develop relational understanding. Others refute this hopeful and optimistic view, arguing that from the very beginning children should be taught to understand relationally and helped to make connections with other ideas in mathematics. This assumes, of course, that such an approach is possible. Skemp claims that instrumental understanding is more easily adapted and transferred to new tasks and problems. It may be that the type of understanding for which a teacher aims in an activity should be determined by the content to be taught and the children's level of understanding.

Children's attitudes

Larcombe (1985) claimed that 'the most significant thing brought to the mathematics lesson by a pupil is a set of feelings and attitudes towards mathematics.' A positive attitude towards mathematics, and its teaching and learning, is the most important aspect of a primary mathematics classroom where attitudes with respect to number are formed, particularly when children's informal pre-school ideas about number are challenged by a more formal classroom approach.

Attitudes are made up of three components:

- the *cognitive or belief component*, where children associate good or bad feelings to the subject, in our case number
- the *affective* or *feeling component*, resulting from emotions and feelings of pleasure, satisfaction, fear, hate, dislike and apprehension when working on a number activity
- the *action* or *behavioural tendency component*, when children exhibit their feelings and emotions when faced with number tasks.

What are your feelings about mathematics? Did you ever show your feelings openly in a mathematics classroom, or did you keep them hidden, fearful that you were the only one who had such feelings? What implications have your own feelings for your teaching of mathematics?

There is little doubt that children who are allowed to develop negative attitudes to mathematics, for whatever reasons, are a constant worry for teachers. They are also unlikely to attain highly. What do you think are possible reasons for children in the primary school developing negative attitudes to mathematics?

To do

Discuss with colleagues your feelings towards mathematics and experiences which have contributed to their development.

Teachers teaching number

Teachers are the most important resource in a classroom, and children who learn mathematics do so mainly as a result of good teaching by effective teachers. Unfortunately, more is known about how children learn mathematics than about the 'best' method of teaching it. This seems strange as one would expect the teaching of a topic – for example, addition facts – to be based upon knowledge of how children learn addition facts and, consequently, effective ways of teaching such facts to develop accordingly. This deficiency in our knowledge is due in no small measure to the amount of research that has been conducted into how children learn mathematics, with little time being devoted to finding how teachers should teach. This book provides a balance between discussing important issues in learning primary mathematics, such as children's errors and misconceptions, and their implications for teaching.

Effective teachers

Effective teachers of number are those who teach in such a way that every child in their class succeeds to the fullest potential and develops positive attitudes for future learning. Such teachers promote both instrumental and relational understanding of conceptual and procedural knowledge of relationships across different aspects of number. They are also likely to acknowledge that there are many perceptions about the nature of mathematics, ranging from the belief that mathematics is a set of rigid rules which children have to learn to mathematics as a way of thinking. Children who experience only one view of mathematics quickly find learning repetitive and barren. The modules in this book describe key issues and activities, covering a number of different ways of viewing mathematics.

Traditional teaching of number consists mainly of teachers demonstrating a procedure and supporting it with explanations while children listen passively, then practise the procedure. Although there are children who respond positively to this approach, it has not been effective with large numbers of children, as you may testify from your own experience as learners.

In contrast, Askew *et al.* (1997) describe effective teachers, who they refer to as 'connectionists', as ones who emphasise children and teachers:

- valuing each other's methods and explanations
- sharing their strategies for doing mathematics
- discussing and demonstrating relationships between different aspects of mathematics.

Clemson and Clemson (1994) provide descriptions of four teaching strategies which are prevalent in primary schools:

- *Individual monitors*, who set work individually, monitor such work, and have a high rate of interaction with individual children
- *Class enquirers*, who use class teaching and questioning and feedback, and who consciously manage the learning which is taking place throughout a lesson
- *Group instructors*, who group children and deliver facts and open questions with little individual attention
- *Style changers*, who use a mix of the above three styles.

Galton and Simon (1980), in their research into the four teaching strategies, found that the greatest gains in a basic mathematics skills test were achieved by children in the 'class enquirers' classes.

Planning to teach

When planning lessons, teachers should have knowledge of the errors that children are likely to make and the possible misconceptions that can develop. Consequently they should target:

- ways children are likely to best understand and make sense of the conceptual or procedural knowledge in the content to be taught
- ways in which children will be able to use their own thinking and reasoning powers
- children's ability to apply their knowledge in solving realistic problems.

In order to teach number effectively, whatever style is considered appropriate and however well planned lessons are, teachers must have a depth of subject knowledge about:

- number concepts and number systems
- the four number operations

To think about

Reflect on your own primary and secondary teachers. Which of the four teaching strategies did they employ? Which strategy did you respond positively or negatively to?

- algebra as a mathematical system
- problem solving in realistic and in mathematical situations.

Teachers should also have an understanding of a variety of teaching strategies, children's errors and misconceptions, and models and representations of number and the operations used to develop mental and written methods.

Models and representations

Every module of this book contains descriptions, illustrations of models and representations which may be used to enhance children's learning. These take the form of apparatus and diagrams. They are tools to help children 'visualise' number concepts and procedures which would otherwise never be understood by many. Threlfall (1996) provides a thoughtful analysis of the place and role of such material, warning of the dangers of teachers assuming that they teach children mathematics when in effect they only teach children how to use apparatus.

The use of models and representations to teach number has its dangers, as Aubrey (1997) warns: 'What is most likely to occur is that children do not relate their classroom interactions with the associated use of structured materials to their existing out-of-school problem-solving.' When using models and representations teachers should constantly draw children's attention to how they match what children already have experienced.

Using and applying mathematics

Central to any mathematics curriculum must be the development of children's ability to use and apply the knowledge and skills they learn 'in practical tasks, in real-life problems and within mathematics itself' (DFE/Welsh Office, 1995). The Scottish guidelines view mathematics 'in the widest sense as a problem-solving activity' (SOED, 1991).

Although the order of the modules in this book explores number concepts and number systems before considering the four operations with number this in no way implies an order of teaching such ideas. Module 11 discusses different types of problems to which children should be introduced, and how problems may be used by teachers to teach mathematics.

Technology and teaching number

Calculators

The debate about permitting primary children to use calculators when working with number will remain with us for many, many years. Governments' attitudes towards calculators in primary schools vary from country to country and often depend on the political party that is in power. At the very least, children should be taught how to use the different functions on calculators and when it is appropriate to use them. In this book we take the view that calculators have an important place as a means of learning mathematics, not as a tool for replacing the need for children to learn mental and written strategies and methods. However, when very large numbers are involved in number problems or investigations, calculators can be a valuable aid as children are then able to concentrate their attention on relationships rather than on the complex calculations

To think about

What are your views about children in primary schools using calculators? Share your views with colleagues.

they might otherwise have to perform. For a more detailed discussion of the role of calculators in the teaching and learning of primary mathematics the reader is referred to the work of Janet Duffin (1997).

Computers

As primary schools vary in the number of computers available at any one time, where they are situated and how they are used, it is not possible to draw firm conclusions about the 'best' way of using them in the teaching of mathematics.

An increasing number of commercial programs aimed at teaching children different aspects of number is available. These programs are usually presented in appealing contexts with children performing tasks or solving problems. They are mainly aimed at children practising knowledge and skills.

Logo

Logo is a simple programming language suitable for primary children. Early-years children may start by playing with a Roamer, or floor turtle, and become familiar with the type of commands such as 'Forward 10' and 'Left 90'. The Logo philosophy is very much one of children exploring and using the language themselves; the initial vision was of children learning mathematics in 'Mathland', rather like people learn French by living in France. The value of turtle geometry is not confined to shape and space. When children direct the turtle (and on the screen this is usually represented by a small arrowhead) they are indeed forced to consider distance, direction and shape but they will also be engaged in estimation of the number of units and will be experimenting with different numbers. They are likely to need to count in fives or tens, and to use large numbers.

Spreadsheets

A spreadsheet is a grid made up of rows and columns where each cell or box can be labelled according to its column and row position. Information can be typed into the cells in the form of numbers, labels or formulae.

A spreadsheet would be very useful, for example, for entering information about the sales made at the school shop or imaginary sales made at the class 'shop'. The goods sold can be written in one column, the number of items sold in the next, and the price in the third column. A simple formula in the fourth column would allow the calculation of sales. Totals and averages are easy to find and a variety of graphs are available for displaying data in a visual and attractive way. A spreadsheet makes calculation and display easy and is ideal for a meaningful investigation such as 'What size of packet gives the best value for money?' or 'What is the price per slice of bread for various different brands?' Spreadsheets also provide powerful environments for the exploration of number patterns (see Module 16).

Classroom environment

Primary mathematics classrooms contain a collection of learners that a teacher should aim to mould into a community of mathematical thinkers in which each child is valued and feels able to share with others their thoughts, suggestions, reasoning, views, opinions, conjectures, predictions and generalisations while accepting that they may or may not agree.

Teachers assessing children

Assessment, teaching and learning are three interrelated and inseparably linked parts of the same whole in that they have the same goal – that of contributing in their own particular way to children reaching their full mathematical potential. Successful teaching is based upon knowing what children already know and can do, what learning difficulties they have and what learning activities should be constructed to take them to their next level of understanding. The cycle then repeats itself. Assessment aims to evaluate children's learning and their difficulties, thereby monitoring teaching outcomes and, necessarily, teaching methods. The danger with all assessment in mathematics is that it focuses on that which is easy to assess, namely knowledge and skills, such as multiplication facts. Teachers should ensure that their assessment of number, whatever form it takes, also covers the more difficult conceptual and procedural areas of learning, such as thinking, reasoning, creativity, guessing, conjecturing, generalising and other investigative processes and skills.

Many of the activities described in the book can provide summative and diagnostic assessment of children. When assessing children working with activities teachers should be clear what they are looking to assess, but should also be prepared for opportunities to assess that which arises incidentally and unexpectedly. The importance of assessing children cannot be over-emphasised, particularly diagnostic assessment, which aims to find out not only errors that children make and misconceptions they develop but also the reasons for them.

Module 1

Learning to teach early number

Contributed by Sally Threlfall

Introduction

When children attending full-time school for the first time encounter the formal knowledge and skills of number, it is inevitable that they will draw on the foundations established in pre-school settings. The better these foundations, the smoother and faster is the growth of their number work. Early number experiences at home and in pre-school education are vital to what can be achieved in primary schools. This module explains what pre-school number experiences should be like and what forms of knowledge develop as a result.

Curricula and early number

Guidelines have been published in England and Wales (SCAA, 1996) concerning the 'desirable outcomes' of pre-school work. The number-related aspects are as follows.

- They 'use mathematical language, such as ... more to describe ... quantity'.
- They are familiar 'with number rhymes, songs, stories, counting games and activities'.
- They 'order, sequence and count using everyday objects'.
- They 'recognise and use numbers to ten and are familiar with larger numbers from their everyday lives'.
- 'Through practical activities children understand and record numbers, begin to show awareness of number operations, such as addition and subtraction, and begin to use the language involved.'

Key terms

cardinality	the 'how many' aspect of whole numbers; used for the quantity of discrete items, the 'numerosity', in a collection
quantity	a general term that includes cardinality ('How many?'), but also measures contexts ('How much?') in which numbers are related to some quality of a single object
invariance or **conservation of number**	the unchanging quantity aspect of a collection or set under transformations such as 'counting in a different order' and 'changing position of objects'
ordinality	the 'positional' aspect of whole number
comparing quantities	the significance of bigger and smaller numbers as representing more and less quantity
numeral	the way in which a number is represented symbolically
order and sequence	the way in which all numbers can be put in order, or sequenced in the number string called counting
counting	recitation of the whole number sequence and its use to determine and compare quantities.

Key issues in early number

Related concepts and issues

The elements of early number work and their interrelationships are shown in Figure 1.1. However, this should be understood differently from the concept and issues maps in other modules in the book, where there is likely to be a notion of a hierarchy of ideas, with some ideas forming building blocks for others. In the context of largely informal understandings, the links in this map are potential areas for connections to be made and understandings to be developed. Knowledge of early number is not so much of identifiable concepts, ideas or actions, but is more the building of loosely characterised connections, extensions and associations. This map shows the range of the domain and some of the areas for development. It does not characterise a child's thinking so much as the adult's teaching.

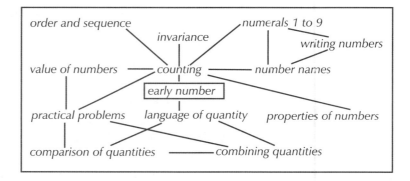

1.1 Concepts and issues associated with early number

The content of pre-school number curricula

The characteristics of experiences with number within the pre-school setting are fundamentally different to the kinds of teaching and learning which are described in Modules 2–21. There are differences

- in ambition, with a dominance in the early years setting of informal aims over formal targets
- in interpretation of children's behaviour, with knowledge in the early years characterised without an expectation of reliable performance on specific tasks and
- in the nature of the activities, with freely chosen activities having equal emphasis with teacher-designed activities, and with very little 'practice' in pre-set tasks.

The desirable outcomes listed earlier represent a reasonable summary of some of the expected characteristics of the average child as he or she reaches statutory school age, and it is indeed desirable that children can do these things before entering compulsory education. However, the listing of specific talents contains the risk that the desirable outcomes may be followed over-literally to determine the provision that is made in the setting, narrowing the focus in the teaching of number-related work for young children. Pre-school children's knowledge and understanding of number is broader and richer than this, and in some cases more advanced.

The actual words of the desirable outcomes are not limiting, as their language does permit a broad and appropriate interpretation, characterisation and categorisation. The SCAA themselves have exemplified this in their supporting documentation (SCAA, 1997). However, if the teaching staff in an early years setting lack confidence in, or knowledge and understanding of, number for the young learner, they may interpret the desirable outcomes more narrowly than intended.

An example of a narrow interpretation of curriculum objectives is one that sees the statements as listing specific learning which is to be manifested in reliable performance (which may be called 'an ability to ...'). The teaching which is designed to lead towards the listed behaviours may then also be specific and focused, oriented to particular skills and knowledge. This is formal teaching towards formal learning, and is a common approach to teaching towards curriculum targets for older children. However, the larger part of number-related teaching in the pre-school setting is necessarily and properly informal in nature. It attempts to develop children's learning in the various aspects of number through interaction that is not just about the specific things that are to be learned. The learning is in a sense incidental to the apparent focus of the conversation. In talking to the teacher about their construction with blocks, for example, children may be learning a great deal about relative size and equivalence. This may have been carefully planned by the teacher, but from the child's point of view they are just talking about their 'garage'.

An experience-led curriculum

Pre-school children are entitled to a curriculum that recognises their nature and meets their needs. This is not achieved by a diet of teacher-set tasks targeted on the items specified in lists of curricula for the under fives. What may be an appropriate activity to do with older children does not become appropriate for younger children just by making the numbers smaller and the mathematics 'easier'. However, this is not an obvious truth. It is possible to approach number work with younger children in a similar way to working with older children, but doing so will under-exploit the potential for learning which the young child brings to any activity, and can result in under-achievement.

In number work young learners most need an experience-led curriculum to build the informal knowledge that will enable formal knowledge to develop later. They must be given the opportunity to 'do

To do

Arrange visits to a pre-school playgroup, a private nursery and a primary school-based nursery. How does each implement the desirable outcomes listed on page 1?

lots and talk about it'. Later knowledge and understanding needs to be well rooted in early play and exploration. Arising from this, there is clearly an issue of identifying and valuing the informal knowledge that each child has, and using this as evidence to inform planning for the child and the number curriculum programme.

The early number curriculum should target specific performance only rarely. It should instead seek to extend and enlarge children's knowledge in a non-specific way by building on the children's previous experiences and perceptions, providing new experiences, and making the essential connections between them. There are three dimensions to this process:

- What are the domains of number knowledge with which the early years curriculum is concerned?
- What are the contexts of experience? What is provided for the children to do? What are the activities?
- How does the teacher teach? What can be said and done to enable learning?

Teaching for informal knowledge requires a set of teacher behaviours different from those used in the transmission of formal knowledge.

Contexts for number

The environment of very young children, both in pre-school settings and outside, has a good deal of number in it, characterised by Ginsburg and Baron (1993) as a combination of:

- *A physical environment of quantity*. Numbers exist for children as both quantities and numerals in the different corners of their world. Quantity matters to them a great deal in both 'how many' and 'how much' forms in food, toys, possessions, distances to walk, stairs to climb, and so on. Quantity makes a qualitative difference in their physical environment. Young children see numerals written on their birthday cards, on clocks, on 'button boxes', telephones, buses and cars, houses and so on. Association of these 'squiggles' with the number names and the number sequence is one of the key steps in early number teaching and learning.
- *A social environment of quantity*. Number is talked about. It is the topic of social arrangements, mealtimes, ages, places, and much conversation with adults and other children.
- *Quantity in literature*. There are numbers in books and other forms of story telling (including some television programmes). Numbers are significant to the characters in the stories children hear, and numbers are found in poems and rhymes of all kinds.

These dimensions of early number experience can be extended in the pre-school setting in the following relevant and meaningful ways.

- *Number songs and rhymes*. From nursery rhymes to the recent creations of some well known poets, there are many songs and rhymes in circulation that have a number theme, or number elements. Many of these are progressive, in the sense that the numbers change up or down with each repetition of the verse. Examples are 'Ten green bottles' and 'Five little speckled frogs'.

- *Stories and books.* Much good children's literature is full of potential for number learning. With rich text and complex illustration children can be provoked into making numerical connections and identifying patterns and sequences of numbers.

- *Number corner or area.* A set-out section of the pre-school setting, resourced with pens, calculators, number dice, spot dice, number cards, spinners, sorting apparatus, and games, will increase the spontaneous activity with and learning about numbers.

- *Areas of play provision that are continuously or regularly available.* Every pre-school setting has some areas of activity that are available on most visits, and the children are free to choose to play in any available area during at least part of each visit. Areas usually include a sand tray and a water tray, unit construction blocks (some large, others small), a 'home' corner, a book corner, outside play, a 'role play' area, and a writing area. Each of these has number potential, which sometimes exists physically, manifesting itself through a child's ambition within the play (e.g. the number of extra blocks to carry across to fill a space), and sometimes socially, manifesting itself in conversations as play is unfolding (e.g. whose water container will fill more cups). The skilled intervention of an adult can maximise these opportunities without losing the child's involvement in their own freely chosen, self-directed play.

These different contexts are not to be associated with particular elements of learning – with counting better learned through stories, and comparison through 'free play', for example. Teachers can develop any of number skills or knowledge through interaction with the children in any of them.

Building on existing understanding

Young children entering nursery or reception classes are not 'clean slates'. They have acquired considerable informal knowledge and understanding of number from having encountered numbers in a variety of everyday circumstances and contexts.

They may know, for example, that numbers are attached or associated with houses, buses, telephones, platforms, shoes, clothes, days, years, and to their birthdays, and may be aware that money has numbers and the things they want have prices.

Children strive to make sense of the number-related information they meet and seek explanations from adults. The nature of these explanations will support their thinking and learning about size, quantity, uniqueness, value and number labelling.

In particular, many children will have had experience of baking, shopping, helping to lay the table or sort the washing. These experiences are the focus of number-related conversations as children seek solutions to practical problems that arise with knives, forks, food and odd socks. They will have acquired language that will structure their understanding in terms of such concepts as more than, more needed, too much, not enough, some missing, enough, just right.

To do

Make a list of all the contexts in which 2–3-year-old children are exposed to spoken numbers.

Children may well also have seen pre-school television programmes featuring numbers and mathematical ideas. Many nursery rhymes and songs that children learn in the home use and contain the language of number. The traditional tales that are central to our oral culture frequently contain numbers: the three bears, the three billy goats Gruff, the three little pigs etc. Many good children's books are rich in number language and early number concepts. Through any or all of these, children accumulate ideas, thoughts and understanding about numbers.

In addition to these everyday opportunities, parents and carers have a seemingly intuitive impulse to engage in counting activities with children. Adults spontaneously count with children as they climb the stairs, fasten buttons, serve food, or look at things of mutual interest.

All of these sources bombard children with numbers, sequences and patterns. As a result, young children are often enthusiastic and interested in numbers, actively seeking number and pattern, and full of ideas about what numbers are, what they mean and why we need them. They demonstrate their understanding through interaction spontaneously. Consider the following conversations, taken from pre-school transcripts.

EVERYDAY NUMBERS

Melvina is just four years old. She has drawn a house and attempted to put a number 11 on the door. She says:

M: Look I've put an 11 on it. I live at 11, Jade lives next door at 9. My Nana lives at number 37.

T: I live at number 122. That's a big number and my house is on a long, long street. Why do you think houses have numbers?

M: So the postman can bring my birthday presents to my house and *not Jade's.*

Daniel is nearly four. He is very pleased with his new trainers. He says:

D: My trainers are 11 G. My old trainers don't fit, they are 10. My feet are big.

The teacher takes off her shoe and places it next to Daniel's foot.

T: Whose shoes are the biggest?

D: Yours are ... yours are ... It's much bigger.

T: But my shoe is only a size 6.

D: Yes but mine is a kid's size 11, yours is a grown up's 6.

T: What is the G for Daniel?

D: It's for ... it's for ...
Daniel reaches down and touches his trainer with his hand span out.

T: Could it be to tell how wide (with emphasis) your shoe is?

D: Yes, yes and it's very, very ...

To do

Identify the 'domains' of number in Figure 1.1 which are being touched on in each of the interactions above.

These children are demonstrating an understanding about number that should be built upon. As a result of such interactions, young children often have much informal knowledge about numbers even before they come to a pre-school setting. Gelman and Gallistel (1978) describe five 'counting principles' that are commonly developed in very young children in relation to small quantities.

- The 1–1 principle – that the numbers in the counting series are used once each for each item in the count
- The stable order principle – that the numbers are always in the same order
- The cardinal principle – that the last number means something, i.e. is the number of items
- The abstraction principle – that not all things can be counted, just sets of discrete things
- The order irrelevance principle – that the order in which the items are 'tagged' does not matter, as the outcome will be the same.

To do

Choose one of the five principles. Devise an activity for 3-year-olds in an appropriate context in which the principle is embedded.

Such informal knowledge is the foundation for later formal work, but it is not universal, reflecting differences in the environments in which young children live and grow. For example, the principles of counting described above can be found in many 3-year-old children, but not in all those of 5. Munn (1994) cites evidence of pre-statutory school age children who do not seem to have realised that the purpose of counting is to find out 'how many'.

The disconnectedness of early number knowledge

It is a characteristic of newly acquired knowledge that it is context specific. We first learn about some new thing in one setting, and associate that knowledge with that setting. As a result what is seen by another person as essentially the same or similar knowledge can be disconnected for any individual into discrete sets, each associated with a different context of acquisition. As we make connections between similar, but previously separated, knowledge sets we develop an integrating concept which enables us to see the separate occurrences as essentially the same.

To do

Make a list of the different contexts in which pre-school children may experience the number 5.

Number work is relatively new for young children, so it is frequently and characteristically disconnected. They have learned different things about numbers in different contexts and have made connections between them in only limited ways. It is common, for example, that the numbers in different contexts are seen by young children as different sorts of things. They do not readily recognise the numbers in counting stairs as being applicable to the numbers of sweets they have. The numbers used to say how old someone is are not always seen to be also used to identify a particular house.

Acknowledging that young children may not have a single integrated concept of number, teaching in the early years setting is best characterised as extending the children's diverse ideas about number and making connections between them, for example the various connections between counting and quantity. The integrated concepts listed in curriculum documents are not *acquired*, they are *developed*.

Some ideas for teaching early number

What we know about young children's learning has strong implications for how we should go about teaching them. We know that young children bring a great deal of knowledge of number to the pre-school setting. Much of it is informal (that is, not reliable under task conditions), and it is often fragmented, with knowledge of number in one context not being related to knowledge of numbers in other contexts. Accordingly, the major purposes of early years work with numbers are:

- to access, extend and develop the knowledge of very young children
- to ensure that all children have the opportunities to develop new informal knowledge
- to make the connections between elements of existing knowledge, and to the new knowledge being acquired, and
- to formalise the portion of number knowledge that is sufficiently developed into a form in which reliable behaviour in task conditions can be expected (this is usually only a small proportion of the number knowledge a child has).

Tasks and freely chosen activities

One of the ways in which the pre-school setting is most noticeably different from school settings is that teacher-set tasks are firmly in the minority, if present at all. In pre-school settings for much of the time, and in some settings for almost all of the time, children are freely choosing activities. Provision will consist of a number of areas of play, set out to enable children to pursue their own activities and purposes:

- sand and water trays, with structured equipment of various kinds
- at least one construction area, with blocks and construction kits that can be used to build and model
- a painting area
- a workshop/technology area for boxcraft and collage
- a food preparation area
- domestic and other 'role play' provision, with clothes that can be worn and resources commensurate with a particular theme (shop, office, etc.) and table-top areas for games and small equipment
- a book area
- a writing area for developing early literacy and, increasingly,
- a numeracy area as described above.

When teaching adults work in these areas there is a fundamental choice open to them. They can either start with each child's purpose in being there, and interact with the children in line with the child's agenda while attempting to develop the child in ways that fit with an adult agenda or offer a stimulus for children to respond to, interacting with the children more obviously with the adult agenda, while remaining sensitive to each child's understanding of the purpose.

In every pre-school setting the adults should spend time in each of the different areas of provision, working with the children in one of these ways. In neither case does this involve giving children a task to do.

When tasks are offered in pre-school settings they tend to be given a different status: the status of school (often in the number or writing area, highjacked for the purpose). Many providers in pre-school settings do not give tasks at all, and are convinced that the educational provision is better for it and that more learning occurs without tasking. Children may comply with tasks but they do not engage intensely with them.

The role of adults in activities

A sound general principle of all teaching is to start where the child is and work from what they know. In the teaching of number in the early years this principle has a particular 'spin'. It does not, and should not, mean giving each child the next task in a sequence of formalised activities, the starting point to be determined by the tasks that can currently be completed successfully without assistance. This is not a suitable approach because young children's knowledge is informal, and is not as readily accessible as it may be for older children. Many young children are reluctant to share their understandings and achievements in the context of focused questioning in a tasked setting. If judgements about future suitable activities are made on the basis of a child's responses to formal tasks, his or her potential will be underestimated. This can be a particular difficulty in the early weeks of school, before the children adjust and settle in. At that time they may allow the teacher little or no clear evidence of achievement, but this does not mean that the knowledge is not there.

A better approach is to acknowledge and appreciate that there is a logic to what a young child can do and that, to start from where the child is, the teacher must find and understand that logic, share in it and use it in their subsequent conversations with the child. This is best achieved through interaction in the context of children's self-chosen play.

To think about

How convinced are you that pre-school children learn without being involved in teacher-set tasks? What are the arguments for and against such an approach?

CONSIDER MANDY

Mandy is nearly four. She can recognise numbers to 10 and can write them down. She is playing engrossed with a plastic spinner with the numbers 1–10 upon it.

T: That's a good game Mandy.

M: Yes I'm getting lots of eights.

T: Are you? You could write the numbers down and see.

Mandy gets some paper and a pencil and proceeds to spin and write down each number. The teacher leaves, but continues to monitor. Mandy continues with the activity until the session ends, writing all the numbers in a random way on both sides of the paper. Mandy is collected by her father, and is observed in heated discussion. Her father approaches a member of staff and requests a spinner to take home. Mandy returns the next day with several pages of numbers and the spinner. She shows her teacher.

M: Look at all these numbers.

T: So many, Mandy. Were there lots of eights?

M: No there was lots of everything.

Starting with and extending the child's agenda can lead to more interesting and more valuable work than designing tasks to fit the supposed range of number work of the young child. Who, after all, would plan for pre-school children an investigation using spinners?

It is also wise to consider that not all children follow the same pathways or share the same interests and enthusiasms. Working from what a child knows and can do will involve pursuing the current enthusiasms of young learners.

OUTSIDE PLAY

Ben is nearly four years old. His main enthusiasm is outside play. He is an active, lively learner. Outside he will make patterns and spirals with numbered pebbles which he can recognise, he will make repeating patterns with natural materials, jump from number to number on the stepping stones shouting them out as he lands, and he will make number plates for the bikes using the letters of his name and the numbers he can write.

Taken from this outside classroom and forced to learn in formal situations inside, Ben might become frustrated and difficult. A single approach that rests on adult-directed activity around a table is likely, by its nature, to reduce individual achievement to a low common denominator. It will underestimate potential levels of achievement in more diverse and freely chosen contexts, and prejudice entirely the achievement of the most active young learners, frequently, but not exclusively, boys.

If the learning experiences, activities and opportunities teachers plan and provide are embedded in their understanding of what the child knows and can do, then the child has a starting point from which to move on and the teacher's knowledge enables them to provide appropriate support. The teacher can bridge and build the child's thinking and learning, translate knowledge from informal to formal forms and build new informal knowledge. By meaningful interaction with children about number in their environment, children will develop. Meaningful interaction draws the children out, persuades them to explain, and challenges them to be consistent and correct, in contrast to interaction limited to a narrow adult agenda. The way in which the informal knowledge of the young child is promoted by 'child-contingent' responsive interaction with an adult in the pre-school setting has been called (among other things) 'motherese' (Meadows, 1986) following studies of 'responsive' mothers.

Talking about numbers

Talk is central to the learning process. Even though the immediate and overwhelming impression for any adult first looking into a pre-school setting is activity, the most important single dimension to the learning that occurs is talk. Children learn not so much by doing as by talking about what they are doing. Talk in the social context will shape their perceptions and understanding. First-hand experiences are essential, but 'experiences' are not granted by the existence of an opportunity; they need talk, and preferably adult talk, to develop them. Number work is active, but has also to be interactive.

The first and most natural focus for the talk is the child's perception of the situation. Skilful teaching introduces the number agenda incidentally, insinuates the specifics of number-related learning into the conversation without altering the child's perception of the talk as relevant and meaningful and pertinent to their play. There can be child-specific content in the talk, arising from the teacher's awareness of the child's point of growth drawn from informal assessment in previous conversations, but the learning purpose is not strict. The awareness is defining the agenda for the conversation, but is not determining exactly what is being said. There is no 'push' for specific learning by forcing the conversation down particular paths, away from the child's purpose. This is why the learning outcomes in early-years number work are conceptualised largely as 'developing' in an aspect rather than 'learning' a particular thing.

The centrality of talk to learning for the young child has important implications for the role of the adults in early-years classrooms, and for the role of the teacher in managing them. Through talk the adult shapes the child's thinking and by so doing creates appropriate learning experiences. They raise children's awareness, support the process of making sense with suggestions and strategies, and help a child to make connections between the ideas, meanings and relationships that are developing. As the adult is crucial to the learning process, all adults working in a pre-school setting should be involved (i.e. have a more than supervisory role).

Making connections

The main agenda of informal number learning in the early years is to make connections between the various number things that children know already to other number things. For example, when singing 'Five little specked frogs' a substantial number of very young learners will chorus 'I'm three!' whenever the number three is sung or said. Numbers signify quantity and position, have a meaning, and tell a story. Through informal number learning young children develop the vital awareness that the same number always tells the same story, has the same meaning, and represents the same quantity or position.

A strong focus of children's number is counting, and as such counting can act as the 'glue' which connects different situations together in the child's mind. Counting is also one of the number skills about which there is some expectation of formal competence by the end of pre-school education. As Figure 1.1 suggests, counting has links with appropriate recording of numerals, understanding of the values of small numbers, comparisons of quantity, ordering and sequencing and (in the 'order-irrelevance' principle) the 'invariant property' of number known as 'conservation'. Counting can also be used by children in problem-solving situations. It is to be exploited, supported with strategies such as the use of fingers, and self-conscious counting valued as a competence.

Activities in contexts

Teachers of children in pre-school education should plan to maximise opportunities for children to gain experience in each of the contexts in a pre-school setting.

Number songs and rhymes

The rich potential for number learning in songs and rhymes is often under-used. Teachers frequently sing number songs and rhymes as 'fill in' or 'carpet time' activities, but rarely plan systematically for them. Songs and rhymes can be supported in action by number symbols, and in follow-up by an interactive display of characters, objects, physical context and words and symbols associated with the songs or rhyme, for subsequent independent enactment. For example, 'Five little speckled frogs' can be sung with numerals alongside the actions. It can also be turned into an interactive display with a log, five plastic frogs, a blue cloth, numerals 1–5, and words from the song.

Stories and books

Stories that have number relevance can be supported with sets of story-specific props for independent enactment. Teachers regularly read good number books to large groups of children, but the real potential lies in sharing these stories with small groups, where the quality of interaction and the pace of and scope for learning is greater. An adult-directed activity that involves sharing a good book (such as John Burningham's *The Shopping Basket*, or Inga Moore's *Six Dinner Sid*) with a small group of children to support and extend their thinking about number would be more meaningful, interesting and motivating than any worksheet.

A number 'corner' or area

With the right quality of resources readily available and easily accessible children play and make up number games. The planned and systematic placement of an adult in the area for playing number games with interested children is another very suitable and appropriate adult-focused activity.

To do

List ten contexts in which it is 'natural' to count. List five others in which it is 'natural' to count backwards.

To do

Choose a well known number song or rhyme, and collect or make a set of 'props' that will enhance it, and encourage the children to play and sing independently.

To do

Make a list of good story books for young children that are rich in potential number learning. Consider the ways you might use these with small groups of children to promote their understanding of number.

COUNTING DINOSAURS

Naomi and Beth have freely chosen to work in a number area. They are playing with the spot die and counting dinosaurs. Each throws the die in turn and takes that number of dinosaurs from the bucket. After each turn they count up the dinosaurs and decide who has more.

This is observed by the teacher, who approaches and joins them at the table. At an appropriate point the teacher intervenes, sensitively, with the suggestion of playing with two dice each. Naomi and Beth accept readily, pleased with the interest of the adult. They quickly adjust to throwing two dice, counting up the total accurately and collecting an increased number of dinosaurs. At the end of each turn the teacher encourages the children to remember how many they had before and to 'count on'. When the children tire they leave the activity, still chattering about their game. This activity involved instruction, but in a context chosen by and meaningful to the children. The teacher then fills in a simple observation sheet (Table 1.1).

To do

Make and use some simple number games using numerals, dice, spinners and counting toys. Note down the achievements children demonstrate on a simple 'Who, What, What Next' sheet. Consider how the rules of your game might be altered: (1) to challenge and extend older or more able children; and (2) to support the developing skills of younger or less experienced children.

Context: Number area		
Who?	What?	What next?
Naomi	Invented number game with spot dice and dinosaurs. Accurate 1–1 counting beyond 20. Played with two dice, counting spots for total.	Set up game tomorrow.
Beth	Beth counting on. Good recall of how many, Beth beginning to be able to count on without support.	Support counting on with strategies. Try with number dice.

Table 1.1

Table 1.1 is evidence of work undertaken and the learning taking place, but also part of the planning process for 'maximising the opportunities' for these children in the context.

Familiar number games are also a very good context for more formal work, as it 'naturally' draws on all available skills. In a formal number game lesson, the teacher should have a set of possible practical tasks and problems from which to select as the session unfolds.

Areas of play provision that are continuously or regularly available

Teachers should explore the potential for number learning in all of the areas of provision in the setting. In outside play, for example, there is scope to number stepping stones, parking bays or pebbles, to mark the playground with numbered grids and lines. In the water tray there is scope to sequence number symbols by ordering and numbering the

To do

Identify areas of provision that allow good opportunities for number learning. Consider how resources in these areas might be organised or labelled to promote young children's numeracy.

bottles, beakers, jugs and funnels, and to state clearly how many of each there are. A basket labelled with six boats will provide the opportunity to develop an awareness of number operations every time the children tidy away. In the home area the play pizza with six pieces enables most regular players to know 'facts to six' without counting one to one. There are many opportunities for number-relevant interaction, and meaningful and relevant use of numbers and number symbols in areas of continuous and regular provision, but these are frequently under-exploited.

Assessing early number

Assessment principles

As a companion to working towards desirable outcomes it is essential to have accurate approaches to assessing and recording the number achievements of young children.

ASSESSING ACCURATELY

A child is playing with wooden unit blocks. She is then taken away from this to a teacher-led activity of counting, comparing and ordering with sorting animals. She does not do this very well, and the teacher decides on that evidence that she needs to be taken out of her play rather more, and given further work with sorting animals and other similar materials, as she 'clearly' needs more 'practice' in counting, comparing and ordering.

This chain of events is rooted in an assumption that the child's level of operation is simplistic, and that she can be taken away from what she had been doing without effect. The results of the formal teacher-led activities seem to 'prove' the assumption, and it is common for the teacher to say 'She cannot even ...'.

An alternative perspective on this scenario is that the child's level of operation can be complex, and that disruption from her engagement in an activity risks a considerable effect on her concentration and interest. From this perspective, unless a generous time is granted to build a new involvement with the new context, the child is unlikely to adjust to the new stimulus quickly. She may even be resentful and distracted, thinking about her construction play and wishing to return to it. She is likely to be confused about the teacher's motives and behaviour. She knows that the teacher knows the answers required in the task, so why is the teacher asking her 'How many'?. Is it possible that the teacher does not know, even though a 'grown-up'? Or is this a test? Is there a response the teacher wants? In such a situation the child's most likely pre-occupation is to discover the course of action that will enable her to return to the block play as soon as possible. She is likely to under-perform.

It is very important to give children time and space to perform so as to gain a true picture of what each child knows and can do, and as a result know which experiences to provide to build on it and extend it. Observing children in freely chosen activity is much more revealing than giving them a pre-determined task. Questioning aimed at eliciting their thinking and related knowledge is much more revealing than questioning aimed at 'testing' a pre-determined specific skill. A child playing with wooden unit blocks can be counting, comparing, estimating and ordering within the play. Taking time with young children to find out the skills and knowledge they are using in their 'play' leads every teacher to increase their respect for the depth and complexity of the thinking of the young child. Following this path can be said to 'prove' that the child's level of operation can be complex: the teacher may then say 'Look at all she can do ...'.

Observation-led assessment is the prime and painless way to obtain evidence of, and information about, the number achievements of young learners. Teachers should value it and ensure that they find time to do it on a regular basis, following a plan for systematic collection of information about all children in a range of contexts and having a system for ad-hoc noting of interesting observations as they occur. Observation should be viewed as a key teaching skill without which it is difficult to function in the early-years classroom.

Baseline assessment

Assessment on entry to full-time schooling is not new. Teachers have always assessed what children know and can do in order to plan for the individual child and to decide an appropriate educational programme for the class group. There is broad consensus around this purpose. However, from September 1998 a 'baseline' assessment within the first seven weeks of full-time schooling became a statutory requirement in England and Wales. Each school must use a scheme accredited by the Qualifications and Curriculum Authority (QCA) to generate one or more numerical outcomes to inform future 'value added' analysis (although it is hoped that it can serve the planning purpose as well).

If 'value added' is to be fair and just, the assessment practice on which it is based must be principled, and take account of the nature of young children as learners and the central importance of context by observation of the child's action in normal work. A series of test questions related to the different elements of the baseline criteria may seem the most straightforward approach, and would certainly give rise to a numeric outcome, but would measure only the formal knowledge of each child, not the much more extensive informal knowledge that is the more significant precursor to their subsequent development. An observational approach can access this critically important informal knowledge. However, as observation in the context of 'normal' work cannot be guaranteed to be about specific pieces of learning, the observation-based schemes of baseline assessment utilise a 'best fit' approach against sets of descriptions characterising different levels, which can be given a numerical value for comparative purposes. Children's behaviour in a range of contexts, including freely chosen 'play' activities, is evaluated against these descriptions to arrive at a single numerical outcome for each 'strand'.

The descriptions related to number in the scheme developed in Leeds LEA (Leeds City Council, 1997), which was accredited as an open scheme by QCA in 1998, and which is used in several other LEAs, are listed in Table 1.2.

Number

1   No observable evidence – may only indicate a reluctance to share achievement

2   Joins in with familiar number songs and rhymes

    Counts aloud to 5, usually accurately

    Counts to 5 using everyday objects arranged in a regular way, using 1–1 correspondence by either pointing to or moving the objects

3   Takes part confidently in number songs and rhymes

    Plays simple number games with support

    Counts aloud to 10, usually accurately

    Counts to 10 using everyday objects arranged in a regular way

    Recognises and uses numerals to 5, with some support

4   Plays simple number games independently

    Counts to 10 using everyday objects arranged either in a regular or random way, usually correctly

    Is familiar with some larger numbers from everyday life

    Recognises, orders and uses written numbers to 10

    Shows an awareness of number operations

5   Accurately counts, orders, adds and subtracts numbers to 10, using apparatus, and can estimate with some success

    Reads, writes and orders written numbers to 10

    Shows an interest in larger numbers, counting and reading numbers to 20 and beyond, and showing some awareness of place value

Table 1.2

Teachers using this scheme gather evidence of achievement in a variety of contexts over the first six weeks of the reception year. They give value to a child's previous experiences by recognising evidence of achievement from parents, nurseries and other settings. Working collaboratively with all staff who may have knowledge of the child, they then make baseline judgements by 'best fit' analysis, comparing the evidence they have gathered with the description in each category.

Review of key points

➤ Although it is similar in content to work with older children, the teaching of number in the early years is qualitatively different

➤ Each aspect of the desirable outcomes for pre-school number work should be understood to be implicit in a range of meaningful practical contexts, and to be best developed through verbal interaction with an involved adult, rather than directly taught

➤ As well as adult-directed activity in the many number-relevant pre-school contexts, it is absolutely essential to connect with children in their freely chosen activities

➤ A curriculum planned around focused activity which is not embedded in children's play will result in a mathematical curriculum that is not meaningful or relevant to them, and which will be far less effective in developing their mathematics

➤ High-quality observation-led assessment is central to a better understanding of the rich complexity of young children's learning about number. It will access for the teacher the logic that underpins each child's activity and learning and will, as a result, guide the teacher towards significant learning, and inform future planning both for the child and the provision

➤ A formal approach to assessment risks cutting across the child's working patterns, being irrelevant and meaningless to the child, and resulting in under-performance. This will lead to under-estimates of potential and subsequent under-achievement

Part 1
Module 2 Learning to teach number concepts and number systems: an overview

Introduction

In many books about the teaching of mathematics you will read how it is believed that children develop the concept of number. Unfortunately, the concept of number to which the authors refer is that of natural numbers, not number concepts in general. A discussion on number concepts is beyond the scope of this book; it is even questionable that there is a single concept of number as there are so many different types of number and number systems. This module considers the relationships between different types of number which, together with number systems, are further explored in Modules 3–10.

Number concepts and number systems in national curricula

Number concepts and systems form the basis of measures, geometry, statistics and probability. Consequently, primary children are rightly expected to be taught the structure and the relationships within and between systems and to develop an intimacy and fluency with numbers. This comes about by:

- understanding the relative magnitudes of numbers
- being able to order numbers according to their magnitude
- developing the ability to write a number in different ways
- developing the ability to recognise when numbers are equivalent, however they are represented
- understanding the similarities and differences between number systems
- developing the skills necessary to write the 'same' number in different systems.

Key terms

The following terms are described in Modules 3–9, to which the reader is referred.

natural numbers Module 3

whole numbers Module 3

zero Modules 3 and 4

decimal numbers Module 5

vulgar fractions Module 6

percentage Module 7

Key issues in number concepts and number systems

Related concepts and issues

Stewart (1975) claims that the natural or counting numbers are likely to have developed as a consequence of the desire and practical need of people to record important events in their lives. Only much later did the idea of number as an abstract concept appear. As the demands of societies increased so did the need for other numbers. It is thought that the Hindus invented the number zero, and the need for fractions arose out of necessity to describe the result of dividing material into parts. Negative 'whole' numbers were required to express the result of subtraction when the first number was smaller than the second number, and division of numbers gave rise to the idea of rational or ratio numbers, popularly known as fractions. The relationship between these systems of numbers is shown in Figure 2.1.

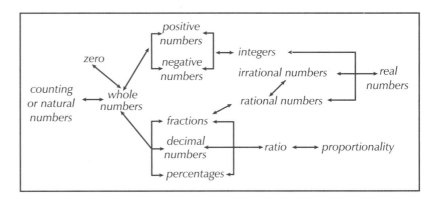

2.1 Relationships between different types of numbers

The idea of real numbers arose from Greek geometry and the study of calculus, and requiring all equations to have a solution demanded that the square root of –1 be given an 'existence' in mathematics and hence 'unreal numbers', known as complex numbers, were invented. The connections between different systems of numbers should continually be brought to the attention of primary children as they are gradually introduced to new numbers. The similarities and differences between different types of numbers should not be hidden from children.

19

Pre-number experiences

A visit to a reception class early in the autumn term is likely to find children sorting objects into sets according to different attributes. This work with sets, together with matching and ordering, has, since the 1950s, been viewed as essential pre-number experience for young children. Thompson (1997) describes how the mathematical and psychological developments of the twentieth century brought about the introduction of practical activities of this kind, and questions the purpose of such activities in the learning of number. There is little doubt, however, that such activities have a role to play in children's learning of number: the issue is, what kind of role?

Aubrey (1997) also challenges the place of 'set theory' activities in the learning of early number, claiming that it fails to take account of the understanding which children have already developed as a consequence of their meaningful out-of-school experiences. She refers to the 'Dutch realistic primary mathematics teaching (which) has avoided entirely the introduction of set theory and stresses rich thematic and concrete contexts, integration of mathematics with other subjects, differentiated leaning processes and working together in heterogeneous groups'.

The '-ing' processes, such as sorting, matching and ordering, are, however, considered by many mathematics educators to be essential tools in the development of children's mathematical thinking and their relationship with 'set theory' is merely historical.

The concept of a unit

Running as a thread through every number concept module is the notion of 'unit', which has a critical role in the development of the different number systems (Watanabe, 1994; Askew, 1998). It is a concept on which little research has been conducted but which is now recognised as fundamental to children's construction of mathematical concepts, knowledge and skills.

At its most primitive level a unit is a singleton, a single element, idea or object. When a child begins to form a group or a collection of units, the group becomes a 'larger' unit. You will immediately recognise this as the basis of the place value system where the collective unit is 10, and where groups of 10 are collected into 10s to form a unit of 100, which in turn are collected into 10s to form a unit of 1000, and so on. Hence, the symbolic representation of whole numbers is constructed by building up units of units of units of ... .

When a singleton is broken down into 'smaller' units retaining the 10 relationship the decimal notation comes into existence. A fraction is the result of subdividing a singleton into a number of parts; a number of these new units collected together to form a composite unit. The ways in which the notion of a unit relates the different number concepts is explored in more depth in each of the modules.

Equivalence and equals

There is much confusion among mathematicians and mathematics educators as to the exact difference between equivalence and equals

To think about

Look at the workbooks of some recent primary mathematics series and the associated teachers' handbooks to see how sorting, matching and ordering are used to introduce children to pre-number ideas.

relative to numerical expressions. Horril (1986) defines 'equal' as 'of the same quantity, amount, or number as another' and 'equivalence' as 'the relation between two statements which are either both true or both false such that each implies the other'. There is little doubt that children become confused, especially on the occasions that the equals sign is used and read as equivalent. This issue is followed up in the modules as another thread running through different number concepts.

Technology

Calculators and computers have an important place in the learning of number concepts and should be considered an integral part of a teacher's armoury and viewed by children as tools to assist their learning. Teachers who believe that calculators can be used only for calculating, which is indeed why they are manufactured, are mistaken. Unfortunately, it is not possible to describe the many calculator and computer activities which children can do with the objective of developing a particular aspect of non-computational number understanding. The *Framework for Teaching Mathematics* (FTM; National Numeracy Project, 1999) describes in the introduction the role of calculators in the primary years and, in the programmes for years 5 and 6, lists the calculator skills that children should develop in order to use a calculator effectively. These are further developed in *Teaching Mental Calculation Strategies: Guidelines for Teachers at Key Stages 1 and 2*, produced by the Qualifications and Curriculum Authority (QCA, 1999). The FTM lists the following ways in which a computer can support teaching and learning:

1 Exploring, describing and explaining number patterns
2 Practising and consolidating number skills
3 Exploring and explaining patterns in data
4 Estimating and comparing measures
5 Experimenting and discussing properties of patterns in shape and space
6 Developing mathematical vocabulary, logical thinking and problem-solving skill.

In the programme for each year, reference is made to when, where and how a computer might be used to enhance children's learning so that its use is 'consistent with the lesson's objectives'.

Models for learning number concepts

Throughout the succeeding modules you will see described ways of using apparatus and diagrams which model or represent, each in their own way, number concepts. The aim of such material is to assist children to develop perceptual and mental images which may result in their understanding of number concepts. These are:

- discrete objects
- pictures of objects
- number rods
- number tracks

- number lines
- number grids, including the 100 square
- base 10 apparatus
- money and measures.

Apparatus and diagrams are not a panacea for the ills of learning about number concepts: if they were, the difficulties children still encounter would no longer exist. As Threlfall (1996) points out: 'The justification for the value of practical materials is theoretical.' In order that the materials have any value as a teaching and learning experience they must have embedded in them the structure of the number concept. This is a criterion that teachers should use when considering the use of any apparatus or diagram. However, having this embedded structure does not guarantee that children will perceive its existence, nor will they necessarily abstract it in such a way that it is assimilated into their schema. It is the role of the teacher to assist children in observing that which they might not 'see', and to articulate the relationship between the embedded structure and its representation in other ways, particularly symbolic.

Review of key points

➤ The concept of number comprises many sub-constructs

➤ Different number systems demand different understandings

➤ Understanding the structure of a number system and its inner relationships is a major aim of the primary curriculum

➤ Children should consider what different number systems have in common and the ways in which they differ

➤ The concept of 'unit' is fundamental to the development of number concepts

➤ There is confusion about the distinctions to be made between the relations equals and equivalence when applied to number expressions

➤ Apparatus and diagrams may help children in their understanding of number concepts, but interaction of child and teacher is an important contributor to this process

Module 3   Learning to teach whole numbers

Introduction

Whole numbers are the 'counting' numbers (one, two, three, four, etc.) together with zero. The need to communicate and remember 'how many' or 'how much' is a fundamental human requirement, and systems of tallying leading to whole number systems have been in evidence from the earliest times. Among the different systems for representing numbers, some have a name and symbol for zero, where others do not.

It is reasonable to consider whole numbers like 203 with thoughts of place value. While numbers have a name derived from a system rooted in base 10, and are symbolised using place value, it is possible to think of them as a system without place value. It seems likely that, for many children, whole numbers are understood as such a system before they develop a deeper insight into how whole numbers are constructed.

Whole numbers in national curricula

Teaching and learning about whole numbers have three main interrelating aspects: (1) the meaning of whole numbers; (2) the names and symbols for the numbers; and (3) the order of whole numbers, in the sequence called 'counting'. The related skills required in most primary curricula include:

- developing the ability to count
- recognising that the cardinality of a set is independent of the order in which the elements are counted
- being able to recognise the smallest and largest of a set of numbers
- placing a set of numbers in order
- understanding the relationships more than, less than and between.

Key terms

cardinality the 'how many' aspect of whole numbers; the quantity of discrete items, the 'numerosity', in a collection or set

natural numbers the numbers that occur 'naturally', 1, 2, 3, 4, ...; often called the counting numbers

whole numbers the counting numbers, together with zero (0, 1, 2, 3, 4 ...); often also used, however, to include the equivalent negative numbers, −1, −2, −3, −4, ...

zero the first number in the whole number sequence; the numerosity of the empty set, represented by the numeral 0

ordinality the 'positional' aspect of whole number

tallying the process of making marks which are in one–one correspondence to objects in a set

---

Key issues in whole numbers

Related concepts and issues

The relationships between whole numbers and other concepts and issues are shown in the map in Figure 3.1. In teaching about whole numbers there are three main interrelating aspects:

- the meanings of whole numbers
- the names and symbols for the numbers
- the order of whole numbers, in the sequence we call 'counting'.

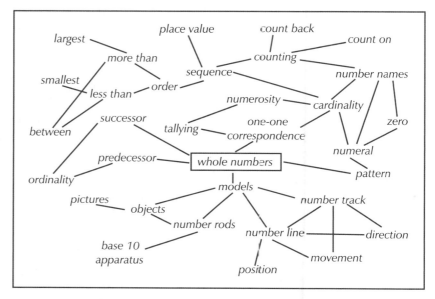

3.1 Concepts and issues associated with whole numbers

The meanings of whole numbers

Whole numbers are used for many purposes:

- for counting
- as a measure of size
- to signify position
- as a measure of quantity
- as a label.

Whole numbers are a sequence of increasing value, starting with the number that represents the absence of value, zero. Each term in the sequence has a value one greater than the previous term, and one less than its successor. The sense of any member in such a sequence is its relationship with the term before it and after it in the sequence. One of the first meanings of 7, for example, is that it is between 6 and 8.

The most important meaning of whole numbers, however, is to describe quantity. Quantity manifests itself in different ways – how many, how much, how long, how far, which position, which size, which level, which route. Numbers are used in different ways in different contexts. Variations can be broadly classified as the cardinal and ordinal aspects of number, together with application in measurement. Numbers are also widely used as labels, and when the system is not known the numbers seem to be arbitrary, e.g. numbers for buses.

Names and symbols

Strictly, '7' is not a number, but a numeral. The number is the concept of seven to which this symbol refers. However, the only way we can refer to 'the number seven' is by using the universal numeral 7, or by a name, which may be different in different languages. In practice, therefore, 7 is called a number.

Apart from 0 to 9, the names and numerals for numbers are based on a place value system, but it is also possible to think of larger numbers just in terms of their position in the number sequence. Children may think of forty-two as the one which 'comes just after' forty-one, in the same arbitrary way that 's' comes just after 'r' in the alphabet. However, they are inclined to notice patterns and regularities in the sequence, so the understanding of larger whole numbers can be in terms of a system, even though not yet a place value system. As a result, if a line of numbers 3451, 3452, 3452, 3453, 3455, 3456, 3457, 3458 is offered, a child who does not know the value of these numbers can still deduce that a number is repeated and there is one missing, and that it is 3454, and know that the next number is 3459.

Models for whole numbers

Discrete objects

Children's first experiences when developing the concept of whole number are with sets of discrete objects, and teachers should take every opportunity to engage children in responding to the questions 'How many?' and 'How much?'. With small numbers (up to 5) an association can be built up between number and sets of objects on the basis of perceptual pattern. This ability of being able to 'see' how many without counting is known as 'subitising'.

Number rods

Using linking cubes as discrete objects (see Figure 3.2a) provides the opportunity to join them together into a continuous number rod having the same cardinality as the discrete set. This is frequently the first experience children have of 'seeing', say, 7 as a 'whole unit' of 1 *seven*, rather than as 7 individual parts or '*ones*' (see Figure 3.2b). Later, number rods can be given values as multiples of a '*one*', or unit, where the individual units making up the number are not apparent (see Figure 3.2c).

To do

Make a collection of the different ways in which each of the numbers 0 to 9 are written or printed in different contexts. Compare these with how the numbers appear in children's textbooks.

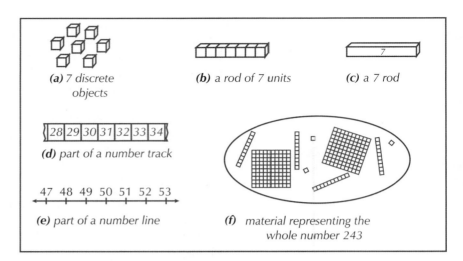

(a) 7 discrete objects

(b) a rod of 7 units

(c) a 7 rod

(d) part of a number track

(e) part of a number line

(f) material representing the whole number 243

3.2 Models for whole numbers

Number tracks and lines

Number tracks and lines emphasise the ordinality aspect of numbers, with a one–one correspondence between a whole number and a 'space', region or point. They incorporate an implicit assumption of direction, as it is usual for whole numbers on a number track or line to increase in value from left to right (see Figures 3.2d and 3.2e). This is only a convention, as is the double arrow head on number lines to imply that what is seen is only a part of a larger (infinitely long) line.

Base 10 apparatus

Although base 10 apparatus (see Figure 3.2f) is specifically designed for developing the concept of place value, its use should be explored for large whole numbers. The collective units of 10s and 100s make it ideal for children to experience large numbers before representing them using a place value system.

Relationships between whole numbers

More than, less than

When whole numbers are thought of in terms of 'how many' or 'how much', the concepts of 'more' and 'less' are important relationships. These are first established:

- by one–one matching
- by the direction to be travelled along the counting sequence ('up' or 'down', 'after' or 'before') or on the number line.

The notions are then extended to 'how many more' and 'how many less' by considering the remainder following matching, as in Figure 3.3a, or by counting how many steps have to be taken between numbers (see Figure 3.3b).

Between

Formally, a 'between' number is more than one number and less than the other. Informally, children may view the 'between' numbers as

5 is 2 more than 3
3 is 2 less than 5
(a)

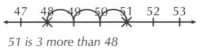

51 is 3 more than 48
48 is 3 less than 51
(b)

3.3 More or less

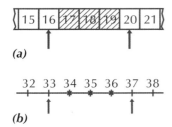

(a)

(b)

3.4 Between

To think about

Is 'first, second, third ...' a different kind of counting from 'one, two, three ...'? When children count a number of objects, which of the two sets of number names is normally used, the cardinal or ordinal? Are the children who do different things displaying different understanding?

somehow sandwiched between the two given numbers in the counting sequence, or on a number track or line (see Figure 3.4).

Counting

The ability to count is essential for every child, but is not often directly taught. It may be fundamental to an understanding of numbers (opinions differ), but at the very least it is important because children use it. Counting strategies in arithmetic are widespread. They depend on counting skills as well as knowledge of the counting sequence. Children who cannot count on (starting at any given number) have been found to struggle with addition. Children who cannot count back have been found to struggle with subtraction. Overall it seems fair to say that the more skilful a child is in counting, the easier they will find number work. It is therefore dangerous to neglect counting, or assume that it is done with once children can count fluently to 100. Learning to count is more problematic in English than in many other languages, because in English the irregularity of the teen words and the ten words, and their similarity, is a source of confusion for many children.

Nevertheless, various features of counting, such as reciting the number names in order, and using that sequence to determine the cardinality of a set of objects, or a size, or a position, are well established procedures for very small numbers even before children come to school.

In the first years of schooling, counting is extended to apply to larger and larger numbers, in three strands of development:

- how much of the counting sequence is known: the range of counting
- how well the counting sequence is known: the skills of counting
- how useful the counting sequence is: the application of counting.

How much

'How much' is concerned with how far children can count reliably and correctly. For the majority of children how much of the counting sequence is known progresses in predictable extensions and 'sticking points' over a period of years up to about age 9, by which time most children can count reliably to at least 10 000. These are listed below.

- young children know that counting is continuous, and keep on counting even though they do not in fact know what comes next: '... twelve, thirteen, seventeen, fifteen, thirteen, nineteen, fourteen, sixteen ...'
- many children soon learn the 'decade sequence' of 'mmty one, mmty two, mmty three' and so on, although there are often consistent omissions, with 'mmty seven' followed by 'mmty nine' in each decade, for example
- the decade order is a greater sticking point, with many children leaping around from tens to tens, much as follows: 'thirty-eight, thirty-nine, seventy, seventy-one, seventy-two, ..., seventy-nine, fifty, ...'. It is common to teach children the tens sequence independently of place value knowledge, but they often recite it as: 'seventy, eighty, ninety, twenty'

- the next common sticking point is just over a hundred, with children commonly proceeding as: 'one hundred and eight, one hundred and nine, two hundred, two hundred and one, ...'
- many children seem reluctant to count over 1000, as if they feel that 1000 is the biggest number possible.

By the time children are counting larger numbers the pattern within counting is well established.

How well

'How well' is about children starting their counting at any number, counting backwards, keeping track of their counting, counting in different-sized steps, such as in 2s, 3s, 5s, 10s, 20s, 50s, 100s, 1000s. The development of counting skills has three important steps:

1 counting on
2 counting back
3 keeping track.

Counting on

The first step is the ability to 'count on', that is to start counting from any number as well as from 1.

In most adults the difficulties children have with counting can be simulated by demanding similar performance with a different sequence – the alphabet. We all know the alphabet sequence all the way through, but how well do we know it?

Counting on is used in calculation, with many children using counting methods to answer problems such as 'What is 7 add 5?'. It is common to encourage children to 'Put one number in your head and start from there', but this is of little use unless the number sequence has been learned to a sufficient degree that counting on can be done.

Counting back

Counting backwards is another important counting ability. Many children know the number sequence well enough to count back, or down, from 5 or 10, as it is part of their early experience in stories, songs and rhymes (and many children end their counting down with 'blast off', suggesting another source of count-down experience), but counting back from 15 or 23 is not so well done.

The difficulty that many children have with counting backwards is not conceptual; it is simply a matter of knowing the sequence well enough to do it. This is achieved, as so much else in this aspect of number, by repetition, with an important contribution from the perception of pattern.

Keeping track

Another important development in the competence of counting is keeping track of a count, knowing how many steps have been taken.

To do

Ask individual 6-year-old children to count starting at 15. Make a record of the different strategies they use. Try to put the strategies into a hierarchy of stages of development. Repeat the activity with some 7-year-olds. Are there any noticeable changes? What happens if you ask them to start counting at 175?

To think about

Start 'counting' at 'S'. Did you have to start from 'A'? Did you start at a letter that you knew to be 'smaller' like 'M' and take a run up? Ask someone else to try. Discuss together the problems you encountered.

The value of doing this when calculating is seen through an example: 'Calculate the difference between 27 and 32.' One would not do this by counting back 27 steps from 32, but by counting up from 27 to 32, keeping track of the number of steps taken. In manifesting this skill children use an interesting variety of methods, only some of which will have been taught. They may:

- use their fingers
- use pictures or objects as tokens
- use a number line
- use double counting ('27 is go, 28 is one, 29 is two, 30 is three ...').

How useful

'How useful' is about children using the sequence of numbers to assign numerosity or position to things. Does children's verbal count have a one-to-one relationship to the items? Do they miss some out or count some twice? The deployment of the skills involved in counting objects and pictures also passes through identifiable phases:

- counting objects
- counting pictures of objects.

Counting objects

When counting objects, the youngest child begins with a real need to move the objects. They create two sets, an 'objects to be counted' set and an 'objects already counted' set, and systematically move the objects from one to the other. A progressive conceptualisation of the process involves the need to touch the objects, but without moving them, followed by pointing at the objects one by one, and finally counting objects just by looking. The objects to be counted and objects already counted are separated in children's minds.

Counting pictures of objects

In counting items in pictures, the activity again involves finding a way to sort the items into those yet to be counted and those already counted, with items changing their classification as the count proceeds. Studies of eye movement when counting have shown that there is a sequence of development:

- children in the first 'stage' randomly pick off items, gradually working through until they think all the items have been counted
- later, children often adopt a 'spiral' approach, either starting at the edge and moving in or starting in the middle and spiralling out
- later still the approach usually involves lines, counting either in a zigzag or moving left to right along successive lines.

These 'stages' are very evident when a child is given a picture and allowed to number the items in order to count them – putting a 1 in or near what they see as the first one, and so on. In some cases the sequence is scattered, in some it is in a spiral, in some zigzag and others in lines, left to right.

To do

Randomly put a 'large' number of objects, say buttons or coins, on a table. Count them, noticing the strategy you use. Count them again, starting at a different object. How did your counting strategy change?

Children and whole numbers

The meanings of whole numbers

The different contexts for numbers that are explored by the young child – numbers on buses, numbers for shoes, numbers of objects, numbers for ages, and so on – give rise to a set of understandings about number. As Fuson and Hall (1983) have detailed, children derive from these experiences a set of different meanings for numbers; separate, simple meanings often associated with specific contexts of use. They understand numbers as labels, numbers as counting, numbers as size, numbers as position, and numbers as quantity of objects, but may not connect the different meanings; they may not see that numbers when they occur in different contexts are all the same 'really'. Keeping the meanings separate may in the short term reduce confusion (is a number 3 bus smaller than a number 4 bus? Does it go less far? Less fast?), but should be removed as soon as possible, as it limits flexibility and efficiency in thinking because children have to learn essentially the same sequences and operations several times over, in each context separately.

Writing number names and symbols

In general children do not have difficulty in writing number names other than those which have a place value element. A difficulty, however, arises in the spelling of such names.

SPELLING

A group of over 100 6-year-old children were asked to write the word for the number 30. These are a selection of the responses:

farley, furty, fitty, firty, thety, fhtti, theretea, fherty, thty, thringty, therty

Is it important that children should learn to spell number names? If so, at what age should they be able to do so? List the reasons for your decisions. Compare them with those of some of your colleagues.

3.5 Number reversals

Reversals

When writing numbers, reversals are very common among younger children. The reversals may be of digits, or of the order of digits in numbers, or a mixture of the two (Figure 3.5; the last example is possibly intended to be 32, or, perhaps, 23). Reversals are worrying as they seem to place a large barrier to a child's learning and, although they should be drawn to a child's attention, experience suggests that they are not as serious as they appear. They may occur naturally as a by-product of developmental aspects in visual orientation and the child can be perfectly clear about what they have written. Reversals do not usually persist beyond age 7.

Counting

Children's progression in learning the counting sequence has been characterised earlier in this module. Errors of various kinds occur when children try to count beyond their range. However, these are not to be treated as errors for remediation purposes, just as indicators of the child's current counting range.

The shared common error in the skills of counting, which occurs in counting on, counting back and keeping track, is to include the starting number in the count. For example, in counting on 6 from 17 the child may hold up 6 fingers and count '17, 18, 19, 20, 21, 22', with an outcome characteristically one less than required. In keeping track of a count from 17 to 23 they may count from 17, putting up one finger for each of 17, 18, 19, 20, 21, 22 and 23, with an outcome characteristically one more than required.

When counting objects, or items in pictures, children can go wrong in three distinct ways:

- the sequence has errors
- the sequence does not correspond to the items changing in category from the 'to-be-counted' group to the 'already-counted' group. The rhythms of moving (or touching, etc.) and speaking are not in line; one is slower than the other. As a result the final word in the count may be greater or less than the number of items being counted. For example, children may say, 'One, two, three, four, five, six, seven' at the same time as they are moving four cubes from one side of the desk to the other
- some items are missed out from the count or are counted twice.

In counting objects this may indicate a premature attempt to use a more sophisticated counting approach. A solution is to adopt a less sophisticated approach, i.e. to encourage the child who is going wrong when pointing to touch or to move the objects, moving gradually back up through the 'stages' later on.

When counting items in pictures, on the other hand, it is more likely that a problem occurs when counting in a random way, or in spirals – the *less* sophisticated strategies, as it is harder when doing so to account for which items have been counted. The solution in this case is for the child to be taught a more sophisticated strategy, so that they come to 'see' lines of items in the pictures, and learn ways of working systematically through them, either in zigzags or in left-to-right fashion.

Some ideas for teaching whole numbers

Activities with cardinality

Cardinality is readily developed by most children through counting. However, children who struggle to be consistent in their counting of objects do not have the basis for a conclusion that a count tells you 'how many'. As well as supporting them in their counting (perhaps physically, establishing a better word-movement rhythm, or organisationally, by

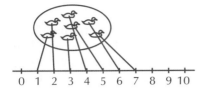

3.6 Mapping a count onto a number line

setting up 'objects counted' and 'objects to be counted' zones or by aligning the objects) it is sometimes helpful to map counts onto a number line, as in Figure 3.6.

Activities with numeral shapes

Learning the shape of the number symbols 0–9 is achieved by repetition, as they make no sense in themselves. As with all 'rote'-learned knowledge, good teaching is a matter of finding ways to endlessly repeat the necessary experience without the children feeling the tedium. With the symbols for numerals this can include:

- numbers on cards
- numbers in the air
- numbers in sand
- numbers in textile materials
- plastic numbers in a feely bag
- numbers in Plasticine and clay
- numbers on dominoes
- number recognition games.

An excellent class activity involves partly obscured numbers written in different ways. A numeral is hidden behind a large card and the child must guess the number as it gradually appears (Figure 3.7).

3.7 Obscuring numerals

Activities for counting

Oral work

The basic activity of counting is not well suited to paper and pencil contexts, as most work will be done in dynamic whole-class or group oral interactive settings, counting in different ways within and around a group. For example, it is simple enough to get a group of children counting so that the 'count' passes from one child to the next around and around (and they only say a number when it is their turn). This can then be extended in different ways: counting up in twos, counting up in twos starting from 3; counting down in fives from 200; adding extra 'rules' such as changing direction when the numbers reach a certain level or when the number ends in zero. Counting is also well suited to odd moments whole-class activity, at the beginning and end of periods, in assembly queues, etc.

Using a calculator

Unusual counting sequences, for example counting in twos or tens, are readily explored using calculators, which can be primed to 'count' using the constant function – by pressing the = button repeatedly following an operation (the exact procedure varies between calculators). So, on simple calculators, 1 + 1 = = = = = = = counts in ones, 2 + 2 = = = = counts in twos, and so on. One of the most constructive ways to use this facility is to get the children to list the 'results' of calculator counting vertically and to examine the outcomes for pattern. This uses the calculator as a data generation device.

To do

'Prime' a calculator of your choosing to 'count' up in threes from two, or to count down in sixes from 100. List the 'results' vertically and find some patterns.

To do

Design a record sheet to monitor counting skills. Will it be an individual or group sheet? Will it be comprehensive or selective? Which particular counting skills are more important? How will changes be noted – with descriptions or on a tick list? Will there be scope for dates, to know when things were learned? Will there be a diagnostic element, noting the nature of errors?

A systematic approach to teaching counting

As a result of its importance, counting should be given rather more attention in schools than is common at present. Time should be spent with individual children on counting (similar to the time spent with individual children on reading), getting each child to count to and with the teacher or another adult, regularly, and every day for some. Each child should be set targets in relation to each of the three strands of counting, and targeted support just beyond his or her current range of skills (equivalent to the support given by teachers to children's 'instructional' level in reading when working with them individually).

The monitoring of each child's development in counting is straightforward, albeit complex, requiring a record-keeping system. The extent of the system adopted to monitor children's development of counting skills can vary, but should include all three aspects: how much, how well and how useful.

The actual assessment to complete a record is best done one-to-one as an interactive interview, which briefly touches on the three aspects. Although it will be different to fit the design of the record, and will also be varied to take account of the individual and what the record says they can already do, the assessment interview may be similar to that shown in Table 3.1.

A class activity

OBJECTIVE	To explore relationships between whole numbers
ORGANISATION	Whole class in a large space
RESOURCES	A set of large number cards, one for each child, prepared so that a card can be hung around a child's neck. The domain of numbers can vary. Examples for sets of 30 cards are:

- six of each number from 1 to 5, three with the number name and three with the numeral;
- three of each numeral (or name) from 1 to 10;
- one of each numeral (or name) from 21 to 50.

ACTIVITY

- The nature of the activity is dependent on the set of number cards used.
- Each child is given a card and the children move around quietly until the teacher gives an instruction, such as, 'Hold the hand of someone who has the same number as you', 'Hold the hand of someone whose number is three less than your number'.
- The children should frequently change cards so that they are continually operating with a different number.

Assessing counting by interview

Instruction	Purpose	Advice
Start counting at 1	To determine if there are any problems with the sequence under 20, and whether she/he can handle the sequence within tens	Allow her/him to get to just over 30
Stop. Start at 37	To determine if she/he can 'count on' and handle the 39–40 and 49–50 bridges	Allow her/him to get to just over 50
Stop. Start at 94	To find out if she/he will go over the hundred, and cope at 109	Allow her/him to get to 123 or so
Stop. Start at 286	To discover whether she/he is coherent when counting larger numbers	Allow her/him to go on to 300
Stop. Can you count backwards? Start at 10	To see if the basic string is established	Allow him/her to count back to 0 (or 'blast off')
Count down from 20	To see how far he/she can go	Stop him/her at 10
Count down from 83	To see how far he/she can go	Stop him/her at 67 or so
Count down from 204	If they can do this they can probably manage anything	Stop child at 195
Can you keep track of your counting? Start at 25 and stop at 33. How many steps is that?	To discover if there are any problems with keeping track, leading to a count that is too small or too large	
Start at 67 and count on an extra 8. Start at 85 and count back 7	To see if keeping track can be managed when counting on or back	
Can you count in twos? Two, four ... Can you count in twos starting at 3?		Allow her/him to go on to 36 if able Prompt with the first few if he/she does not understand, and stop at 21 or so
Can you count in tens? Start at 10		Allow her/him to go beyond 100. If she/he goes '80, 90, 20' note it and move on. If they stop at 100, suggest she/he carries on
Count in tens starting at 6		If the child does not follow, start him/her off but stop at 96
Now look at these objects (about 8). How many are there?	To determine the 'level' of organisation into 'to-be-counted' and 'already counted' groups	If the child moves, touches or points, continue as 'What about these (about 8 again) – can you count them without touching them, just by looking?'
Here is a larger group (about 18). How many are there?	To see if the child has a grouping strategy	
Now look at this picture. How many ... are there?	To determine the 'level' of visual organisation of the items	After the reply, ask 'How did you do it? Did you count round and round, or what?'

Table 3.1

A group activity

OBJECTIVE To recognise numerals when presented in different forms

ORGANISATION Individuals or pairs

RESOURCES Each individual or pair has a set of numeral cards and a large sorting grid (see Figure 3.8).

one	two	three	four	five
1	2	3 3	4 4	5 5
1 1	2 2	3 3	4 4	5
1 1	2	3	4 4	5 5
1	2 2	3	4	5 5

3.8 Sorting numerals

ACTIVITY

- The teacher talks about the objective, discussing some of the numerals with the children and the number names on the sorting grid.
- The children then sort the numerals.
- On completion the teacher discusses with the children what is the same and what is different about all the 'ones', all the 'twos', etc.
- The children end by designing their own numerals.

Test your own knowledge: whole numbers

1 These are the number names for 1–9 in the Korean language:

1 (il), 2 (ee), 3 (sam), 4 (sah), 5 (oh), 6 (yook), 7 (chil), 8 (pal), 9 (goo)

a Work with a colleague to learn the names and then ask each other questions about which numbers come after, before, are more than, less than and come between given numbers.

b What difficulties did you encounter? What relationships were the easiest/most difficult for you to learn? Try to offer explanations why this might be.

2 The set of whole numbers is in one–one correspondence with the set of even numbers.

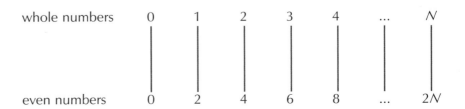

whole numbers   0   1   2   3   4   ... N

even numbers   0   2   4   6   8   ... $2N$

This suggests that there are the 'same' number of whole numbers as even numbers. How can that be when the even numbers are a subset of the whole numbers, the other subset being the odd numbers? Discuss this apparent contradiction with your colleagues.

Review of key points ➤ Very young children have a sense of small whole numbers without being able to say or write them

➤ Whole numbers are independent of any representational system

➤ Numerals are the way that numbers are represented, but the word 'number' is used for both the concept and its representation

➤ The set of whole numbers provides a counting system where each successor is one more than its predecessor

➤ Cardinality and ordinality are different, yet closely related, systems

➤ Counting is an essential skill that all children should master and teachers should raise its priority

➤ Children should work with whole numbers beyond the domain of 0–20 before they are introduced to place value concepts

Module 4   Learning to teach place value

Introduction

Whole numbers greater than 9 are represented systematically in our number system, and calculation would be more difficult if this were not so. The ancient Roman numbers, familiar to us because they are still sometimes found on clock faces, were systematic in what they represented, but the system did not make calculation easy. The current system, used in Europe since the Middle Ages, and usually referred to as 'Hindu-Arabic', is more sophisticated because of its place value structure. Place value is perhaps the most important concept children need to understand in their early learning of mathematics, but many children are slow to accommodate its meaning. Its very sophistication could be a reason why many children find it a difficult concept to learn despite efforts over many years to improve the teaching of place value.

Place value in national curricula

Place value pervades the number curriculum, and its importance in the development of children's understanding and ability to work with multi-digit numbers cannot be overemphasised. Most primary mathematics curricula stress the following aspects of place value:

- understanding that the position of a digit signifies its value
- ordering numbers
- approximating numbers to a multiple of 10
- multiplying and dividing by powers of 10
- applying place value in money and measures.

Key terms

grouping   grouping of single objects or of sets of objects produces a collective unit

base   a base is the repeated use of the same collective unit forming a number system. The base for our number system is 10

place value   used to describe the idea that the value represented by any particular digit in a number is dependent on the position or place of the digit in that number. Thus, in 275 the 5 is in the 'ones' place and represents five, the 7 is in the 'tens' place and represents seven tens (seventy), the 2 is in the 'hundreds' place and represents two hundreds

zero   in place value the zero symbol, '0', is used as a place holder to signify the absence of value in a particular position. Thus, in the number 207 the 'tens' position is 'empty'

powers   as we move from the 'ones' place to the left in the written recording of whole numbers, successive places represent increasing powers of the base 10 (see Table 4.1)

Key issues in place value

Related concepts and issues

Counting in whole numbers is naturally an important basis for arithmetic, not least place value. The representation of these numbers immediately involves digits for ones, tens, hundreds, and so on. But the idea of representing numbers so that grouping into batches of ten has great significance forms the essence of beginning to come to terms with the way we record larger numbers, and this is encapsulated within the concept of base. Zero also emerges as a critical concept, with its function as a place holder within the system. Much effort needs to go into developing language as the system becomes more and more elaborated. All of this is illustrated in Figure 4.1, with the understanding that language is an essential feature in every concept and issue.

Number base 10

It appears reasonable to assume that humans adopted base 10 because of early counting which used ten fingers (including thumbs). Indeed, we even refer to the symbols 0 to 9 as digits, the same word as may also be used for fingers and toes.

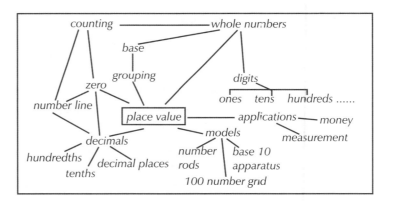

4.1 Concepts and issues associated with place value

Representations of the base 10 number system

Millions (1 000 000)	Hundred thousands (100 000)	Ten thousands (10 000)	Thousands (1000)	Hundreds (100)	Tens (10)	Ones (1)
$10 \times 10 \times 10 \times 10 \times 10 \times 10$	$10 \times 10 \times 10 \times 10 \times 10$	$10 \times 10 \times 10 \times 10$	$10 \times 10 \times 10$	10×10	10	1
10^6 Sixth power of 10	10^5 Fifth power of 10	10^4 Fourth power of 10	10^3 Third power of 10	10^2 Second power of 10	10^1 First power of 10	$10^?$? power of 10

Table 4.1

Reasons why our number system might be claimed to be superior to any previous system, like the Roman or Babylonian, include the following:

- it is built around a very limited number of symbols
- it incorporates a symbol for zero
- it has a convenient 'base' (10)
- it uses a place value system which makes written recording and calculation easy.

Table 4.1 shows a variety of written representations of the first six place value positions in our base 10 number system.

In number work, we take for granted that the number base is ten, although other number bases are possible. In base 10 arithmetic, we have ten digits (and therefore only ten symbols, namely 0, 1, 2, 3, 4, 5, 6, 7, 8, and 9). The counting number following 9 has to be represented by the symbol 10, representing one 'ten' plus zero 'ones'. Thus, for numbers greater than 9 the same symbols 0 to 9 are still used, but in combination according to rules which children have to learn.

To do

What 'symbols' did the Romans use for 1, 5, 50, 100 and 1000? How did they combine the symbols to represent other numbers?

Understanding place value

There are four key processes that are central to children's understanding of place value:

- counting
- partitioning
- grouping
- number relationships.

Counting

There is always a danger that counting is restricted to the sequence 0, 1, 2, 3, ... It is important that children move from using one as a counting unit to using other powers of base 10 such as ten, hundred, and thousand. In other words, they should frequently count 10, 20, 30, ...; 100, 200, 300, ...; and 1000, 2000, 3000, ..., as well as in sub-units such as in 2s, 5s, 20s, 25s, 50s, 200s and 500s.

Partitioning

There are two stages in partitioning which develop understanding of place value. The first is called 'unique partitioning'. This is the standard representation that occurs at the initial stage of learning when children write a number as the composition of a tens value and a ones value. For example, 59 is written as 5 tens and 9 ones. This is often called the expanded form of a number. 'Multiple partitioning' is a later development when children begin to extend their ability by writing 59 as 4 tens and 19 ones, or 3 tens and 29 ones. Partitioning is a very important tool for mental strategies.

Grouping

Many children appear to see the process of grouping as having relevance only when involved with objects or pictures of objects. However, grouping goes much beyond this being part of many activities with multi-digit numerals. The 'doing' and the 'undoing' of groupings contributes to both mental and written strategies. For example, 30 − 8 may be viewed as 20 + 10 − 8 = 20 + 2 = 22.

Number relationships

The understanding of relationships between numbers should be an objective in children learning about place value in particular and number sense in general. Ordering of numbers is one of the most important of these relationships.

Jones *et al.* (1996) conducted a research study which validated a framework for 'nurturing and assessing' the development of place value in children based upon the four key processes just discussed. It will be helpful for you to see this in detail as it makes a valuable contribution to teachers' understanding of how the concept is gradually built up. A modified version of the framework is reproduced in Table 4.2.

A framework for developing place value

	Counting	Partitioning	Grouping	Number relationships
Level 1: Pre-place value requiring the use of single digits	Count and count on in ones; count informally in tens	Make numbers in different ways: 5 is 4 and 1	Estimate numbers of objects in a group using 5 and 10 as benchmarks. Count in 5s and 10s. Group to make it quick and easy to check	Determine numbers more/less than 5 or 10; a 'lot more/less'; numbers 'in between' 0 to 10
Level 2: Initial place value using ten as a composite unit	Count groups of ten as though they were single items; forming and counting groups of tens and extras; count on in tens and ones	Make multi-digit numbers in different ways, especially tens/ones	Estimate number of objects in a group using an appropriate unit (e.g. 10). Count to check. Group to make it quick and easy to check	Order multi-digit numbers within and across decades

continued on opposite page

Table 4.2

Table 4.2 continued

	Counting	Partitioning	Grouping	Number relationships
Level 3: Developing place value extending the use of two-digit numbers to mental addition	Count, count on, or count back by tens to add/ subtract mentally	Make multi-digit numbers different ways (most less than 100). Find the missing part of a number (most less than 100)	Determine whether the sum of two two-digit numbers is in the thirties	Order multi-digit numbers (especially those under 100 formed by interchanging digits)
Level 4: Extending place value to three-digit numbers	Count, count on, or count back by hundreds and tens to add/ subtract hundreds and tens mentally	Make multi-digit numbers different ways (many up to 1000). Find the missing part of a number (many up to 1000)	Determine whether the sum of two three-digit numbers is more or less than 250, for example. Given 31 tens and 12 ones, determine the number of units without reference to materials	Order multi-digit numbers (including those up to 1000 formed by interchanging digits)
Level 5: Essential place value requiring flexible approaches to written and mental number problems with numbers to 1000	Count on, or back by hundreds, tens and ones to add/subtract mentally	Make multi-digit numbers (some beyond 1000) different ways	Determine whether the sum/difference of two two/three-digit numbers is more or less than (e.g. 350). Given 2 hundreds, 23 tens and 9 ones, determine the number of units without reference to materials	Order multi-digit numbers up to 1000 (especially determining which of two numbers is closer to a third)

The role of zero

The concept of zero is a vital one in calculation, yet in itself it creates difficulties for many learners. Zero is sometimes referred to as a 'place holder', thus emphasising both its connection with place value and its use in ensuring that a particular position (place) in the number system is held and not lost when calculations are carried out. If, for example, the outcome of a calculation is 104, the 0 in the middle is vital, yet is not spoken in the description 'one hundred and four'. The history of mathematics suggests that the concept of 'zero' was not only an extremely significant development but was also a surprisingly late 'invention', and this in itself is enough to warn teachers that the concept and use of zero is not such an obvious idea. Many of the difficulties children experience in number calculations are with zero rather than with other features of the place value system.

Models for place value

Number rods and base 10 apparatus

Number rods based upon a unit (ones), together with collections of that unit (tens), are essential for children working within the tens and ones stage of place value. These may appear as linking cubes, or base 10 apparatus, where the 'ones' unit is retained in a 'ten' as 10 ones (Figure 4.2a), or as numbered rods (see Figure 4.2b). Children should collect 'tens' and 'ones', recording how many they have using number cards (alternatively, they may start with the cards and find the rods to match). The use of number rods for 100s, 1000s and above requires that the tens rods are bundled together. This has advantages as children must constantly be collecting 10 tens to make a hundred. However, the most convenient apparatus is the base 10 material extended to using the 100 square and then to the 1000 block, which can be used in a similar way to that described above (see Figure 4.7).

Number tracks

Number tracks used to represent whole numbers inevitably show place value in the symbols they use. To stress the relationship between the different decades and the structure of the place value system a 0–20 number track can be cut to form a number grid as in Figure 4.3. This should be repeated with number tracks from 0 to 30, 0 to 40 and so on, as larger numbers are explored.

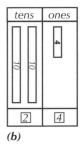

4.2 Place value using linking cubes and number rods

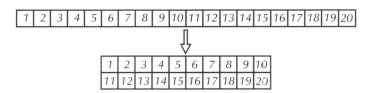

4.3 A number track becomes a number grid

To do

Compare different textbooks to see if and how number tracks, number grids and number lines are used.

Number lines

The 0–10 number line should be extended to include firstly numbers to 20, then to 30, and so on up to 100. On all occasions the relationships between numbers in the different decades should be discussed with children in the way they are represented symbolically and how they are said and written in words. Figure 4.4 shows a number line constructed to bring out the infinite nature of numbers and the base 10 structure of the number system by emphasising the different decades in different ways. Teachers often use alternating colours for adjacent decades on a number line placed around the classroom wall.

*0 1 2 3 4 5 6 7 8 9 **10 11 12** 13 **14** 15 **16 17 18 19** 20 21 22*

4.4 Decades on a number line

Metric measurement

A wide variety of collective units have been used in the past, some of which are still in use today. Imperial units such as 12 inches to 1 foot and 3 feet to 1 yard, and miles (1760 yards) are still used to measure longer distances; there are 60 seconds to one minute, 60 minutes to 1 hour, 24 hours to 1 day, and so on. However, we always use the ten digits to perform calculations based on these systems of measurement, and this tends to obscure the fact that we are nevertheless working with a variety of collective units. The metric system is now encouraged for measurement, both because the collective unit and base is always 10, and because the system is more international than any other. It is sometimes claimed that money and measurement with metric units on the one hand, and the concept of place value on the other, may be taught in a kind of mutually supportive combination. If there is a problem with metric measurement in this regard it is that some of the powers of 10 are given particular names, for example 'centimetre' and 'kilogram', which sometimes obscure the use of 10 as base for the whole system.

The British system of money

The British 1p, 10p and £1 coins illustrate the use of both place value and base 10 in coinage. There are, however, other collective units: 2p, 5p, 20p, 50p and £2. There are good practical reasons for having these 'additional' coins and the £5, £20 and £50 notes, but they can obscure the base 10 structure of our money system. This illustrates how money, like the metric system, might not provide the ideal illustration of place value, and how the combination referred to in the previous paragraph might not always provide the hoped-for support.

Number names and symbols

In general, the language of numbers (in English) emphasises the place value system in base 10 yet at the same time obscures it through lack of consistency. There are nine words (one, two, three, ..., nine) for the nine counting numbers (1, 2, 3, ..., 9) and these same nine words are represented within the names for subsequent groups of numbers like 11–19, 21–29, 31–39, and so on – except that the words for 11 and 12 don't fit the system (cf. the corresponding words in many other European languages). Thus there is a problem of seemingly arbitrary words, and such inconsistencies cause difficulties for children. What is more, the words for numbers following 12 *end* in 'teen' (and not 'ten'), whereas the words for numbers following 20 helpfully *begin* with 'twenty', or 'thirty', and so on. This is a difficulty of tens–ones reversal.

The language of the numbers greater than 10 therefore needs to be explored and explained throughout, and in particular at the first stage the link between 'teen' and 'ten'. Some teachers might decide to employ temporary alternative descriptors, for example 'ten-one', 'ten-two', ten-three', and so on, to help the accommodation period, though this will probably have to be done alongside the usual terminology in order not to confuse, given that many children will have already encountered the 'proper' words outside school. 'Eleven' and 'twelve' can only be explained as peculiarities, perhaps numbers which people a long time ago considered so special that they warranted individual words.

There are other idiosyncrasies, too, like 'thirteen' and 'fifteen', which don't follow the pattern of the other 'teens', and 'ten', 'twenty', 'thirty' and 'fifty' which don't follow the pattern of the other multiples of 10 ending in 'ty' (and the four in 'forty' even loses its 'u'!). Thus we find there are irregular spellings and pronunciations. Subsequently, as larger numbers are encountered, 'twenty', 'thirty', 'forty', 'fifty', 'sixty', etc., also require discussion, both from the point of view of their pattern and also from the point of view of the exceptions. In these, we find '-ty' instead of 'ten' and thus the modifications of 'ten', first into 'teen' and then into 'ty', create another difficulty. 'Thirty' and 'fifty' conveniently correspond to the modifications of spelling found in 'thirteen' and 'fifteen', but 'forty' is a new variation. Eventually, 'one hundred' needs to be introduced, a completely new word for a completely new magnitude, the smallest three-digit number.

> ### To think about
>
> Compare, for complexity and likely pitfalls, the number words in the English language and in any other languages with which you are familiar. Compare your knowledge with colleagues who may know languages which you do not.

Children and place value

Learning difficulties

Branford, as long ago as 1908, wrote: 'Teachers of arithmetic are familiar with the difficulty most children have in mastering the use of the principle of place-value and of the zero.'

The Concepts in Secondary Mathematics and Science Project (CSMS) provided much evidence of young secondary school children struggling to add and subtract in situations such as 6399 + 1 and 3597 + 10 (Brown, 1981b). For primary school teachers, these examples need to be taken not only as an indication of difficulties, which clearly may still remain as children move from primary to secondary education, but also as helping to define objectives.

DIFFERENCE SPOTTING

Orton (1992) reported a research study which asked 11–12-year-old children to identify pairs of four-digit numbers that differed as in Table 4.3.

This provides more detailed information on the attainment of many primary pupils in place value. With older children, it was observed that in every age group the order of difficulty was the same, but that performance generally improved steadily through the years.

Sets of four-digit numbers	
Difference requested	**Facility (%)**
Set 1: numbers that differed by 10, such as 1246 and 1256	65
Set 2: numbers that differed by 100, such as 2136 and 2236	45
Set 3: numbers that differed by 1000, such as 5337 and 6337	72
Set 4: numbers that differed by 10, and crossed a boundary, such as 6497 and 6507	30

Table 4.3

Reading and writing numerals

Children's difficulties with reading and writing numbers are the cause of many later errors when operating with numbers.

WRITING NUMERALS

Barker (see Orton, 1992) tested and interviewed a large group of children in the age range 7–9 years across a number of schools on their place value abilities. One revealing question concerning the writing of numerals, posed orally, was: 'There are five boxes on your paper. In the first box I want you to write the number fifteen.' Questions proceeded similarly for the numbers 'thirty-six', 'four hundred and thirty-two', 'two hundred and nine' and 'four thousand and sixty'.

The first two numbers, 15 and 36, were within the grasp of most of the children. There were 11 different responses to 432, with 27% of the children writing 4032 or 40032. About the same proportion of the 7–8 year olds wrote 2009 for 209, but the proportion dropped to 5% for children of 8–9 years. There were 21 variations for 4060, with 40060 and 400060 being common. Again the 8–9-year-old children were much better than those of 7–8, but this is a difficulty which, for some children, recurs unexpectedly, and sometimes persists into secondary school. It seems that numbers below 100 are much less likely to present this kind of difficulty, but Ginsburg (1977) found at least one child writing 23 and 35 as 203 and 305, respectively. Such findings illustrate how difficulties with place value and with zero can often not be separated.

Are the errors that children make 'reasonable' and 'logical'? How would you convince children that what they consider 'logical' is not correct?

In the reading of numbers, there are obvious difficulties with larger ones such as 18523 and 27564398. Here, the digits need to be grouped in threes from the *right* hand end, a method which children need to learn. The reason for grouping in threes, as in 27,564,398 is that we can now clearly see the millions (27 of them, in the group on the extreme left), the middle group is then the thousands (564 of them), and the final group on the right comprises the hundreds, tens and ones. This grouping may be done by spacing rather than by using commas (because of internationally accepted conventions), i.e. 18 523 and 27 564 398. Note that one thousand, and later one million, both act, in a way, as subsidiary bases. This suggests first that children need to be very secure with numbers below 1000 before venturing beyond, and second that the use of 'thousands', 'ten thousands', and 'hundred thousands' as labels for successive places moving further leftwards beyond 'hundreds' (and the similar structure for millions) needs to be explained carefully.

Value of digits

Without an understanding of the value of digits in a number little progress is possible in mathematics.

DIGIT VALUE

In the CSMS Project (Brown, 1981b) this question was asked:

5214	The 2 stands for two hundreds
521 400	The 2 stands for two ...?

It produced only 22% correct responses from 11–12 year olds (and still less than 50% from those of 14–15 years). However, we must not imagine that reading problems lie only with very large numbers. Dickson *et al.* (1984) record several errors from primary school sources, such as 4001 being read as 'four hundred and one', and 8030 being read as 'eight hundred and thirty'.

Kouba *et al.* (1989) asked the following questions:

What digit is in the tens place in the number 2059?

What digit is in the thousands place in the number 43 486?

They reported 64% and 45% success rates, respectively, from a sample of 9-year-old children. These results perhaps indicate that children are less successful in stating the value of a digit given its position than in finding the position of a digit when its place value is given.

Are both these aspects of place value covered in primary textbooks? How are they dealt with and what size of numbers are used?

Misconceptions involving zero

A difficulty with reading and writing numbers involves the use of zero as a place holder. One complication inflicted by social convention is that zero is sometimes loosely referred to as 'nothing', and this may not be helpful to children – 'nothing' suggests the absence of anything at all, not even a representation of that nothingness. If there are no objects on the desk, you do not see anything, but the representation of that nothingness in mathematics is the visible and readable symbol '0'. Even the words 'nought', 'none' and 'no' to some extent carry similar dangers, yet children meet all of these words and ideas, in the home and the street if not in school. A further complication is that even the letter 'O' (pronounced 'oh!') is used to describe the symbol '0', for example in the widely used method of reading telephone numbers. What is clear is that '0' must be treated with scrupulous correctness, and many children need considerable guidance in accommodating its meaning.

Ordering whole numbers

The ability to place numbers in their correct relative positions as on a number line is also an important aspect of understanding place value.

ORDERING

Sixty-one 9–10-year-old pupils from two schools were asked to write these numbers in ascending order (smallest to largest):

26 945 49 562 24 659 25 964 9654

As many as 23% of the children were unable to produce the correct order. This was the most common incorrect response.

24 659 25 964 26 945 49 562 9654

What was the thinking which produced the error? What are the implications for writing assessment items to test ordering of numbers?

Ordering of a set of numbers demands more than merely asking for either the largest or smallest of a set, particularly when the numbers are written vertically beneath one another as they were in the following.

THE LARGEST

Ward (1979) asked 10-year-old children the question 'which town has the largest population?'

Aberdeen	183 800
Bath	151 500
Fleetwood	28 800
Walsall	184 600
Winchester	31 000

Only 65% of the children were successful in this task. It seems that the more digits the given numbers have, the more difficulty children experience with ordering. If it is tempting to blame lack of success on the magnitude of the numbers, however, the work of Bednarz and Janvier (1979, 1982) is sufficient to point out that numbers less than one thousand can also provide problems for 9-year-old children.

How may the format of presentation of numbers influence children's responses to questions about ordering?

Some ideas for teaching place value

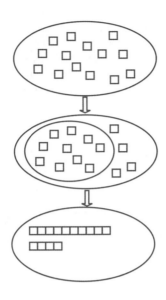

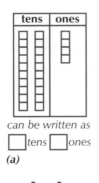

4.5 Grouping in 10s

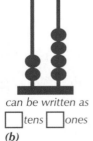

can be written as

☐tens ☐ones

(a)

can be written as

☐tens ☐ones

(b)

4.6 Symbolising pictorial representations

Textbooks and place value

There can be no doubt that the emphasis given to activities on place value in textbooks is limited. These activities tend to fall into four types:

- grouping in tens
- symbolising and pictorial representation
- using a picture of an abacus
- writing numbers in expanded notation.

Grouping in tens

As we have seen, only ten symbols are required to represent all whole numbers because of the system of place value and because the base is 10. It is the idea and practice of grouping which manifests the base. For children, the critical first step in understanding our system of recording of numbers beyond 9 is to link grouping into batches of ten with the position of a digit in a numeral; in other words to link the 1 in 14, for example, with one batch of ten in the counting (see Figure 4.5). Thus the batches or bundles should be finally placed to the left of the 'ones', in order to assist recording. Many experiences with collecting objects together into batches of ten with ones left over is required, and later extended to collecting tens into hundreds (ten tens). This needs to be done concretely for some time, using a variety of objects each time and recording the total as a number. If rods (like match sticks or short straws) are used, it may be helpful to fasten the bundles of ten together in some way, perhaps with elastic bands. A possible sequence for recording the number of objects in symbols is:

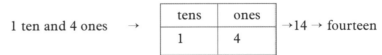

	tens	ones	
1 ten and 4 ones →	1	4	→14 → fourteen

Linking cubes, which both allow ten units to be made into a 'fixed' rod, can usefully be employed at this stage as well. Many experiences with totals between 10 and 19 naturally come first, then totals between 20 and 29, and so on. The importance of batches of ten is eventually reinforced on rulers, in the 'hundred square', on graph paper, and in countless other ways in mathematics, but this early stage of grouping is when its importance is first established.

Symbolising and pictorial representation

Children are presented with pictures of tens and ones (Figure 4.6a), and are required to write the 'quantity' as a number of tens and ones. This activity mirrors that with the base 10 apparatus described earlier. The activity is sometimes reversed, with children given the number and asked to draw the ten rods and the ones.

Using a picture of an abacus

This is a similar approach to the above, but with some important cognitive differences. It is illustrated in Figure 4.6b.

To do

Discuss with colleagues the four different teaching activities. Make a list of the differences in the cognitive expectations of each activity. How is it possible for children to answer questions correctly in each approach without understanding place value?

Expanded notation

This is the most popular textbook activity, possibly because it takes less space than the two above activities. It uses words and/or symbols, and appears to be regarded as the final step in developing children's understanding of place value. Children are required to write in the missing numbers, and there are many variations, some of which are shown here:

$$478 \quad = \quad \square \text{ hundreds} \qquad \square \text{ tens} \qquad \square \text{ ones}$$
$$= \quad \square \,(100) \qquad + \quad \square \,(10) \quad + \quad \square \,(1)$$
$$= \quad \square \,(10 \times 10) \quad + \quad \square \,(10) \quad + \quad \square$$
$$= \quad \square \times 100 \qquad + \quad \square \times 10 \quad + \quad \square$$

hundreds	tens	ones
▦▦		▫▫▫▫
2	0	4

two hundred and four $\Rightarrow$ 204

4.7 Place value using base 10 apparatus

Activities with apparatus

The use of discrete objects, number rods, number tracks, the hundred square and number lines are sufficient to support the early stages of grouping into tens, and tens of tens, etc. Subsequently, however, more sophisticated base 10 apparatus should be introduced to children. It is important that they become familiar with and understand its structure before it is used for the four operations on number.

Whatever concrete materials are used, it is essential to heed the evidence which clearly indicates that apparatus in the form of a model or representation on its own may not lead automatically to sound understanding (see Module 11). It is not sufficient to provide the materials and hope that they will promote learning. Considerable effort needs to go into developing children's understanding of the progression from materials to tabulation to symbolism, as shown in Figure 4.7.

The particular example here requires emphasis on the use of zero. At the same time, the structure of numbers should be emphasised through writing in 'expanded notation'; that is, $14 = 1 \times 10 + 4 \times 1$, and $134 = 1 \times 100 + 3 \times 10 + 4 \times 1$.

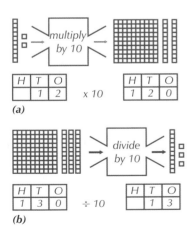

4.8 Multiplication and division by 10

Activities multiplying and dividing by powers of 10

Both mental and written methods for the four operations may require knowledge of multiplication and division by multiples of 10. Reference has already been made to the unique expanded notation which sums up the structure of numbers, and which children need to learn:

$$238 \quad = \quad 2 \times 100 \quad + \quad 3 \times 10 \quad + \quad 8 \times 1$$
$$= \quad 2 \times 10^2 \quad + \quad 3 \times 10^1 \quad + \quad 8$$

Both multiplication and division by 10 can be seen diagrammatically in Figure 4.8. A knowledge of indices (see Module 10) helps understanding of multiplication by 10 by showing how each power of 10 in the unique expanded notation becomes one higher power of 10 throughout. For example,

$$238 \times 10 \quad = \quad (2 \times 10^2 \quad + \quad 3 \times 10^1 \quad + \quad 8) \times 10$$
$$= \quad 2 \times 10^3 \quad + \quad 3 \times 10^2 \quad + \quad 8 \times 10^1$$
$$= \quad 2 \times 1000 \quad + \quad 3 \times 100 \quad + \quad 8 \times 10$$
$$= \quad 2380$$

To think about

Analyse a set of textbooks and the teacher's guides to see what coverage they give to place value. What models do they recommend?

This is one way of understanding why multiplication by 10 is sometimes ill-advisedly described as 'adding a nought' – in no sense are we 'adding' a nought, and we are certainly not subtracting a nought when we divide by 10. This kind of approach contributes to misleading rules for children to remember, including the equally unhelpful 'to multiply by 10 move the decimal point one place to the right' (see Module 5). What has certainly happened is that *digits have moved into new places*, and this should be the focus of the children's observations and consequent analysis of the transformation of the numbers involved.

A class activity

OBJECTIVE   To make the largest number using five given digits

ORGANISATION   Whole class working individually

RESOURCES   Teacher has a set of ten digit cards, one each of the digits 0 to 9. Each child has a sheet on which there are sets of five boxes for writing five-digit numbers:

ACTIVITY

- Teacher states the objective (i.e. to make the largest number) and, if necessary, writes numbers on the board
- Teacher then shows five of the digit cards in turn from the set
- As a card is shown the children decide where to write the digit in one of the five boxes
- When complete the children's numbers are put on the board and everyone reads them
- The winning number is the one satisfying the objective

Similar activities may be based on finding the smallest number, a number in between two given numbers, a number less than a given number, a number more than a given number, a number that is nearer to one of two given numbers.

A group activity

OBJECTIVE   To make and order two-digit numbers

ORGANISATION   Small groups

RESOURCES   Each child has ten digit cards 0–9, and a recording sheet with grids for writing two-digit numbers and space for writing each number in words. For example:

3	1

thirty-one

ACTIVITY

- Each child makes five two-digit numbers, using any card only once.
- Each child records the numbers made and writes them in words.
- The five numbers made are then written in order.
- Lists are then compared to see who made the largest and the smallest numbers.

Test your own knowledge: place value

1 The number 275 when expanded is $2 \times 10^2 + 7 \times 10^1 + 5 \times 10^?$. What power of 10 represents the 'ones' place? Explain your reasoning to a partner.

2 A base eight (octal) number system would need only eight digits, so for convenience we could use 0, 1, 2, 3, 4, 5, 6, and 7.

   a Write out the representations of numbers in octal notation for the base ten numbers from 1 to 100.

   b Explore octal addition and subtraction.

   c Next, really test yourself on octal arithmetic by trying out some multiplication questions like 23×6, 23×65 and 123×57, and also some division questions like $365 \div 7$, $1004 \div 14$ and $717 \div 36$. The last task requires fractions or octimals (not decimals, of course) to express the answer.

   To what extent does this exploration of octal arithmetic indicate to you what demands we are making on children when they work in base 10?

3 Hexadecimal numbers (base 16) are difficult to handle, because they require 16 digits (including 0), and we have only ten obvious ones. In order to try out hexadecimal arithmetic, it is necessary to invent extra symbols, and often the following are used: 0, 1, 2, 3, 4, 5, 6, 7, 8, 9, a, b, c, d, e, f.

   a Write out the representations in hexadecimal notation for the base 10 numbers from 1 to 100.

   b Now comes the real crunch! Make up and try to answer some addition and subtraction questions. If you feel brave, try out some multiplication questions.

   c The easiest way to investigate division is to work through your multiplication tasks 'in reverse'. This really brings home to us not only the sophistication of our place value system in base 10 but also how much we have had to learn and understand, and how much we are expecting of children.

4 To the ancient Babylonian civilisation, 60 was an important base, and it is believed that we owe our measures of both time and angle to this feature. Investigate the Babylonian number system.

51

Review of key points ➤ Understanding place value incorporates understanding of the use of ten as the collective unit or base for everyday calculations

➤ Understanding place value incorporates understanding of the significance and use of zero as a place holder

➤ Some children require considerable time and effort to absorb the concepts of place value, base and zero

➤ Once introduced, the concepts of place value, base ten and zero are constantly involved in calculations, and eventually link up with studies of money, the metric system and decimals

➤ The language of our number system is not entirely helpful to learners, because of inconsistencies and exceptions to the rules of construction, but it nevertheless must be developed alongside and used to support place value work

➤ Reading large numbers requires arranging digits in threes from the right before it is possible to read from the left

➤ The value of positions in which digits are placed may be thought of as powers of the base, so powers are involved in a thorough understanding of the place value concept

➤ Useful concrete apparatus to assist the learning of place value does exist, but remember that the objective is always to illuminate and support the development of written arithmetic

➤ Work with other number bases and a variety of systems of measurement may be used to illuminate place value and base 10, but they should be used with care. For many children the focus needs to be almost exclusively on working in base 10 until that is mastered

Module 5   Learning to teach decimals

Introduction

Consideration of whole numbers requires us to think of 'ones', 'tens', 'hundreds', 'thousands' and so on, with each successive unit in this list not only getting larger but also having a '10 times' relationship with the units on either side. As we move to the left in a numeral, the value of the position of each successive digit is ten times the previous one, and in this way we are able to represent numbers as large as we like. These units, however, do not always provide us with small enough quantities with which to measure and to calculate. It is theoretically simple to solve this problem, because if 'one hundred' is 10 times 'ten', and 'ten' is 10 times 'one', then we can easily invent a unit so that 'one' is 10 times bigger than it; it is these smaller units we call decimals. Decimals provide us with a way of continuing a 10 times relationship and dealing with quantities and measurements which are as small as we like.

Decimals in national curricula

National curricula in primary mathematics stress the following aspects of learning decimals:

- extending the place value system to units smaller than one
- recognising and using decimals in money
- understanding of decimals to two decimal places
- working with decimals in measurement applications
- rounding of decimals
- equivalence of decimals with fractions and percentages.

Key terms

decimal number a number which includes a decimal part will be referred to in this module as a decimal number. Thus 7 is a whole number, but 7.2 is a decimal number

decimal point a mark, usually a 'dot' which separates the whole part of a number from the decimal part

decimal fraction a decimal number consists of a whole number part and a decimal part. The decimal part is strictly a decimal fraction, because its magnitude is less than 1, for example the decimal part of 7.2 is the decimal representation of the vulgar fraction 2/10, or 1/5

rounding a decimal number may be rounded to any given number of decimal places. Thus, if the answer 7.2318695 is obtained from a calculation it may be rounded to 1 decimal place, say, thus yielding 7.2

Key issues in decimals

Related concepts and issues

Figure 5.1 shows the prior and dependent concepts and issues. The notion of decimals arises from the extension of the number system to units smaller than 'ones', and therefore depends on place value with base 10, and on zero. A large part of the time spent by children in learning about decimals is simply to do with this extension to smaller positive numbers. The introduction of decimals immediately requires the introduction of the separator, or marker (the decimal point), and requires the naming of the new 'units' as tenths, hundredths and thousandths. Their use in calculations, involving the four operations of addition, subtraction, multiplication and division, may be regarded by teachers merely as an extension of work on the four operations applied to whole numbers, but pupils do not always see it as so straightforward. Children often need a considerable amount of time to accommodate this extension to decimals. In particular, long multiplication and long division by pencil and paper methods require much time and effort. The distinctions between decimals that are rational numbers (or fractions) and those which are irrational numbers may never be articulated in the primary school, but children nevertheless need to be encouraged to think about the different kinds of numbers they are using. The links with both fractions and percentages are considered in Module 7.

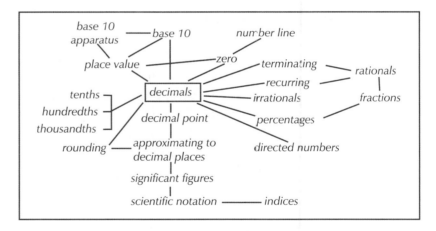

5.1 Concepts and issues associated with decimals

Decimal place value

The place to the right of the 'ones' in the place value system, the 'first decimal place', is the 'tenths'. This is an obvious description to use, given that the relationship is that each unit in the system is 10 times the one on its immediate right. In this way, as much expansion to the right as could ever be required may be achieved. The 'hundredths' obviously come next, in the 'second decimal place', with the 'thousandths' after that, in the 'third decimal place', and so on. This is a very significant development of the number system.

When dealing only with whole numbers, there is always a 'next number', for example the next number after 13 is 14, and the next number before

48 is 47. With the introduction of decimal numbers we can no longer talk of the next number, for example after 2.6 or before 0.35. This is a much larger step in the development of understanding numbers than we might immediately think. It brings with it the notion that one can always find a number between any two given numbers, for example between 5.3 and 5.4, or between 5.378 and 5.379. Indeed, there is no limit to the number of numbers between 5.3 and 5.4, or between 5.378 and 5.379, or between any given pair of numbers. This notion of decimals also revolutionises the concept of a 'number line', but unfortunately carries with it conceptual difficulties for many primary children.

The expanded place value system involving decimals, and the associated relationships with powers of 10, referred to in Module 4, are now shown in Table 5.1. The symmetry around the 'ones' column (and not around the decimal point) stands out clearly.

Extending place value to decimals

Thousands	Hundreds	Tens	Ones	Tenths	Hundredths	Thousandths
1000	100	10	1	0.1	0.01	0.001
$10 \times 10 \times 10$	10×10	10	1	$\frac{1}{10}$	$\frac{1}{10 \times 10}$	$\frac{1}{10 \times 10 \times 10}$
10^3	10^2	10^1	10^0	10^{-1}	10^{-2}	10^{-3}

Table 5.1

Note the potential for mis-hearing when speaking about decimals, which is something to guard against with children. 'Tens' and 'tenths' sound so very similar, as do 'hundreds' and 'hundredths', and 'thousands' and 'thousandths'. This is a very unfortunate feature of the language of decimals; it is necessary to articulate very clearly, and at the same time to continue to emphasise the distinctions in magnitude.

Decimal point

With whole numbers, the place alone is sufficient to indicate the magnitude which any digit represents. In the number 2364, it should be clear that the 2 represents two thousand, the 3 represents three hundred, the 6 represents sixty, and the 4 represents four. When a number includes decimal places, a clear written 'marker', the decimal point, is required to separate the whole number part from the decimal part, as there is no other distinguishing feature.

The dot, full stop – or 'point', which is how it should be described – is placed 'on the line', as in 8.15, in just the same way as a full stop at the end of a sentence. This has not always been the case, however, and the older notation of placing the point 'half way up', as in 8·15, is still sometimes found, particularly in primary textbooks. In both representations, the number would be read as 'eight point one five'. It is important *not* to read it as 'eight point fifteen' as the digits 1 and 5 in no sense represent the whole number 15. It does, however, represent 'eight plus fifteen hundredths', or 'eight and fifteen hundredths', which

To think about

Explain to a colleague why 'ones' must be represented by 10^0 and 'tenths' represented by 10^{-1}.

55

illustrates how careful teachers need to be in their use of language. The decimal point does not act as a separator between two whole numbers, a common misunderstanding in children which needs to be corrected constantly. Here, the 1 in the first decimal place is one tenth, and the 5 in the second decimal place is five hundredths, and the decimal number is equivalent to the fraction (mixed number) $8^{15}/_{100}$.

Clearly, numbers may include digits on both sides of the decimal point, as in 8.15, or on one side only, as in 8 and .15. In decimal numbers with a zero whole number part, it is common practice to incorporate that zero before the point, as in 0.15 (rather than just .15), 0.06 (instead of .06), and 0.605 (instead of .605). This is purely a convention, and serves only to clarify and emphasise. It is important in writing decimal numbers, however, as otherwise the decimal point might be overlooked.

Unfortunately, dots or points are also used in other ways, for example children see time written as 6.15 am. Cricket enthusiasts will recall that the number of overs remaining in an innings appears on television screens, for example, as 6.2 where the 2 represents the number of balls and the 6 the number of overs. Similarly, the numbering of tables and figures in books (this one included) often depends on using dots as separators. Teachers should not keep these applications hidden from children, but should use them to discuss the different ways a dot is used.

Models for decimals

Number rods

Two types of number rod are useful in introducing children to tenths. In both types the choice of the rod to represent 'one', that is the base unit, is important as the 'one' is broken down into parts, not built up as with whole numbers. Figures 5.2a and 5.2b show both types, with the one rod ('long') and a tenths rod ('unit'). The 'long' built with linking cubes shown in Figure 5.2a retains its 'tenness', which can be both an advantage and a disadvantage.

Base 10 apparatus

This module makes it clear that decimals need to be introduced as an extension of the place value concept with whole numbers. The extension of the place value system 'one place further to the right' through the introduction of tenths is a natural first step. Base 10 apparatus allows a 'long' to represent 'one', which is then equivalent to ten 'tenths', ten of the small cubes, as in Figure 5.2a. Ultimately, however, and perhaps even from the start, it may be appropriate to use a 'flat' (10×10 'units') to represent 'one', as in Figure 5.2c. This approach has the advantage that a tenth is represented by a 'long', and a hundredth by the smallest cube without any re-definition of what is to be regarded as the 'one'. The base 10 apparatus may then be used to introduce and represent written numbers to two decimal places, like 1.47.

Number lines

When the idea of a number line is first introduced, as in Figure 5.3a, it is only with whole numbers (positive integers, with zero as the start or 'origin'). When decimals are introduced, we are faced with an issue

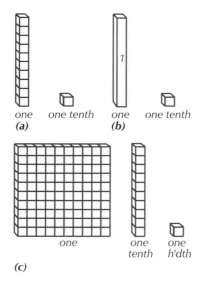

one   one tenth   one   one tenth
(a)   **(b)**

one   one   one
                 tenth   h'dth
(c)

5.2 Varying the representation of 'one'

raised earlier. There is now an unlimited set of numbers which we might wish we could place between any two given numbers. For example, between the whole numbers 1 and 2 the numbers with one decimal place are 1.1, 1.2, 1.3, ..., 1.9. Then, between 1.1 and 1.2 the numbers with two decimal places are 1.11, 1.12, 1.13, ..., 1.19. Such listing could go on indefinitely. Children need to appreciate the infinite nature of such an exercise, but this takes time. It is helpful to begin by marking the positions of 'tenths', because they occur at regular intervals like the whole numbers. The first problem is that marking all the tenths between 0 and 10, say, is not only a very big job, which can easily lead to loss of interest, but it is also difficult to place them all within the spaces available.

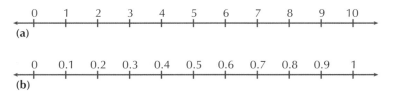

5.3 Tenths on a 0–10 number line

A more restricted picture of a limited part of the number line might be more appropriate, as in Figure 5.3b, but positioning hundredths presents the same problem all over again! There is no way that tenths, hundredths and thousandths can be marked easily and distinctly by hand on a 0–10, or any other, number line. One method which appeals to children is the magnifying glass, or zooming in, approach as shown in Figure 5.4. This provides justification for choosing a section of the first attempt at marking a number line. It also provides opportunities for practice in marking a variety of sections of the original line.

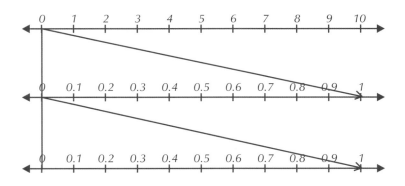

5.4 Magnifying number lines to show decimals

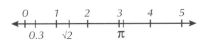

5.5 Placing recurring decimals and irrationals on a number line

When it comes to marking recurring decimals and irrational numbers, however, the problem gets even worse. Although 0.3..., or 0.3̇, representing ⅓, can be marked reasonably well, it is more difficult to mark 0.142857..., or 0.1̇42857̇, representing ⅐, and irrational numbers such as √2 (1.4142...), and π(3.14159...) are even more difficult, as seen in Figure 5.5, because the exact positioning is difficult to achieve.

The role of zero

When dealing only with whole numbers, zero is used as the 'origin' in listing numbers (0, 1, 2, 3, ...), and is also used as a place holder to the right or in the middle of other digits, for example in 10, 70, 100, 104, 160, 1001 and so on. It is rarely found to the left of other digits, for example 05, and is not required in such a position when doing pencil and paper arithmetic. (In recording, and often because a computer is going to be used to analyse the data, you will sometimes find that, for example, a birthday needs to be recorded in two-digit numbers, such as 03-05-98. Children do need to be made aware of this form of recording as an occasional specialised use of zero which is unlikely to be relevant to their study of mathematics.)

When dealing with decimals, however, zero is often absolutely essential in the left-most position(s) in a number after the decimal point. The whole numbers 07 and 7 may be regarded as representing the same concept, and the zero is not really required, but in .07, or better still 0.07, the zero before the 7 cannot be discarded.

When dealing with money, or when rounding, there are also times when a decimal number must have (an) additional zero(s) in the right-most position(s). Thus, the meaning of £3.2 can only be guessed. It might represent an incorrect attempt to record three pounds and twenty pence (when calculators are used for money problems the answer, if in pounds, may appear as 3.2), or it might be an incorrect attempt to record three pounds and two pence. The 'extra' zero, in £3.20, is essential. Likewise, when the number 3.2996 is rounded to two decimal places the approximation must be recorded as 3.30, and when rounded to three decimal places the approximation is 3.300. Children sometimes seem to be very careless with zeros when working with decimals. This apparent carelessness may be the outcome of an incomplete understanding of how zero is used in mathematics, however, and great care needs to be taken to help children to greater awareness and deeper knowledge.

To do

Make a list of the different ways children may meet zero in everyday life. In each instance describe the role the zero plays.

Expanded notation

In Module 4, the issue of the use of expanded notation was introduced. The purpose of requiring children to use expanded notation is to emphasise the value of the digits in a number, and in particular the importance of place value. It is therefore equally important to provide experiences and practice when dealing with decimals. The activities are comparable to those in the previous module, for example:

$$3.16 = (3 \times 1) + (1 \times 0.1) + (6 \times 0.01)$$

The British system of money

Children want and need to learn about money very early in life. Thus, in one sense, money can act as an introduction and motivation for decimals, and this is accepted in national curricula. However, some of the features of how we use and talk about money do not help in the study of decimals.

- For most of us, there are only ever two decimal places when handling money; it is not an infinitely extendible system like decimals
- The digits in the decimal places represent distinctly named coins

known as 'pence', which suggests that in a way there are two bases to the system, 'pound' and 'penny'. Thus £3.72 is read as 'three pounds seventy-two pence', or just as 'three pounds seventy-two', and not as 'three point seven two pounds', as the study of decimals would demand. In fact, translating £3.72 into 'three pounds seventy-two' actively encourages the abuse of reading decimals referred to earlier. Treating the amount as a decimal number, the decimal part would need to be read as 'seven two', and not 'seventy-two'

- The separation of the amount into two distinct units, pounds and pence, can interfere with the development of an understanding of the × 10 relationship between consecutive places. Thus 65 pence may be thought of entirely concretely, as coinage, and not as 6 tenths plus 5 hundredths of one pound

- It is sometimes suggested that the decimal system can be modelled by using pound coins, 10 pence coins and 1 pence coins, but this can easily lead to children writing money as, for example, £1.3, which is not acceptable. Nevertheless, when there is an advantage to be gained in using money as a real-life example of decimals in action, we need to grasp it.

Metric systems of measurement

The metric systems of measurement provide better examples of decimals in action, though they are usually encountered some time after first meeting and using money. Indeed, a consideration of metric units of measurement leads to the conclusion that a decimal system of coinage does not provide 'measurement' opportunities in the true sense of the word; that is, on a continuous scale. Using money involves exchanging physical objects, whereas metric units involve dealing with more abstract equivalences and continuous measures.

In length, the metre is the standard unit and, using decimals, this is all that is required to represent any length. However, it is likely that the centimetre (one hundredth of a metre) and millimetre (one thousandth of a metre = one tenth of a centimetre) will be encountered in measurement, whether in the classroom or elsewhere. The kilometre is one thousand metres, and will be encountered by children, but it is a very long distance for practical classroom activities! In liquid measure, the litre is the standard unit, and the prefixes milli- (one thousandth) and kilo- (one thousand) are in common use. In mass (weight) the standard is the gram, and again the prefixes milli- and kilo- are regularly used. Remember that the smaller and larger units, involving the prefixes milli-, centi- and kilo-, may not be appropriate when using metric units to reinforce decimals. Indeed, the common practice of using metres and centimetres for most classroom measurement is again like using two bases, somewhat comparable to pounds and pence, and may not help if decimals form the focus of study.

Other applications

Real-life examples of decimals, such as car trip mileage indicators or skating competition scores, are very useful examples with which most children are familiar. These examples will need to be discussed in detail. Car mileage is particularly useful because, even on local journeys, each 0.1 of a mile can be clearly seen clicking by quite rapidly, but with

To do

Make a collection of applications of decimals for use in the classroom.

To do

Collect together a group of three or four of your colleagues. Go round the group by counting up by zero point seven, starting at zero until the first whole number is said. What will this be? Repeat the activity but count down this time from the whole number as a start. Repeat with other decimal fractions. Try to predict who will be the first to say a whole number.

To think about

What fraction is equivalent to the decimal 0.1111...? What fraction is equivalent to the decimal 0.9999...? Some people find this last result startling.

sufficient time to enjoy watching it all happening. A class competition, scored in the way skating is scored, may also help to provide practice in the use of tenths, and both timing and measuring distances at school sports may provide a wonderful opportunity for children to appreciate measurement with decimals in action.

Many sporting events involve timing using decimals of seconds to at least two decimal places. World records in the 100 metres and the lap times of Formula One cars are just two examples.

Counting in decimals

In previous modules great stress was put on children counting in whole numbers, whatever the size of the numbers. Decimals should be no exception to this. Thus, children should begin by counting in tenths up and down using different starting numbers. Be prepared for the 'natural' error of '...zero point eight, zero point nine, zero point ten'. This can be extended to counting up and down in two tenths, three tenths, ..., and later to counting up and down in two decimal places, such as zero point three one.

Terminating and recurring decimals

The numeral 8.15 incorporates a decimal part which 'terminates'; that is, it ends after the second decimal place. The number quite clearly consists of eight ones plus one tenth plus five hundredths.

Not all decimals terminate. The decimal 0.3333... (the dots signify the digits continue without end), alternatively written as $0.\dot{3}$, does not terminate – it 'goes on for ever', with the digit 3 in every decimal place. This decimal is usually read as 'zero (nought) point three recurring'. The reason why recurring decimals are important in mathematics is that, like terminating decimals, they represent fractions, sometimes quite simple fractions. One-tenth is 0.1, one-fifth is 0.2, one-half is 0.5 and one-quarter is 0.25, none of which recur, but one-third is 0.3333.... The decimal 0.090909..., which is the decimal form of the fraction one-eleventh, and in which the digits 0 and 9 repeat for ever, would be written more briefly as $0.\dot{0}\dot{9}$. The decimal 0.142857142857142857..., which is the decimal form of the fraction one-seventh, would be written as $0.\dot{1}4285\dot{7}$. All terminating and recurring decimals are also fractions, and therefore are also rational numbers (see Module 8).

Irrational numbers

Some numbers cannot be represented by either terminating or recurring decimals. For such numbers one can literally continue writing digits for ever, without there being any pattern to the repetitions of digits. These numbers cannot be written as fractions. In other words, they are not rational, and they are therefore described as 'irrational'. Such numbers may not be encountered by many primary pupils, but they are important in mathematics and you need to know a little about them. The easiest way to generate an irrational number is to take the square root of a simple prime number, such as 2 or 3 or 5. (In case you have forgotten, the square root of 2 is the number which, when multiplied by itself, produces exactly 2 as the result.) Try this, using a calculator. Your calculator might yield 1.4142136 as the answer, for example, or 1.414213562, depending on the number of

To do

Use a calculator to find √2. Write down the number showing in the display. Now clear your calculator, type in the number you have written down, and then square it. Does the display now show 2? If not, why not? After all, you found √2 and then squared it. Try similar experiments starting first with 3, then with 5, and then with numbers of your own choosing.

decimal places available in the display. The calculator display can, of course, show only a certain number of decimal places, and therefore can provide only an approximate value for this square root although, for all practical purposes (like measuring) we hardly ever need more than three decimal places. In fact, there is no way of producing a decimal number which is a completely correct value for the square root of 2, which is why such numbers are often written as √2, √3 and √5, as the only way to express them accurately.

The number π, necessary for all calculations relating to circles, is another example of an irrational number. It is often approximated to the fraction $\frac{22}{7}$ or to the decimal number 3.14, but this disguises the fact that it is not a rational number, and, using digits, cannot be written exactly. Primary teachers may never be formally involved in teaching about irrational numbers, but when children have access to calculators on the one hand, and elder siblings on the other (as they might at home if not in school) their activity might provoke questions. Irrational numbers can in no way be considered obscure or remote, when simply taking a square root can produce one. It is sometimes said that the phenomenon of being absolutely unable to avoid contact with irrational numbers seriously troubled Greek mathematicians 2000 years ago. We hope it will not trouble you.

Children and decimals

Relating decimals to money

Thyer and Maggs (1971) commence their chapter on teaching money to young children by stating, 'Money is much more difficult to teach than length or capacity, for example, because the relationship between coins cannot readily be seen.' Unlike centimetres and millimetres, whose inter-relationships can be clearly seen on a ruler, 10 pence and 1 pence coins are discrete objects with no visual relationship to model the relationship between their values. The view expressed by Dickson *et al.* (1984) is that '... money may not necessarily be a good medium for introducing elementary number ideas.' The dilemma in the context of this section is how to anticipate the problems which might ensue from trying to build an understanding of decimals on this prior knowledge of coinage.

MONEY PROBLEMS

Brown (1981b) found that about half of the secondary school pupils interviewed confused 'tens' and 'tenths' at some stage, and drew attention to the fact that with money, for example £0.75, the 7 represents both seven tenths (of one pound) and seven tens (of pence). There is also the potential for confusion between the five hundredths (of one pound) and five pence (units). In fact, when asked for a real-life example of the use of a number like 6.4, around 10% of the pupils used money to explain. Unfortunately, only half of these pupils interpreted the number as six pounds and forty pence, with the other half interpreting it as six pounds and four pence, with some of these even writing it as £6.4. The established evidence about confusion, when money is used to illustrate or make more concrete the decimal concept, is not huge, but there is some indication from research that great care is needed, as suggested earlier.

Decimal words and positions

Successive tenths are read and written as 'zero point one, zero point two, zero point three, ..., zero point nine', but 'zero point ten' does not follow in this sequence! In other words, any apparent comparability with reading and writing whole numbers breaks down. There is no obvious documented research evidence concerning children's errors here, but there is also no doubt that this is a difficulty which is very familiar to teachers. It is important that children learn the similarities and differences between reading and writing decimals and whole numbers, and to do this they need to list, by both saying and writing, and perhaps with reference to a number line, sequences of decimals such as the following:

0.1, 0.2, 0.3, ..., 0.9, 1.0, 1.1, 1.2, ..., 1.9, 2.0, 2.1, ...

0.01, 0.02, 0.03, ..., 0.09, 0.10, 0.11, 0.12, ..., 0.19, 0.20, 0.21, ...

The relationship between decimals and the fractions 'tenths', 'hundredths', 'thousandths', and so on has always been considered vital. The evidence from research is that only about half of all children aged 12 years are comfortable with the idea of equivalence.

DIFFERENT NUMBERS

In a CSMS question (Brown, 1981b), for which pupils had to say what the 2 represents in (a) 0.260, and (b) 0.412, the facilities were 53% and 48% respectively (ages 12–15). The nature of the deficiencies in knowledge and understanding is clearer from the information that in (a) 23% answered 'hundredths', and in (b) 21% answered 'units (ones)'. The summary by Brown is important: 'The major difficulty that weaker children seemed to have was in understanding that the figures after the point indicated that part of the number which was less than one unit, even though the names of the decimal places in relation to diagrams showing units, tenths and hundredths had been explained to them at the beginning ... Instead, children seemed to think that the figures after the point represented a 'different' number which also had tens, units etc.'

What questions does this raise about the use of money as an illustration of decimals in action?

Ordering decimals

One of the interesting features of the findings of research into children's misconceptions and errors with decimals is the universal nature of the results.

ORDERING RULES

Studies by Sackur-Grisvard and Leonard, cited in Resnick *et al.* (1989), found that about half of the 10–11-year-old children tested used one of three incorrect rules to order decimals which have the same whole number digit (e.g. 3.214 and 3.8).

- The first rule, subsequently named the whole number rule by Resnick *et al.* in the course of continuing this research, is that the number with more decimal places is the larger, therefore 3.214 > 3.8. It was suggested that the occurrence of the whole number rule was due to children seeing the decimal parts as if they were whole numbers

- The second rule, named the fraction rule by Resnick *et al.*, is that the number with fewer decimal places is the larger, and hence 3.8 > 3.214. Since one-digit decimals are read as tenths, and two-digit as hundredths, it was suggested that children who understand fractions may infer that longer decimals are smaller

- The third rule, the zero rule to Resnick *et al.*, is that the number with one or more zeros immediately to the right of the decimal point is the smallest and, if the numbers of zeros are the same, then apply the first rule. Thus for 3.09, 3.8 and 3.214, the smallest is 3.09 and the largest is 3.214. It was suggested that the adoption of this rule was associated with the place holder function of zero, so the decimal with zero next to the decimal point must be the smallest. The whole number rule was found to occur frequently and early in learning, but in comparing American, Israeli and French children Resnick *et al.* found that the fraction rule was used least frequently by the French. It was suggested this might be because decimals precede fractions in the French curriculum, and other studies cited by Dickson *et al.* (1984) support this suggestion.

In what ways could you use this evidence to ensure that the children you teach do not make the same mistakes?

Misconceptions and errors using a number line

Teachers are encouraged to use number lines to assist children in their development of number concepts. Yet there is considerable evidence to indicate that the number line is a complex model making high cognitive demands on children. What does not appear to have been established, however, is why children find the number line model so difficult. It may be, for instance, that children who have been tested using a number line have not experienced, over many years, a progressive use of number lines as their knowledge of numbers increases. What other possible reasons do you think could explain the evidence from research such as that described overleaf?

ESTIMATING DECIMALS

The position of decimal numbers on the number line was tested by Brown (1981b). In these items, shown in Figure 5.6, a section of the number line was shown, and an arrow clearly indicated which number was required. Table 5.2 summarises the facilities for children aged 12 and 15 years, respectively. The purpose of showing these two age ranges is to indicate the post-primary development, and thus to suggest likely levels of competence among primary pupils.

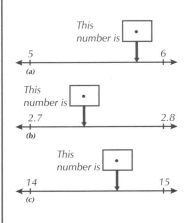

(a)

(b)

(c)

5.6 Estimating decimals

Facilities for estimating decimals		
Number indicated	Facility (%)	
	12-year-old children	15-year-old children
5.8	62	85
2.74	31	71
14.65	24	61

Table 5.2

List the concepts, knowledge and skills required to answer each of the questions. How does your list help to explain the order of difficulty of the questions?

The work by Brown used number lines with numbers greater than 1 and involved secondary school children.

DECIMAL ESTIMATES

A study of 91 9–10-year-old students conducted by the authors used a number line from 0 to 1 and provided a half-way mark and an arrow at 0.6 (Figure 5.7a). The question was:

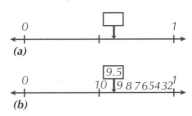

(a)

(b)

5.7 A child's estimating strategy

'Estimate the decimal number the arrow is pointing to.'

Some 38% of the children gave an accurate estimate of 0.6, with a further four children writing 0.7. Some children drew marks on the line, indicating a strategy. Figure 5.7b shows one child's incorrect response.

What was the child's strategy? What skills and knowledge are required to answer this question successfully?

Some ideas for teaching decimals

Textbooks and decimals

Although there are those who advocate the introduction of decimals to 7–8-year-old children through reference to money and measurements, most textbooks make no mention of decimals until children are 10 years old, and long after they have learned about fractions. Activities with money are commonplace in textbooks from an early age, but they are seldom related to decimals.

Some textbooks develop the place value of 'tenths' by considering the tens relationship between thousands, hundreds, tens and ones leading to the introduction of tenths as being 10 times smaller than 1. The value of this tenths place is often written as $\frac{1}{10}$ rather than 0.1 as authors see it building upon earlier work with fractions. Indeed, very quickly children are expected to write numbers, such as $2\frac{8}{10}$, as decimals and 62.8 as a fraction. The language used is frequently misleading, using fraction to mean both vulgar fraction and mixed number, and decimal to mean both decimal fraction and decimal number. The addition and subtraction of decimals involving tenths quickly follows, with few applications to enable children to relate decimals to their everyday lives.

Other textbooks use models to help children understand how decimals relate to whole numbers, but even these books move very quickly to requiring children to deal with decimals in an abstract symbolic mode.

Activities with money

The most valuable coins in relation to decimals are the 1p, 10p and £1. Some children may arrive at school with considerably more acquaintance and knowledge than that, but it is still possible to focus particularly on these three and to ignore, to some extent, other coins. Coin recognition comes first, in learning about money and then progress in the mastery of the concept of money in relation to exchange for goods and services, making use of a class shop and similar activities when appropriate. Having developed the necessary language, emphasis then needs to be placed on value and equivalence. In particular, the 10 times relationship needs to be developed.

In terms of progression in learning about money, it is clear that larger and larger amounts will be used over time, and that the other coins (2p, 5p, 20p, 50p and £2) will have to be used when their time comes in this progression, yet still the ten times aspect can be emphasised. In this way, when written recording is introduced, it will follow on naturally from the main focus first on 1p and 10p, and then £1 coins. Abstract problems involving the four operations are not likely to be as valuable as practical experiences in handling and using money. Certainly, given the caution expressed by so many authors about using money to illustrate decimals, it is not wise to place too much emphasis on approaching decimals through children's knowledge of money.

Activities with practical measurement

A metre stick, marked off in tenths (as shown in Figure 5.8) and later hundredths, can also be used to carry out practical measuring and recording activities. The metre sticks can be made by children from a

5.8 A metre stick

'master' stick drawn on a wall or board. In a topic on 'Ourselves', body measurements can be taken first using tenths of metres, and later tenths and hundredths of metres, with consequent practice in recording. Similarly, the liquid capacities of containers can be measured, using a 1 litre measuring jar or jug marked off in tenths. It may also be decided to engage in weighing activities, though there are awkward and difficult features involved in handling real scales and heavy weights.

The value of measuring activities at this stage lies not only in the practice gained in measuring using tenths but also in the way this measurement will inevitably lead to the justification for even finer subdivisions – hundredths, and perhaps even thousandths. Eventually, such practical activities can lead to the 'centimetre' being introduced as a special word for one hundredth of a metre, and perhaps even the 'millimetre' and 'millilitre' as one thousandth of a metre and litre, respectively. As already mentioned, real-life examples of more than one decimal place do exist, for example in athletics, in skiing and in motor racing, and these should be harnessed to illustrate the greater precision which these subdivisions allow. Questions involving judgements (like 'Who or what is the fastest?') and based on lists of numbers involving one decimal place, and then more decimal places, are also important; these can be based on the real-life examples suggested earlier.

Activities with number lines

It is easy to say that a number line involving decimals is merely an 'extended' calibration of the pre-existing whole number line. Whilst that may be true, the practical difficulties of finding the space to write all the subdivisions, referred to earlier, will quickly become apparent. Some attempt to do this, however, using only the tenths, and perhaps extending only part way along the classroom number line (some of which go all round the classroom) is an important experience for children to take part in or, at the very least, to witness. Children need to be provided with opportunities to think about both the theoretical and practical aspects of this activity. In theory, there is no end to how many times one can subdivide and subdivide again, but in practice the space required to record the numbers prevents progress beyond a certain stage. Children need to experience and think about situations like this, involving infinite processes, without the teacher introducing complicated language or explanations. Indeed, such activities provide relatively painless introductions to important ideas like limit and infinity, and these should be addressed in the primary school.

Activities with expanded notation

Alongside all of the ways of introducing the concepts and notation, it is important that children are constantly given the opportunity to rehearse the connections. The number 3.25 not only represents $3 + \frac{2}{10} + \frac{5}{100}$, it also represents $3 + \frac{25}{100}$. And the number 3.251 not only represents $3 + \frac{2}{10} + \frac{5}{100} + \frac{1}{1000}$, it also represents $3 + \frac{251}{1000}$, and also $3 + \frac{2}{10} + \frac{51}{1000}$, and so on. The link with measurement, say in metres, is also important. Thus, 3.25 m = $(3 + \frac{2}{10} + \frac{5}{100})$ m = $3\frac{25}{100}$ m = 3 m 25 cm. Note that the question 'How many hundredths are there in 3.251?' may be confusing. The clever answer might well be '325', but this is not an answer we should ever expect from children who are still learning about decimals.

To do

Make a list of sporting activities where decimals are used.

To do

Choose several different textbooks which use number lines for work with decimals. Develop a progressive use of number lines for decimals which you can use with children.

Activities with multiplying and dividing by powers of 10

Children need to appreciate that the simple operations of multiplying or dividing by 10 can be understood in a variety of ways. Unfortunately, pupils sometimes learn 'rules' which might appear to summarise the outcomes of these operations without this appreciation, and this can lead to errors. For example, multiplying 30 by 10 produces 300, hence the misleading 'rule', 'to multiply by 10, add a 0'. Thus, when multiplying 0.3 by 10, some children are tempted to write 0.30 instead of the correct answer, which is 3. The equivalence $0.3 = \frac{3}{10}$ provides another perspective, and 0.3×10 might then be better understood as $\frac{3}{10} \times 10$, from which we obtain the answer 3. The following two further examples of equivalences may be helpful, though the second is much more 'advanced' than the first:

$$300 \times 0.1 = 300 \times \tfrac{1}{10} = 300 \div 10$$
$$300 \div 0.1 = 300 \div \tfrac{1}{10} = 300 \times 10$$

Other misleading rules concern 'moving the decimal point'; hence when 0.35 is to be divided by 100, it is sometimes said that 'you move the decimal point two places to the left', but there is only one number to the left, resulting in total confusion for some children. Children also forget which direction to move. Thus, instructing the children to 'move the decimal point' is not a helpful long-term strategy, though it is legitimate to discuss keeping the decimal point fixed and moving the numbers, once knowledge is secure and as a summary of what has been learned. Table 5.3 illustrates the clarity and consistency of recording the outcomes of the operations of multiplying and dividing by powers of 10 when the decimal point remains in the same place. When 30.8 is multiplied by 100, it is necessary to fill the space in the ones column with a 0. When 30.8 is divided by 1000, it is also necessary to fill the space in the tenths column with a 0. Both of these are normal uses of zero in its place filling role.

Multiplication and division by multiples of powers of 10										
			3	0	.	8				
Operation	Outcome									Comments
× 10		3	0	8	.					The decimal point is superfluous in these two outcomes.
× 100	3	0	8	0	.					
÷ 10				3	.	0	8			
÷ 100				0	.	3	0	8		The zero before the decimal point is a convention (see earlier), but the zero after the point in the last row is essential.
÷ 1000				0	.	0	3	0	8	

Table 5.3

A class activity

OBJECTIVE   To develop the idea of decimal numbers being between whole numbers

ORGANISATION   Whole class

RESOURCES   Teacher has a set of number cards 0–9; each child has two sets of cards, a whole number set from 0–8, and a decimal fraction set from .0–.9

ACTIVITY

- Teacher holds up two consecutive numbers, say 4 and 5, the 4 in the right hand and the 5 in the left hand.
- Teacher then asks the children to make a decimal number between 4 and 5 using their cards and to hold it up for everyone to see.
- Children can be asked to say their number.
- The activity can be extended by asking children for a decimal number between 4 and 5, but nearer to 5, say.
- Children should explain how they know their number satisfies the requirements.

A group activity

OBJECTIVE   To place decimals in order

ORGANISATION   Small groups

RESOURCES   Two sets of number cards, each set on a different-coloured card, one set of 20 cards for the whole number part of a decimal with two each of the numbers 0–9, the other set of 20 for the decimal part of a number with two each of .0–.9

ACTIVITY

- All the cards are placed face down in the middle of the children in two piles, whole numbers in one pile and decimals in the other.
- One child chooses a whole number card and a decimal card to use as the starter number, say 3.8.
- The next child chooses one card from each set to make another decimal number.
- If the number is larger than the starter number the child puts the number next to the starter number and gains one point, if not the two cards are put on a discard pile.
- This continues until all 20 cards in each set have been used. The winner is the one with the most points.

Test your own knowledge: decimals

1 Use your calculator to write $\sqrt{3}$, $\sqrt{5}$, $\sqrt{7}$, $\sqrt{9}$, and $\sqrt{11}$ as decimals to three decimal places. Now use your calculator to write $\sqrt[3]{2}$, $\sqrt[3]{4}$, $\sqrt[3]{8}$, $\sqrt[3]{12}$, and $\sqrt[3]{16}$ as decimals to three decimal places.

2 Use your calculator to write the following fractions as decimals to four decimal places: $\frac{1}{3}$, $\frac{1}{6}$, $\frac{1}{7}$, $\frac{1}{12}$, $\frac{1}{13}$.

3 Find fractional forms for: 0.25, 0.125, 0.05, 0.02, 0.00625

4 The recurring decimal $0.\dot{2}\dot{3}$ may be converted into a fraction as follows:

Let the required fraction,	F	=	0.232323…
Then, by multiplying by 100,	100F	=	23.232323…
Thus by subtraction,	99F	=	23
And so	F	=	$\frac{23}{99}$

Use this method to find fractional forms for the decimals $0.\dot{0}\dot{9}$, $0.\dot{7}$, $0.\dot{6}$, $0.\dot{0}\dot{6}$, $0.\dot{0}7692\dot{3}$

5 In a calculation of the circumference of a circle of diameter 2.6 cm, and taking π as 3.14, the product 3.14×2.6 is required. The normal procedure involves ignoring the decimal points, calculating the product as if for the whole numbers 314 and 26, and then inserting the decimal point three places from the right. Yet it is not necessary to use such a procedure, shrouded as it is in mystery. The decimal point can be correctly inserted into each line, as below, and can be explained:

$$
\begin{array}{l}
3.1\,4 \\
\underline{\times\ 2.6} \\
6.280 \quad (3.14 \times 2) \\
\underline{1.884} \quad (3.14 \times 0.6) \\
8.164 \quad (3.14 \times 2 + 3.14 \times 0.6)
\end{array}
$$

Work with a partner, and set each other decimal numbers multiplication questions to explain in a similar way.

Review of key points

➤ Decimals may be regarded very simply as an extension of our base 10 number system to positive numbers smaller than 1

➤ Decimal currency requires great care when used to illustrate decimals

➤ Measurement and calculation with metric units are good sources of meaningful practice in using decimals

➤ The language of decimals requires great care, because of the potential for confusion between 'ten' and 'tenth', etc.

➤ Decimals may or may not 'terminate'. Decimals which terminate or recur may be expressed as fractions

➤ Some children find it hard to understand that the decimal point merely serves to separate two parts of the same number

➤ The same apparatus as for teaching place value may be helpful when teaching children about decimals

➤ Placing decimal numbers on number lines introduces important new concepts

➤ Teaching rules to children may not lead to understanding and insight, and may even not lead to satisfactory performance in routine calculations

➤ Calculators provide an excellent support to children learning about decimals

Module 6   Learning to teach fractions

Introduction

Apart from 'half' and 'quarter', fractions are little used outside the classroom. The language of fractions, including 'halves' and 'quarters', is employed by adults and children in a very loose manner. In many cases fractions are used to indicate a small part, or two or four parts, without the parts being the same in size or value. Thus, it is common to hear adults use expressions such as 'only a fraction of the cake has been eaten', or for young children to say that they want the 'bigger half'.

Children meet the notions of 'half' and 'quarter' frequently in many different situations outside the classroom. Half-past, quarter-past and quarter-to are part of telling the time; measuring scales, such as those on the side of electric kettles, have divisions of half pints as well as showing the amount of water as a decimal of a litre; shoes can be bought in half sizes; some petrol stations show the cost of petrol in tenths of one penny. Also many children will be familiar with the signs that appear regularly in supermarkets and retail stores offering goods at half price, or with one-third off.

Fractions in national curricula

The most common references to fractions in primary curricula include:

- understanding and using fractions in contexts
- estimating fractions as proportions of a whole
- measuring using fractions for accuracy
- halving numbers for mental strategies
- calculating fractions of quantities
- writing one quantity as a fraction of another.

Key terms

fraction	formed when a unit (a line, region or set) is partitioned into a number of parts
vulgar fractions	a vulgar, or proper, fraction is a number whose value lies between 0 and 1
numerator	the name given to the number above the line. Thus in the fraction $\frac{3}{7}$ the numerator is 3
denominator	the name given to the number below the line. Thus in the fraction $\frac{3}{7}$ the denominator is 7
mixed numbers	'fractions' greater than 1 are written as a combination, a mixture, of a number of wholes and a fractional part of the whole
improper fractions	mixed numbers can be written as improper fractions, in that they are not proper, having a numerator greater than the denominator. Thus $2\frac{1}{2}$ can be written as the improper fraction $\frac{5}{2}$, as $2\frac{1}{2}$ is equivalent to five halves

---

Key issues in fractions

Related issues and concepts

Figure 6.1 shows the relationships between the different concepts and issues that contribute to the development of the concept of a fraction. Most of these are considered at some stage in this module.

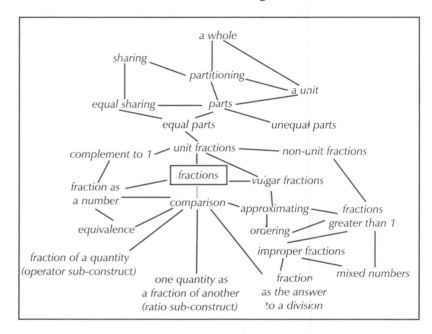

6.1 *Concepts and issues associated with fractions*

Much of children's early learning of fractions is based around a continuous model using regions, in the form of shape, length, volume and capacity, and discrete models using real objects or representations of objects. Only later should they meet the more complex idea of a fraction as a number represented on a number line relative to other numbers and a fraction as an operator and a ratio.

Different types of fractions

There are five different types, or sub-constructs, of fractions:

- fraction as part of a 'whole' or a 'unit'
- fraction as a number
- fraction as the result of division of whole numbers
- fraction as a ratio
- fraction as an operator.

Fractions as part of a 'whole' or a 'unit'

When a region or any continuous quantity, such as area, is taken to be the unit and valued as 1, it is subdivided into an equal number of fractional parts with one or more of the parts collected together, as shown in Figure 6.2.

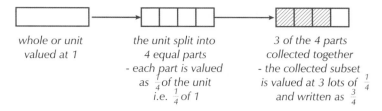

whole or unit
valued at 1

the unit split into
4 equal parts
- each part is valued
as $\frac{1}{4}$ of the unit
i.e. $\frac{1}{4}$ of 1

3 of the 4 parts
collected together
- the collected subset
is valued at 3 lots of $\frac{1}{4}$
and written as $\frac{3}{4}$

6.2 Subdividing a continuous quantity

When a set of discrete objects is taken to be the unit and valued as 1, the set is subdivided into subsets, fractions of the whole set, each containing the same number of objects or quantity with one or more of the subsets collected together. Figure 6.3 illustrates this subconstruct.

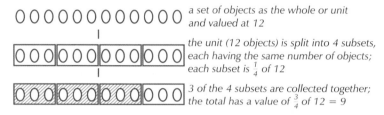

a set of objects as the whole or unit
and valued at 12

the unit (12 objects) is split into 4 subsets,
each having the same number of objects;
each subset is $\frac{1}{4}$ of 12

3 of the 4 subsets are collected together;
the total has a value of $\frac{3}{4}$ of 12 = 9

6.3 Subdividing a set of discrete objects

Fraction as a number

A fraction when considered independently of its relation to 'objects' can be viewed as a number, just like whole numbers, and as such each vulgar fraction has a position on a 0–1 number line. The position of the fraction ⅔ is arrived at as shown in Figure 6.4.

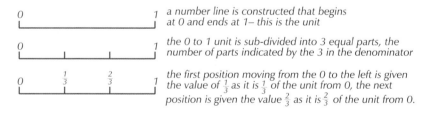

0   1
a number line is constructed that begins
at 0 and ends at 1– this is the unit

0   1
the 0 to 1 unit is sub-divided into 3 equal parts, the
number of parts indicated by the 3 in the denominator

0          $\frac{1}{3}$ $\frac{2}{3}$ 1
the first position moving from the 0 to the left is given
the value of $\frac{1}{3}$ as it is $\frac{1}{3}$ of the unit from 0, the next
position is given the value $\frac{2}{3}$ as it is $\frac{2}{3}$ of the unit from 0.

6.4 Positioning thirds on a 0–1 number line

Fraction as the result of division of whole numbers

Children's early experience of division involves the restricted set of whole numbers so that the problems of remainders, and later fractions, do not obscure and overwhelm the development of the concept of division. If, however, the second number in a division is not an exact divisor of the first then the system of whole numbers is no longer closed because the answer involves a fractional part, so the whole number system is extended to include fractions. For example, if two cans of cola

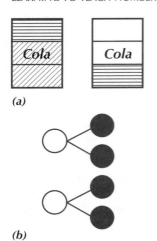

(a)

(b)

6.5 *Fractions as division and ratio*

are shared equally among 3 children, then each gets 2 lots of ⅓ of each can, i.e. ⅔ of a can as in Figure 6.5a. (Note: each gets only ⅓ of the two cans.) Thus 2 ÷ 3 is written as ⅔, the 2 (the whole part) having been subdivided into three equal parts and two of the parts collected for each child.

Fraction as a ratio

The two sets shown in Figure 6.5b are in the ratio of 1 to 2, as for every one white object in the first set there are two black objects in the second set. We say that the number of white objects is ½ the number of black objects and the ratio of white objects to black objects is 1 to 2, and written as 1:2.

Fraction as an operator

Figure 6.6 models how a fraction can be viewed as a combined operator on a quantity, with the numerator acting as an enlarger and the denominator acting as a shrinker.

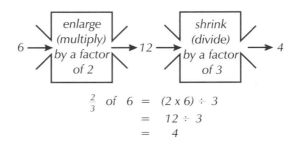

$$\tfrac{2}{3} \text{ of } 6 = (2 \times 6) \div 3$$
$$= 12 \div 3$$
$$= 4$$

6.6 *Fraction as an operator*

Children learning about fractions

Children bring to their learning of fractions many experiences from everyday life. Consequently, they develop informal conceptualisations of fractions that on occasions are in conflict with the more formal concepts they encounter in the classroom. The influences of these early conceptualisations, together with that of a pre-existing knowledge of the whole number system, are often barriers to children learning the mathematics of the fraction number system. Initially children do not view fractions as an extension of the whole number system; nor do they perceive fractions as numbers.

The concept of a fraction

The word *fraction* is derived from the Latin *frangere* meaning 'break'. There are other words, such as fracture, that have a similar derivation and may provide help with children's understanding of the fraction concept.

To do

Make a collection of words, like fracture, that would be of help when introducing the idea of a fraction to children.

A fraction has a variety of forms and takes on more meanings than the commonly understood belief that a 'fraction is a part of a whole'. Children's development of the concept of a fraction can only be successfully achieved over many years by them experiencing the variety of meanings and forms in which fractions occur. The concept of fraction is a conjunction of many interrelated subconcepts, and a misconception in one of these subconcepts leads inevitably to misconceptions in the fraction concept itself.

The representation of a fraction, such as ⅔, requires a learner to make a leap forward in mathematical understanding as ⅔ is an entity and does not mean two different and separate numbers, albeit that the numbers do have independent meanings within the overall concept of the fraction.

To think about

Figure 6.7a represents two cakes. Each cake is cut into four equal pieces. The pieces shown in Figure 6.7b are eaten. Has 1¼ or ⅝ been eaten? Explain why both answers could be correct.

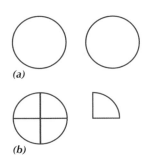

(a)

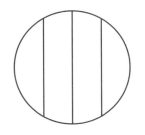

(b)

6.7 What fraction is eaten?

The unit or whole
The most fundamental idea on which fractions are based is that of the 'unit' or 'whole'. All fractions are relative to a unit. When writing a fraction symbolically the unit is assumed to be the number 1.

Partitioning
Fractions are created when a unit is partitioned into parts. The fractional value of each of the parts is only the same when the parts are equal.

PIZZAS

6.8 Quarters of a pizza!

Jacob claims that he has cut up the pizza in Figure 6.8 into quarters. How would you convince Jacob that he is wrong?

Comparing unit fractions
Unit fractions have a numerator of 1. They are some of the earliest fractions that children encounter, both in everyday life and in their school work.

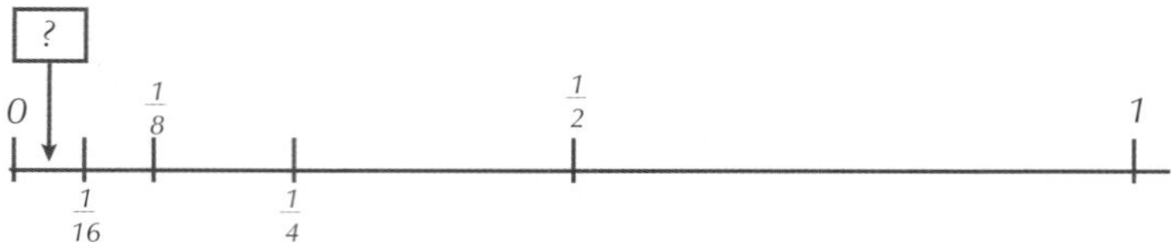
?
0
$\frac{1}{8}$
$\frac{1}{2}$
1
$\frac{1}{16}$
$\frac{1}{4}$

6.9 Unit fractions on a 0–1 number line

To think about

Figure 6.9 is a number line from 0 to 1 with some fractions shown. Draw the number line. What is the fraction that the arrow is pointing to? Mark on your number line where you think $\frac{1}{3}$, $\frac{1}{5}$, $\frac{1}{6}$, $\frac{1}{7}$ will be. Reflect on your strategy. Did your colleagues use the same strategy?

Equivalent fractions

Fractions that are equivalent look different symbolically, but have the same value. For example $\frac{4}{5}$ is equivalent to $\frac{8}{10}$. We write $\frac{4}{5} = \frac{8}{10}$, where the equals sign means 'is equivalent to'. The sign '[' is often used to signify 'equivalent to', but is not introduced to children until much later in their learning of mathematics.

The idea of a family of equivalent fractions is well illustrated using a fraction wall as in Figure 6.10. This 'fraction wall' shows some of the fractions that have the same value as $\frac{1}{2}$. All the fractions that are equivalent to $\frac{1}{2}$ belong to an equivalence class called the 'one-half family'. The fraction wall illustrates many different relationships, such as $\frac{1}{2} = \frac{1}{4} + \frac{1}{4}$, $\frac{1}{4} - \frac{1}{8} = \frac{1}{8}$.

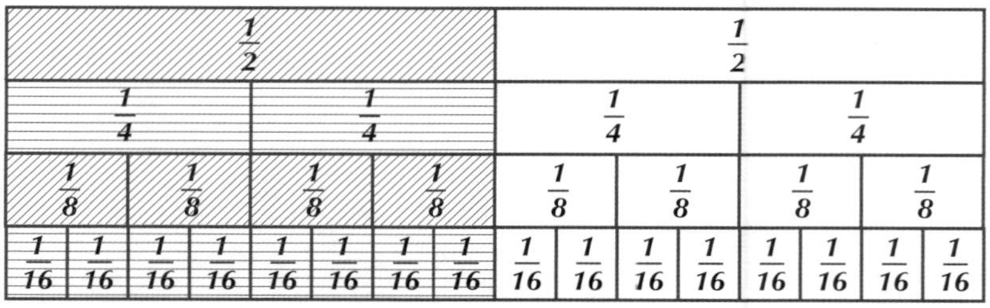
$\frac{1}{2}$ $\frac{1}{2}$
$\frac{1}{4}$ $\frac{1}{4}$ $\frac{1}{4}$ $\frac{1}{4}$
$\frac{1}{8}$ $\frac{1}{8}$ $\frac{1}{8}$ $\frac{1}{8}$ $\frac{1}{8}$ $\frac{1}{8}$ $\frac{1}{8}$ $\frac{1}{8}$
$\frac{1}{16}$ $\frac{1}{16}$ $\frac{1}{16}$ $\frac{1}{16}$ $\frac{1}{16}$ $\frac{1}{16}$ $\frac{1}{16}$ $\frac{1}{16}$ $\frac{1}{16}$ $\frac{1}{16}$ $\frac{1}{16}$ $\frac{1}{16}$ $\frac{1}{16}$ $\frac{1}{16}$ $\frac{1}{16}$ $\frac{1}{16}$

6.10 A fraction wall

To think about

Is $\frac{3}{5}$ less than, equal to, or more than $\frac{2}{3}$? List the concepts and processes you used to arrive at the answer. Compare your reasoning with that of a colleague. A strategy might be: the 3 is more than the 2 (comparing numerators), and the 5 is more than the 3 (comparing denominators). Hence $\frac{3}{5}$ is more than $\frac{2}{3}$.

Discuss with colleagues what you think about this strategy. Discuss with each other different incorrect strategies that children might use and the 'logic' of such strategies.

More than, less than

Comparison of the size of fractions is difficult for some children as they think of the numerator and denominator of a fraction in terms of whole numbers. Is, for example, $\frac{3}{5}$ less than, equal to, or more than $\frac{2}{3}$?

A symbolic approach uses the idea of equivalent families of fractions. Each fraction is written as equivalent fractions until the denominator of one of the fractions in the $\frac{2}{3}$ family is the same as the denominator of one of the fractions in the $\frac{3}{5}$ family.

$$\frac{2}{3} = \frac{4}{6} = \frac{6}{9} = \frac{8}{12} = \boxed{\frac{10}{15}} = \frac{12}{18} = \frac{14}{21}$$

$$\frac{3}{5} = \frac{6}{10} = \boxed{\frac{9}{15}} = \frac{12}{20} = \frac{15}{25} = \frac{18}{30} = \frac{21}{35}$$

As $\frac{2}{3} = \frac{10}{15}$ and $\frac{3}{5} = \frac{9}{15}$, then $\frac{2}{3}$ is more than $\frac{3}{5}$ by $\frac{1}{15}$.

Finding a fraction of a quantity

In primary mathematics curricula the stress is not on the four operations, but on finding a fraction of a quantity which is an application found more readily in real life than performing, say, addition of fractions. What, for example, is ⅔ of 150 cm?

The denominator, 3, tells us how many equal parts the whole, 150 cm, has to be partitioned into. The numerator, 2, tells us how many of the parts are to be collected together. Once again a diagram, as in Figure 6.11, helps. Thus ⅔ of 150 cm can be found by dividing 150 by 3 and then multiplying by 2.

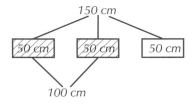

6.11 Two-thirds of 150 cm

We can write ⅔ of 150 = $(150 \div 3) \times 2$ *or* $2 \times (150 \div 3) = 100$

Writing one quantity as a fraction of another

How would you find what £75 is as a fraction of £300? The £300 is the whole and the £75 a fraction of that whole. A diagram (Figure 6.12) is helpful, showing the £300 as the whole with the £75 as a fractional part of that whole. The £75 becomes the numerator and the £300 the denominator of the required fraction. We write the fraction as £75/£300. The units, in this case £s, are the same and the fraction becomes ⁷⁵⁄₃₀₀, which can be written as ¼, an equivalent fraction. Thus, £75 is ¼ of £300.

6.12 One quantity as a fraction of another

Children and fractions

Misconceptions of a unit

Many errors occur when children work with fractions because of the lack of understanding of the concept of the unit involved.

UNITS

Olimpia Figueras (1989) lists a number of misconceptions associated with the different units involved in the recognition or construction of a fraction (see Figure 6.13). Three examples are given of responses that illustrate the types of errors children make.

When you are next visiting a school try one of Figueras' examples on a small group of children. Compare your results with those of a partner, analysing any misconceptions the children may have. Try to conjecture what may be the cause of the misconceptions.

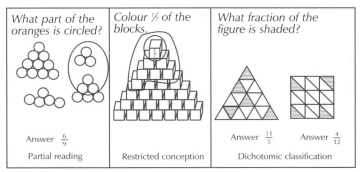

6.13 Misconceptions associated with the idea of 'unit'

Children make these kinds of errors more frequently with the discrete objects model than with the region model. Reading and matching the meaning of the instructions to the totality of the picture creates problems for children who appear to focus on only part of a picture when it is not obvious to them what the unit is meant to be. This is apparent with the set of oranges where there is a lack of precision in that it is unclear what the whole number of oranges is.

A restricted conception of the whole leads to children trying to make sense of the whole unit in relation to the numbers in the stated fraction. In the case of the blocks the child used the 7 in the denominator to count 7 blocks as the whole and circling 1 (the numerator) block as ½ of their restricted whole.

The 'What fraction of the figure is shaded?' question refers to two shapes, the answers being given by the same child. Many children make the same kind of error, partitioning 'the whole into two disjoint sets: a set of elements with a certain property and its complement' (Figueras, 1989). Such children do not perceive the whole unit as having any part to play in the derivation of the fraction. In effect they are writing a ratio of the two different kinds of triangles.

PIZZAS AGAIN

Nancy Mack (1990) describes an interview she conducted with Julie (11 years old) who, when asked what fraction of a 1-foot board would be left if ⅞ was cut off, replied that she did not know, but could do it if was to do with pizzas. When the whole was a pizza Julie responded correctly. Children's informal knowledge appears to be of assistance to them in correctly identifying the different kinds of unit when asked about fractions. However, when presented with 'identical' situations represented symbolically and concretely with classroom materials they are disposed to regard all the parts represented as units. Thus when asked 'How much of this is shaded?' (see Figure 6.14) a child may reply 'five-eighths', but the question 'How much is shaded of these pizzas?' is more likely to elicit the answer, 'one and a quarter'.

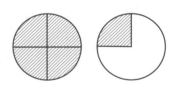

What would you do to help Julie overcome her misunderstandings?

6.14 Julie working with pizzas

The nature of the whole in fraction problems creates its own particular difficulties.

Young children are also likely to change the whole unit as they proceed through a problem, particularly when what they have produced does not match their expectations. Dagmar Neuman (1991) relates the response of some young children to the task of giving him a half of a piece of string. They cut the string into two pieces, acknowledging their understanding of the need to produce two parts. The, then put the two lengths together and discovered that the parts were not the same length. Here they recognised that the two parts had to be equal. In order to produce two equal parts they then cut the longer piece to match the length of the shorter piece. The equality of the two pieces was then established to their satisfaction, but the fact that the whole had now been changed did not concern them.

CHANGING UNITS

6.15 *Four quarters make a whole*

6.16 *Thirds!*

Nancy Mack (1990) claims that children 'often arbitrarily shift the unit so that the unit is comprised of all the elements identified in the problem, or in pictures and materials representing the problem.' She illustrates her contention by describing an interview she had with Jane. She said to 11-year-old Jane, 'You have one whole chocolate cake with strawberry icing, and you eat a quarter of the cake. How much of the cake do you have left?' Jane got out fraction circles and produced one whole circle with four quarters as in Figure 6.15.

She moved one piece away, indicating her understanding of the problem, and replied 'One third ... because there's three pieces left ... three pieces in the whole thing ... so they are called thirds' (see Figure 6.16).

Despite putting the piece back and taking it out again and again, Jane was adamant that the pieces were quarters when there were four in the whole, but were thirds when one of the quarters was removed. On both occasions Jane concentrated her attention on the 'whole' that she was able to perceive and, in that sense, was correct in her conclusions about the value of each part; she saw no contradiction in shifting the whole depending on what was visible to her.

What would you do to convince Jane that her reasoning is faulty?

From the very start of their formal learning of fractions it is essential that children are given experiences of a wide variety of shapes and different ways of partitioning the same shape, and of discrete sets of objects partitioned in many different ways, yet showing the same fraction. In this way an emphasis can be placed on the different kinds of units involved in the fraction concept, contributing to a richer experience than many children get at the present time.

The process of partitioning a unit

A basic process in the creation of a fraction is the partitioning of the whole. This process is sometimes known as subdividing or dissecting. Children should experience partitioning of different wholes, both continuous regions and discrete quantities, into smaller units well before they are introduced to the idea of a fraction. Children's informal experiences are often associated with the act of sharing and frequently the resulting shares are not equal; a young child's life is like that. Thus to build upon their experiences initial activities should involve the process of partitioning without the demand that the parts created be equal. The equal parts requirement should be added to learners' experiences at a later stage.

There is a great deal of evidence to show that when both children and adults meet problems that appear to be fractional in nature their response is to behave as if they were whole number partitioning problems.

SHARING PIZZAS

Kieren (1988) describes how children reacted to such a problem that asked them to share equally eight pizzas among five people. Figure 6.17 models the informal strategy that many of them used.

What strategy do you think the children used to solve the problem?

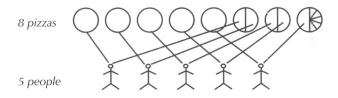

8 pizzas

5 people

6.17 Sharing eight pizzas among five people

If the problem is treated as a fraction problem the answer can be written immediately as ⅝ or 1⅗. However, the context of the problem appears to suggest to children that a fractions approach is inappropriate, and that a more suitable strategy is to share pizzas as though they represent independent units, rather than treating the eight pizzas as the unit. The informal strategies that children adopt for 'real-life' problems suggest that, although such problems may be a starting point for the learning of fractions, children may view the use of fractions as irrelevant to the situation. When this occurs children feel that they are being asked to learn a method for solving a problem which is in conflict with one that they already know and use successfully. Children then reject the fraction approach.

Partitioning into equal parts

Children's early partitioning activities result in them producing parts that are unequal, although frequently they are convinced that the parts are equal and no amount of 'logical' reasoning on the part of a teacher will convince them otherwise. Children also do not have the skill or technique to dissect shapes into equal parts with any degree of accuracy and are easily satisfied with their attempts to do so. The strategies children use to partition a continuous region into equal parts appear to be a function of the nature of the region. Thus, when asked to divide a square into three equal parts the responses shown in Figure 6.18 are typical. Children adopt similar strategies for partitioning circles into 'equal' parts.

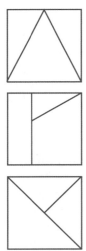

6.18 Dividing a square into three equal parts!

PARTITIONING CIRCLES

Peck and Jencks (1981) illustrate the sketches a 13-year-old made when asked to draw the fractions ½, ⅓, ¼ and ⅕ of a circle (Figure 6.19). What is the child's strategy?

It is interesting to note that the strategy works for ½ and ¼, but not for the other two fractions. Why is this?

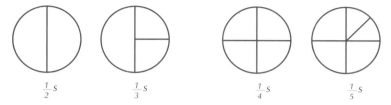

$\frac{1}{2}$s $\frac{1}{3}$s $\frac{1}{4}$s $\frac{1}{5}$s

6.19 A strategy for finding fractions of a circle

Partitioning into a number of parts that is not a power of two often demands knowledge of measuring that is more difficult than the concept of the fraction involved in the partition. For this reason textbooks restrict themselves to the very simplest of fractions. However, this misleads children, both in the limited partitioning strategies that they devise and in the restricted examples of the fraction concept from which they are expected to generalise. A solution to the problem of fraction concept development lies in practical activities that make it possible for children to operate on continuous material such as paper, string or bottles with water, allowing them, through trial and improvement, to experience actions, such as folding, cutting, and filling, that lead to equality of parts.

Naming and symbolising fractions

Many of the errors that children make are the result of

* too early an introduction of symbol representation
* insufficient experience with real-life examples, concrete models and diagrams, and a command of the language of fractions.

Children's informal knowledge of fractions often goes unrelated to their knowledge of symbols. Names of the common fractions are used and learned from an early age and in themselves do not appear to cause difficulty for learners despite being used for two different purposes: for example, 'a third triangle' and 'a third of a triangle'. However, problems arise when children are confronted with making sense of the relationship between symbols and names for the less common fractions, such as 'two-sevenths'. There are obvious connections between the oral name for a fraction and the symbol that represents it and children appear to have little difficulty in understanding that a written symbol for a fraction involves two numbers separated by a line.

$$\text{two-sevenths} \rightarrow \frac{2}{7}$$

The obstacle to children learning a symbolic representation of a fraction is their inability to understand the meaning of each of the two numbers, and to give a meaning to the line, both as independent entities and in relation to each other.

Children's early experience of numbers is concerned with single digits and a way of combining digits for numbers greater than 9, e.g. the number forty-two is written as 42 with a rule of place value attached to the position of each digit. The digits are written side-by-side horizontally. The symbol for a fraction has two numbers, one vertically beneath the other. The meaning of each has a kind of 'place value' in that the bottom number, the denominator, represents the number of equal parts that the whole has been partitioned into, and the top number, the numerator, is the number of parts under consideration. The relationship between the two numbers produces a new number. A common error when representing a fraction is due to a misunderstanding of the meaning of the denominator. When this occurs children write ½ for the fraction of the shape in Figure 6.20 which is shaded. This misconception perceives a fraction as the ratio of the shaded to the unshaded parts.

6.20 A half!

Equivalent fractions

Children's everyday experiences of fractions contain little that contributes to the idea of equivalence of fractions, beyond that of two quarter-hours making half an hour. Yet knowledge and understanding of equivalent fractions is essential as it is a key concept for children to progress in their comprehension of much of their future learning in this area of the curriculum. Thus children's learning of equivalent fractions is mainly the domain of the mathematics classroom and any misconceptions that children develop can be laid at the door of the teaching they have received.

The learning of equivalent fractions is often restricted to symbolic exercises in a textbook, leading children to seek algorithmic strategies for converting one fraction to an equivalent fraction. These exercises take the form of 'finding a missing number', as in the following examples.

$$\frac{1}{2} = \frac{\square}{4}, \quad \frac{2}{3} = \frac{4}{\square}, \quad \frac{3}{\square} = \frac{9}{12}, \quad \frac{\square}{7} = \frac{20}{35}$$

There is much evidence to show that children reject the methods that they are taught in the classroom in favour of their own invented methods.

INVENTING STRATEGIES

Ohlsson and Bee (1991) found children inventing strategies in order to answer questions on equivalent fractions even after being taught the early ideas of fractions including equivalent fractions. They were presented with problems in the form

$$\frac{n_1}{d_1} = \frac{?}{d_2}$$

The task of the 10–11-year-old children was to find the missing numerator n_2 to make the fractions equivalent. Table 6.1 lists those procedural strategies which were described by more than one child.

Strategies for finding equivalent fractions

Problem, and child's answer in bold	Explanation given by the child	The strategy represented algebraically
$\frac{1}{5} = \frac{1}{10}$	Top numbers have to be the same. Bottom numbers don't.	$n_2 = n_1$
$\frac{1}{5} = \frac{2}{10}$	Two times five is ten.	$n_2 \times d_1 = d_2$
$\frac{1}{5} = \frac{5}{10}$	One time five is five.	$n_2 = n_1 \times d_1$
$\frac{1}{5} = \frac{5}{10}$	Because five can go into one, and one can go into five, and five can go into five.	n_2 is a whole number divisor of n_1 and d_1
$\frac{12}{15} = \frac{2}{5}$	Because I subtracted ten from this to get five, and I subtracted ten from twelve and I got two.	$d_2 = d_1 - 10$ implies that $n_2 = n_1 - 10$
$\frac{12}{15} = \frac{3}{5}$	Three times five is fifteen.	$n_2 \times d_2 = d_1$
$\frac{12}{15} = \frac{32}{5}$	Five times three is fifteen, and three times twelve is thirty-two.	$Y \times d_2 = d_1$ implies that $n_2 = Y + n_1$
$\frac{4}{8} = \frac{8}{2}$	Bottom number and top number have to be the same.	$n_2 = d_1$
$\frac{4}{8} = \frac{12}{2}$	I added them (4 and 8) together.	$n_2 = n_1 + d_1$

Table 6.1

To think about

Discuss with colleagues the thinking behind each strategy in Table 6.1.

Unless what children are taught is understood and accepted by them as sensible and appropriate, matching their existing schemas, they invent their own strategies in preference to techniques presented to them in the classroom.

Comparing fractions

In order to conceive of fractions as numbers children need to develop a feel for the relative size of fractions and be able to order a set of fractions written in symbols, particularly those having the same numerator or the same denominator. Many children when ordering fractions resort, understandably, to the knowledge they have for ordering whole numbers. In the case of fractions with like denominators there is no conflict. Thus ⅘ is greater than ⅖ because 4 is more than 2. This reasoning is appropriate as the 'unit' of comparison is the same in both fractions, i.e. fifths. It is common for children to use similar reasoning when it is inappropriate to do so. In response to the question 'Which fraction is larger, ¼ or ⅙?' Susie responded by saying '⅙ as 6 is more than 4'. With more complex fractions children will argue that ⅔ is less than ⅗ because 2 is less than 3, referring to the numerators. This is extended to saying that 4/7 is more than ⅔ as 4 is more than 2 and 7 is more than 4. In both these cases children are using their knowledge of whole numbers inappropriately.

The aim should be for children to be able to think about fractions independently of physical and diagrammatic models. However, many children need to resort to their use when confronted with comparison problems, even when they have been taught about equivalent fractions. Errors still occur when children use materials to assist their thinking about the relative sizes of fractions.

QUARTERS AND FIFTHS

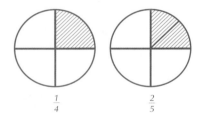

Peck and Jencks (1981) describe a 12-year-old boy who claimed that ¼ was the same as ⅖ and justified it by using the diagrams in Figure 6.21. The boy pointed out that he was aware that some of the fifths were smaller than the others, but that this was not important.

How would you respond to this explanation?

$$\frac{1}{4} \qquad \frac{2}{5}$$

6.21 ¼ is the same as ⅖!

A salient lesson to be learned from such misconceptions is that they can as easily occur when children are using physical or diagrammatic aids as when only written symbols are involved. This is further reinforced in the example quoted by Nancy Mack (1990) of 11-year-old children who happily responded that a pizza cut into six equal pieces gives larger pieces than one cut into eight equal pieces. But when asked 'Tell me which fraction is bigger, ⅙ or ⅛?', said that ⅛ is bigger as eight is a bigger number than six. The children did not, or could not, relate their experience with pizzas to the similar situation with symbols, and consequently saw no contradiction in the different answers.

Fractions as positions on a number line

There is much evidence to indicate that children find the notion of a fraction as a number having a position on a number line more difficult to understand than the continuous and discrete models for fractions. This is to be expected as most fraction experiences children have both in and out of school involve concrete objects, pictures or diagrams where the whole and the equal parts are visible. All children see when using a number line is some kind of mark to represent the position of a fraction on that line.

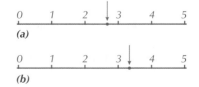

6.22 Two-thirds on a 0–5 number line

Children appear to find marking the position of, say, ⅔ easier when given the 0–1 number line than when asked to position the same fraction on the 0–5 number line with each whole number shown. The most common errors are:

To think about

What may be the thinking of a child who places ⅔ in these positions?

- marking ⅔ between 2 and 3, usually ⅔ of the way from 2 to 3 (see Figure 6.22a).
- marking a point that is ⅔ of the whole length from the 0 end toward the 5 position (see Figure 6.22b). This error may be due to children believing that they were being asked to mark ⅔ of a length of line 5 units long.

Some ideas for teaching fractions

Textbooks and fractions

Although there are variations in the way textbooks approach the teaching of fractions there is much commonality, particularly in certain important aspects of the development of the concept. Not every textbook series, for example, considers the important idea of partitioning independently of the teaching of fractions, nor that a whole should be subdivided into equal parts. Many assume either that the teacher is responsible for drawing children's attention to this or that it is so obvious there is no need to mention it.

The first fraction children meet in textbooks is halves, followed very quickly by quarters. It is at this stage that different content directions are taken, with some textbooks introducing children to thirds, others considering eighths, and a few moving to tenths.

The actions that children are asked to perform are very limited and are summarised below.

To think about

Look at two textbook series comparing the kind of shapes that are used to develop the fraction concept.

- Fold paper shapes to make halves, quarters and eighths
- Determine the fraction that is shaded when shown a shape with one or more parts shaded
- Copy a shape and divide the shape into a given fraction
- When shown a picture or drawing of a set of real objects with a subset ringed to say what fraction is ringed

The relationship between oral language and written symbolism is frequently omitted, with children being introduced immediately to the symbolism when shown a fraction of a shape shaded.

Seldom do textbooks deviate from the use of common shapes. Occasionally other shapes are used, but often they are symmetrical ones. Thus, children are faced with generalising the concept of one-half and other fractions from a restricted set of experiences based in the main, on activities involving squares, circles, rectangles and equilateral triangles.

To think about

Analyse a set of textbooks and the teachers' guides to see what coverage they give to fractions. What models do they recommend?

Very few series provide children with experience of fractions in settings other than with shapes and discrete objects. The ideas of a fraction resulting from a division problem, viewed as a number on a number line, or modelled as an operator are significantly absent from the majority of textbooks and are seldom mentioned in teachers' guides.

6.23 Fraction circles

Activities with fraction circles

Fraction circles consist of a whole circle and sectors of circles that are fractional parts of the whole circle (Figure 6.23). If the pieces are left unmarked then a choice can be made as to which piece represents a whole, thus extending the use of the fraction circles.

Activities with geoboards

The three pin by three pin square grid is the most suitable for developing the concepts of halves and quarters with young children. Different-coloured elastic bands are used to create shapes representing whole and fractional parts – as illustrated in Figure 6.24 on 3 × 3 and 4 × 4 geoboards.

To think about

You may also find fraction boards and fraction rods in use in schools. Find out what these look like and how they can be used.

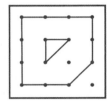

6.24 Fractions on geoboards

A class activity

OBJECTIVE	To develop the concept of equality of parts
ORGANISATION	Whole class followed by group work
RESOURCES	• A set of ten large flashcards or OHP slides. Each card shows a shape (square, triangle, rectangle or circle), partitioned into two, three or four parts, the parts being equal, or not equal, in area (Figure 6.25)
	• A set of 20 small cards for each group of four children similar to the above for children in a group to sort. For larger groups more cards are needed
	• Two sorting grids for each group (Figure 6.26). Each group has only one sorting grid at a time

6.25 Examples of fraction cards

	equal parts	unequal parts
square		
circle		
triangle		
rectangle		

	1 part	2 parts	3 parts	4 parts
square				
circle				
triangle				
rectangle				

6.26 Sorting grids

ACTIVITY

- The teacher uses the large flash cards to discuss with the whole class the number of parts in a shape and the equality or otherwise of the parts.
- Each group then works with a small set of cards, sorting them on one of the sorting grids.

A group activity

OBJECTIVE	To develop the concept of sixths
ORGANISATION	Small groups
RESOURCES	Each child needs an activity sheet comprising congruent circles partitioned into six equal parts

ACTIVITY

- Discuss with children the circles on the sheet, emphasising the number of parts in each circle and that the parts are equal.
- Everyone must shade in one part in the first circle, discussing how many parts out of the six are shaded and how they would write this as a fraction.
- Everyone shades any two parts in the second circle, discussing how to write the amount shaded.
- The groups work together, shading as many parts as they wish in each circle. Each time they must write the fraction that they have shaded and confirm what they have done with the rest of the group.
- Gather the children together and, in turn, select what each group has successfully done with one circle and discuss the example with everyone.
- Repeat this, but with some fractions that have been incorrectly recorded.

Test your own knowledge: fractions

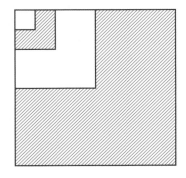

6.27 *A sequence of squares*

1 Draw a 0–1 number line. Mark the position of ½. Put a cross nearer to ½ than ¾. Estimate the fraction that is marked by your cross. What fraction of the whole line is your cross away from ¾? Try to find an alternative approach. Write a comparison of the two approaches.

2 Draw a diagram to illustrate how to find 2 kg as a fraction of 18 kg.

3 Draw a diagram to illustrate how to find 8 ml as a fraction of 2 litres.

4 Draw a diagram to illustrate how to find ¾ of 1500 metres.

5 Figure 6.27 is constructed using a sequence of squares. Each square is one-quarter of the area of the previous square. What fraction is each of the shaded 'L shapes' of the largest square? Predict what fraction of the largest square the next two L shapes would be if they were constructed. Discuss your reasoning with a friend.

6 Write a fraction that is nearer to 0 than to ½. Draw a number line to show where your fraction is positioned relative to 0 and ½

7 **a** Find the fraction that is half-way between ½ and ⅓. Find the fraction that is half-way between ⅓ and ¼. Find the fraction that is half-way between ¼ and ⅕. Find the fraction that is half-way between ⅕ and ⅙. Have you developed a strategy? If not talk with a partner to see if you can work one out together.

b Apply your strategy to find the fraction that is half-way between 1/99 and 1/100

c Generalise your strategy by applying it to the fraction that is half-way between $1/n$ and $1/(n + 1)$, where n is a whole number.

Review of key points

➤ National curricula put the accent on the understanding and use of fractions in everyday contexts

➤ It is important that children's informal knowledge of fractions is built upon in the classroom

➤ The concept of a fraction is difficult to learn as it extends children's ideas of number in ways which differ from those of whole numbers

➤ There are a number of subconcepts, such as a 'unit' and equal partitioning, that children should understand in order to successfully develop the fraction concept

➤ There are five meanings that can be associated with the fraction concept: as part of a unit, as a number, as the result of a division, as a ratio, and as an operator

➤ Children find positioning of a fraction on a number line extremely difficult

➤ The concept of equivalent fractions is a cornerstone of children's understanding of fractions

➤ During the ages of 5–11 years children should experience a multiplicity of activities using the five meanings of a fraction using concrete and pictorial models in order that they can apply their knowledge in a variety of real-life contexts

➤ Children do not readily relate their understanding of fractions in concrete and pictorial situations to similar experiences that use symbols

➤ Learning experiences limited to partly shaded shapes which have some regularity about them leads to children developing misconceptions and strategies and skills that have limited applicability

➤ Errors and misconceptions can often be traced to children attempting to apply their knowledge of whole numbers to fractions when it is inappropriate to do so

---

Module 7   Learning to teach percentages

Introduction

Percentages are widely used in the 'real' world. Interest rates, mortgages, inflation, discounts, income tax, VAT – the list of everyday applications relevant to adults is long, with even road gradients now being expressed as percentages!

The difficulty associated with teaching percentages to children is that the applications mentioned above are encountered by adults on a very regular basis but rarely affect children directly. Thus there are few regular, relevant, everyday experiences for children which teachers can call upon to illustrate and consolidate the ideas and practices they might wish to introduce.

Percentages in national curricula

The emphasis in primary national curricula is on:

- understanding and using percentages in contexts to estimate proportions of wholes
- calculating percentages of quantities mentally, and with paper and pencil
- exploring relationships between percentages and decimals and fractions.

Key terms

ratio   the comparative size of quantities (numbers or measures) of the same kind. It is frequently recorded in the form 3:2 (or 2:5:3, etc. – any number of quantities may be compared), but when only two quantities are compared the ratio may be recorded as a single number – e.g. 1.5 instead of 3:2

proportion   expresses the equality of ratios. Thus the two sets of numbers (2, 3, 5, 7) and (4, 6, 10, 14) are in proportion because corresponding elements are all in the same ratio (1:2). The word 'proportion' is sometimes used to mean 'ratio'

percentage   a proportion (ratio) expressed out of 100. Alternatively it may be thought of as a fraction with denominator 100

equivalence   suppose two objects are in proportion, with the ratio 7:20 expressing the relationship between corresponding lengths. This means that lengths on the smaller object will be 7/20 of the corresponding lengths in the larger. In other words, the lengths in the smaller are 35% of the lengths in the larger. This example illustrates the equivalence of the ideas of ratio and proportion, fraction and percentage

---

Key issues in percentages

Related concepts and issues

Figure 7.1 reflects the inter-relationships discussed in the previous sections of this module, and therefore sums up the work so far. Note that 'percentage' is not a word which appears in all books concerned with teaching mathematics to young children, suggesting that the amount of time spent on the topic in primary schools in the past has been limited.

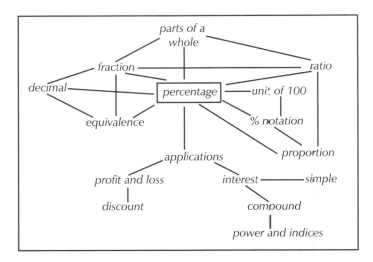

7.1 Concepts and issues associated with percentages

To do

With a colleague, calculate 17½% of £166.50. If you feel this is too demanding, wait until you have read the whole of the section on key issues in percentages, and then return to the question.

The concept of percentage

For most people, percentages are understood first and foremost as being derived from fractions with denominator 100. Thus, for example, $\frac{1}{2} = \frac{50}{100} = 50\% = 0.5$. Also, if 12 people out of a sample of 20 go to work by car, we can translate that into 60%. That is simply because of the equivalence of fractions: $\frac{12}{20} = \frac{60}{100}$. Similarly, if an item costing £5.00 is reduced by 10%, it will cost £4.50, because the reduction is 10% of £5.00 $= \frac{1}{10}$ of £5.00 $=$ £0.50. Percentages like 60% and 10% are relatively easy to apply, and problems involving such simple percentages can often be solved mentally, without using taught methods. Difficulties arise with more complicated numbers, like 12½% and 6.666...%, where it is harder to see the equivalent fractions $\frac{1}{8}$ and $\frac{1}{15}$, respectively, and by percentages like 3.75% which might arise from interest rates. Children are often taught routine procedures so that they can, theoretically, cope with any percentages that occur, but sometimes this concentration on formal, taught procedures only serves to obscure the basic concepts. Thus, when adding 17½% VAT onto an item costing £166.50, panic sets in and conceptual understanding goes out of the window.

The word 'percentage'

The word 'percentage' represents its meaning exactly, because 'per cent' means 'per hundred'. In this sense, life might be thought to be relatively easy for teachers, compared with trying to introduce many other terms used in mathematics which cannot be so easily related to simpler word forms. Many children will have travelled to destinations overseas, and may have met the word 'cent' (or similar) to describe a coin. Always a 'cent' coin is one hundredth part, usually of the basic unit of currency, for example the dollar in North America. The word 'cent' is of Latin origin, and is therefore not surprisingly the basis of many other words to do with 100, for example century (100 years, or 'runs' in cricket), centimetre (already encountered as one-hundredth of a metre), centigrade and centipede.

However, the word 'per' might cause more problems than anticipated. It occurs frequently as the beginning of a word, but there is not the same constancy of meaning as with 'cent'. In percentage, 'per' means 'for each', 'in each', or 'out of each', so 20 per cent is 20 in each hundred. In a similar way, one-quarter is 'one in four' or 'one out of each four', which is equivalent to twenty-five in each hundred, and thus 25 per cent. Children need more time to grasp this idea of equivalence than you will initially anticipate. In short, the more problematical aspect of the meaning of 'per cent' is likely to be the proportionality implied by the 'per' rather than the association with one hundred.

The % symbol

The % symbol will be new to many children despite it being part of everyday advertising. The symbol needs to be explained with understanding and relevance in order for it to have meaning. Basically, the three units of the symbol (°, / and ₀) are the same as the three units of the number 100 (1, 0 and 0), though in a different order. This might be used to explain to children why we use the symbol, though the actual development is more complicated.

Percentages as proportions of wholes

Children need to meet percentages of wholes in a variety of contexts. These can often involve simple numbers, in which case there is much to be said for demanding mental rather than paper and pencil or other methods. Figure 7.2 shows a rectangle subdivided into squares, with some squares shaded. It is legitimate to ask what percentage of the rectangle is shaded, just as one might ask what fraction is shaded, or even what proportion is shaded. Similar questions may be based on other rectangles, on squares, on circles, and in many other spatial contexts.

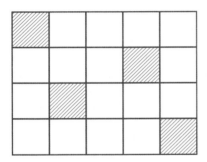

7.2 What percentage is shaded?

The opportunity of using the word 'percentage' in simple numerical situations needs to be grasped regularly. An example of a number activity is to investigate what percentage of a set of whole numbers are in the '3 times table'. In the numbers from 1 to 10, the '3 times table' numbers are 3, 6 and 9, so 30% are in the '3 times table'. In the numbers 1 to 20, there are six '3 times table' numbers, that is 30% again. Does this proportion stay the same for 1 to 30, 1 to 40 and so on? Here the working out of percentages is reasonably straightforward as the number is always out of a multiple of 10. This activity can readily be extended to the other 'tables' and all the information graphed.

In the same way, when working with measures of many kinds, questions may be couched in terms of percentages. A simple example which also incorporates the important skill of estimation is, when drinking, to estimate what percentage is left each time the cup or bottle is put down. Although the first example in this section has been classified as spatial, because it is based on area, it is also a measurement context. Contexts involving area and volume are easy to invent.

Decimals and percentages

Decimals are parts of wholes represented in tenths, hundredths, thousandths, etc. Thus, 0.37 represents 3 tenths plus 7 hundredths, and therefore also 37 hundredths (see Module 5). But by definition, percentages are hundredth parts of wholes, too. The equivalence with percentages is therefore superficially simple, for 0.37 is 37 hundredths is 37 per cent. Many adults never realise that the correspondence between percentage notation and decimal notation is so straightforward. Unfortunately, in unthinking approaches to teaching mathematics, children are often mistakenly given rules rather than made to think about what they are doing, so converting 37% might become 'drop the % and put a decimal point in front'. It should not surprise us that 6% then becomes 0.6 and not 0.06, as it should be. The correct conversion is that 6% is six hundredths, which is 0.06. Corresponding errors also occur in reverse, in converting decimals to percentages.

Fractions and percentages

Again, the equivalence is mathematically straightforward, but often presents more problems than with decimals, simply because fractions are not always tenths or hundredths. In order to relate a fraction to its equivalent as a percentage it is necessary to convert the fraction into decimal form, as tenths plus hundredths, etc. Thus, to choose a simple fraction which cannot easily be converted into decimal form, but which we have met in earlier modules, ⅓ (one third) is 0.3333..., which is therefore 33.33...%. This may naturally also be written as 33⅓%. Much time has traditionally been spent in schools, in trying to teach children how to convert fractions into percentages. The simplest conversion, as we have already seen, is from decimals to percentages, and vice versa, and therefore one alternative when dealing with a vulgar fraction is always to convert the fraction into decimal form first, by division. The calculator makes this very simple:

$$3/7 = 3 \div 7 = 0.428571 ... \approx 42.86\%$$

In most circumstances this would be rounded to 43%. (The symbol $\approx$ means 'is approximately equal to'.)

The commonly taught instruction 'to convert from fraction to percentage, multiply the fraction by 100 and insert the % symbol':

$$3/7 = 300/7\% \approx 42.86\%$$

is clearly equivalent to the method above, but it can be seen by children as a typically mysterious mathematical process.

Uses and abuses

Percentages may be informative with small numbers, but they are particularly valuable when dealing with large numbers. Budgeting at any level, whether domestic, school, local authority or national, can sensibly refer to increases and decreases in term of percentages. If the school budget for next year is 5% greater than the current year, and inflation over the year has averaged at 3.5%, then all interested parties have a simple basis on which to draw conclusions. Other factors may need to be taken into account, but percentages provide basic numerical information in a conveniently easy form.

At the same time, percentages can provide a doubtful basis for comparisons. Is it fair that the entire working population should receive the same percentage salary increase in any particular year, when the disparities between the salaries before the increase are so great, and thus the actual increases are so different?

School examination results are usually expressed in percentage form to make comparisons easier. If one subject is marked out of 65 and another out of 110, comparisons are very difficult, but conversion to percentages makes life much simpler for all concerned. Yet, at the same time, such comparisons may be completely invalid for other reasons if, for example, the marks on the first paper range from 40 to 65 and on the second from 40 to 95. So expression in percentage form does not automatically validate previously invalid comparisons.

Percentages are usually less valuable for small numbers. If there are four people in your family group, then you constitute 25% of that group (that is indisputable), but there is little value in expressing the information in such a way. On the other hand, if a child obtains a mark of 7 out of 10 in a mathematics test, and then obtains 12 out of 15 on a similar test a week later, the percentages (70% and 80%, respectively) might reveal the improvement more clearly.

A useful source of real-life examples of the use of percentages is newspapers, but it is wise always to think very carefully about whether the use is a valid one or whether it is an abuse, either deliberate or unwitting. Sometimes percentages are spoken of outside a numerical context, just as a form of speech, for emphasis or effect. Thus, an athlete might claim to be intending to work, not at 100% of the maximum rate possible, but at 110%, in order to win the event. Clearly, no-one can really work at 110% of their maximum possible rate: here, 110% is used just to make a point. Yet percentages greater than 100 can exist. If a school has an extra 5% in the budget for the new year, it is legitimate to claim that the budget is 105% of that of the previous year.

Applications

Many real-life applications involve calculating percentages, often of money. For example, for many parents, their salary rise in a particular year might be expressed as a percentage of the previous year's salary. Or it might be that, in a particular year, car manufacturers decide to put up the prices of their new cars by a certain percentage. Or we might find that we need to take VAT at the current rate into account in our budgeting. The VAT rate is currently 15%, which at first sight isn't the easiest of figures to deal with. Thus, with children, if applications are introduced, it is likely that it will be necessary to use quite simple numbers. For teachers, using VAT is a good way to revise how the

To do

Collect examples of the use of percentages from newspapers and journals for use in the classroom. Make a poster which can be used for a display on a classroom wall. Discuss with colleagues how each is being used and its validity.

equivalencies discussed above might provide different methods. Three contrasting methods are shown here, but there are many other legitimate methods.

CALCULATING PERCENTAGES

A computer printer is advertised at £120 + VAT. What is it actually going to cost? (Note that it would be more normal for the advertised price to be £119.95, or similar!) Three methods that children use are shown in Table 7.1.

Three methods of calculating the cost of a computer printer

Method 1	Method 2	Method 3
The VAT amounts to 17½% of £120. This extra may be calculated separately, as 10% + 5% + 2½% (which conveniently is successive halving), and added on to the advertised price:	The VAT is 17½/100 of £120, and that is equivalent to $^{35}/_{200}$ of £120.	The VAT of 17.5% is 0.175 of the advertised price (by converting the percentage to a decimal). The sale price is therefore 1.175 (1 + 0.175) of the advertised price, that is:
	Then $\dfrac{\overset{7}{\cancel{35}}}{\underset{40}{\cancel{200}}} \times \overset{3}{\cancel{£120}} = £21$	
advertised price: £120.00 10% addition: £12.00 5% addition: £6.00 2½ % addition: £3.00	TOTAL: £141.00 Thus the cost is: £120 + £21 = £141	1.175 × £120 = £141.00 by using a calculator

Table 7.1

Children and percentages

To do

If a local computer store is selling £175 printers at a 10% discount, calculate the sale price. Find as many ways of working out the answer as you can. Discuss these with a colleague. If you did not complete the earlier task involving VAT, see if you can complete it now.

Fundamental misconceptions

Research evidence into children's understanding of the meaning of percentage is very limited, particularly at the primary stage. Perhaps the most telling evidence comes from Sewell (1981), who interviewed adults to collect evidence for the Cockcroft Report (1982). She discovered that about 30% of her sample of 100 inferred that they regarded all percentages as meaningless.

The evidence of children's misconceptions and errors with percentages relates to older children as the topic is given more prominence in the secondary curriculum.

This essential meaning of percentage is often supported by tasks such as that in Figure 7.3a. Shading 20% of 100 squares, however, implies shading 20 squares, and the meaning might not be adequately conveyed by such a simple example. The concept needs to be supported by other shading tasks such as that in Figure 7.3b. Here, if a child shades 20 squares we can be sure the idea of percentage has not yet been grasped.

Calculating percentages

A percentage of a quantity

Much of the research data on percentages concerns finding a percentage of a quantity, an important aspect of the primary and secondary curriculum.

The National Curriculum tests at the end of Key Stage 2 in England and Wales usually have questions on percentages. In the SCAA (1995) report on the 1995 Key Stage 2 Tests, we find, 'many children were not able to

(a) Shade 20% of the squares in this grid.

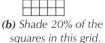

(b) Shade 20% of the squares in this grid.

7.3 Shading percentages

calculate 15% of 80 children', and that 'a common incorrect answer was 15 which showed a lack of basic understanding of percentages'. Most errors were in 'the attempted application of the standard method: 15/100 × 80'.

CHILDREN'S CALCULATIONS

In 1996 Key Stage 2 tests a question asked children to calculate 70% of 130 kg. The SCAA report (1996) wrote that 'many children did not know a correct method to calculate 70% of 130 kg. Those who were able to answer it correctly used a range of effective, if not always efficient, methods which demonstrated an understanding of percentages.' The report described the methods of four different children, as shown in Table 7.2.

Four methods used by children to calculate 70% of 130 kg

Susan used a standard method:

$$\frac{\overset{13}{\cancel{130}}}{1} \times \frac{\overset{7}{\cancel{70}}}{\underset{\underset{1}{\cancel{10}}}{\cancel{100}}} = \frac{91}{1} = 91 \text{ kg}$$

Adrian did not use fractions, choosing instead to use multiplication for 130 × 70 and then dividing by 100:

```
    130
  x  70
    000
   9100
   91·00
```

Rosie partitioned 70% into quantities that she could more easily handle:

```
  70       65          65
 -50     2)130         26
  20                   91
        13 × 2 = 26
        10)130
```

How did Rosie partition 70%?
Raksha also partitioned 70% but used a different partition and method:

```
                26      26      91
                26      13      39
26 halved is    26      39     130
13 which is     13
                91

                        26
               10%     5)130
```

How did Raksha partition 70%?

Table 7.2

Older children in the secondary school continue to have problems solving questions involving percentages of quantities.

SCHOOL DINNERS

A question used by the CSMS project was: '6% of children in a school have free dinners. There are 250 children in the school. How many children have free dinners?' Hart (1981) reports only a 38% success rate amongst 13-year-old students.

In another question the children were asked: 'The price of a coat is £20. In a sale it is reduced by 5%. How much does it cost now?' For this, the success rate in the same age group was only 20%.

It appears that when children leave secondary school it is not possible to claim that everyone has mastered percentages. Indeed, the evidence suggests that many children have been unable to overcome their difficulties with the topic.

One quantity as a percentage of another

Apart from the work of the Assessment of Performance Unit (APU) and CSMS there is little research data available for this aspect of percentage work.

FAULTY CARS

The APU (1980) found that 15% of the 11-year-old children asked could work out what percentage 50 is of 250, but that in general 'no more than one third of the pupils got the percentage questions right'.

This is confirmed by the CSMS, which included this question: 'The newspaper says that 24 out of 800 Avenger cars have a faulty engine. What percentage is this?' Only 32% of the 13-year-olds questioned were able to answer this correctly.

Decimals, fractions and percentages

Calculations involving percentages almost invariably require some knowledge of equivalence, which seems to be another aspect of percentages that children find difficult to master, even for fundamental equivalences, such as $\frac{1}{10}$, 0.1 and 10%.

PERCENTAGE CONVERSIONS

Some relevant data is contained within the first APU primary survey report (1980), where we find: '50 per cent of pupils correctly wrote the fraction ¼ as a percentage while about 25 per cent knew its decimal equivalent. Conversions of decimals to percentages and vice versa were carried out successfully by half the pupils for familiar fractions ... Facilities of just over 40 per cent were obtained for the conversion of tenths to decimals and less for converting hundredths to decimals (30%).'

Some ideas for teaching percentages

To think about

Analyse a set of textbooks and the teachers' guides to see what coverage they give to percentages. What models do they recommend?

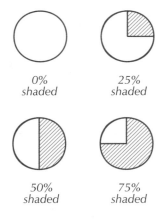

0% shaded

25% shaded

50% shaded

75% shaded

100% shaded

7.4 Matching a percentage to a proportion

Textbooks and percentages

Percentages are not usually found in primary school textbooks until those written for 10–11-year-old children, and then sometimes the work is suggested only for high achievers. There is no evidence that primary school children cannot cope with percentages any earlier, nor that fractions and decimals must be comprehensively taught before percentages can be introduced. The order of teaching seems to be based more on established practice than on evidence from working with children. We therefore do not know whether earlier introduction to percentages would offer any advantages.

The order of introduction of ideas is generally:

- state that, for example, 40 out of 100 may be recorded as 40%
- use a 10 × 10 grid to shade regions and record as percentages
- write one quantity as a percentage of another
- the equivalence between percentages and fractions
- calculating percentages of quantities
- applications.

Activities with proportions as percentages

Working with shapes and proportions of shapes is a good early introduction to the ideas and language of percentages. A possible sequence is outlined here.

1. Matching a percentage to a proportion of a shape (usually but not necessarily a circle) as in Figure 7.4

2. Estimating, using words like 'nearly' and 'about' – for example, 'about 50%' as in Figure 7.5

3. Extending the previous idea to use phrases such as 'just less than' and 'just more than'

4. Introducing 'between' – for example, 'between 40% and 50%', and even 'between 33% and 50%' (that is, using the approximate percentage equivalents of one-third, and perhaps also two-thirds)

5. Extending all the above to estimating percentages in pie charts

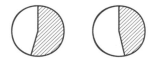

7.5 *About 50%*

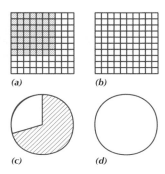

(a)   *(b)*

(c)   *(d)*

7.6 *Percentages of shapes*

Activities with percentages and shapes

Early emphasis needs to be placed on the idea that percentages are based on fractions with denominator 100, or on proportions of 100. Thus, a 10 × 10 square grid can provide a simple form of concrete apparatus to support this idea. What percentage is shaded in Figure 7.6a, for example? Can you shade in 20% of the square in Figure 7.6b? Care must be taken to vary the 'dimensions' of the square grid, so that the exercise does not become one of simply counting squares to obtain the answer.

Other shapes may also be used, such as a rectangle for both accurate measures and estimates, and circles for estimates. Approximately what percentage of the circle is shaded in Figure 7.6c? Can you shade in 75% of the circle in Figure 7.6d? Any object which provides a whole which has clearly been subdivided into 100 equal parts, or multiples of 10, can be used, and this can lead to imagining the subdivisions of a whole into 100 parts. Even lines of, say, 10 cm, divided into millimetres, could be used. At the same time, the notation using '%' can be introduced, and set alongside other forms such as decimal and fractional.

Simple equivalences may be introduced next. If '5 per cent', written as 5%, means 5 out of every 100, and there are not 100 but 200 children in the school, how many children does that 5% represent? What if it were 6%, or 12%, or 20%, or 21%, or 21½%? There is no limit to the number of questions of this type, which may be based on a simple (contrived) real-life situation. As long as the complexity is built up slowly and carefully, the concepts may be steadily strengthened and developed. Similar questions may then be asked the other way round. If 16 of the 200 children are absent on a particular day, what percentage is that? Such activities as described in this section are sufficient for a first introduction.

Activities with percentages, decimals and fractions

Some authors recommend a concentration on learning the common equivalences. There is no doubt that committing such equivalences to memory can be a great asset when it comes to calculations, but if equivalences are to be learned with meaning, and not by rote, then they must be built up from the kinds of activities discussed in the previous section. One way in which children should be helped to learn equivalences is by means of a conversion chart (Figure 7.7, which shows a 'vertical' line relating 75%, 0.75 and ¾).

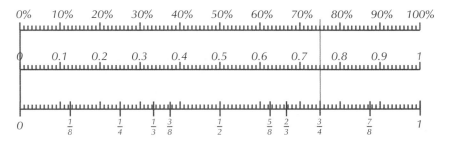

7.7 *Relating percentages, decimals and fractions using number lines*

99

Useful equivalences to try, ultimately, to remember are shown in Table 7.3, but children should build this information up themselves over a period of time. The last two in the list may not be inserted into the table until much later than the others. Clearly, additional ones may be added if desired, though the most likely basic and important ones are all included here.

Equivalences between percentages, decimals and fractions		
Fraction	Decimal	Percentage
1/10	0.1	10%
1/100	0.01	1%
1/2	0.5	50%
1/4	0.25	25%
3/4	0.75	75%
1/5	0.2	20%
3/10	0.3	30%
2/5	0.4	40%
3/5	0.6	60%
7/10	0.7	70%
4/5	0.8	80%
9/10	0.9	90%
1/20	0.05	5%
1/3	$\approx$ 0.333	$\approx$ 33.3%
2/3	$\approx$ 0.667	$\approx$ 66.7%

Table 7.3

Activities with percentage of a quantity

Estimating

A valuable first stage, as with many methods of calculation, is to demand estimates for percentages of quantities. Some examples are provided here:

- 30% of 20 is 6, therefore 30% of 19 is 'about' 6
- 10% of £14.00 is £1.40, therefore 9% of £14.00 is 'about' ...
- 7% of the children in the school is about how many?

When children are accustomed to estimating, and are reasonably proficient, the expectation should be that they should always use estimation as a check when calculating.

Calculating

Suppose a dealer sells bicycles at a 10% discount in a short-term promotion event. Let us assume that a child is interested in the cost of a bicycle which is normally sold at £230. There are many possible variations that children can use for calculating the actual cost.

BUYING A BICYCLE

- The most obvious approach to finding the new price is to deduct 10% (= $\frac{1}{10}$) of £230, that is £23. Thus, the new price is £230 – £23 = £207.

- Alternatively, $\frac{9}{10} \times$ £230 = 9 × £23 = £207.

- A very different alternative, as we have seen earlier, is to convert the percentage to a decimal; then we have 10% = 0.1. The decrease is then 0.1 × £230 = £23.

- Alternatively the new cost, using a calculator, is 0.9 × £230 = £207.

- If the price decrease is 7½%, again there are many alternative strategies. One is to use 10% of £230 is £23, so 5% is £11.50 and 2½% is £5.75. Thus, 7½% of £230 is (5% + 2½%) of £230, that is £17.25, and the new price is £212.75.

- Another method is to use 1% of £230 = £2.30, so 7½% of £230 is 7½ × £2.30 = £17.25, and the cost is then £212.75.

- If we wished to use decimals throughout, we would need to use the conversion 7½% = 0.075 (think about it!), then the new price is 0.925 × £230 = £212.75.

- A very different approach is to use 7½% = $\frac{7.5}{100}$ = $\frac{15}{200}$ = $\frac{3}{40}$. Then the decrease is $\frac{3}{40} \times$ £230 = ¾ × £23 = ¼ × £69 = £17.25.

Percentage problems can always be tackled by breaking them down into manageable subsections, and children should be taught to think about situations in this way, rather than taught routines which are not properly understood. Conversion into decimal form always provides a good method, as long as the decimal is not too difficult. Always, the teaching emphasis should be on thinking about how to solve the problem, rather than rushing into a routine procedure.

Interest on savings

Interest on savings is a common application of percentage increase. Rates are in reality always disappointingly small, and often involve fractions of per cent, so that 2½% and 5% are the only realistic simple percentages which you might use in problems with children. Note that interest is usually 'compounded'. That means that you gain interest on the previous interest. If £100 is invested at 5% per 'annum' (year), then the interest in the first year is £5, which gives a new 'capital' of £105. In the second year, the interest is therefore 5% of £105, which is £5.25. The capital is now £110.25, so the interest in the third year is 5% of £110.25. It is clear that the interest is becoming more and more complicated to work out as the years go by. In real life, the capital sum invested would also change for other reasons. Nevertheless, interest forms a relatively motivating application of percentages, and should be used. A calculator naturally helps when the calculations become complicated. Sometimes 'simple interest' is used, in order to avoid the increasingly complicated calculations as the years go by. In simple interest situations, the interest is always based on the original sum invested, no matter how many years are involved. This is not the kind of interest most people look for, but it does give rise to easier questions.

Activities with one quantity as a percentage of another

Estimating

Estimation, once again, should be the normal introduction to this kind of calculation, and should provide a check whenever calculations are demanded. For example, 6 out of 25 is 'about' 25%, 12 out of 110 is 'about' 10%, 133 out of 250 is about 50%, and so on. Examples are very easy to invent but are a very important challenge to thinking mathematically.

Calculating

One good reason for the customary exclusion of this topic at the primary level is that there is no doubt that real-life examples can be quite difficult. Another reason may be that the knowledge may be of much less practical use than that of the previous section. Here we have to suppose that, for example, we know the actual increase but want to know the percentage increase. If a car costing £12 250 is found to have gone up in price, overnight, to £12 750, and this is claimed to be 'the first increase since this time last year' (in the way that manufacturers might), does that seem fair? Is it in line with inflation? Under such circumstances, we might want to be able to satisfy ourselves that the increase is not extortionate. Naturally, children might need to practise on many simpler questions before tackling this particular 'real life' example. Here is a simple example to illustrate possibilities. If a £200 bicycle goes up to £212, the percentage increase may be calculated by first obtaining the actual increase, namely £12. The increase as a fraction of the original is

$$\frac{12}{200} = \frac{6}{100} = 6\%$$

This is a very simple example, which reveals a reasonable price increase, but one which might nevertheless be greater than inflation. Note that, once we have the denominator 100 in the fraction we may, in effect, take the numerator as the percentage. You may check its correctness by calculating 6% of £200, in the way we did in the previous section.

A class activity

OBJECTIVE	To find the percentage of a grid which is shaded
ORGANISATION	Whole class
RESOURCES	Teacher has a number of OHP slides of different-sized rectangular grids made of unit squares; the number of squares in a rectangle should be a factor or a multiple of 100

ACTIVITY

- Teacher shows a slide on the OHP.

- One child suggests how many squares the teacher should shade.
- Children say what percentage of the rectangle is shaded.
- One child explains why.

A group activity

OBJECTIVE   To find the percentage shaded of a 100-square grid

ORGANISATION   Small groups

RESOURCES   Each group has a sheet on which there are a number of large 100-square grids

ACTIVITY
- Children take it in turns to shade in a number of squares on one of the grids. The number shaded should be more than 10 and less than 20.
- Each time, the child has to say what percentage they are shading and how much is shaded altogether.
- The winner is the child who shades the last square.
- The activity can be extended to using a 50-square grid.

Test your own knowledge: percentages

1 Find the actual cost of a household item which is advertised as £166.50 + VAT. Use the current rate of VAT. (You may have already done this question!)

2 A driver notices that a downhill road gradient warning sign reads '14%'. What do you think the corresponding older, fractional (ratio) sign would have been?

3 Convert the following fractions to percentages: $\frac{3}{8}$, $\frac{7}{8}$, $\frac{1}{6}$, $\frac{5}{6}$, $\frac{3}{20}$, $\frac{11}{20}$

4 A car is advertised at £12 000 but, when a customer shows interest, the salesperson says that the price has just gone up by 5%. However, the customer is offered a special 'Privileged Customer' deal of 4% off the new price. How much would the car now cost this customer?

5 A car costing £12 250 goes up in price, overnight, to a new price of £12 750. Is that a reasonable price rise for one year? Give reasons for your answer.

Review of key points ➤

➤ Percentages are widely used in the 'real world', so children need to be given all the help possible to understand their meaning and use

➤ Because percentages are widely used in the 'real world', suitable examples from that world, such as are found in the media, should be used in lessons

➤ Children should always be encouraged to think about percentages in the simplest possible way, perhaps by informal methods

➤ The bottom line for all explanations about percentages is that 'per cent' means 'per hundred'

➤ Equivalences between fractions, decimals and percentages are important, and need to be practised frequently

➤ Often the simplest method of applying a percentage is to convert it to a decimal, and then use a calculator

➤ The simple equivalence between a decimal thought of as hundredths and the corresponding percentage needs to be particularly emphasised

➤ There is never just one way to apply a percentage, and thus there is never just one way to solve a problem involving percentages

Module 8   Learning to teach ratio and proportion

Introduction

This topic draws together a number of connected ideas, and looks at them in a new light. The time devoted to ratio and proportion in the national curricula for primary school children is relatively small, yet the concepts involved in looking at old ideas in these new ways are very significant mathematically. Some children, of all ages, find the ideas amongst the most difficult they encounter at school, yet they are vital if children are to become numerate adults.

Ratio and proportion in national curricula

Primary national curricula vary widely on the amount of reference to ratio and proportion. Ratio and proportion are important in drawing together previous work on fractions, decimals and percentages. The stress in primary schools should be on:

- describing and comparing proportions using fractions, percentages, decimals and ratio in appropriate and relevant contexts
- understanding the equivalence between different ways in which proportion is represented
- finding ratios between quantities
- using simple unitary ratio.

Key terms

ratio   the comparative size of quantities (numbers or measures) of the same kind. It is frequently recorded in the form 3:2 (or 2:5:3, etc. – any number of quantities may be compared), but when only two quantities are compared the ratio may be recorded as a single number, e.g. 1.5 instead of 3:2

rate   a correspondence between two different measures. Speed is a simple example, recorded as miles per hour, centimetres per second, or similar units

proportion   compares a part of a quantity with the whole. Thus a ratio of 1:2 results in the proportions 1 out of 3 and 2 out of 3. The word is also used to express the equality of ratios. Thus the two sets of numbers (2, 3, 5, 7) and (4, 6, 10, 14) are in proportion because corresponding elements are all in the same ratio (1:2). Proportion is sometimes mistakenly used to mean 'ratio'

scale   records the ratio of corresponding measures between those on a model (or plan) and the actual, usually in the form 1:n.

similarity   two geometric shapes (plane or solid) are similar if one is an enlargement of the other with corresponding measurements in the same ratio

rational numbers   numbers which can be written as the ratio of two integers

irrational numbers   numbers which cannot be written as the ratio of two integers

---

Key issues in ratio and proportion

Related concepts and issues

Figure 8.1 shows that the growth of understanding of ideas of ratio and proportion may be encouraged from familiar roots. The main core emerges from the consideration of decimals, fractions and percentages in a slightly new light, with the even more elementary ideas of partitioning and division feeding in. Equivalence, viewed often as equality, allows ratios to be defined as the same – in other words, measurements of objects are in proportion. Some of the applications such as photographs and maps can be used as a way into the study of ratio and proportion, but in Figure 8.1 they are shown as if they follow on from the basic concepts, because they are certainly also applications.

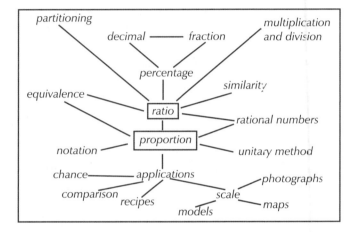

8.1 Concepts and issues associated with ratio and proportion

Ratio, rate and rational numbers

The three mathematical ideas of rate, ratio and rational number are all related, and are all generally implied in mathematics curricula. *Rate* is frequently used in both everyday and business conversation, together with per, for example in rate of pay, and in discussions of a minimum wage of so much per hour. On the other hand, *ratio* is more of a mathematical word but ration, representing fair shares for all, is an idea familiar to many. Mathematicians often do not like to talk of fractions, but prefer to talk of *rational numbers*, because a rational number can be thought of as the ratio of two whole numbers. Usually there are two numbers involved in rate, in ratio, and in rational numbers. Cooking provides us with simple examples of the use of ratio and rate with which we are all very familiar, for example when flour and milk must be mixed in the ratio of two parts flour per one part milk, no matter how many people the end product is to feed.

Most of us drive a car, so we know all about speed limits of 30, 40, 60 or 70 miles per hour. Speed is an expression of rate: 30 miles per hour is 15 miles per half hour, and is 60 miles per 2 hours etc., and these are equal rates. Maps and plans, too, are drawn to a particular scale, which expresses the ratio between the distances on the map or plan and those on the ground.

It is when we wish to talk about equal ratios that we imply proportionality. Two heaped tablespoons of flour to one (level!) tablespoon of milk and four heaped tablespoons of flour to two tablespoons of milk express the same proportions, because 2:1 = 4:2. Proportion is the name we should use when referring to the equality of two ratios, and this is the only way the two terms 'ratio' and 'proportion' can sensibly be distinguished. Teachers and children need to understand all these ideas, and use the associated words appropriately, as well as experiencing the contexts in which the ideas and words arise.

Partition and ratio

One of the elementary ideas which underlies those of ratio and proportion is partitioning. In a situation where a parent has five sweets to give to two children, it is necessary to partition and allocate in some way. Let us suppose it is decided that the older child should be given three of the sweets, then there is a partitioning of the five into two groups of three and two, respectively (see Figure 8.2).

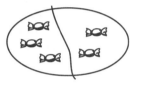

8.2 A partition of five

In another way, however, when we consider the situation multiplicatively, the ratio of allocations of older to younger is 3:2, that is, the older receives ³⁄₂ times as many sweets as the younger (i.e. 1.5 times as many). If that rule was adopted for any number of sweets, the older would receive three for each two which the younger received. The emphasis on looking at situations 'multiplicatively' (rather than 'additively') is the essence of ratio. It is also one aspect of what children find difficult in coming to terms with ratio. Why should they think about two numbers in terms of 'how many times bigger' one is than the other, when the straightforward 'how many more than' is easier and more familiar? The answer is that there are times when a multiplicative approach is the right one. We do sometimes need to know how many times one thing is bigger than another. The principles of household cooking and professional map drawing are both examples of this.

Division and ratio

Ratio and division are closely related concepts, but there are two different ways of looking at this relationship. In the example of the sweets given above we have 'divided up' the total of five sweets into two groups of three and two, and thereby we have established a ratio of 3:2. This is one common way in which we use the word 'divide' in everyday speech and usage, simply in the act of partitioning.

It is not what we usually mean by division as the inverse of multiplication, however. Mathematically, division means dividing one number by another, in the sense of finding how many times one number is 'contained in' another. The mathematical meaning is applied when we convert the ratio 3:2 to 1.5:1, that is, 3 contains 2 'one and a half times', or, 'there are one and a half 2s in 3'. Any dictionary should make it clear that we do use the word 'divide' in these two different ways, and that they both come together in the topic of ratio and proportion. This means that we have to be exceedingly careful when talking about ratio and division with children.

The mathematical use is important when it comes to simplifying ratios, for example 12:3 is equivalent to 4:1, and may be expressed more simply as 4:1. It is also important in the sense that a ratio may be regarded as a single number (not necessarily whole), for example π, the ratio of circumference:diameter in circles, which is usually obtained practically in school by dividing the circumference by the diameter in many different circles.

Fractions and ratio

If a supplier wishes to partition ('divide up'!) 80 cartons containing ball-point pens to two retailers in the ratio of 3:2, the fractions ⅗ and ⅖ are likely to be used. In this case, ⅗ of 80 is 48, and ⅖ of 80 is 32, so the first retailer gets 48 to sell, and the second gets 32. It is then easy to check that 48:32 is equivalent to 3:2. Such a method of using fractions is the only practical general method which one could apply to a situation like this, and this example illustrates one way in which a ratio problem may be changed to a fraction situation for its solution. In one way this helps, because children are happier with the language of fractions.

Contrastingly, when we draw a plan, using a scale of 1:10 say, distances on the ground become ¹⁄₁₀ of that distance when we draw a line on the plan. Here, the fraction we would use to calculate plan distances is taken directly from the ratio, and indeed the technical term 'representative fraction' is sometimes used in such situations instead of 'scale'. The correspondence between ratio and fraction is close, though once again, in the two examples here, the ratio has provided us with fractions to use in calculations in two slightly different ways.

Percentage and ratio

Percentages are now used on road signs which give warnings of steep gradients, and these replace the older signs based on ratios, thus emphasising another equivalence, this time between percentage and ratio. The older signs were of the form '1 in 7' (representing 1:7), indicating a vertical 'rise' or 'descent' of 1 unit for every 7 units travelled. The newer signs are of the form 10% as in Figure 8.3. The basic hypothetical advantage of this new method should be clear – the larger the percentage the steeper the hill. In the older system, using 1:*n*, the smaller the value of *n* the more danger.

Rational numbers

Mathematicians talk of fractions as 'rational numbers' – that is, numbers which are formed from ratios of two other numbers. Certain advantages of this terminology should be clear straight away. The important distinction in mathematics is between rational numbers, which can be expressed as the ratio of two whole numbers (or integers), and irrational numbers, which cannot. Sometimes learners think that the important distinction is between fractions and decimals, but it can be seen from Module 5 that decimals are either rational (because they either

8.3 A road sign showing a gradient

108

terminate or recur) or irrational. The only decimals which cannot also be expressed as fractions are the irrationals.

The connection between fraction and ratio is all the more clear when we consider equivalent fractions, for example:

$$\frac{2}{3} = \frac{4}{6} = \frac{6}{9} = \frac{8}{12} = \frac{10}{15} = \ldots$$

This could be interpreted just as easily as an expression of equivalent ratios (proportionality):

$$2:3 = 4:6 = 6:9 = 8:12 = 10:15 = \ldots$$

We shall see in a later section that children find formal proportionality difficult, and it is because proportionality underlies work with fractions that fractions themselves often cause more problems for children than teachers expect.

Unitary method

If a packet of 12 ball-point pens costs £2.52, and a shopper wants one pen for each of the five members of her family, one method to work out the cost of five pens is to find the unit cost – the cost of one pen – first:

	12 pens cost	£2.52	=	252 pence
∴	1 pen costs	252 ÷ 12 pence	=	21 pence
∴	5 pens cost	5 × 21 pence	=	105 pence
			=	£1.05

This method, when the cost of one item is calculated first, is often known as the *unitary method*. Here, the calculation is based on the constant ratio 1:21. It can clearly be used not only with monetary situations but also whenever two variables are in a ratio relationship with each other, for example in calculating times and distances. The advantage of teaching the unitary method is that children can be taught it as a procedure, though their understanding of its connection with ratio may be non-existent.

Scale

Scale has already been quoted as an example of ratio being used in the real world. Scale drawing is a common and valuable classroom activity for many reasons. It provides added interest if the plan is of an area known to the children, it illustrates a genuine use of mathematics (which incidentally also acts as a link with geography), it provides much-needed concrete practice in handling ratio and proportion, and it provides an opportunity to become accustomed to expressing ratios in the 1:*n* or *m:n* form.

Photographs also form a good visual example of an everyday manifestation of scale. Familiar friends and places are instantly recognisable in a photograph, because the proportions remain the same on the photograph as in real life. Photographs of people seen through the distorting mirrors of a funfair illustrate how proportions must stay the same. This is the principle of map drawing: the proportions on the map must be the same as the proportions on the ground.

To think about

VAT calculations, based on a VAT rate of 17½%, may be carried out by adding 10% + 5% + 2½%. An alternative is to use a unitary method, that is to calculate 1% and then multiply by 17.5. Compare these two methods of calculating the VAT by applying them to sums of money of varying complexity.

To think about

What scales are in common use in the maps and plans that are available in shops? What scales would you use when children are asked to draw (a) a scale drawing of the classroom, (b) a scale drawing of their route to school, (c) a scale drawing of their trip to a holiday destination?

109

Chance

When a coin is tossed, for example at the start of a sporting contest, it is often said that there is a '50–50' chance of calling correctly. This expression of the comparative likelihoods of success and failure is rarely seen written down outside of mathematics lessons, so it is not always appreciated that it is really the ratio 50:50. It is interesting that a percentage form is used in this common expression (there is a 50% chance of success and a 50% chance of failure) rather than the much simpler equivalent, 1:1.

The 3-times table in ratio form		
1	:	3
2	:	6
3	:	9
4	:	12
5	:	15
6	:	18
7	:	21
8	:	24
9	:	27
10	:	30

Table 8.1

Probability uses both ratios and fractions to express the relative likelihoods of particular outcomes. Thus, the probability of obtaining a 6 when throwing a die (with faces numbered 1–6) is usually expressed as the fraction ⅙, representing an expected success rate of one 6 for every six throws. In the same way, the probability of obtaining a head when tossing a coin is ½, or 0.5, representing the expectation that a head will occur on average in one out of every two tosses. The chance of obtaining a 6 on a die, in ratio form, is 1:5, representing the comparative likelihoods of success and failure on each throw. The comparative likelihoods of success and failure, in ratio form, are sometimes known as 'odds'.

Multiplication tables

Multiplication tables record multiplicative relationships, and therefore form a simple introduction to the idea of ratio. As an illustration, Table 8.1 records the '3-times table' in ratio form, each pair of numbers being in the ratio 1:3.

Children and ratio and proportion

Performance

Nunes and Bryant (1996) report on a number of studies involving primary children, largely within a discussion of multiplication.

RATIO COMPARISON

One particularly novel study which Nunes and Bryant discuss was that by Noelting (1980), involving taste tests of different concentrates of orange juice, in which as many as 86% of 8-year-old children were able to say which mixture would taste more orangey when 1 cup of water was mixed with first 2 and then 3 cups of concentrate. However, in the comparison of 3 cups of water with 2 cups of concentrate and 3 cups of water with 4 cups of concentrate performance was poorer; for example, less than 25% of 10-year-olds were successful.

The APU (1980) looked at primary children's understanding in a more formal setting.

PRIMARY PROPORTIONALITY

The APU used 33 items relating to proportionality with primary children. On the item 'A lorry uses 1 gallon of petrol every 9 miles; how many gallons would it use on a journey of 108 miles?' they report a 70% facility. In general, a fraction introduced into items similar to this illustration lowered the success rate to about 45%, and use of the 1:n notation lowered the facility to less than 30%. One particular feature commented on was the wide range of performance on these proportionality questions.

Many of the studies of children's understanding of ratio and proportion have been carried out with secondary school children, because the ideas pervade much of their curriculum.

SOUP RECIPE

In Hart (1981) there is considerable discussion of the results of the CSMS Ratio Test. One question was based on a recipe for Onion Soup for 8 persons:

8 onions
2 pints water
4 chicken soup cubes
2 dessertspoons butter
½ pint cream

The test questions were:

'I am cooking onion soup for 4 people.
  (a) How much water do I need?
  (b) How many chicken soup cubes do I need?
I am cooking onion soup for 6 people.
  (c) How much water do I need?
  (d) How many chicken soup cubes do I need?
  (e) How much cream do I need?'

Responses to parts (a)–(d) were quite good, with facilities ranging from around 95% in (a) to 75% in (d) across the entire 13–15-year age group, but answers to part (e) were very poor, with only 24% of 13- and 14-year-olds answering correctly. In other words, many pupils found it was not difficult to halve the quantities in the recipe, or even to halve, halve again and add, and that was often their preferred method, but it became exceedingly difficult to do this when the original quantity was not a number which divided easily.

Misconceptions and errors

At the secondary level proportionality is one of the most researched areas of mathematics, not only in Britain but around the world. The universal conclusion is that children on the whole find metric (to do with measurements) proportionality very difficult but, more importantly, this research has thrown light on the misconceptions and errors which affect performance.

PAPER CLIPS

Figure 8.4 shows an apparently simple question which illustrates this world-wide research, which also captures the essence of what needs to be understood, and which clearly reveals common errors. It was created by Karplus in the 1970s (see, for example, Karplus *et al.*, 1977).

The essential numerical relationship is summed up in Table 8.2.

Mr Short and Mr Tall

You can see the height of Mr. Short measured in paperclips. Mr. Short has a friend, Mr. Tall.
When we measure their heights with matchsticks:
Mr. Short's height is four matchsticks,
Mr. Tall's height is six matchsticks.
How many paperclips are needed for Mr. Tall's height?

Mr Short

Heights in matchsticks and paperclips		
	Matchsticks	Paperclips
Mr Short	4	6
Mr Tall	6	?

Table 8.2

8.4 A ratio question

The task requires the missing number in a statement of the equivalent fractions

$$\frac{4}{6} = \frac{6}{?}$$

The correct answer is 9, but very large numbers of secondary schoolchildren respond with 8. This is because they are interpreting the situation additively, as $4 + 2 = 6$, so $6 + 2 = 8$, instead of multiplicatively, which ratios and equivalent fractions demand, namely $4 \times \frac{3}{2} = 6$, so $6 \times \frac{3}{2} = 9$.

Only 28% of the 13-year-olds tested obtained the correct answer.

Discuss with some colleagues how you could help children to recognise the difference between additive and multiplicative situations.

The additive approach to ratio is so prevalent that teachers need to work hard to provide experiences from which children will begin to appreciate the need for a multiplicative approach. In coming to appreciate the multiplicative nature of the relationship, one common method is, in the words of one child interviewed: 'Four and half of four add up to six, so it must be six add half of six, which makes nine'. Ingenious though the method is it still retains an additive component. In the longer term it is helpful if it can be replaced by the kind of approach which dispenses with addition altogether and encourages multiplication by $\frac{3}{2}$. One way in which children might be encouraged to do this is to compare their body measurements with those of their parents, or to use soft toys and model cars to think about the idea of ratio.

Another valuable finding from CSMS and elsewhere is that there is a clear hierarchy of difficulty in ratios expressed numerically in that 2:1, 3:1, 4:1 are relatively easy, 3:2 is not particularly difficult, but others may be much more difficult. Thus it is necessary to use more complex ratios like 2:5 and 4:3 in order to provide a challenge, and performance on 2:1 and 3:1 tasks might mislead teachers. On the other hand, we do have a very clear progression to work through with pupils, starting with 2:1, 3:1, 4:1 and the like, moving to 3:2 and 2:3, and then finally moving on to harder ratios. The danger with this progression, however, is that children, although taught to use the multiplicative approach, find the additive approach works successfully some of the time with the easy numbers. With more difficult numbers they then prefer the additive approach as it is easier to perform.

Discussion

The moral for primary teachers is clear. Ratio and proportion should at first be approached on the basis of previous knowledge, perhaps quite informally, making use of familiar real-world and mathematical situations. It is only in the secondary school that the situations need to become more formalised. Primary school teachers may therefore look at the evidence here not with an eye on how their children are ever going to cope, but more for ideas of how children might be confronted with situations which are going to provide elementary experiences that will enable a more formal approach later. It is in this regard that situations like the use of orange juice mixtures might be appropriate. It is possible to use very simple practical situations (like recipes) to encourage pupils to think about how to maintain the same proportions, no matter how many people need to be fed, and by gradually increasing the complexity of the ratio to encourage an understanding of how proportion works. Above all, there is no need to complicate the situations by expecting such a difficult calculation as the $\frac{1}{2} + \frac{1}{2} \times \frac{1}{2}$ required in part (e) of the soup question mentioned previously.

Müller (1979) wrote a persuasive article on how good primary children can be at appreciating the essence of proportionality, as long as the tasks are not complicated by difficult numbers. Over a varied collection of proportion tasks of a largely practical nature and which did not involve calculation, such as cutting a giant stick of 'rock' into sections to ensure a fair distribution, the children were able to complete the tasks successfully – that is, so as 'to ensure a reasonably fair distribution'. Metric proportion needs to be handled with care.

Teachers should be under no illusions about the importance of the topic, however. In trigonometry, in probability, in geometry, in graphs (conversion, pie chart, etc.), in calculus, indeed throughout the whole of mathematics, the ideas of ratio and proportion form a vital cornerstone in the development of the subject.

Some ideas for teaching ratio and proportion

To think about

Analyse a set of textbooks and the teachers' guides to see what coverage they give to ratio and proportion. What models do they recommend and what contexts do they use?

Textbooks and ratio and proportion

There is little commonality in the content and approach of textbooks when considering ratio and proportion. Most books tend to set the topics in contexts which may have appeal to children. These are:

- simple recipes
- distance/time graphs leading to speed
- plans of desks, classrooms, playgrounds and schools
- enlarging photographs
- comparing maps drawn to different scales.

Activities with number tables

Finding the missing numbers in tables which are based on a proportionality relationship is a very obvious exercise for children. The simplest of these are really just multiplication tables, but they may be made as easy or as difficult as you like, and some examples are shown in Figure 8.5. There is no suggestion that children will find all such questions easy, particularly when fractions are involved. The first example is simply an extract from the 3-times table, and this unfortunately allows unthinking completion by continuing the number pattern in the right hand column. The other two are more demanding, and enable the teacher to move attention onto the ratio property. What is being suggested is that it is possible to look at such arrangements of

2	6		2	10		4	3
3	9		4	20		6	$4\frac{1}{2}$
4	12		7	35			9
5			5			10	$7\frac{1}{2}$

8.5 Missing numbers in multiplication tables

numbers and encourage a focus on the multiplicative or proportional relationships, without using complicated language. Such questions illustrate the fact that numerical ratio tasks are in a sense but one stage removed from the study of multiplication.

Vergnaud (1983) discusses, in some detail, multiplicative structures and the difficulties children experience in coming to terms with the relationships between the numbers in tables such as those above, though his examples were generally based on problem situations. He concludes with several important general points:

- concepts develop through solving problems
- appropriate problems for children may justifiably be 'far removed from an advanced mathematical point of view'
- if children's understanding is to develop it is a mistake not to challenge pupils with complex concepts.

Activities with recipes

Recipes clearly provide a very good example of ratio and proportion being used in the real world. Here is a down-to-earth problem-solving situation, far removed from an advanced mathematical point of view, which still provides a challenge to pupils. In practice, cooks usually do not consciously use mathematics, and often approximate when adapting recipes for different numbers of people. Yet they stray extravagantly from the stated proportions at their peril.

The onion soup recipe of the CSMS test is a good example of what can be done with children, and there is no end to the possibilities which the children themselves might bring from home recipes. It is possible, and perhaps advisable, to structure the development of ideas, so that simple multiplication is all that is required at first. If one egg is required in a recipe for two people, then two eggs are required for four people, three eggs for six people, and so on. However, if three eggs are required in a recipe for two people, and we need to adapt for three people, the proportions require a little more thought – and if two eggs are required for four people in a recipe we need to adapt for five people, the situation is more difficult still. Yet the challenge is essential for prompting the kind of thinking on which the development of ratio concepts depend.

Activities with similarity and enlargement

Mathematicians speak of two shapes (including solids) being 'similar', when they mean that corresponding lengths are in the same proportions. In Figure 8.6, there are two rectangles. These two rectangles are mathematically 'similar' because each side in the larger is twice the length of the corresponding side in the smaller. A less precise but very common way of describing the relationship is that they both have exactly the same shape, although one is a bigger version of the other. Of course, there are always dangers when precision is lost in mathematical definitions. In the case of similarity, particular care is needed anyway, because the 'everyday' definition of similarity is in a sense a less precise version of the mathematical definition. Thus, to children, any two rectangles might be regarded as being similar, purely and simply because they are both rectangles, and they could therefore be said to have the same shape! It is

8.6 Similar rectangles in the ratio 1:2

To do

Make a list of contexts in which the word 'similar' might be used in an everyday sense.

possible to focus simply on the enlargement of shapes, as a drawing or computer exercise, producing new shapes which are twice, three times, one and a half times, two and a half times, etc., as big as the original, and then to use these to discuss the relationships between corresponding lengths. It is also possible to use shapes, either of thin plastic or in picture form, in order to make comparisons.

Activities with unitary ratio

The unitary method, described earlier in connection with buying pens, is a practical approach to solving many proportion problems. Hart (1981) reports, however, that no child quoted the unitary method in the solution of tasks, though some children did seek a $1:n$ relationship, which is the first step in the unitary approach. At the same time, the children also generally avoided multiplying by a fraction, and much preferred building up, as described in connection with the onion soup task. The unitary method involves a kind of building up, after an initial conversion to $1:n$. Thus there is no reason at all why simple applications of the unitary method should not be practised as it is a usable practical method which provides experience in handling proportion situations.

Activities using a topic approach

Streefland (1984) describes how a topic such as the study of the problems of being a giant might be harnessed to study ratio and proportion with 8–9-year-old children. This would link up well with the appeal of stories like *Jack and the Beanstalk* and *Gulliver's Travels*. Here are some of the possible activities:

To do

Look through children's reading books to see possibilities for introducing early ideas of ratio and proportion.

- estimating and determining the giant's height, given a print of his hand
- comparing a number of objects from the giant's world with our world (sole of shoe, newspaper, handkerchief, etc.)
- exploring and composing cake recipes
- comparing the giant's length of pace and speed of movement with ours
- comparison of the giant and his daughter – aged 8–9 of course
- using the purchase of items of food to introduce the concept of 'best buy', and how to work it out.

A class activity

OBJECTIVE	To use ratio in a practical context with toy model cars
ORGANISATION	Small groups
RESOURCES	A variety of toy cars made to scale and either the real cars (staff car park) or brochures of the cars containing true measurements; calculators

ACTIVITY
- The whole class decide which measurements of the models will be taken.

- Every group measures their models and, using the scale and a calculator, works out what the lengths on the real car should be.
- The lengths are compared with lengths measured on the real cars or with those given in a brochure.
- Percentage errors can be calculated to compare each group's accuracy.

A group activity

OBJECTIVE   To produce distorted enlargements of pictures or photographs

ORGANISATION   Small groups

RESOURCES   Each child in a group needs the same picture or photograph, and squared paper

ACTIVITY
- Children draw a square grid on their picture or photograph (this may be done on tracing paper if the picture is precious).
- They draw enlargements of the photograph on the squared paper, each child in the group using a different pair of ratios, such as 1:2 'vertically' and 1:4 'horizontally', or 1:3 'vertically' and 1:2 'horizontally'.
- Members of each group compare their final distorted pictures.

Test your own knowledge: ratio and proportion

1   Investigate some cookery books for suitable recipes for children to think about reducing and increasing quantities for different numbers of people

2   Use the unitary method to perform any day-to-day enlargement calculations which you might need to carry out

3   One common and very important application of ratio is in conversion graphs. The fact that 0° Celsius (Centigrade) is equivalent to 32° Fahrenheit, and 100° Celsius is equivalent to 212° Fahrenheit is sufficient information to draw a straight-line graph. Draw this graph, and use it to find the Celsius equivalent of room temperature (about 65°F) and body temperature (about 98°F). Is there a place on the graph where the two values, °C and °F, are numerically the same? What other conversion graphs might be appropriate to use with children?

4   Pie charts are used when the data represent proportions of a whole. Choose a context such as 'How I spent my day', and draw a pie chart. What do you think would be the difficulties of trying to draw pie charts with primary children (they are not easy, unless an appropriate computer software package is used)?

5   An understanding of the rate of exchange is essential for foreign travel. Use this concept either in planning your next overseas holiday or with children to budget for a school trip.

117

6 Design a small robot, in whatever proportionality relationship with humans that is appropriate for the age of children.

7 Investigate the relationships between the surface areas and volumes of similar solids. Cubes are easiest, so you could begin by comparing a unit (1 × 1 × 1) cube with a 2 × 2 × 2 cube.

Review of key points

➤ Ideas of ratio and proportion should grow out of earlier, familiar ideas such as fraction

➤ Ideas of ratio and proportion should grow out of real and fantasy-world interests of children

➤ The emphasis should be on the investigation and discussion of ideas such as enlargement, equivalence and scale

➤ Teachers need to continually draw children's attention to the differences between additive and multiplicative situations

➤ Accuracy is important, but should not be the first aim

➤ Above all, confidence in the appreciation of a new way of looking at things is vital

---

Module 9　　Learning to teach integers

Introduction

Calculators are common in many homes, and at school 'pupils should be given opportunities to use calculators as a means to explore number...' (DES, 1995). Such exploration will sometimes yield a negative result. A pupil constructing a sequence by continually subtracting 3 from a given starting number will eventually be presented with negative numbers, e.g. 13, 10, 7, 4, 1, –2, –5, or a pupil who presses the keys 4 – 9 may be surprised by the 'minus' sign. No longer is 4 – 9 'impossible'!

The early appearance of numbers which are not natural numbers raises fundamental questions as to how they should be explained and what language should be used. Is the answer to 4 – 9 'minus 5' or 'negative 5'? What is the best position to write the negative sign? Does the child see the '–' sign as an instruction to subtract? Children may be familiar with negative numbers from the winter temperatures shown on TV weather forecasts so this may be an early context for discussion of integers. Other models to assist children in learning about integers are discussed later in the module.

Integers in national curricula

Negative numbers were for many years not considered appropriate for most primary children. Even now, the inclusion of negative numbers, leading to ideas of integers, varies considerably between different primary mathematics curricula. The aspects of integers common to many curricula include:

- extending understanding of the number system to negative numbers, particularly when in context
- developing work with negative numbers in the context of rise and fall of temperature
- considering methods of adding and subtracting negative numbers.

Key terms

negative numbers　numbers that are less than zero are called negative numbers

positive numbers　positive numbers are numbers greater than zero

integers　an integer is a positive or negative 'whole' number, together with zero

directed numbers　an expression which appears to have no agreed definition. We will use it to describe the set comprising all numbers with a positive or negative sign, together with zero

---

In the rest of this module all examples use integers, but the arguments apply equally to all directed numbers.

Key issues in integers

Related concepts and issues

Children's understanding of the natural numbers, for example the number 3, is rooted in concrete experiences, but there is no similar concrete model for ⁻3. There is a conceptual leap for children in coming to terms with the concept of negative integers. As a symbol a negative number may be met when using a calculator or seen on the television weather forecast, but there are no familiar props (like fingers) to help pupils visualise a negative integer. The temperature scale is the obvious model to use but children do not find it easy to read scales (APU, 1980). Pupils who own a calculator may have made their own discoveries about the 'new' numbers which exist below zero, but others will need considerable accommodation to adapt their ideas of whole numbers to negative numbers. Figure 9.1 shows a map for some of the concepts and issues associated with the integer concept.

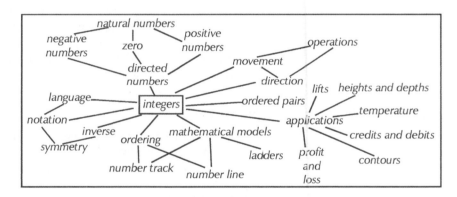

9.1 Concepts and issues associated with integers

Signs

A positive number is sometimes shown by preceding the numeral with a '+' sign. There is no agreed position for the '+' sign and you will find the number positive 3 shown as either +3 or ⁺3. In a similar way a negative number, such as negative 5, is written as –5 or ⁻5. We shall use the raised position for the signs to avoid confusion with the '+' and '–' operation signs. Figure 9.2 shows the different sets of numbers modelled on a number line. Only integers are labelled. It is immediately apparent that there is a one-one correspondence between the natural numbers and positive integers that enables, for example, 3 to be viewed as ⁺3.

Language

The signs '+' and '–' already have words attached to them: '+' is read as 'and', 'add', or 'plus', and '–' as 'take away', 'subtract' or 'minus'. It is not uncommon for such language to be transferred to positive and negative integers, so that ⁺3 is read as 'plus 3' and ⁻5 read as 'minus 5'. There are

To do

Explore ways of producing +3 and –3 in the display of many different types of calculator.

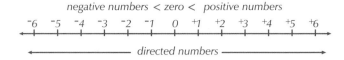

negative numbers < zero < positive numbers

$$^-6 \quad ^-5 \quad ^-4 \quad ^-3 \quad ^-2 \quad ^-1 \quad 0 \quad ^+1 \quad ^+2 \quad ^+3 \quad ^+4 \quad ^+5 \quad ^+6$$

directed numbers

9.2 Positive and negative integers as reflections in zero

obvious dangers with these expressions as both plus and minus are words associated with operations, whereas the symbols preceding positive and negative numbers are an indication of the nature of numbers relative to zero. To avoid this danger we shall refer to $^+3$ as positive 3, and $^-5$ as negative 5.

There are also problems when referring to negative numbers increasing or decreasing. For example, the temperature is said to decrease from $^-5°C$ to $^-7°C$, despite the fact that 7 is numerically greater than 5. Similarly, the change from $^-3°C$ to $1°C$ is an increase in temperature although 1 is numerically less than 3. The words increasing and decreasing need to be used with great care when talking about negative numbers.

Ordering

The ordering of natural numbers is often achieved using concrete material, such as counters. Such material is not applicable to negative integers and considerable accommodation may be required before pupils feel confident to compare negative integers. Initially, discussion related to ordering should be related to some appropriate context or model. Which is higher (or warmer), a temperature of $^+8°C$ or a temperature of $^+11°C$? Which is lower (or colder), a temperature of $^-3°C$ or a temperature of $^-7°C$? With experience of a thermometer scale pupils begin to appreciate which direction gives higher temperatures and which direction gives lower temperatures. Some children invent their own rules.

SARAH'S RULE

Sarah was asked to look at negative and positive numbers on a thermometer scale and to say what she noticed. Her response was 'With negative numbers it's the other way round. Big numbers are smaller.'

To think about

What is the inverse of $^-7$? What is the inverse of $^+4$? What is the inverse of 0?

Additive inverse

Children often observe that a negative number is the same distance from zero, but on the opposite side, as its corresponding positive number. This is an indication of the important mathematical concept of additive inverse. On a number line negative integers can be viewed as the images of the positive numbers reflected in zero (see Figure 9.2).

121

To think about

An important distinction is made in the interpretations given to the addition sign and to the positive and negative signs attached to a number when two integers are added. What different interpretations are given to the different signs?

Addition

Using a number line

Addition of natural numbers can be illustrated as jumps or movements on a number line. For natural numbers $2 + 3$ can be thought of as a movement of 2 followed by a movement of 3, which has the same result as a movement of 5. This same addition can be seen on the extended number line as $^+2 + ^+3$. The starting point is taken as zero, looking in the positive direction, and then a movement of forward 2 is followed by a movement of forward 3. Some children quickly realise that the process can be shortened by starting at the position of the first number and then moving forward 3 from there. A negative number has to be seen as a movement in the opposite direction so $^+2 + ^-3$ would be forward 2 followed by backward 3, which is equivalent to a movement of backward 1, or $^-1$. Similarly, $^-3 + ^+4$ would be seen as a movement of backward 3 followed by forward 4, which is equivalent to a movement of forward 1 or $^+1$.

Figure 9.3 shows two additions of integers and highlights the differing interpretations of the signs.

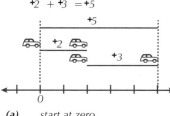

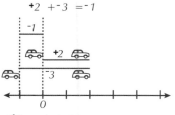

(a)   start at zero
face the positive direction
move forward 2
face positive direction
move forward 3

(b)   start at zero
face the positive direction
move forward 2
face positive direction
move backward 3

9.3 Modelling addition of integers

To do

Use number lines to show that $^-2 + ^+3 = ^+1$ and that $^-2 + ^-3 = ^-5$

Children should experience moving on a large floor number track and a number line in order to develop the ideas of direction and movement related to the addition sign and the sign of the numbers. This should be followed by them using a model car or person with a direction built into it. Only then should working on a number line be considered without the support of models.

Addition using inverses

Adding the inverse to an integer has the effect of undoing the number to give zero. This suggests another method for the addition of integers. If the integers have opposite signs it is possible to use an inverse to undo the smaller integer. For example, in $^-3 + ^+4$ the $^-3$ can be undone by using a $^+3$ of the $^+4$, leaving $^+1$. Writing it in full we have:

$$^-3 + ^+4 = ^-3 + (^+3 + ^+1) = (^-3 + ^+3) + ^+1 = 0 + ^+1 = ^+1$$

To think about

What assumptions are built into the additive inverse approach?

Subtraction

Using a number line

If a number line is used for subtraction of integers the subtraction sign has to be seen as an instruction to turn around to face the negative direction. For addition the direction faced is right, towards the increasing positive numbers and movement is forward or backward according to the sign ($^+$ or $^-$ respectively) of the integers. For subtraction start by facing right for the movement for the first number, but turn around for the subtraction sign before moving for the second integer. The movements forward or backward are again according to the sign of the integer, as for addition. For example:

- $^+2 - {}^+3$ would entail a movement of forward 2, a change of direction to face the negative numbers and a movement of forward 3 to $^-1$ (Figure 9.4a)

- $^+2 - {}^-3$ would entail a movement of forward 2 to $^+2$, a change of direction to face the negative numbers and a movement of backward 3 to $^+5$ (Figure 9.4b).

To do

Use number lines to show that $^-2 - {}^+3 = {}^-5$ and that $^-2 - {}^-3 = {}^+1$.

To think about

Compare the two additions in Figure 9.3 and two subtractions in Figure 9.4. Discuss with a colleague similarities and differences. Explain the mathematical reasons why these occur.

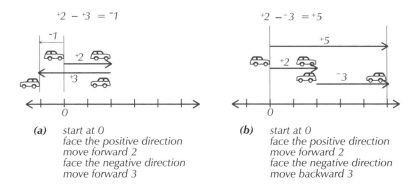

(a) start at 0
     face the positive direction
     move forward 2
     face the negative direction
     move forward 3

(b) start at 0
     face the positive direction
     move forward 2
     face the negative direction
     move backward 3

9.4 Modelling subtraction of integers

Primary school children are normally only expected to work with examples which can be related to some context like temperature, although it can be argued that negative integers are in context when represented on a number line. Thus, the example in Figure 9.4a could be reworded as 'If the temperature is $^+2$ and the temperature falls by 3 degrees what will be the new temperature?', but the example in Figure 9.4b would not be appropriate for a temperature fall. Instead we could ask 'What is the difference between the temperatures $^+2$ and $^-3°$C? Compare the temperatures on a temperature scale or number line to find the difference'; or 'The temperature falls from $^+2$ to $^-3$. How many degrees does the temperature fall?' In both cases there are difficulties in interpreting the fall of 5 as $^-5$.

Subtraction by adding the inverse

Another approach to subtraction of integers is to avoid it! If you realise that subtraction of an integer gives the same result as the addition of its inverse it is always possible to convert a subtraction problem into one of addition.

To think about

What is the inverse of $^-2$? What is $^+5 + $ (the inverse of $^-2$)? Is this the same as $^+5 - {}^-2$? What is the inverse of $^+4$? What is $^-1 + $ (the inverse of $^+4$)? Is this the same as $^-1 - {}^+4$?

123

Signs and language

The position of the negative and positive signs to indicate the nature of an integer may not seem important to those of us who have succeeded in distinguishing between these and the operation signs for addition and subtraction. We readily read ⁺5 + ⁺3 as 'plus 5 plus plus 3' and understand that we are using the plus in front of the 5 and in front of the 3 to mean something different from the operation of 'plus'. This does not mean that we should, therefore, not recognise that there is an opportunity in such usage for children to become confused and meet an insurmountable barrier in their learning of integers. Despite the fact that many textbooks fail in the notation and language they use to emphasise the differences between the signs and the operations, we strongly recommend that you adopt the convention of writing the signs in a raised position, referring to them as positive and negative, not plus and minus. Thus ⁺5 + ⁺3 should be read as 'positive 5 plus positive 3'. Similarly, ⁺5 − ⁻3 should be read as 'positive 5 minus negative 3'. This terminology for directed numbers links with the names positive and negative axes used in Module 19.

Models and applications

The concept of zero as the reference point from which numbers can go in either direction is of fundamental importance. It is when we need numbers below zero, in the opposite direction to the natural numbers, that we are required to use directed numbers with a sign attached.

The thermometer

A picture of a thermometer showing °C above and below zero is an excellent model for directed numbers but care should be taken, if a thermometer is drawn in a 'horizontal' position, to match the direction of the numbers on the number line (Figure 9.5).

9.5 *What is the temperature?*

Lifts

Most children enjoy going in a lift and this model provides a natural vertical orientation for work with integers. The floors are often labelled 1, 2, 3, etc. Unfortunately the ground floor is usually labelled G and not 0 and if there is a floor below ground level it may be labelled B or LG.

Contour lines

If the number on a contour line shows the distance of points on the line above sea level what sign should be given to the number when the points are below sea level? What would a contour line labelled 0 mean?

Credit and debit

Children's familiarity with banking words like credit, debit, withdraw and overdraft may vary but the idea that if all your money is taken out of your account you will be left with nothing and that debts can be cancelled if more money is put into the bank may be helpful for understanding how positive and negative numbers undo each other.

Sporting applications

Football and hockey enthusiasts may be aware of the need to calculate goal differences when teams have the same number of points in a league, and this could be a motivating context for the ordering of integers. Scores in golf are referred to as being above or below par. These are recorded using positive and negative signs. However, once again the signs appear in the middle, not raised.

Ladders

Ladders provide a useful half-way stage to the use of a number line, with the rungs being given an integer value. The movements take place from rung to rung across the gaps.

Number tracks

Very young children are able to suggest the need for names of regions on a number track to the 'left' of zero.

INVENTING NAMES

A group of Year 1 children had a large floor number track on which they placed number cards in order and moved according to instructions. They had placed the number cards 1 to 8 as in Figure 9.6.

Children took turns to stand on a number facing the increasing numbers and were asked to guess the number behind them. They then moved back to this number and the question was repeated. When they reached the number 1 it was unanimously agreed that the next number was zero. There was much discussion as to what the next one should be called. Eventually it was agreed to call it 'one before zero'. This was continued for the next number.

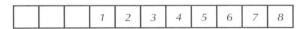

9.6 Inventing names for numbers less than 1

Number lines

The use of number lines to introduce the concept of integers is very popular (see Figure 9.2), but success depends heavily on children having worked with them for whole numbers. Their use for operating with integers is less common and care must be exercised if this model is adopted. The cognitive demands of a number line, where a number can be either a position or a movement, are often overlooked by teachers. When integers are introduced an extra demand occurs as the movements also have direction.

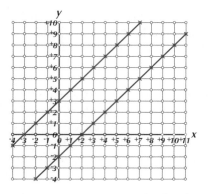

9.7 Two integers as sets of ordered pairs plotted on a graph

Integers as ordered pairs

Another way of defining an integer is as a set of ordered pairs of natural numbers (Mathematical Association, 1970). This approach was favoured some time ago when the concept of a set was seen as a basic pillar for the development of number and an important unifying idea at the heart of mathematics, and when set notation was more commonly used in primary schools. For example:

- $^+2$ is the name for the equivalence class of ordered pairs {... (9,7), (8,6), (7,5), (6,4), (5,3) ...}. So $^+2$ is the set of ordered pairs with a difference of $^+2$ with the larger number first, or the set of ordered pairs with the first number 2 more than the second number

- $^-3$ is the name for the equivalence class of ordered pairs {... (6,9), (5,8), (4,7), (3,6), (2,5), (1,4) ...}. So $^-3$ is the set of ordered pairs with a 'difference' of $^-3$, or the set of ordered pairs with the first number 3 less than the second number.

Each integer can thus be illustrated as a set of points taking the first number in each ordered pair as the x co-ordinate and the second number as the y co-ordinate (see Figure 9.7).

Children and integers

To think about

What is special about each set of points? What is special about the integer zero as a set of ordered pairs? How is the integer $^+2$ related to the integer $^-2$ as sets of ordered pairs? Compare your answer about $^+2$ and $^-2$ with the symmetry of $^+2$ and $^-2$ shown on the number line.

Some misconceptions and errors

Using a temperature scale

The ability of children of 11 years of age to read a temperature from a thermometer scale was tested by the APU (1980). Over 80% were successful when the temperature was marked on the scale, but if the temperature was at an unmarked point the facility fell to about 30%, and if it was a negative temperature to 20%. When reading up the scale the temptation was for children to ignore the sign and to read from, for example, –10° to 11°. In using a temperature scale, to help children's understanding of integers, pupils may need a lot of help in labelling the numbers correctly and in inserting missing numbers. We cannot assume that the temperatures between those marked are self-evident.

THERMOMETER PROBLEM

A class of 37 children, aged 9–10, were asked by the authors to write the temperature shown on the thermometer in Figure 9.8.

9.8 Reading a negative temperature

Eight children gave the correct answer of –6, with one child writing M6 as her answer. The most common incorrect answers were –14 (three children) and 14 (eight children).

Look up the different types of scales on thermometers used in textbooks. What are the concepts and skills required to read each temperature scale? Which concepts and skills were lacking in the children who wrote –14 and 14?

A temperature scale drawn horizontally with negative numbers to the left of zero is very like the number line, but the use of the number line for addition and subtraction of integers is not without criticism. Hart (1981) suggests that pupils aged 13–15 could indeed use integers as points on the number line and most could cope with addition of integers, but their understanding of subtraction was very limited. The operation of subtraction as 'turn around and continue' has a different interpretation from that of addition, 'followed by', and the integers are more likely to be seen as points on the number line than movements or shifts.

The recommendation is that at an early stage of development integers should be seen as discrete entities, for example pounds (credits or debts) or coloured counters which 'cancel' each other out. To keep the same colour code as bank accounts, a positive number could be represented by black counters and a negative number by red counters.

Inventing notation

It is often recommended that children should, when meeting new concepts, be given the opportunity to invent their own notation. In the research described below children using such an approach were compared with others using a number line for negative numbers.

NEGATIVE NOTATION

Liebeck (1990) explored the understanding of 9–11-year-old children using a card game based on scores and forfeits. A child winning 3 scores would take 3 black counters, whereas if 2 forfeits were awarded the child would take 2 red counters. Children worked out their score at the end of each go and also devised methods of recording their progress. These were the recordings devised by two children. What do they mean?

$$4 + ⑤ = Ⓜ① \text{ and } ③ - 1 = ④$$

Another group of 9–11-year-olds were introduced to negative numbers through the use of number lines. A post-test after 6 weeks showed a significant difference in favour of the scores and forfeits group.

What are the different cognitive and mathematical demands of the two approaches?

Errors using a number line

Number lines are known to be models of the number system that make great demands on children's understanding of the continuous nature of number and the order relationships associated with it. For those children who have yet to master the principles underlying number lines, using them to model negative numbers can be of little value.

ESTIMATING NEGATIVES

The authors asked the following question of 26 children in an above-average class of 10–11 years who had been taught about negative numbers. The exact answer was −40.

'Estimate the number the arrow is pointing to.'

9.9 *Estimating a negative number*

Five children wrote a positive or natural number as the answer and one child wrote 0. The negative answers, together with their frequency in brackets, are listed below:

−5(1), −10(1), −30(1), −40(3), −45(1), −50(4), −60(1), −78(1), −80(2), −90(3)

As a teacher what would please you about the answers given? What would disturb you? What would you accept as a correct answer? What explanations can you offer for the incorrect answers?

There are advantages in using the number line. Çemen (1993) suggests that it clearly distinguishes between subtraction (minus) and negative numbers (negative). The method also reveals that subtraction is equivalent to addition of the inverse. Of course this is something which children may also discover for themselves from playing with red and black counters. Subtracting 3 black (⁺3) has the same effect as adding 3 red (which would then cancel 3 black) and subtracting 5 red (⁻5) has the same effect as adding 5 black (which would cancel 5 red). Subtraction of negative numbers has not been found easy at the secondary level. Malpas (1975) describes his attempt and failure to use a number line combined with ideas of bank transactions. High-attaining children with an intuitive understanding of number, however, may experience no problems. High-attaining 8-year-olds discussing the subtraction of negative numbers have been heard to say 'Well, if you take away something negative it's got to make it more positive'.

Some ideas for teaching integers

Textbooks and integers

Most primary text books introduce the concept of negative numbers in relation to temperature or using a number line. There is a dilemma here in the use of everyday experiences as to whether to use the language of everyday life or the more precise mathematical expression. Teachers could refer to both, drawing children's attention to the mathematically accurate language as that which avoids the confusion inherent in using the same words, plus or minus, for both the operations and the signs of numbers. It also seems preferable, as already discussed, to raise the +

To think about

Analyse a set of textbooks and the teachers' guides to see what coverage they give integers. What models do they recommend?

and – signs so that they are more easily identified with the number and not with the operations of addition and subtraction. This again is a departure from the usual central positioning of the signs on a common thermometer scale and teachers may be torn between copying the notation of the everyday-life model or developing less ambiguous mathematical notation. A decision will also have to be made as to whether to label the natural numbers as directed numbers with a + sign, in contrast to the negative numbers, or to leave them (as most textbooks do) in their familiar form with no sign. The aim must be to help children to feel confident with the new numbers, but also to accept an unsigned number as equivalent to the number with a + sign.

A class activity

OBJECTIVE	To order integers
ORGANISATION	Whole class
RESOURCES	Teacher draws a strip of ten boxes on the chalkboard in which integers are to be written by the children:

smallest   largest

Also a set of 62 cards containing two each of the integers $^-15$ to $^+15$, including 0

ACTIVITY

- Each child is given one card.
- Teacher selects children to come out one by one.
- The first child shows his or her card to the rest of the class and writes the integer in any box.
- Succeeding children show their card to everyone, but can write their integer in a box only if the written numbers are then in order from smallest to largest.
- The activity continues until no more boxes can be filled.

A group activity

OBJECTIVE	To discover how to multiply integers
ORGANISATION	Small groups
RESOURCES	Each child has a copy of the two patterns and the incomplete Table 9.1.

Patterns in multiplication of integers									
X	‾4	‾3	‾2	‾1	0	⁺1	⁺2	⁺3	⁺4
⁺4						⁺4	⁺8	⁺12	⁺16
⁺3						⁺3	⁺6	⁺9	⁺12
⁺2						⁺2	⁺4	⁺6	⁺8
⁺1						⁺1	⁺2	⁺3	⁺4
0									
‾1									
‾2									
‾3									
‾4							‾8		

Table 9.1

ACTIVITY

- Children complete the patterns and write a reason for their answers.
- Children discuss their reason with other children in their group. Answers may be checked using a calculator.

$$
\begin{array}{ll}
4 \times 4 = 16 & 2 \times 3 = 6 \\
3 \times 4 = 12 & 2 \times 2 = 4 \\
2 \times 4 = 8 & 2 \times 1 = 2 \\
1 \times 4 = 4 & 2 \times 0 = 0 \\
0 \times 4 = 0 & 2 \times {}^-1 = ? \\
{}^-1 \times 4 = ? & 2 \times {}^-2 = ? \\
{}^-2 \times 4 = ? & 2 \times {}^-3 = ? \\
{}^-3 \times 4 = ? & 2 \times {}^-4 = ?
\end{array}
$$

- Table 9.1 is completed using patterns in the numbers going across and down the table.
- Children justify their answers.
- Children use their table to write a set of rules about multiplying negative and positive numbers.

Test your own knowledge: integers

1 Write a short description of the differences between natural numbers and integers.

2 Table 9.2 is a sorting grid. Where possible, write integers that belong in each region.

Sorting integers according to two criteria			
	$< {}^-6$	$= {}^-6$	$> {}^-6$
$< {}^-2$			
$= {}^-2$			
$> {}^-2$			

Table 9.2

3 a What is the integer name for the equivalence class {... (2,7), (3,8), (4,9), (5,10), ...}?

  b Draw the equivalence class on an *x–y* co-ordinate system.

  c What is the equation of the line that passes through all the ordered pairs in the equivalence class?

  d How does the equation of the line relate to the integer name? Will this always apply?

4 a Find the missing numbers: ${}^+7 + {}^-4 = \square$; ${}^-5 + \square = {}^-8$; $\square + {}^-3 = {}^-1$

  b Invent other questions to cover all possible addition types.

5 a Find the missing numbers: ${}^-7 - {}^+4 = \square$; ${}^+5 - \square = {}^-8$; $\square - {}^-3 = {}^-1$

  b Invent other questions to cover all possible subtraction types.

Review of key points ➤ It is possible to introduce early ideas of negative integers to young children

➤ Most primary mathematics curricula require children to understand negative numbers and to add and subtract them

➤ Negative numbers in context is the recommended means of introducing children to the concept

➤ The language and signs used in everyday examples of negative numbers frequently differ from those recommended for use in the classroom

➤ Possible confusion can arise unless the language used to name operations is different from that used to name the negative and positive signs

➤ There is lack of agreement as to the position of the positive and negative signs in front of integers

➤ The number line model involves recognising that an integer has a unique position on the line. It is usual to have the positive integers to the right of zero and the negative integers to the left. These are then viewed as directions, positive to the right, negative to the left

➤ When adding and subtracting using a number line there are further cognitive demands of movement and direction associated with the operation and the sign of the integers

➤ Care should be taken when using models involving number scales as children find difficulty in reading such scales

➤ Integers can be defined as an equivalence class of ordered pairs and represented on a co-ordinate system

Module 10   Learning to teach indices

Introduction

The concept of indices is one of the first that children meet in their mathematics learning that is mainly restricted to the classroom. The word 'index' and its plural 'indices' are seldom used in everyday speech. When they are, it is usually in connection with economic affairs, e.g. the retail price index or the cost of living index. This usage derives from statistics. It does not have the same meaning as the mathematical meaning.

Indices in national curricula

Indices as a topic of study is only infrequently found in national curricula for primary children. However, the ideas of square and cubic numbers are an early part of the development of indices and are often included in curricula as part of number patterns and number shapes. Primary curricula are likely to include:

- square and cubic numbers
- square roots and cube roots
- simple representations of indices involving areas and volumes
- writing and use of the indices 2 and 3.

Key terms

base   the number which is repeatedly multiplied by itself in a product is called the base. Thus, in $10 \times 10 \times 10 \times 10 \times 10 \times 10$, 10 is the base

index   the number of times a base is repeated in a product is called the index; sometimes known as 'exponent'. Thus in $10 \times 10 \times 10 \times 10 \times 10 \times 10$, the index is 6 as there are 6 tens

power   the numerical value, the product, of a repeated multiplication

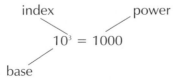

square number   the result of multiplying a number by itself, for example $5^2 = 25$, is a square number. 5^2 is read as 'five squared', or 'five to the two'

cubic number   the result of multiplying a number by itself and then by itself again, for example $5^3 = 125$, is a cubic number. 5^3 is read as 'five cubed', or 'five to the three'

Key issues in indices

Related concepts and issues

The idea of powers is inherent in the structure of place value, although they are seldom expressed in index notation. Figure 10.1 shows the connections between powers and indices and other areas of the curriculum.

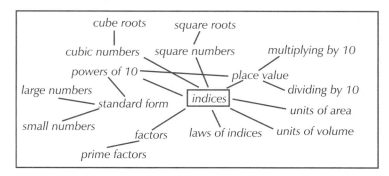

10.1 Concepts and issues associated with indices

What do indices mean?

Indices are simply a shorthand way of writing multiplication of a number by itself a number of times. For example, $6 \times 6 \times 6$ can be written as 216 or 6^3, depending upon which is most convenient. Writing $6 \times 6 \times 6$ is long-winded, with 216 expressing the result of the calculation. However, 6^3 is very compact and preserves the structure of the original expression.

Index notation

Index notation is little different from that of 3×4, which can be thought of as a shorthand way of writing $4 + 4 + 4$, the sum of three 4s. Similarly, when we have $4 \times 4 \times 4$ the question asked is, 'What is the product of three 4s?' The notation must involve a 3 and a 4 in some way. Exploring shorthand ways of writing expressions such as $4 \times 4 \times 4$ provides an interesting activity for children, involving them in seeing how notation may have been developed.

Standard form

Very large and very small numbers are frequently written in what is called standard form. To express a number in standard form it is written as a number between 1 and 10 multiplied by a power of 10, where the index is a whole number, positive or negative. For example, it is believed that our solar system was born about 5000 million years ago. The number 5000 million would be written in standard form as: 5 000 000 000 $= 5 \times 1\,000\,000\,000 = 5 \times 10^9$. The 5 is the number between 1 and 10 and the 9 is the whole number index of the power of 10.

Atoms are very, very small. About 5 million hydrogen atoms placed side by side would be only 1 cm in length. One hydrogen atom is 1/5 000 000 cm long, which, written in standard form, is 2×10^{-7} cm.

Calculators often display the results of calculations in standard form if the answers are too big to fit in the display. For example, an answer which reads 1.2 E+8 means:

$$1.2 \times 10^8 = 1.2 \times 10 \times 10 \times 10 \times 10 \times 10 \times 10 \times 10 \times 10$$
$$= 1.2 \times 100\,000\,000$$
$$= 120\,000\,000$$

The 1.2 is the number between 1 and 10, the 'E' stands for exponent, the 10 is understood or implicit in the notation; and the +8 is the index of the power of 10. The length of a hydrogen atom, 2×10^{-7} cm, written on a calculator would be 2E–7.

INVENTING NOTATION

The challenge of finding a shorthand way of writing repeated multiplications in a product, such as $4 \times 4 \times 4$, was presented to a class of 10–11-year-olds who knew nothing about indices. They recalled that 3×4 was a shorthand for $4 + 4 + 4$. They then practised writing similar sums in the multiplication shorthand form.

The class was then split into pairs and challenged to create a shorthand notation for $4 \times 4 \times 4$. They were told that they had to be able to say why they thought their method was a good one and why it could not be confused with other ways of using numbers. Much discussion took place before the class was brought back together to consider all the suggestions. Each pair's notation was recorded when it differed from those already listed. When all suggestions had been written on the blackboard the advantages and disadvantages of each were discussed, with pairs defending their suggestions. At the end of the lesson it was agreed that the two most acceptable notations were 4^3 and 3^4, with each digit in a pair being the same size. The possibility of both methods being mistaken for fractions gave rise to writing the 3 smaller than the 4, i.e. 4^3 or $^3 4$ with the first then introduced as the conventional one. You may recognise the second method as similar to the way of writing the 'cube root of 4'.

Area and volume

The word 'square', as in 'square number', is used when an area is calculated. Thus a rectangle of length 8 cm and width 5 cm has an area of 40 square centimetres (see Figure 10.2a). The standard way of writing this is 40 cm². It is read as '40 square centimetres'. Note the mismatch between the order in the notation, 40 cm², and the expression, 40 square centimetres.

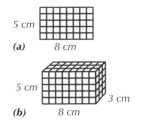

5 cm
(a)   8 cm

5 cm   3 cm
(b)   8 cm

10.2 Area and volume in square and cubic centimetres

Similarly, the word 'cubic', as in 'cubic number', is used when a volume is calculated. A rectangular box of length 8 cm, width 5 cm and height 3 cm has a volume of 120 cubic centimetres (see Figure 10.2b). The standard way of writing this is 120 cm^3. It is read as '120 cubic centimetres'.

Powers of 2

Doubling

In mental methods emphasis is placed upon children knowing doubles and halves. A popular classroom oral activity for developing the ability to double and halve involves giving children a starter number and then asking them to repeatedly double it, stopping at some agreed number. The order is then reversed, starting with the 'stop' number and repeated by halving.

When doubling, the answer each time is the starter number multiplied by a power of 2. For example, the sequence 2, 4, 8, 16, 32, 64, 128, 256, ... in index notation is 2, 2^2, 2^3, 2^4, 2^5, 2^6, 2^7, 2^8, ... The pattern in the indices suggests that 2 should be written as 2^1. In mathematics this is adopted as a definition.

Patterns in powers of 2

A table of powers of 2 (Table 10.1) highlights some interesting patterns.

Tabulating powers of 2 in the search for patterns		
Index form	Index	power
2^1	1	2
2^2	2	4
2^3	3	8
2^4	4	16
2^5	5	32
2^6	6	64
2^7	7	128
2^8	8	256

Table 10.1

There is an obvious repeating pattern in the unit digits 2, 4, 8, 6, 2, 4, 8, 6, ... with a cycle of period 4. Why is this?

Graphing powers of 2

Repeated addition of 2 produces a linear graph, in effect the 2 times table, which has a constant rate of increase. The rate of increase in the value of the power of 2 as the index increases is very different, as can be seen in Figure 10.3.

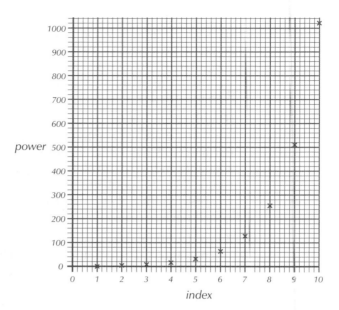

10.3 Graphing powers of 2

To think about

The graph plots points for positive integer values of indices having obvious interpretations as the number of 2s in the product that gives the power. Can negative integers and decimals be used as indices? If so, what do they mean?

Mental methods

There are very specific multiplications that lend themselves to a mental strategy which uses powers of 2 by doubling or halving the numbers in the product. The strategy changes the product into other products which have the same answer, eventually ending with a multiplication that is simple to do. Here is how the method works with 28×16.

To think about

Estimate 49×32. Use the doubling/halving method to calculate 47×32. Describe how you did it to a colleague.

$$28 \xrightarrow{\text{double}} 56 \xrightarrow{\text{double}} 112 \xrightarrow{\text{double}} 224 \xrightarrow{\text{double}} 448$$

$$\times \underline{16} \xrightarrow{\text{double}} \times 8 \xrightarrow{\text{halve}} \times 4 \xrightarrow{\text{halve}} \times 2 \xrightarrow{\text{halve}} \times \underline{1} \atop \underline{448}$$

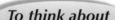

INVESTIGATING MULTIPLICATION

A class of 10–11-year-old children, who had been introduced to indices, was given a table to complete (part is shown in Table 10.2). They were asked to work with a partner to search for a relationship between the questions and the answers and then to complete further questions without doing any working. Most of the children were not only able to see a relationship between the indices but were also able to write it in words as a generalisation and to explain why.

In words write a general statement about multiplying numbers to the same base. Try writing your statement in symbols. If correct, you have written the first law of indices.

Multiplying numbers which have the same base

It is thought by many primary teachers that operating with 'indices' is too difficult for primary children. The episode described above shows that this may not be the case.

Searching for the first law of indices		
Question	Working space	Answer in index form
$3^2 \times 3^3$	$3 \times 3 \times 3 \times 3 \times 3$	3^5
$5^4 \times 5^2$	$5 \times 5 \times 5 \times 5 \times 5 \times 5$	5^6
$2^5 \times 2^3$	$2 \times 2 \times 2 \times 2 \times 2 \times 2 \times 2 \times 2$	2^8
$7^5 \times 7^4$	$7 \times 7 \times 7 \times 7 \times 7 \times 7 \times 7 \times 7 \times 7$	7^9
$4^2 \times 4^6$	$4 \times 4 \times 4 \times 4 \times 4 \times 4 \times 4 \times 4$	4^8

Table 10.2

To do

Work with a partner. Copy and complete Table 10.3. Discuss any patterns you have seen. Write in words a general statement describing a rule for the division. When you have written the general statement compare it with colleagues. Write the agreed statement in symbols. This is the second law of indices.

Dividing numbers which have the same base

A similar activity explores the division of numbers having the same base with the aim to write a general statement or 'law'.

Searching for the second law of indices		
Question	Working space	Answer in index form
$2^4 \div 2^3$	$\dfrac{2 \times 2 \times 2 \times 2}{2 \times 2 \times 2}$	
$4^6 \div 4^2$		
$7^5 \div 7^4$		
$3^9 \div 3^5$		
$5^7 \div 5^2$		

Table 10.3

To do

A negative index appears in a^{m-n} when m is less than n. Work with a colleague to find a meaning for a power which has a negative index such as 5^{-3}. Write in words a general statement describing the meaning of negative indices. Write the statement in symbols. This is the third law of indices.

What does a negative index mean?

To enable a meaning to be given to a negative index it is necessary to use the second law of indices which you have just 'discovered'. This second law can be written as $a^m \div a^n = a^{m-n}$.

What is a^0?

You are now in a position to consider a value for 10^0. What is the answer to $10^2 \div 10^2$? This is 100 divided by 100, which is of course 1. Using the second law of indices we have

$$10^2 \div 10^2 = 10^{2-2} = 10^0$$

Thus, we have two different forms of answer to the same calculation. In order that there are no possibilities of contradictions mathematicians give them the same value. Thus, $10^0 = 1$.

As there is nothing special about the base 10, we can replace it with a 'general' number, say 'a'. This gives us the fourth law of indices, $a^0 = 1$.

Thus any integer (excluding 0), no matter how big or how small, when calculated to an index of zero, has the value 1. It is strange to think that $1\ 000\ 000^0$ is equal to 1, but it is.

Children and indices

To think about

Use a scientific calculator with an index button to find the value of powers such as 10^2, until you think you know how it works. Explain how it works to a colleague. Find the value of different numbers to zero index. Does the calculator confirm what was 'proved' above? What value, if any, does it give to the number 0^0?

There is very little research into the difficulties primary children encounter when working with indices.

Misconceptions and errors

The most common error that children make is to forget the meaning of the shorthand notation and interpret the index as meaning multiply by the index rather than multiply the base by itself a number of times equal to the index. Thus, children will often say the 5^3 is 15 rather than 125, or 3^2 is 6 rather than 9. There is no easy remedy for this and very little research to help. The one thing that you can do as a teacher is to ask the pupil what the index means and get them to write out in full the equivalent expression, for example $5^3 = 5 \times 5 \times 5$.

INCORRECT RESPONSES

In a small case study the authors asked a class of 32 10–11-year-old pupils these two questions: (a) What is $5^2 + 2^2$? (b) Calculate 4^3

The facility for question (a) was just over 80%, but for (b) it dropped dramatically to 15%, with many answers given as 12. Two incorrect responses for question (a) that occurred many times were $10 + 4 = 14$ and $7^2 = 49$. Many children wrote 12 as the answer to question (b). Explain the thinking of the children who made these errors.

Some ideas for teaching indices

Textbooks and indices

Few primary textbooks introduce children to indices.

To think about

Analyse some textbooks and the teachers' guides to see what coverage they give to indices. What models and approaches do they recommend?

Activities with place value

Writing the value of each place value position can be the starting point for exploring patterns in the index notation (see Module 4):

ten thousands	thousands	hundreds	tens	units
10^4	10^3	10^2	10^1	1

Continuation of the pattern of the indices would suggest that $10^0 = 1$.

If the children have met decimal numbers, then the pattern can be further extended (see Module 5):

thousands	hundreds	tens	units	tenths	hundredths	thousandths
1000	100	10	1	0.1	0.01	0.001

The pattern of the indices would suggest that $0.1 = 10^{-1}$, $0.01 = 10^{-2}$, $0.001 = 10^{-3}$.

Activities with measures

The use of indices can be reinforced through units of area and volume: a square of side 1 cm has an area of 1 cm by 1 cm = 1 cm^2, or 1 square centimetre. Similarly, a rectangular box which has sides each of length 1 cm has a volume of 1 cm by 1 cm by 1 cm = 1 cm^3, or 1 cubic centimetre. It is important that children not only use index notation to express both area and volume but also understand its derivation.

A class activity

OBJECTIVE
To match a number written in index notation with its expanded product

ORGANISATION
Whole class

RESOURCES
Every child has a set of 16 cards on which are written powers in index form using all pairings of the numbers 2, 3, 4 and 5. For example,

$$3^2 \quad 5^4 \quad 2^2 \quad 4^3 \quad 3^5$$

The teacher either writes products on the chalkboard or OHP or has product cards that match the indices cards

ACTIVITY
- The teacher holds up a product card.
- The children hold up the index card that matches the product.
- One child is chosen to explain why the cards match and to say both expressions.

A group activity

OBJECTIVE
To match squares and cubes with their indices representation

ORGANISATION
Small groups

RESOURCES
Each group has the 'flats' and 'blocks' for the bases 2, 3, 4 and 5 from a multi-base arithmetic set, a set of eight matching indices cards, such as

$$2^2 \quad 3^2 \quad 2^3 \quad 3^3$$

and a set of eight number cards equal to the power of the indices cards, 4, 8, 9, 27, etc.

ACTIVITY

- One child chooses a flat or block and places it in the centre of the group.
- The next child matches the 'shape' with its appropriate indices card and explains the choice.
- A third child matches the shape and the indices card with the 'power' number card and explains the choice.
- The activity is repeated until all shapes and cards are used.

Test your own knowledge: indices

1   Evaluate each of the following in two ways so as to be able to check your answer:

$$\text{e.g. } 10^2 \times 10^2 = (10 \times 10) \times (10 \times 10) = 100 \times 100 = 10\,000$$
$$10^2 \times 10^2 = 10^4 = 10 \times 10 \times 10 \times 10 = 10\,000$$

a 103×10^3 **b** 10×10^2 **c** $10^5 \div 10^3$ **d** $10^6 \div 10^5$ **e** $10^3 \div 10^4$ **f** $10^3 \div 10^3$

2   Write down 1000 and 100 as powers of 10. List the place values from one million down to a thousandth as powers of 10. Explain why 10^0 represents the value of the 'ones' place.

3   Write the following numbers in full, and then write them in standard form (a number between 1 and 10 multiplied by a power of 10). **a** two million **b** three hundred thousand **c** six million two hundred thousand **d** twelve million **e** two hundred million **f** sixty five thousand two hundred.

4   Investigate patterns in the ones digits of powers of 3, powers of 4, ..., powers of 9. Investigate relationships between the patterns of different powers. Explain the relationships.

5   A chess board has 64 squares. One penny is put on the first square, two on the second, four on the third, eight on the fourth, and so on, until all the squares are covered. How many pence will be on the 64th square as a power of 2? How much is this is pounds? How much will be on the whole board?

6   Discuss with a colleague the value of $9^{1/2}$ and $8^{1/3}$. The first law of indices may be of help. Investigate how you could use a calculator to find their values.

Review of key points

➤ The concept of indices is seldom met by children outside the mathematics classroom

➤ Very large and very small numbers are often written in standard notation which uses indices

➤ Square and cubic numbers can be used to introduce indices

➤ A very basic introduction to indices can come from units of area and volume

➤ The idea of a common base is an extension of base 10 in the place value system

➤ Children can be given the opportunity to suggest a shorthand notation for writing repeated products, leading to the conventional notation for indices

➤ Powers of 2, which are directly associated with doubling, are useful for mental methods when multiplying numbers

➤ The laws of indices can be 'discovered' by children

➤ The laws of indices show how it is possible to give a meaning for:
  - negative indices
  - the index zero
  - fractional indices

resulting in a powerful shorthand notation used throughout the study of mathematics

Part 2

Module 11 Learning to teach number operations: an overview

Introduction

The ability to calculate mentally and in a written form is considered by politicians, business and society, and by the vast majority of teachers and educators, to be the most important objective by far in a primary mathematics curriculum. The advent and availability of cheap calculators and, to a lesser extent, computers, appears to have had little effect on such people's views. For many years the argument will continue about the place of number operations in primary schools and the role of calculators in the teaching of number.

National curricula and number operations

Number operations are central to the primary mathematics curriculum. The specific aspects which apply to each of the number operations are considered in detail in Modules 12–15. There are, however, some common issues which relate across the four operations. These are:

- understanding the operations, including the commutative, associative and distributive properties, and where they apply and do not apply
- knowing how the numbers 0 and 1 combine with other numbers
- learning number facts for rapid recall
- developing mental and written methods of calculating
- using facts and methods for solving problems in number, money and measures
- understanding the relationships between the four operations.

Key terms

addition see Module 12

subtraction see Module 13

multiplication see Module 14

division see Module 15

known fact a number relationship between three numbers which can be recalled from memory

derived fact a number relationship between three numbers which can be inferred or deduced from known facts by using knowledge of the number system

mental methods methods or strategies that can be performed 'in the head' without using any written form of recording

142

written methods paper and pencil methods, procedures or algorithms for calculating

informal methods methods which children have developed independently of any teaching

standard algorithms methods of written calculation to be taught to every child

models apparatus or diagrams that are used to represent methods of calculating

Key issues in number operations

What is a number operation?

One mathematical definition of a binary number operation is: 'A rule or process assigning to two numbers another number.' With some children the definition is all too plain to see in action as, not understanding what they are doing, they search for a rule, and in many cases are happy with any rule as long as they produce an answer.

A number operation sign is the indicator of the rule and informs children that they have to combine the two given numbers according to a predetermined ordinance. Children then select whichever of the four rules they have learnt is meant by the sign. Having made this decision they then proceed to recall from memory a known fact, derive a new fact, or perform a procedure using the rule. For most children knowing or finding the answer is what is important, not the process of how they arrived at the answer. This is also true of many teachers. The result is children behaving as 'machines' when working with numbers, not as reflective thinkers. This is not to claim that correct answers are not an essential feature of number operations, only to stress that following rote procedures is not conducive to engendering in children the desire to think and operate mathematically.

> ### To think about
>
> It is accepted that the order of difficulty of the operations is addition, subtraction, multiplication and division. Why do you think this is?

Teaching number operations

Ever since formal schooling was established people have been advising on the 'best' method to teach children how to calculate quickly, effectively and efficiently. Such counsel tends to change with the fashion of the times. Perhaps we should recognise that, despite all the knowledge we now have about how children learn about computation, there does not appear to be a 'best' method. This could be due, to a large extent, to the fact that the most important resource in any classroom is the teacher and, by their very nature, teachers vary considerably in many respects. A further significant variable is, of course, the child. No two children are alike in the way they learn and consequently teaching computation needs to take into account the learning requirements of individual children. When teaching methods of calculating:

- acknowledge and respect children's informal methods
- ensure that children have the awareness, knowledge and fluency with number concepts required before embarking on teaching computation
- use a variety of models and apparatus for children to experience operations and demonstrate how they function
- encourage the sharing of children's informal mental and written methods

143

- base standard methods (mental and written) on children's own methods
- use calculators and computers to enhance children's learning, not to replace their need to learn computational skills
- set calculations in realistic, appealing, meaningful and relevant contexts.

Meanings of number operations

Each of the four number operations has what might be termed basic meanings. These are interpretations of a number operation arising from restricted (and sometimes inadequate) experiences in everyday life. Young children's limited experience requires that teachers enlarge children's encounters with number operations and, in doing so, present them with opportunities to experience more sophisticated meanings of a number operation. The outcome should be an integrated meaning of an operation which enables children to respond to any situation requiring the use of the operation. In doing so children come to a better and more secure understanding of the world in which they live.

Models for learning computation

In Modules 12–15 ways of using apparatus and diagrams which model or represent, each in its own way, one or more of the four number operations will be described. The aim of such material is to assist children develop perceptual and mental images of how operations function on numbers – which, it is claimed, will result in their understanding of an operation and in the development of computational skills independently of the model or representation. These materials are:

- discrete objects
- pictures of objects
- number rods
- number tracks
- number balance
- number lines
- number grids, including the 100 square
- function machines
- base 10 apparatus
- money and measures.

Apparatus and diagrams are not in themselves the solution to teaching number operations successfully (Threlfall, 1996). If they were, the errors and misconceptions that children make would never occur. In order for the materials to have any value as a teaching and learning experience they must have embedded in them the structure of a number operation and reflect very closely the processes that are used in the standard algorithm it is intended to teach. These are two criteria that teachers should use when considering any apparatus or diagram. However, having an embedded structure and reflecting the essential processes does not guarantee that children will perceive their existence in the models, nor will they necessarily abstract them in such a way that they assimilate them into their schema. It is the role of the teacher to assist children in consciously observing that which they may not 'see' and to articulate the relationship between the embedded structure, the processes and their symbolic representation in standard algorithms.

Relationships between the number operations

Addition and subtraction are part of the system of 'additive structures' in mathematics. At a higher level are multiplication and division, part of what is referred to as 'multiplicative structures'.

Addition is inevitably the first operation that children meet in schools. Subtraction quickly follows and, although addition and subtraction are the inverse of each other, subtraction is initially taught unrelated to its 'sister' operation. In problem contexts the operations of addition and subtraction always involve numbers related to the same 'object'. For example, 'Charlotte has 3 chews. She buys 2 more. How many chews has she now?' The 3, the 2 and the answer 5 are about 'chews'.

Problems involving the higher level operations of multiplication and division include numbers which relate to different 'objects'. For example, 'Raj has 2 bags of biscuits. Each bag has 4 biscuits. How many biscuits has he altogether?' The 2 refers to bags, the 4 to biscuits, and the answer 8 to biscuits. This is one reason why the operations are considered to be of a higher order. A second reason stems from each of them having a meaning, usually the first children meet, based upon the repetition of addition for multiplication, and subtraction for division. A consequence of this is that division is the inverse of multiplication. Figure 11.1 shows a diagrammatic representation of the two levels of operations and the 'repeating' and 'inverse' relationships that exist between them.

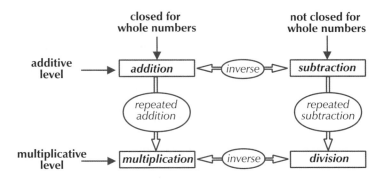

11.1 Relationships between the four operations

Properties of number operations

Closed systems of numbers

Children's first experiences with numbers involve the set of natural numbers (see Modules 1 and 3). Both addition and multiplication are closed in the system of natural numbers in that when any two natural numbers are added or multiplied the answer is always a natural number. This enables children to work in the two systems with the confidence

To think about

Take a look at the subtraction exercises in some textbooks for younger primary children. You are unlikely to find questions with the first number less than the second number as in 4 – 7. Discuss with some colleagues whether this stance is justifiable. Is your judgement based upon mathematical, cognitive, manageability grounds, or are your reasons based purely on tradition?

To think about

Discuss with a colleague the closure of proper fractions, mixed numbers, decimal numbers, integers, rational numbers, and irrational numbers with each of the four number operations.

that they can readily interpret the answer as it will always be like the numbers they had to start with. When the natural numbers are extended to include zero the set is known as the whole numbers. The system of whole numbers is also closed in addition and in multiplication.

The same is not true, however, when the operation is subtraction. For example, consider the subtraction 4 – 7. The answer is not a natural number. For this reason the natural number system is extended to include negative numbers.

Similarly, division of whole numbers may result in a quotient (the answer) being a decimal number. Thus, the set of whole numbers is extended to include decimal numbers.

What is commutativity?

Addition and multiplication

Soon after working with addition of simple numbers early years children may 'discover' a pattern in the answers to additions which use the same numbers. For example, $4 + 5 = 9$ and $5 + 4 = 9$. That the additions $a + b$ and $b + a$ have the same answer is one of the first discoveries that children make in mathematics and which they generalise in words. However, the statement $4 + 5 = 5 + 4$ does not automatically follow for children as they do not immediately perceive the '=' sign as saying 'has the same value as'. This is an important step for children to make as it is a recognition that numbers are commutative in the operation of addition. The commutative property in addition is stated as:

$a + b = b + a$, for all numbers a and b.

Multiplication has the same property, namely:

$a \times b = b \times a$, for all numbers a and b.

The two statements above have been expressed algebraically. How do you think children might express these identity relationships using words? Ask some children and compare their responses.

Subtraction and division

The operations of subtraction and division are *not* commutative. It is as important for children to know and understand this as it is to know that addition and multiplication are commutative. It appears that children reason that because addition is commutative then so must be the other three operations. Unfortunately, exercises in textbooks do little to discourage this misunderstanding. In subtraction, for example, although children will be asked to find 8 – 3 they will not be asked to find 3 – 8. But the two calculations should be discussed and compared, using calculators or number lines, to 'disprove' that 8 – 3 = 3 – 8.

What is associativity?

The associative property is helpful when finding answers to questions such as $246 + 159 + 41$, as 159 can be added to 41 before then adding 246 to the answer. This is because $(246 + 159) + 41 = 246 + (159 + 41)$. Primary children appear to have an intuitive understanding of the associative properties of addition and multiplication which are stated as:

$a + (b + c) = (a + b) + c$, for all numbers a, b and c
and $a \times (b \times c) = (a \times b) \times c$, for all numbers a, b and c.

Textbooks do not dwell on the associative property as much as on the commutative property, leaving children to develop awareness of it from working with examples. To some extent this does not matter – until children meet examples in subtraction and division, such as $9 - 4 - 1$ and $8 \div 4 \div 2$.

What is the distributive property?

While the commutative and associative properties relate to one operation, the distributive property results from considering combinations of two operations. For example, 7×58 can be calculated using the property $7 \times (50 + 8) = (7 \times 50) + (7 \times 8)$. Without a working knowledge and understanding of the distributive property, either conscious or intuitive, children are unable to develop sophisticated methods of multiplying and dividing large numbers. The general statement which expresses that multiplication is distributive over addition is:

$a \times (b + c) = (a \times b) + (a \times c)$, for all numbers a, b and c.

The distributive property considered above combines only multiplication over addition. There are other pairings to consider, such as division over subtraction.

What is special about 0?

The number 0 has a property in addition and subtraction that it does not have in multiplication and division. When the number 0 is added to any number N, that is $N + 0$, the answer is N. The commutative property of addition also tells us that $N + 0 = 0 + N = N$. As the sum in both additions is equal to N, leaving the number N unchanged (or identical) when 0 is added to it, then 0 is called the identity for addition.

Similarly, when 0 is subtracted from any number N the answer is N, that is $N - 0 = N$. However, $0 - N \neq N$, unless $N = 0$. Because N remains unchanged only when 0 is on the right of the subtraction sign, 0 is called the right identity for subtraction.

Although zero is not an identity in multiplication and division it has a special property when operating on any number N in each operation. In multiplication $N \times 0 = 0$ and $0 \times N = 0$. This property has led to 0 being called the zero element under the operation of multiplication.

Similarly, $0 \div N = 0$, but $N \div 0 \neq 0$ (what is the value of $N \div 0$?). Zero is known as the left zero element of division.

What is special about 1?

The number 1 has a property in multiplication and division that it does not have in addition and subtraction. When any number N is multiplied by 1, that is $N \times 1$, the answer is N: $N \times 1 = N$. The commutative property of multiplication also tells us that $N \times 1 = 1 \times N = N$. As the product in both multiplications is equal to N, leaving the number N unchanged (or identical) when multiplied by 1, then 1 is called the identity for multiplication.

Similarly, when any number N is divided by 1 the answer is N, that is $N \div 1 = N$. However, $1 \div N \neq N$, unless $N = 1$. Because N remains unchanged only when 1 is on the right of the division sign 1 is called the right identity for division.

Methods of calculating

Informal methods

Many teachers, when introducing children to methods of calculating mentally or using standard written algorithms, ignore the fact that children may already have developed their own informal methods. Despite valiant efforts on the part of teachers, children frequently continue to use such methods inappropriately even after being taught other, more efficient, methods. Informal methods have a part to play in children's personal calculations, but often become unsuitable when large numbers are involved. They can (and should) be used as starting points for teachers, providing a stepping stone to the development of more formal methods. The aim of every teacher should be to provide children with:

- a variety of mental methods
- standard written algorithms
- the ability to decide which informal or formal mental or written method is appropriate to answer a particular problem.

Figure 11.2 shows a process for teaching formal methods.

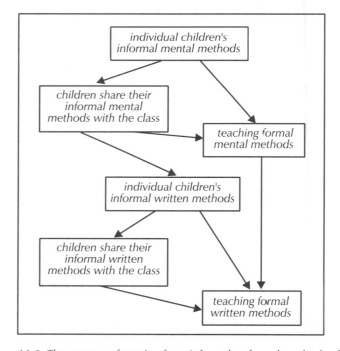

11.2 The process of moving from informal to formal methods of calculation

Mental methods

Mental methods or strategies begin with knowledge of facts that can be easily and quickly recalled. These are then combined with inferences based on:

- awareness of how the number system functions, including place value
- breaking numbers into parts and operating on the parts separately
- the derivation of new knowledge by changing the numbers in systematic ways.

Threlfall and Frobisher (1998b) classify mental methods as:

- those that involve splitting a number into parts
- those that adjust a number to a nearer number
- special methods that apply only to particular problems.

PARTS AND NEAR

Here is an example of a 7-year-old girl using a parts strategy in which she isolated a 10.

'What is 3 less than 60?'

'I took away 3 from 10, that made 7. I added 7 to 50 which is 57.'

Here is a 9-year-old's strategy which used 600 as it was near 590, the number in the question.

'What is twice 590?'

'I would round it up to 600. Twice 600 is 1200, then take the 20 away equals 1180.'

Special methods

These methods apply only to particular numbers and operations. For example, a 10-year-old boy found the answer to 96 divided by 4 as follows, 'I halved 96 which equals 48, then I halved 48 to get 24'.

Teaching mental strategies

There is considerable debate about whether it is possible to teach mental strategies to primary children. The issue revolves around the conflict that might occur between the method teachers describe, explain and use to solve a problem and that which children already have in their informal repertoire. Possible solutions to this difficulty are for children to share their methods with other children in the class and by:

- providing practical activities that demand that children work mentally
- requiring children to draw pictorial representations of the method used to solve a problem when apparatus is used
- asking children from an early age to make pictures 'in their heads' of what they did in a calculation
- insisting that children describe to others the pictures they 'see'
- challenging children to explain why their method worked.

None of these processes comes easily to children. Only through continued encouragement of teachers will a child become a reflective thinker and consequently develop the ability to use and apply mental methods appropriately and accurately.

There will be occasions when teachers should insist that children make no written records or jottings to help them with their mental calculations. There will also be times, particularly when large numbers are involved, that children should be encouraged to assist their thinking by making notes of numbers in the process of calculating. The decision of where to draw the line between no writing and some writing is a difficult one for teachers as it should be based upon knowledge of an individual child and not of the class as a whole.

Teachers also need to be prepared for children who, 'even when they have learned more sophisticated strategies, occasionally combine these with counting techniques' (Thompson, 1997).

Written methods

Thompson (1997) writes, 'A key idea in distinguishing between mental and written methods concerns the notion of 'direction'. In the case of the standard written algorithm ..., the sum is set out vertically and is tackled from right to left, whereas in the mental version it is usually set out horizontally and the answer is calculated from left to right.' This change of direction in presentation and operation is acknowledged as a potential difficulty by the FTM (National Numeracy Project, 1999) which delays introducing written algorithms until children have developed a competence with mental methods, at about 8–9 years of age. Before that age the beginnings of written algorithms are introduced by children counting on in multiples of 100, 10 and 1 on number lines. This is illustrated for the addition 86 + 57 in Figure 11.3.

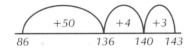

11.3 Adding 57 to 86 on a number line

Anghileri (1997) describes research in the Netherlands which supports the use of unmarked and unnumbered number lines for children developing methods of calculating with larger numbers. These give children the freedom to choose the size of jumps and to be unconcerned about scale.

Written methods and standard algorithms are often called pencil and paper methods. As with mental methods, there are two views about written methods. One school of thought advocates children developing a variety of written methods with which they feel secure, understand and can work with successfully; others are strongly of the opinion that the ultimate aim, however it is achieved, is for children to be taught a standard algorithm which is described in detail in the curriculum, and no deviation should ever be tolerated. It is not sufficient, however, to teach only the standard algorithm, as children should develop the skill to recognise when it is appropriate to use such an algorithm and when to use a mental method. Once again, the ultimate decision when faced with a problem to be solved lies with the individual child, but children are unable to make this decision unless they

- have the algorithmic skill to achieve success
- have had opportunities to experience the need to make such a decision
- have been guided in their choice of decision by a teacher sensitive to their skill and ability.

To think about

Discuss with some colleagues what you consider to be the similarities and differences between calculating mentally and calculating with a standard algorithm. How does this knowledge help you to teach both methods?

The processes for developing the skills of calculating and making appropriate decisions are similar to those for developing mental methods:

- providing practical activities which demand that children record their working in a written form
- requiring children to draw pictorial representations of the method used to solve a problem when apparatus is used
- asking children to make pictures 'in their heads' of the calculations in an activity
- insisting that children describe to others the pictures they 'see'
- challenging children to explain why their method works
- relating children's methods to a standard algorithm
- using and applying the standard algorithm in problems for practice
- using a calculator for self-checking, *not* for doing the calculation.

The role of calculators

The FTM claims that 'the calculator's main role ... is not as a calculating tool, since children are still developing the mental calculation skills and written methods that they will need throughout their lives. But it does offer a unique way of learning about numbers and the number system, place value, properties of numbers, and fractions and decimals.' On the basis of this claim, the FTM concludes that 'schools should not normally use the calculator as part of Key Stage 1 (ages 5–7 years) mathematics but should emphasise oral work and mental calculation.' One could argue that, as calculators enhance learning about numbers, they should be used as an integral part of children's development of mental calculations at all ages.

To think about

Discuss with colleagues your views about the use of calculators in the primary years.

Problems and number operations

Matthews (1967), writing as director of the Nuffield Mathematics Project, asserted that 'The solution to genuine problems and the judgement-making involved are integral parts of living.' The genuine problems to which Matthews refers can be categorised as:

- routine problems
- environmental, or real-life, problems
- process, or reasoning problems.

Routine problems

These are problems that appear to be written specifically for textbooks and have little or no relevance to situations which children will ever meet. They mostly appear as word problems and are often said to be contrived for the sole purpose of practising a known technique or procedure. For example, 'Theresa has 72 football cards. She gives half to her sister and one third to her brother. What fraction of the cards has she left?', could be claimed to be contrived as would Theresa, or anyone else, ever want to know what fraction she had left?

To think about

Try this problem for yourself. What knowledge, processes and reasoning did you use? Did you find more than one solution? How many possible solutions are there? How can you be certain?

Environmental, or real-life, problems

Problems that fit into the category of environmental problems are those which are either a part of a child's world or are problems which children are motivated to solve even though they may belong to someone else's world, perhaps the world of adults. You will also see them expressed as 'realistic problems', although there appears to be no agreed definition of 'realistic'. An example of an environmental problem is, ' Jessica helped her mother bake 3 trays of buns. Each tray had 6 buns. How many buns did Jessica help her mother bake?'

Process or reasoning problems

These problems occur within the field of mathematics and require process or reasoning skills to solve them as well as calculations. Here is such a problem.

'Find what the missing digits could be: $\boxed{}\boxed{}\boxed{7} \times \boxed{9} = \boxed{1}\boxed{}\boxed{3}$.'

What should teachers expect of children when they present them with problems? Certainly they would hope that children have the algorithmic skill necessary to solve the problem accurately. But before this children have to decide what operation is appropriate for a solution. It is this latter requirement that is a weakness for many children: they could do the problem if only they knew what calculation to perform. Unfortunately, the fault for this can be traced back to children being taught algorithms divorced from the ability to correctly decide which algorithm to use.

There are two extreme approaches to the 'skill/apply' dilemma.

- One approach teaches children a written procedure; they then practise it until the teacher is convinced they can perform it successfully on most occasions

- The other approach challenges children to solve problems before they learn how to calculate. Thus the need to be able to calculate arises out of the desire to solve the problem. Initially, when involved in this style of teaching, children use informal methods which teachers then use as the basis for developing a formal algorithm.

To think about

Choose a textbook series together with the teachers' guides. What approach do they suggest or is implicit in the way they present problems? What approach do you favour? Why?

Review of key points ➤ Learning to calculate efficiently and effectively is the major aim of a primary mathematics curriculum

➤ Knowledge of the properties of number operations contributes to the development of methods of calculating

➤ Children need knowledge of number facts to develop mental methods and written algorithms

➤ All primary children should be able to calculate accurately, choosing the mental or written method that is appropriate to the situation

➤ Knowledge of the relationships between the four number operations is an important factor in using number operations

➤ There is no 'best' method of teaching children to calculate

➤ Each operation has a number of different meanings, which should be integrated for a fuller understanding of an operation and in order to recognise and apply the appropriate operation in any situation

➤ Apparatus and diagrams assist children's learning of number operations, but do not replace the need to learn a standard algorithm

➤ Children should learn to calculate mentally and with written algorithms

➤ Children's informal methods are the starting point for learning formal methods

➤ Knowing how to calculate is of little value without the ability to use and apply computational skills

➤ Calculators can be used to support the learning of mental and written methods, but only where appropriate should they be used for calculating

Module 12   Learning to teach addition

Introduction

Addition is the first and most obvious of the four operations on number and, perhaps, the one that children use most frequently in their everyday lives. The ability to add successfully is a basic skill, and it is a reasonable expectation that the vast majority of primary children should master addition with whole numbers. Success in addition creates a sound foundation for the development of many other numerical skills.

Addition is considered by many adults, including teachers, to be relatively easy; this may be a major source of difficulty when teaching it. Addition is a sophisticated concept and, perhaps because it is the first operation children meet in school, a difficult skill to learn.

Addition in national curricula

Primary curricula include as aspects of addition:

- understanding of the operation of addition, including its commutative and associative properties
- acquiring knowledge of addition facts for rapid recall
- developing mental and non-calculator written methods
- using facts and methods to solve problems
- applying addition in number, measurement and money
- relating addition and subtraction as inverse operations
- adding decimal and negative numbers.

Key terms

addition a mathematical operation performed on two numbers, usually the numerical result of combining two quantities, or by increasing a quantity by a given amount

the '+' sign between two numbers to be added; read correctly as 'add' or 'plus', but children often say 'and'

augend the first number in an addition

addend the second number in an addition

plus used as another name for add, but suggests an increase, the augmentation form of addition; it is a Latin word meaning 'more'

and used as an 'early' word for add and often found together with 'make' instead of equals

sum the result of adding two or more numbers; suggests the combination aspect of addition

total again, the result of adding two or more numbers

zero the additive identity which, when added to any number, leaves the number unchanged

---

Key issues in addition

Related concepts and issues

It is clear that learning addition is not a matter of acquiring a series of separate ideas one by one but is a gradual extension of competence, involving a complex web of concepts, knowledge, skills and understanding. Connections between some of the most important related concepts and issues are shown in the map in Figure 12.1.

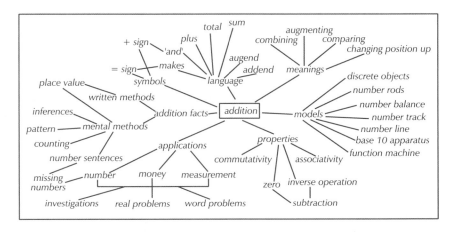

12.1 Concepts and issues associated with addition

To do

Consider a typical challenge, such as the ability to calculate 16 + 35 mentally, or to work out 253 + 168 using a standard paper and pencil method. List all the knowledge (and not just 'off by heart' knowledge) that would be needed to succeed.

Elements of competence

Addition is so intuitive that almost all children of school age can add successfully to some extent, and it is feasible to consider children in terms of their place on a continuum of competence in calculation, from 1 + 1 up to multi-element addition with decimals. At any point in the process of development there is expectation of the level of problem that children will be able to do, as well as an expectation about the approach they will use. It is important to recognise that each of these is supported by the children's knowledge, and there is a commensurate implicit expectation of how much they know, which is not always on the surface.

Children's development in addition also includes their extending understanding of the meaning of addition, their understanding of addition in real situations, and their improving ability to solve addition problems. In turn, this may relate to their skill in using a calculator, since some problems which are outside the calculation range of the child may still be understood well enough, and could be answered correctly, if a calculator were available.

The concept of addition

Young children do not understand addition in the simple, undifferentiated way that adults do. A typically adult conception of addition is purely numeric, as ordered triples. For example the numbers 4, 5 and 9 have an addition (and subtraction) relationship which may be written in different ways, thought about in different ways, and used in different ways. Stripped of these variations, however, the relationship between the numbers is that of numbers-that-fit-together in that way (as opposed to the sets of numbers that fit together in a multiplication/division way such as 4, 5 and 20). Children however, tend to see addition less simply. Their conceptions may be bound up with calculation, with addition as the process of getting an answer when there is a '+' sign. Additionally, they may understand addition in terms of the situations in which they find it. However, just as they understand cardinal and ordinal numbers initially as if they are different things (Fuson and Hall, 1983), they may understand additions in different situations as being different things.

When addition applies to real things in the world there are functional variations, which carry the different kinds of meaning to which children are sensitive. The real-world contexts are not as simple as the number relationships themselves, which are an abstraction of what they all have in common. The real contexts have variations to do with the nature of the objects and the structural, conceptual and temporal arrangements between them.

Meanings of addition

There are four different kinds of meaning for addition.

Combining (part–part–whole)

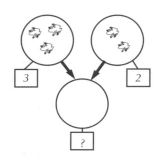

12.2 Addition as the combination of two sets

This can be seen diagrammatically in Figure 12.2, where the cardinal numbers of two sets are added to form the cardinal number of the union. In a word problem this could appear as, 'John has 3 marbles and Sally has 2 marbles. How many marbles have they altogether?'

Augmenting (addition function)

The function machine in Figure 12.7 illustrates this form of addition. This may appear in a word problem as 'John has 3 marbles and buys 2 more. How many marbles has he now?'

Comparing

The number rods in Figure 12.3 model a combination quantity with an equivalent single quantity (commonly measures). As a word problem it may occur as 'This bag of 5 marbles is equivalent to (has the same number as) two bags with 3 and 2 marbles in them.'

Changing position down (ordinal addition)

Figure 12.5b shows this form of addition using a number line. As a word problem this could be, 'A person in position 3 in a queue moves down 2 places. What is the new position?' (Note the directional ambiguity.)

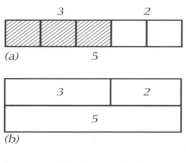

12.3 Modelling addition with number rods

Children's first intuitive understanding of addition is of augmenting (add something to a collection): when they first work with addition as combining (adding together two collections) they may not see this as the same thing and so have no expectation that the numbers will work out the same! Teachers do not always recognise the complexity that the child sees in the different meanings of addition, because we impose our simple integrated numerical meaning onto the different situations and

156

language to make sense despite the variations. In other words, since we know that 15 + 7 is 22, whether we are referring to two collections being combined or one collection being augmented, we ignore any incongruities which may arise. For example, the use of vocabulary that does not really fit the situation (such as saying 'makes' when it is not a change situation). For a child the characteristics of the situation are noticed more, and they may become confused if there is a structure which they have not seen before, or if the 'wrong' language is used.

Language and symbols

There are complications of vocabulary and symbolism for addition, particularly in the early stages of development. Children in pre-school settings demonstrate a common intuitive understanding of addition with small numbers. When it comes to formalising this into school knowledge teachers face a dilemma. Should they use the child-friendly language of 'and' and 'makes?', which have sense for children but constrain their understanding to concrete augmental and combination situations, or should they use the proper words 'add' and 'equals', which are broad and all encompassing but, to a young child, unfamiliar outside the classroom and relatively meaningless?

Similarly, it is suggested by Hughes (1986) that children start off on the wrong foot with addition because there is a premature emphasis on working meaninglessly with the received symbols, using '+ 2' and '='. It is argued that the power of conventional symbolism integrates different kinds of situation to which the same number relationships apply; this is too sophisticated for young children to even begin to understand. They need the symbolism to be clearly related to their perceptions and actions, and the structure of the situation itself. For this reason 'child-friendly' symbolism such as brackets and arrows may appeal at the early stages of learning of addition, as they reflect what children seem to relate to and understand readily. However, this then raises the question of how to 'wean' children onto conventional forms. Examples can be found of almost all the possible alternative combinations of these options used by teachers to reflect their view of the best way out of the dilemma. Here are some examples of an approach from children's books.

$$(5,3) \quad \xrightarrow{\text{add}} \quad \square$$

which may later become

$$(5,3) \quad \xrightarrow{+} \quad \square$$

followed by

$$5 + 3 \quad \longrightarrow \quad \square$$

and finally

$$5 + 3 \quad = \quad \square$$

The issue is particularly important as Hughes (1986) concludes that 'low achieving' children's problems with arithmetic and 'subsequent difficulties in school are more to do with how these symbols are introduced and used than with any deep rooted limitation in the children.'

> **To think about**
>
> Choose a textbook series and analyse how the authors have developed the progression towards the conventional way of recording addition. Then look at the teachers' guides to see if they give further advice.

Models for addition

There are a number of different kinds of apparatus which can be used to model addition, including:

- discrete objects
- number rods
- number balance
- number lines
- the 100-number grid
- function machines
- base 10 apparatus.

Discrete objects

It is usual to find children using discrete objects, such as pebbles and acorns, and then semi-structured material such as cubes, to experience the first stages of addition. The objects are 'dynamic' in that they can be moved from one set to another, or added to an existing set.

An important feature of using discrete objects to model addition is that when the objects are combined the original sets are 'lost', being subsumed in the union of the sets. Thus it is important that a record of the number of objects in the original sets is made before the combining takes place. A difficulty also arises when the number of objects becomes large as counting errors can occur. For large quantities the appropriate apparatus to retain the dynamic nature of discrete objects is the base 10 material described later.

Number rods

Rods made from linking cubes are popular in schools, and offer a way of modelling different forms of addition. However, they are again in effect sets of discrete objects, which may lead to counting-based conceptions and strategies. Cuisenaire rods, which are not marked, encourage children to see numbers as wholes, and the meaning of addition as relating to quantities as wholes. For that reason Cuisenaire rods promote knowledge of facts as a strategy for finding answers to addition problems, rather than counting.

If children start with the 5 rod and investigate pairs of rods which make 5 they are working with the comparison form of addition (see Figure 12.3b and 12.3c). If the 5 rod is made up of linking cubes it is possible for children to partition the 5. However, if the 5 is a whole unit then the actions available to them to 'break' down the 5 into two or more rods are very different, involving a search process as well as a visualisation of 'length'.

Number balance

A number balance (Figure 12.4) has no obvious units to count, and children use existing knowledge or trial and error to find positions in which weights balance, recording these as number sentences. The number balance gives a clear example of the comparing meaning of addition.

To do

Find a set of Cuisenaire rods and any instruction books. What are the important features of the rods, physical, mathematical and cognitive?

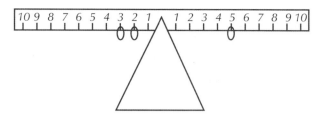

12.4 Modelling addition with a number balance

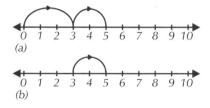

12.5 Two ways of using a number line for addition

Number lines

A number line is a suitable model for showing the augmenting meaning of addition, either showing both steps (as in Figure 12.5a) or by starting at the position of the first number (Figure 12.5b). If the number line is interpreted as an ordinal sequence, the movements may also be thought of as the changing position down meaning. Equally, the comparison meaning of addition can also be modelled on a number line, when two jumps are found that are equivalent to one jump.

The 100-number grid

Figure 12.6 shows how the 100 grid can be used to model addition. The grid has great potential for developing mental strategies for the additions of related number combinations, such as 4 + 9, 14 + 9, 24 + 9, 34 + 9, and so on.

1	2	3	4	5	6	7	8	9	10
11	12	13	14	15	16	17	18	19	20
21	22	23	24	25	26	27	28	29	30
31	32	33	34	35	36	37	38	39	30
41	42	43	44	45	46	47	48	49	50
51	52	53	54	55	56	57	58	59	60
61	62	63	64	65	66	67	68	69	70
71	72	73	74	75	76	77	78	79	80
81	82	83	84	85	86	87	88	89	90
91	92	93	94	95	96	97	98	99	100

34 add 10

12.6 Addition on a 100-number grid

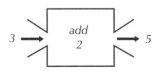

12.7 Modelling addition with a function machine

Function machines

A function machine (Figure 12.7) models addition using the second number, the addend, as an operator which changes the 'input' number, the augend.

Base 10 apparatus

This apparatus, as set out in Figure 12.8, enables children to see addition at work in a concrete form with large numbers and provides a

159

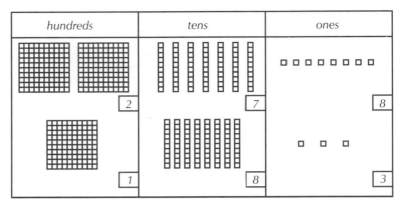

hundreds	tens	ones

12.8 *Using base 10 apparatus for addition*

visible means of modelling exchange and carrying, which can cause children many problems when symbolised.

Mental methods

Mental methods or strategies are based on knowledge of facts that can easily and quickly be recalled, combined with inferences rooted in:

- awareness of how the number system functions, including place value
- breaking numbers into parts and operating on the parts separately
- changing the numbers in systematic ways.

As well as being an important skill to develop in children, work with mental methods is also very revealing to the teacher about children's addition knowledge and reasoning. It appears to be a skill that children may develop without the intervention of a teacher.

MENTAL STRATEGIES

A class of 10-year-old children who had not been explicitly taught any mental strategies were asked to calculate 55 + 38 and 67 + 76 in their heads and then to write down how they did it. These are a selection of the many different responses.

55 + 38: 'Fifty and thirty is eighty, five and eight is thirteen, thirteen and eighty is ninety three.' 'Five off fifty five is fifty, add thirty eight is eighty eight, then add five is ninety three.'

67 + 76: 'Six add six is twelve, so six add seven is thirteen. It is the same in the other column, only there is a hundred, so it is one hundred and forty three.' 'Fifty and fifty is a hundred. Take twenty from the twenty and ten from the seventeen and that is thirty. That leaves seven and six, put them together is thirteen, added to the thirty is forty three, so it is one hundred and forty three.'

The wide variety of strategies used called upon considerable mathematical knowledge combined with insightful reasoning. What was the knowledge and reasoning used in each strategy?

Written methods

An important aspect of learning addition is the ability to calculate addition using a 'paper and pencil' method. Different methods for manipulating symbols on paper in order to calculate additions have been developed over the years, yet children often invent methods of their own based on their approaches to mental addition. In teaching, however, there is a degree of consensus about the 'right' method to learn, mostly that which was established as the fastest, in the days when that mattered (i.e. before calculators). It is arguable whether the method usually taught is also the most reliable, the one most likely to produce correct answers every time, but that nettle is yet to be grasped by the profession.

Set yourself a set of addition calculations, to cover a range of difficulty. Calculate each one both mentally and using a written method. As you complete each one, keep a note of how you do it, the steps you take, the skills you employ, the knowledge you draw on. In what ways do the calculations become more demanding?

Some of what you did in the written calculations will have been a convention. For example, where did the 'carry figures' go? Within the one basic method almost universally adopted in Britain, there are in fact small variations in where the 'carry figures' are placed (on the line, at the top, at the bottom, etc.).

CARRYING

Here are some examples, from different schools.

$$
\begin{array}{c}
\overset{1}{} \\
58 \\
\underline{17} \\
5
\end{array}
\qquad
\begin{array}{c}
58 \\
17 \\
{}_1\underline{} \\
5
\end{array}
\qquad
\begin{array}{c}
58 \\
17 \\
\underline{} \\
5 \\
1
\end{array}
$$

You will notice that the '+' sign has been omitted from each of the examples. Where do you put the sign? Conduct a small survey of your colleagues to find out where they put the '+' sign. How many variations are there which combine the different positions for the '+' sign and the carry figure? Where do textbooks recommend that children put them? Does it matter where the sign and carry figures are put? Should there be a policy about it? Should it be a school policy, a feeder schools policy, a local area policy, an LEA policy, a national policy? What is the alternative? Discuss these issues with colleagues.

A suggested progression

The FTM (National Numeracy Project, 1999) suggests some methods which may assist children in the development of their understanding and skill with the conventional addition algorithm, and which correspond with some of the mental methods that children use. The four illustrated below use the addition of two two-digit numbers, but can readily be extended to larger numbers.

Method A: add the most significant digits first	**Method B:** compensation (add too much, take off)	**Method C:** add the least significant digits first and preparing for carrying	**Method D:** 'carry' with figures below the line

$$\begin{array}{r} 87 \\ +35 \\ \hline 110 \\ 12 \\ \hline 122 \end{array}$$

$$\begin{array}{l} 87 \\ +35 \\ \hline 100 = 87 + 13 \\ 22 = 35 - 13 \\ \hline 122 \end{array}$$

$$\begin{array}{r} 87 \\ +35 \\ \hline 12 \\ 110 \\ \hline 122 \end{array}$$

$$\begin{array}{r} 87 \\ +35 \\ \hline 122 \\ {\scriptstyle 11} \end{array}$$

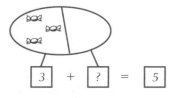

12.9 Modelling a missing number problem

Missing number problems

One missing number

Many published materials contain exercises for calculating 'missing number' problems of this kind, and these pages often cause children, and their teachers, many difficulties. For simple additions there are six variations with one missing number. For example:

1 $a + b = \square$

2 $a + \square = c$

3 $\square + b = c$

4 $\square = b + c$

5 $a = b + \square$

6 $a = \square + c$

Missing number problems, or open sentences as they are also known, can be introduced to children using objects or pictures. Figure 12.9 shows a typical approach that can be found in many textbooks for 6 year olds.

Two missing numbers

Problems with two numbers missing are also popular, particularly as they have an 'open' nature, having more than one possible correct answer. For example:

$$\square + \square = 5$$

This type of open missing number problem provides early pre-algebra experiences and opportunities for exploring patterns in addition with all whole number solutions collected and ordered.

Such problems are well within the capabilities of early years children (see Threlfall and Frobisher, 1998a). For older primary children this activity can become an investigation as children find how many different solutions there are for a given answer. For example, there are six solutions when the answer to the addition is 5. How many solutions are there when the answer is 1, 2, 3, 4, ..., n?

12.10 How far is it from Atown to Bville?

Word problems

Primary mathematics curricula place emphasis on children recognising addition situations and using their skill to solve problems. Problem solving is a vast topic and there is only space in this module to consider a very narrow aspect, namely word problems such as, 'In a library there are 123 fiction books and 345 story books. How many books is that altogether?' Many children who are very capable calculators go to pieces when faced with such problems. Despite children's intuitive understanding of additive situations when very young, the connection with real situations is lost in the exercises used to develop the calculation skill. They lose the ability to recognise the need to add, even though they could work the numbers easily enough. For example, the 'signpost problem' 'How far is it from Atown to Bville?' (Figure 12.10) is not well answered, with many children giving the answer '4'.

The difficulties that children have in working with such examples concern

- understanding and relating to the situation
- knowing which numbers from the situation to calculate with
- knowing which operation(s) to use to calculate
- interpreting the outcome of the numerical calculation correctly in terms of the situation described.

The best way to help children with addition 'word problems' is to root their early experience of addition in a range of concrete, imaginable, settings and to keep the addition connected to real situations by exposure to a range of problems and discussing the different ways they might be solved. Children should be:

- experiencing problems of many kinds and of different structures
- being supported by talking about how they see problems
- constructing visual representations of problem situations
- discussing what mental images they create
- describing how they turn images into a decision about what kind of number operation to perform.

For a more detailed analysis of addition word problems the reader is referred to Dickson *et al.* (1984).

Children and addition

Counting errors

It cannot be assumed that children who are learning addition have successfully learned how to count, and many errors in calculation addition arise from children adopting a counting-based strategy but then counting incorrectly.

SYLLABLES

A child sought the answer to 5 + 4 by putting out 5 counters, then 4 more counters, and then proceeding to count all of them matching with fingers as he went along in the following way: 'one two three four five six se-ven eight.'

He concluded that 5 + 4 = 8.

What was the reason for the error? What would you do with the child to remedy the mistake?

Counting errors can also occur with larger numbers, particularly when either count on or count back is being used as a mental strategy. This is vividly illustrated in the following episode.

CHOCOLATE BARS

A child was asked the total cost of two bars of chocolate, one at 15p and the other at 10p. Starting at fifteen, the child attempted to count on ten, but went as follows: sixteen, seventeen, nineteen, twenty, twenty-one, twenty-two, twenty-three, twenty-four, twenty-five, twenty-six (counting off ten fingers). This was observed by the teacher who asked the child a further question that demanded counting in the 'teens' and the result was the same, the number eighteen was always omitted in the child's sequence of counting numbers.

What activities would you provide for the child to remedy this error?

Calculating errors

Errors in using an algorithm for addition are sometimes the result of slips in concentration on particular problems of a type with which the child concerned is normally competent. More often, however, errors occur when children are required to add something which is outside their current range of competence. Of course, under those circumstances some children just say they cannot do it, and do not attempt a solution. On the other hand many others engage in what Van Lehn (1990) calls 'repair', making do with what they can do to make a stab at it. In that sense most errors in children's arithmetic are 'intelligent', they arise from an attempt to make sense and proceed in ways that they have been taught, or have learned. In terms of the answers the children give, errors often present intriguing challenges to a teacher to recognise the thinking that has given rise to the error, sometimes only (and always better if) resolved by asking the child to tell you what they did.

For each of the following examples, taken from observed responses, try to work out the nature of a child's thinking that could have given rise to the error.

$$32 + 25 = 12 \qquad\qquad 56 + 57 = 103$$

27	128	128
+94	+71	+71
1111	99	899

The typical non-counting errors that children make when adding arise from three different sources:

- lack of holistic understanding
- confusion about methods
- insufficient knowledge to support the method being attempted.

In the examples above the inability to see numbers as wholes, and to treat the elements separately contribute to all the errors. Confusion about methods – what to do with 'spare tens' or 'carry figures' – contributes to the second and third examples, and lack of knowledge, in terms of how to deal with 'missing' numbers, contributed to the last two.

Some ideas for teaching addition

Textbooks and addition

Traditionally, following a brief attempt in the early years to teach what addition means, addition work for primary children consists of exercises which practise calculation.

In these practice exercises children work out answers to specific number questions, at first using objects, pictures or actions to 'help', then later following set procedures, in a sequence of steadily increasing complexity and demand, such as listed in Table 12.1.

To do

Compare and contrast the sequence of addition in Table 12.1 with the sequence described in the FTM (National Numeracy Strategy, 1999)

A sequence for teaching addition

Content	Example
Non-carrying to 10	3 + 2
Carrying to 20	7 + 6
Non-carrying to 50	23 + 1
Carrying with zeros to 50	24 + 16
Non-carrying to 100	45 + 32
Carrying to 50	25 + 18
Zeros to 100	53 + 27
Carrying to 100	44 + 38
Addition of three of more addends to 100	28 + 41 + 9
Everything to 1000	
Any whole numbers	
Decimals	

Table 12.1

To think about

Analyse a set of textbooks and the teachers' guides to see what coverage they give to addition. What models do they recommend?

Primary school mathematics for many children now also includes opportunities to explore addition through investigations, in which the child is expected to make comparisons among addition outcomes by trying different values within a given structure, organising the results and drawing some conclusions about addition. For example, one can take sets of dominoes and explore them in terms of the dominoes that have the same total number of spots. By collecting and ordering the collections made under a criterion, patterns in addition may be revealed.

Actual addition calculation in explorations and investigations is usually taken to be incidental, and calculators are often employed when larger numbers are involved. The purpose of such exploratory work is related to a broader sense of numeracy than mere calculation competence. The Cockcroft Report (1982) gave 'at-homeness with number' as one aspect of numeracy. As such, exploratory work is a break with the traditional approach.

Activities for teaching for meaning

The number relationships implied by addition take different forms in different concrete situations, so there are a number of different contexts for learning addition, each with their own functional characteristics. In order that children are able to apply their number skills to different kinds of situations they need to have knowledge of different contextual forms of addition. Number apparatus and models can be used to give this experience deliberately, in a teaching activity, as can pictures, diagrams and number stories, if appropriately chosen. It must be remembered that the ultimate aim of teaching addition is not just that children will be able to calculate successfully, but that they will be able to calculate *usefully* in situations that they are likely to face in their lives. For that reason the meaning dimension, which relates to problem solving contexts, is important.

The purpose of teaching for meaning is not, however, to make children aware of the differences between how addition is manifested in practice (the augmenting/combining/comparing/ordinal increase meanings described above) but to ensure that each kind is represented in the child's experience of addition, so that a meaning develops which is rich enough when finally integrated under a number banner that the need for addition will be recognised as such in different kinds of problem situation.

The basic activity for teaching for meaning to is to generate addition sentences in the context of the chosen piece of apparatus, picture, or story situation. That is, to allow the child to explore with the apparatus to see what 'works', and to write down the addition combinations that fit together as an addition sentence using the language or symbolism felt by the teacher to be appropriate at that point.

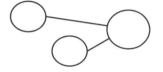

12.11 A diagram to assist addition

If, for example, children are using conventional symbols, when given three weights and a number balance, and asked to 'make them balance', they write down the combination each time they make the weights balance. On another day children may be working with base 10 apparatus, on a diagram such as in Figure 12.11. The children place a quantity of the apparatus in each of the smaller shapes, record how much is in each one, then combine it all in the larger shape, recording the total.

It should be noted that the emphasis in these activities is definitely *not* on calculating the 'answers': the situation should be set up so that the 'answer' can simply be 'read' out of the situation. This is best done if the child is given some choice in the selection of the numbers to use, rather than these being given by the teacher, because that might be interpreted as a request to calculate.

The reason that calculating the answers is not required is twofold:

- firstly, the children would make calculating answers the priority, and would find answers in any way that they could, paying no attention to the structure of the situation, which as a result cannot contribute meaning to their developing conception of addition
- secondly, calculating with apparatus may lead to a lessened ability to calculate mentally or on paper.

Generating addition sentences using a range of apparatus or models establishes a complex meaning for addition. It is also the case that in doing so there is exposure to the sets of addition combinations which are helpful in developing and extending children's knowledge base of addition facts. The results from the children's addition sentence generation should be sorted, ordered and examined to find patterns.

The generation of addition sentence models can be supplemented by using a calculator. This is a context-free way to arrive at the same numbers, and serves to emphasise that the contexts are not necessary to decide the outcome. The other advantage of calculators is that of speed and the consequent ease with which patterns can be created, which also help to enhance the child's growing understanding of the operation of addition.

To do

Make a set of number cards, 1–5. How many addition triples which do not repeat a number, such as 1 + 3 = 4, are possible? Extend the number cards to include 6, then 7, then 8 and finally 9. Is there a pattern? Try this with different-aged groups of children.

Activities for counting-based addition

Initially children's addition is heavily based in counting, and developing counting skills is the best thing to do to help. When children first add two numbers (e.g. 4 and 5) they can be seen to hold up four fingers on one hand and five fingers on the other hand, and starting with the first finger, count through to nine. The limitation of this approach comes when the two amounts to be added are more than ten, or when either one is more than five.

The liberation of being able to count on from a number (see Module 3) is that only one of the amounts has to be on the fingers. The other amount can be 'in the head'. Children can then start with the amount 'in the head' and count through the fingers to the answer. Many children learn spontaneously to put the larger number of the two in the head, and the smaller number on the fingers. This 'min' strategy is rarely taught, but could be by getting children who 'discover' it to share it with the group or class, and then getting everyone to try.

The skill of counting on thus enables any addition where one addend is ten or less to be calculated, quite a step from additions where the total has to be ten or less. Work with children to teach them that counting on repays handsomely.

Similar extensions to the ability to calculate by counting occur when children become able to 'keep track' when counting, and when they are able to count up in tens starting from any number (49 + 33 can then be 49 ... 59 ... 69 ... 79 ... 80 ... 81 ... 82!)

A sequence of development

The developing awareness of the meaning of addition and the beginnings of addition knowledge should prompt the development of other forms of calculation, both mental and written. Methods for addition that rely wholly on counting are very limited, as can be illustrated by the sequence of development as increasing counting skills extend the range of additions which can be calculated using counting (see Table 12.2).

A sequence for using counting to add		
Counting stage	**Range of addition that can be calculated**	**Example**
Counting from 1	Addition to no more than 10	7 + 3 : hold up seven fingers and three fingers ... 7 + 5 : not enough fingers
Counting on	Addition by no more than 10	9 + 8 : hold up eight fingers. Start from nine ... 29 + 8 : hold up eight fingers. Start from 29 ... 29 + 11 : not enough fingers
Counting in tens (with an ability to switch to ones when necessary)	Addition of numbers with a digit total no greater than 10 (e.g. 46 or 73)	45 + 37 : hold up three fingers and seven fingers. Start from 45 in tens. 45 ... 55 ... 65 ... 75. Switch to ones. 75 ... 76 ... 45 + 38 : not enough fingers

Table 12.2

In other words it is possible to see development in counting-based methods, but there are always constraints based on the number of fingers that one can use. These constraints are absent when a number line or base 10 apparatus is available, and children can learn to use counting methods to add any numbers when such apparatus is there to help them. This, however, is not a productive avenue for development, as such equipment is not available outside the classroom, and is in any case too slow. Children need to learn to calculate by non-counting-based methods.

Sadly, in such circumstances, some teachers do not teach children an alternative, but merely forbid the use of fingers. Children are expected to develop an alternative to counting by themselves. Some succeed, motivated by the pressure of having to get correct answers. However, the teaching approach creates anxiety, and for children who take time to take that step it can be particularly damaging. The non-counting approach to addition needs to be taught, systematically, beginning with numbers under 20.

Activities for non-counting methods of addition to 20

When calculating the addition of larger numbers with the 'standard' algorithm there is still an 'irreducible' requirement to calculate the addition of two single-digit numbers. It is best if this part of the calculation can be done quickly and accurately. Primary curricula documents emphasise the value of knowing addition facts to 20. Unfortunately, the ambition to know 'off by heart' all the addition facts to 20 is not achieved in a single step. Addition facts can be memorised, but there is a limit to how far memorisation can go. There is a sense in which connected and meaningful learning can go on and on but memorisation, even when supported by pattern, reaches a point of saturation. For that reason, knowledge of addition facts to 20 should be approached in a different way – through a mixture of knowledge and inference, by using a combination of memory of some facts with inferences from them based on the structure of the number system to derive new facts. Inferred knowledge, while not quite as 'instant' as memorised knowledge, is sufficient for the purpose of enabling success with mental and written methods for the calculation of addition of larger numbers.

Memorisation

It is sufficient that children memorise the following addition facts:

- facts which add by one, and two, rooted in their knowledge of the counting sequence: $3 + 1, 5 + 2$
- facts to 5: $1 + 4 = 5$; $2 + 3 = 5$
- facts with 5: $5 + 1 = 6$; $5 + 2 = 7$; $5 + 3 = 8$; $5 + 4 = 9$
- 'ties' or doubles: $1 + 1 = 2$; $2 + 2 = 4$; $3 + 3 = 6$; ...; $9 + 9 = 18$.
- facts to 10: $1 + 9$; $2 + 8$; $3 + 7$; $4 + 6$ and $5 + 5$
- facts with 10: $10 + 1 = 11$, $10 + 2 = 12$, ...

Together with the children's 'min' awareness that reversed facts are equivalent ($4 + 6$ and $6 + 4$ have the same answer). All the other addition facts to 20 can be worked out by inference.

> **To do**
>
> How many addition facts are there up to and including 2, 3, 4, ...? Is there a pattern? Generalise for up to and including n.

The memorisation of addition facts for rapid recall is achieved through exposure and practice, reinforced by pattern. Starting with the smaller numbers, patterns of facts can be made using the fingers on the hands, holding some fingers down and others up. Patterns may be also made with pictures, with apparatus, with calculators, or in a whole class interaction with the teacher (see Module 17).

For example, number rods may be used in building 'walls'. Figure 12.12a shows part of the '10 wall'. When making walls like this, children see patterns in the arrangements spontaneously, and rearrange the order of the rods accordingly as in Figure 12.12b. Patterns can then be searched for and the facts within it rehearsed, with pattern contributing to memorisation.

In making such patterns it is important to recall the purpose, which is to help children to remember addition facts, and to make sure that this aspect is present in the way the pattern is treated. This means repetition of the elements, both orally and written, and discussion of how they are related. This is most effective if the children are involved in

- creating the 'knowledge sets'
- helping to decide how to organise the 'data'
- observing patterns
- explaining the reasons for patterns.

Activities for inference

The inference of other addition facts from the set of known addition facts involves a set of 'strategies'. These strategies draw on

- an awareness of how facts are related to one another
- how you can take numbers apart, operating with the bits separately before putting them back together at the end
- how you can change the question without changing the answer (e.g. add one to one number and take one from the other, which turns 7 + 9 into 8 + 8 – a known fact).

As a result children 'know' facts without having memorised them.

(a)

(b)

12.12 The story of 10

ADDITION STRATEGIES

Here are some strategies used by some children when adding single digit numbers:

'I know 7 add 8 is 15 because 7 add 7 is 14 and that is one more.'

'I know that 9 add 5 is 14 because 9 add 1 is 10, take one off the 5 is 14.'

'I know that 8 add 5 is 13 because 8 is 5 add 3, and 5 and 5 is ten, so it is three more, 13'.

List the mathematical properties that each child uses in each strategy. Does your list agree with your colleagues?

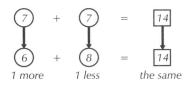

12.13 Raising a strategy 'to the surface'

With these inferences from a set of memorised facts, children can work out the addition of any two single-digit numbers without counting.

It is common for inferences to be spontaneously invented by a proportion of young children. In order that all children can work in this way it is necessary for the teacher to teach how to make inferences. The children need to know about strategies, and to have practice in using them. This can be approached fairly directly, with a lesson on a particular strategy, followed by opportunities to use it. An alternative way to teach strategies is to get children to 'show and share' their range of approaches to a problem. The teacher can then pick up on and elaborate any inferences that were used, and talk with the children about how and why they work. The children then relate the approaches that make sense to them. If encouraged to try different methods with other examples, and to talk about it in a group or possibly a whole class context, they extend their repertoire more 'naturally' and quickly than through direct teaching. The articulation by children of their mental methods is very effective. A further suggestion is to use diagrams to raise strategies 'to the surface', as shown in Figure 12.13.

The calculation of additions up to 20 should be performed mentally, often in an oral context, and always recorded horizontally as an addition sentence such as 7 + 8 = 15. Vertical recording should be retained for the column-by-column procedures needed for larger numbers.

Working out of an addition, either by knowing the answer or by using what is known to derive other knowledge, complements counting. Children who can work out most things still count sometimes. Different strategies live side-by-side and even adults have been shown to use (in more difficult problems) a mix of knowledge, inference and counting.

Activities for addition over 20

The addition of numbers to an answer greater than 20 may be done mentally or using paper and pencil. Both written and mental methods draw, in different ways, on the ability to add numbers up to 20 mentally.

Mental methods

The methods that are used to calculate addition above 20 are parallel to those used for addition below 20.

Written methods

When children have developed meanings of addition, learned addition-related knowledge, and practised efficient ways of adding mentally, they are ready to be taught an addition algorithm appropriate to their stage of development. Initially this will be with numbers to 50 and then 100, extending to all whole numbers and eventually decimals.

Addition algorithms do not reflect the intuitive and meaningful approaches of mental work, which tend to begin with the larger elements first, but have developed as efficient mechanisms for getting answers quickly.

At the start consistency and accuracy are more important than speed, and these are developed through understanding. It is possible to teach an addition procedure as a meaningless sequence of actions. This is the traditional approach, and it can be successful as long as sufficient time is allowed for practice. However, when the procedures are extended to new cases (larger number or decimals for example) the procedure becomes more and more complicated and difficult to remember. When the procedure is understood, on the other hand, when the different steps make sense, then the extension to new domains and complex examples is more straightforward. Using rote methods brings quicker results in the short term, but it is more efficient in the longer term to make the investment represented by teaching children from the start why the algorithm works as it does, what the 'carry figures' actually mean, and so on.

You will find much reference in teachers' books and in textbooks to the use of base 10 apparatus to model an addition procedure. A helpful approach is to manipulate the apparatus alongside the paper and pencil procedure in order to demonstrate it meaningfully. Figure 12.14 shows this at work, combining 10 *ones* and changing them into 1 *ten*.

> **To think about**
>
> These additions use the same digits: 1467 + 2936 and 14.67 + 2.936. Set out the additions vertically and complete them. What differences are apparent?

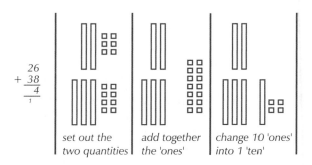

12.14 *Demonstrating addition with base 10 apparatus*

> **To do**
>
> Work through a 'demonstration' of the addition algorithm with base 10 apparatus. What would you say to the child at each stage to draw their attention to the written method? How would you use the apparatus to illustrate the 'carry figure' aspect?

Note that the point of the 'demonstration' approach is not to show the children a method of calculating addition using apparatus; neither is the apparatus being used to 'show' the meaning of addition. The purpose is to bring meaning of the written procedure to children.

Children need to practise using the paper and pencil method independently of any material support – and if you adopt the demonstration approach it is *vital* at this point that the apparatus is removed. They should *not* be allowed to use the apparatus to 'help' (Threlfall, 1996). Paper and pencil addition should be practised as a paper and pencil exercise, with the apparatus brought back for demonstration purposes *only* if systematic errors suggest some misunderstanding, and then put away again as soon as it has been used to overcome the misunderstanding.

An alternative to the demonstration approach allows children to work with the base 10 apparatus whenever they are having difficulties with the written symbols. Advocates of this approach argue that only by working with the apparatus can a child's perceptions and actions relate to that mirrored in the written algorithm.

Estimating and approximating

A further important aspect of addition calculations is approximations, or addition using rounding that gives an estimate of the answer. Approximate calculation is a limited mental method. Mental methods typically deal with the larger numbers first, just as when counting money one 'naturally' starts with the largest coins. One benefit is that by doing so you get an idea of roughly how big an answer is going to be. In other words, this approach concentrates attention on the significant numbers. The traditional ways of doing additions, by contrast, operate on parts of numbers, and the whole is recovered only at the end by reading off what has been written. Approximate calculations begin a mental method, but finish it early.

When faced with a problem, such as $691 + 293$, it is reasonable to argue that as 691 is approximately 700, and 293 is approximately 300 then the answer is approximately 1000. It is further possible to say that the answer is less than 1000, as each number was rounded up. The next level of refinement is to conclude that the answer is between 980 and 1000, as each element was rounded up by less than 10. At this stage one is almost at the point of working out the exact answer.

A class activity

OBJECTIVE	To add mentally a pair of two-digit numbers
ORGANISATION	Whole class
RESOURCES	Teacher has 20 number cards, two sets of 0 to 9

ACTIVITY

- The two sets are mixed and placed together in one pile.
- The teacher chooses two cards to make a two-digit number which is shown to the children.
- A second pair is chosen and shown to the children, who add the two numbers 'in their heads'.
- One child comes out, writes the answer on the board and explains how he or she calculated the answer.
- The activity is repeated until all cards have been used.

A group activity

OBJECTIVE	To find the value of letters written as an addition
ORGANISATION	Small groups
RESOURCES	Each group has a sheet containing the following three additions written with letters. In each problem the same letter represents the same digit, with different letters representing different digits.

$$AB + AB = CD \quad AB + AC = BC \quad AB + BA = ABC$$

ACTIVITY

- Each group works together to solve the three problems finding all possible solutions.
- One member of each group comes out to explain how they solved a problem.
- Each group then makes up some of their own to challenge other groups.

Test your own knowledge: addition

1 Three four-digit numbers are made using the same four digits. The third number is the sum of the first two numbers. What are the three numbers? (An initial digit 0 is not permitted.)

2 Use the digits 1 to 9 once each to write an addition with a sum of 225

3 Arrange the nine digits 1 to 9 to complete this addition:

4 Arrange the digits 1 to 9 into two sets of numbers so that the sum of both sets is the same.

5 Using three 1s it is possible to make only two whole number additions which have different totals:

$$1 + 1 + 1 = 3 \quad 11 + 1 = 12$$

a How many additions can you make using four 1s, five 1s, six 1s, ...?

b What happens when you use 2s instead of 1s?

c What happens if you are allowed to use fractions or decimals?

6 Arrange the digits 0 to 9 into two five-digit numbers whose sum is

a the least possible sum of any arrangement

b the greatest possible sum of any arrangement.

7 Using the digits 1 and 2 it is possible to make the two two-digit numbers 12 and 21, whose sum is 33. With 1, 2 and 3 it is possible to make six three-digit numbers: 123, 132, 213, 231, 321 and 312. The sum of these numbers is 1332. Can you predict the sum of the 24 possible four-digit numbers using the digits 1, 2, 3 and 4? Generalise for all the digits 1 to 9

8 Arrange the numbers 1 to 51 into 17 triads so that the sum of the numbers in each triad is the same.

9 Goldbach's conjecture (not yet proven) states that every even number greater than 2 is equal to the sum of two prime numbers. Find two such prime numbers for the numbers 6, 88, 474 and 3502

Review of key points ➤ Success in addition provides a foundation for success with the other three operations

➤ Addition is a gradual build-up of related concepts, knowledge and skills

➤ There are four different meanings for addition: combining, augmenting, comparing and changing position down

➤ It is important that children are able to associate the language and symbols used in addition with the perceptions and actions they perform with materials and models

➤ Mental addition methods are based upon awareness of the place value system, knowledge of addition facts and inferences

➤ Developing an efficient and effective addition algorithm is important

➤ In calculating, just being able to get an answer is *not* enough; children must know when and how to use an algorithm

Module 13   Learning to teach subtraction

Introduction

The ability to subtract successfully is, like addition, a basic skill, and a reasonable expectation of primary education with respect to almost all children. Unlike addition, however, there are conceptual as well as procedural challenges to subtraction: subtraction is less intuitively obvious, there are distinct variations in meaning, and some of the elements of calculation, particularly when dealing with numbers with zeros, can be awkward to teach and difficult to learn. Consequently, some children who are successful with addition have difficulty with subtraction.

Subtraction in national curricula

There are six major objectives in teaching subtraction:

- acquiring knowledge of subtraction facts for rapid recall
- developing mental and non-calculator written methods
- using facts and methods to solve problems
- applying subtraction in number, measurement and money
- understanding the concept and operation of subtraction
- subtracting decimal numbers.

Key terms

subtraction	a mathematical operation performed on two numbers, usually the numerical result of taking away one quantity from another, or by reducing a quantity by a given amount
the '−' sign	placed between two numbers to be subtracted; read correctly as 'subtract' or 'minus', but children often say 'take away'
minuend	the first number in a subtraction
subtrahend	the second number in a subtraction
take away	represents a physical action of removing objects; is also used as a name for the '−' sign
difference	numerical comparison of two sets of objects or measures to decide how many or how much more or less one is than the other
decomposition	the breaking down of a unit into smaller units, such as 1 ten into 10 ones. Trading, exchanging and regrouping are other words used to describe the same process

---

Key issues in subtraction

Related concepts and issues

It is apparent from the way subtraction is introduced in some classrooms that there is an implicit assumption that experiences with addition provide a basis for this new operation. However, evidence suggests that in the early stages of learning about subtraction children do not relate the two operations in any way. As with addition, children bring to their learning of subtraction a collection of real experiences of the concept in operation. Intuitive ideas of subtraction have been formed, but the relationships between the different meanings of subtraction have yet to be abstracted. The connections between other concepts, operations and issues are shown in Figure 13.1.

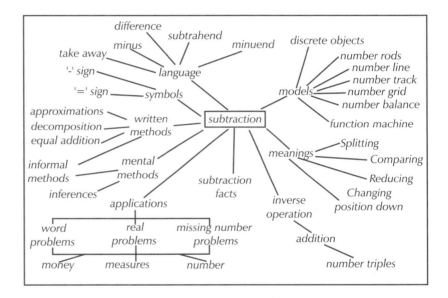

13.1 Concepts and issues associated with subtraction

Meanings of subtraction

Most adults have a conception of subtraction which is integrated under a number understanding, and do not spontaneously recognise some of the differences in the forms in which subtraction appears, both in the use of models and in problem situations. Subtraction, like the other three number operations, is a multi-faceted concept having a variety of meanings. It is important for teachers of young children to know about the different meanings and how they relate to possible problem situations. It is equally important that teachers recognise that, although children have had many pre-school subtraction experiences, they may not have the mathematical language to describe them.

There are five different kinds of meaning for subtraction:

- splitting a quantity
- reducing a quantity
- comparing quantities

177

- changing position up
- inverse of addition.

Splitting a quantity (whole–part–part)

Figures 13.2a and b illustrate this meaning. The splitting or partitioning meaning of subtraction may appear in a word problem as, 'A box contains 17 marbles, of which 9 are Sally's and the rest are John's. How many are John's?'

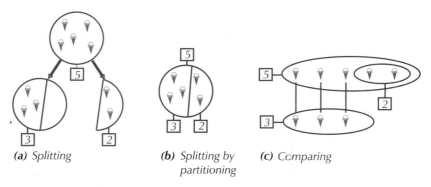

(a) Splitting   (b) Splitting by partitioning   (c) Comparing

13.2 Subtraction as splitting and comparing

Reducing a quantity (subtraction function)

When a number of objects are removed or taken away from a set to leave a subset of the original set the original quantity is reduced. This meaning is identified with the action of 'take away'. This meaning is the reverse of the augmenting meaning of addition. It relates to situations where a quantity is reduced by a given amount, as illustrated in Figure 13.3a. As a word problem this could be, 'There are 275 children in a school. Fifty of them go on a trip. How many are left in school?'

Comparing of quantities

Comparing takes place when a question such as 'How many more marbles does John have than Sally?' is asked. The answer is the numerical difference between the two quantities. Figures 13.2c and 13.3b show this diagrammatically. The difference meaning of subtraction is very common, but causes children many difficulties.

Comparison between two different quantities can in fact fit different sorts of situations. In some cases there is to be an equalisation down, comparing the groups to decide how many to remove from the larger group to make them equal; in another, comparing to decide how many to add to the smaller group to make them equal; in still others one is just comparing. In this context the difference may be found by adding some to the smaller set or removing some from the larger set. It can also be seen by direct comparison

Change position up (ordinal subtraction)

Figure 13.4 shows this form of subtraction using a number line. As a word problem it may appear as 'A team in position 5 moves up 2 places.' (Note the directional ambiguity.)

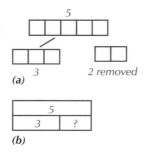

(a)

(b)

13.3 Reducing with number rods

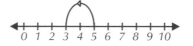

13.4 Subtraction on a number line

Inverse of addition

The inverse of addition applies when the sum and one quantity is known and the other quantity has to be found. This may appear in a missing number problem such as

$$75 + \square = 100.$$

Addition and subtraction are inverse operations in that, given any number N, if I add another number and then subtract the same number I am left with N. Symbolically this reads: $N + n - n = N$, and $N - n + n = N$, what ever numbers N and n are. Primary children do not readily understand this apparently simple relationship.

Language and symbols

Children's pre-school experiences with subtraction of small numbers need to be built upon and extended by introducing language and symbols appropriate to the context and to the stage of development of the children. The difficulty begins for children when we by-pass meaningful and appropriate language and fail to make the connections for them with symbols.

Although young children have many experiences of comparing sets of objects to find out who has more and how many more this is seldom related to subtraction. The question 'How many more?' suggests to children that they need to count a set of objects, not to take away one set from another. The expression 'take away' suggests a physical action (the reducing meaning), although the '–' sign has no directly apparent connection with the words or the action; it is, once again, a sign to be learned by being set in meaningful experiences. The word 'leaves' is often used in an attempt to indicate to children that the result of a 'take away' is what is left. However, the decision has to be made as to when any child is ready for the more formal words ' subtract' and 'equals'. As with addition it is helpful for children to understand that 'equals' can be read as 'has the same value as'.

Many children find difficulty in associating 'difference' with the operation of subtraction. You will often hear them saying that the difference between 7 and 3 is that 7 is straight and 3 is rounded, interpreting the question 'What is the difference?' as a request for a descriptive statement. Children find it helpful in the early stages to use 'number difference' to stress the numerical property of difference. A question asked in the form 'Calculate the difference ...' can also remind children of what is meant.

Models for subtraction

A number of different kinds of mathematical apparatus can be used to model subtraction, including:

- discrete objects
- number rods
- number lines
- function machines
- base 10 apparatus.

To think about

Look through the workbooks and textbooks of a primary mathematics series and analyse the 'subtraction' language used. Is it possible to notice any progression or, perhaps, lack of consistency?

To think about

Select some children's workbooks to see how the writers have attempted to use pictures of objects to model subtraction. Discuss with some colleagues the problems the pictorial models have created that may cause learning difficulties for children.

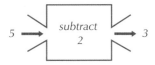

13.5 *Modelling subtraction with a function machine*

To think about

Work out how to use Base 10 apparatus to model the comparing (difference) meaning of subtraction. Would you use different language to describe the subtraction in the two 'versions'? Does the word 'leaves' fit in both cases? How about 'less', 'take', 'subtract', 'minus' and so on?

Discrete objects

Objects can readily be used in the development of the splitting, reducing and comparing aspects of subtraction. It is more difficult to use pictures of objects to model subtraction in a comprehensible form for a child. Writers of textbooks try to overcome this in different ways, however.

Number rods

The actions children perform on linking cube rods for splitting, reducing and comparing are similar to those on discrete objects (see Figure 13.3a). Labelled rods, as shown in Figure 13.3b, model only the comparison meaning of subtraction. After only a short time using trial and error children are able to correctly visualise the rod to fill a gap.

Number lines

Figure 13.4 shows how a number line can be used to model subtraction, effectively as counting back, or the ordinal position change meaning of subtraction.

Function machines

A function machine (Figure 13.5) models subtraction using the second number as an operator and (although this is not strictly reducing, or a decrease) it is readily seen as such by children as it closely relates to the physical action of taking away from a set.

Base 10 apparatus

Base 10 apparatus enables children to see subtraction at work in a concrete form with large numbers and provides a visible means of modelling decomposition which can cause children many problems when symbolised. Figure 13.6 models 165 – 48 with the 165 as material and the 48 in symbols. The 'reducing' subtraction involves removing 48 from the 165 and placing it with its symbols. What is left is the answer to the subtraction. However, you will notice that the amount left is not in its original position, but has been transferred to an 'answer' box.

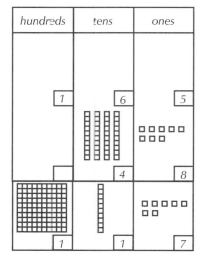

13.6 *Subtraction with base 10 apparatus*

Base 10 apparatus can also be used for modelling the comparing aspects of subtraction.

Mental methods

Mental subtraction methods are based on knowledge of facts, which are then combined with inferences rooted in:

* understanding of the number system, including place value
* breaking numbers into parts and operating on the parts separately
* the derivation of new knowledge by changing the numbers in systematic ways.

MENTAL SUBTRACTION

Here are some responses from a group of 9 and 10-year-old children who were asked to calculate 83 – 35 and 650 – 380 mentally.

83 – 35:

'Take thirty off eighty is fifty, add on three is fifty three, take off five is forty-eight.'
'Eighty take thirty-five is forty-five, add on three is forty eight.'
'I added five to make forty, then forty to make eighty, three more, so it is forty-eight.'
'Eighty minus thirty is fifty, and fifty minus five is forty-five, and add three which is forty-eight.'

650 – 380:

'Six hundred take three hundred is three hundred, three hundred and fifty take eighty is two hundred and seventy.'
'Take eighty away from six hundred and fifty to leave five hundred and seventy, then take three hundred away from five hundred and seventy, to leave two hundred and seventy.'
'Six hundred and fifty is three hundred and three hundred and fifty. Take three hundred and fifty, and the sum is three hundred minus thirty, which is two hundred and seventy.'

What strategies do you think each child used? Were the same strategies used in the same way?

To think about

Ask a group of 9–11-year-old children to do some subtraction calculations mentally, and describe to you how they did them. Try to discern how they approached the problems and keep a note of the different approaches used. What does this tell you about the knowledge that they have, or their awareness of the number system?

Children are not always wholly explicit in their descriptions, so their methods are not always easy to spot. In the last example above, it appears that the two numbers were seen as having common ground, 350 as part of both, so that when that was removed from each element, the problem that remained was easier to do. Expressed in symbols, in full, this is:

$$650 - 380 = (300 + 350) - (30 + 350)$$
$$= (300 - 30) + (350 - 350)$$
$$= 300 - 30$$
$$= 270$$

It is valuable sometimes to share a full version of a child's method with other children, in order to make explicit elements which are usually left implicit. This draws attention to strategies so that others might adopt them.

Written methods

Standard methods

Two distinct methods have been widely used and taught in schools, but one of them is now much more common than the other. However, it is perfectly possible that the method used by some children's parents is different from that which is normally taught in school. The two methods are described below.

Decomposition

The decomposition method splits the 'top' number up, so that a quantity can be displaced to another column where it is added to what is already there, and so give an amount large enough to subtract in that column. This approach changes the appearance of the numbers, while retaining their value. Consider 57–18 written vertically. Fifty-seven, 57, becomes forty and seventeen, 4¹7. Some children do not recognise this fact about the method, and become very confused about when it is acceptable to change a number. Other children are confused by the existence of ¹7 in a column, when all of their place value work suggests that the largest number in a column should be 9.

Equal additions

The equal additions method finds an extra amount, often said to be 'borrowed', to supplement the deficient column quantity in the 'top' number. This is equalised by adding an equivalent amount to the left adjacent column in the 'bottom' number. This approach in effect changes the problem to a different one which is easier to do. Fifty-seven, 57, becomes sixty-seven, 5¹7, and eighteen, 18, becomes twenty eight, ₂8, retaining the difference between the two numbers.

To think about

Before reading about written methods, try this subtraction:

```
  3017
-1409
```

Reflect on the knowledge and the processes you used.

CASE STUDIES

Different methods

Here is an example of each with the same subtraction.

```
    5¹7                4̸5¹7
- ₂1̸ 8             -  1 8
  ───               ───
   3 9                3 9
Equal addition      Decomposition
```

Which of these is familiar to you? Talk to a number of people and find out which method they know, and whether they know of and/or can do the other one.

Despite now being out of favour, the equal additions method copes rather more effectively with subtractions where there are several zeros in the 'top number' as illustrated in the subtraction 5000 – 1987 set out below.

```
4̸5 1̸0⁹ 1̸0⁹ 10        5 ¹0 ¹0 ¹0
-   1 9 8 7         - 2̸1 ¹0⁰9 9̸8 7
  ─────────          ─────────
   3 0 1 3            3 0 1 3
Decomposition        Equal addition
```

The disadvantage of the 'decomposition' method under these circumstances is that one has to do all of the 'decomposing' at the start before any calculation can take place, with the real risk of losing track in the mess of symbols which the method produces. The 'equal additions' method, on the other hand, can proceed as always, one step at a time, and is also far less messy.

Ensure that you can follow both of the examples above, and know why all the figures have been placed where they have, and what they all mean. Then try some further examples of each, at a similar or greater level of difficulty, including some with numbers with decimal elements.

A suggested progression
The FTM (National Numeracy Strategy 1999) suggests that methods for subtracting numbers vertically should build on mental methods and that a variety of such methods should be discussed over a period of time before moving to an agreed method. These are three such methods:

Counting up	Compensation	Approximating
465	465	465
−197	− 197	− 197
3 (to make 200)	300 (465 − 165)	265 (465 − 200)
200 (to make 400)	− 32 (165 − 197)	+ 3 (200 − 197)
65 (to make 465)	268	286
268		

It is suggested that the final method for decomposition should be developed by firstly using an expanded form, as follows:

$$465 = 400 + 60 + 5$$
$$-197 \quad 100 + 90 + 7 \qquad \text{leading to}$$

$$= 400 + 50 + 15 \qquad 4\,5^15$$
$$100 + 90 + 7 \qquad -1\,9\,7$$

$$= 300 + 150 + 15 \qquad 3^15^15 \qquad 4^36^{15}5^{15}$$
$$100 + 90 + 7 \qquad -1\,9\,7 \qquad -1\,9\,7$$
$$\overline{200 + 60 + 8} \qquad \overline{2\,6\,8} \qquad \overline{2\,6\,8}$$

To think about

Use the expanded form to subtract 1968 from 5152. Discuss with colleagues the advantages and disadvantages of using the expanded form as a stage before the final method.

Informal methods

One disadvantage of standard written methods is that none of them has a clear relationship to the mental methods that a child might on another occasion use for exactly the same problem.

INVENTED METHOD

A 10 year old 'hated' doing the algorithm he had been taught as he could not understand how and why it worked. He invented his own method, writing his working horizontally like this:

61	4 − 1 = 3	151	8 − 1 = 7	
−24	60 − 20 = 40	− 68	60 − 50 = 10	
37	40 − 3 = 37	83	100 − 10 − 7 = 83	

How does his method work? Will it always work? Would you allow him to continue to use the method or would you wish to try to convince him that he could do 'decomposition'? How would you achieve this?

To do

Write a set of six subtraction open sentences, one of each type with all numbers less than 10. Predict the order of difficulty of the six questions, recording your reasons. Give the questions to a small group of children. Talk to them about their methods. Write a report of your research.

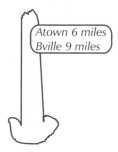

Atown 6 miles
Bville 9 miles

13.7 How far is it from Atown to Bville?

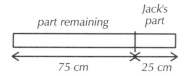

part remaining | Jack's part

75 cm | 25 cm

13.8 The 'blocks' method for subtraction problems

Missing number problems

There are six types of open sentences involving the subtraction sign.

1 $a - b = \square$

2 $a - \square = c$

3 $\square - b = c$

4 $\square = b - c$

5 $a = b - \square$

6 $a = \square - c$

The first open sentence is the standard subtraction sentence. The rest, for various reasons, cause children many difficulties whatever the domain of numbers used.

Word problems

Most primary mathematics curricula place an emphasis on children developing the ability to recognise subtraction situations and use their skills to solve problems. Textbooks contain examples that we classify as word problems, such as, 'In a library there are 423 fiction books. One day 247 are on loan. How many books are still on the shelves?' Many children who are very successful when using a subtraction algorithm are unsuccessful when faced with such a problem. For example, in the problem shown in Figure 13.7 ('How far is it from Atown to Bville?') many children give the answer 15 miles.

This kind of difficulty can only be overcome by children

● experiencing problems of many kinds

● supported by talking about how they 'see' problems

● constructing visual representations of problem situations

● discussing what mental images they create

● describing how they turn that into a decision about what kind of number operation to perform.

Older children, outside the primary age range, can learn to answer word problems by representing the problem situation algebraically. This is not really a feasible ambition for primary children. However, it is possible to get them to represent the situation diagrammatically. One suggested approach is called the 'blocks method' and is widely used in schools in Singapore. In this the children are encouraged to 'map' the numerical elements of the situation onto one or more 'blocks' which represent the situational elements. It is then clearer to see what calculations one must do. For example, the problem 'Jill has a length of string. Jack takes from it a piece 25 cm long. It is then 75 cm long. How long was the piece that Jill started with?' can be represented as in Figure 13.8. It can be seen that the effort to interpret the situation is not avoided, but the physical reference is helpful to children to sustain their imagery of the structure of the situation.

A more detailed analysis of subtraction word problems can be found in Dickson *et al.* (1984).

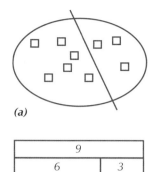

(a)

9	
6	3

(b)

13.9 Relating addition and subtraction

Relating addition and subtraction

One significant feature of the work on subtraction meanings using diagrams and apparatus is that the arrangements are closely related to those for addition. In some cases they are the reverse, and in some they are exactly the same. The part–part–whole meaning exemplified in the partitioned picture, and the arrangement of number rods in Figure 13.9, can be seen either as addition or subtraction. Do these pictures represent $6 + 3 = 9$, or $9 - 3 = 6$, or $9 - 6 = 3$ or $3 + 6 = 9$? The answer is, of course, 'Yes' to all the number sentences. The picture situation is all four, and can switch between them depending on the transient perception of the moment, without any change to the situation itself. This can be exploited by the teacher in creating families of related number sentences with a range of situations to which the part–part–whole meaning applies.

Children and subtraction

Counting errors

SUBTRACTING

A group of 5–6-year-old children were talking about subtracting 3 from 7 by counting. Some said 7, 6, 5 (the answer), others said 6, 5, 4 (the answer). How would you help them understand the difference between their reasoning? How might you use a number track or number line to show which is required?

To think about

For each of the examples in Table 13.1, work out the nature of a child's thinking that could have given rise to the error.

Algorithmic errors

Van Lehn (1990) categorised the different kinds of errors that children make when using an algorithm, many of which relate to problems containing zeros. The most common are shown in Table 13.1.

Categories of subtraction errors

Smaller from larger	Stops borrow at zero	Borrow across zero	Borrow from zero	Borrow no decrement
404	$^3\cancel{4}^1\cancel{0}^14$	$^{\lambda^2}{}_2\cancel{4}^1\cancel{0}^14$	$4^9\cancel{0}^14$	$4^1\cancel{0}^14$
−187	− 1 8 7	− 1 8 7	−1 8 7	−1 8 7
383	2 2 7	1 2 7	3 1 7	3 2 7

Table 13.1

Some ideas for teaching subtraction

Textbooks and subtraction

Invariably, subtracting two-digit numbers is introduced with both 'top' numbers greater than their corresponding 'bottom' numbers:

TU $\qquad$ TU

3 9 $\quad$ always precedes $\quad$ 3 2 $\quad$ by some time.

−2 3 $\qquad\qquad$ −1 7

For some children this order is a cause for difficulty. They develop a strategy that subtracts the smaller number from the larger number, not as teachers believe, the 'bottom' number from the 'top' number. There is a subtle difference here in the perceptions of children, and of teachers, about the order of the elements on which the actions are being performed. Children then apply their successful method to the second type of example – which then proves to be unsuccessful, leaving them at a loss to understand why.

Most textbooks provide word problems, both contextual and mathematical – e.g. How many less than 8 is 5? There is, however, a great deal of variation across textbooks in the use and demands of missing number problems in subtraction.

Activities for teaching for meaning

The number relationships implied by subtraction take different forms in different concrete situations, so there are a number of different contexts for learning subtraction, each with different functional characteristics. It is important for future usefulness that children experience subtraction in a range of forms, so that the meaning which they develop is full and multi-faceted, with an understanding for recognition of the subtraction dimensions in problem contexts. If children only deal in number relationships in the abstract to which the differences do not apply, they may be unable to detect the need for subtraction in the context of real problems.

Opportunities must be taken by teachers to use children's everyday experiences in the classroom to develop the different meanings for subtraction in realistic and meaningful contexts. Children absent from school, pencils missing from work trays are two very simple and recurring 'subtraction' events which can be discussed and recorded in symbols.

Another effective way to teach the meaning of subtraction is to use number apparatus to create subtraction sentences. The basic activity is for the child to make an arrangement with the apparatus, and to record the arrangement as a subtraction statement using the language and symbolism with which they are currently familiar (6 – 4 = 2, perhaps). Using the different forms of number apparatus and models echoes the range of functional variations in real situations, and also enables the sameness between different situations to come through.

The emphasis is definitely not on calculating the 'answers', so the situation should be set up so that the 'answer' can simply be 'read' out of the situation. This is best done if the child is given some choice in the

To think about

Evidence has suggested that authors of textbooks do not provide a balance of subtractions involving all possible combinations of digits, frequently having a bias to some pairs. Survey a recent textbook series to see if all possible combinations of subtractions pairs are adequately covered on the basis of their presumed difficulty.

To think about

Examine the subtraction word problems in two textbooks series. Compare the two series in relation to the teaching approaches used and the progression of difficulty.

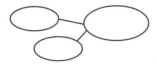

Addition: place quantities in the smaller ovals and combine them in the largest oval.

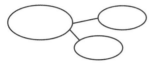

Subtraction: place a quantity in the largest oval and split them into the smaller ovals.

13.10 Diagrams for addition and subtraction

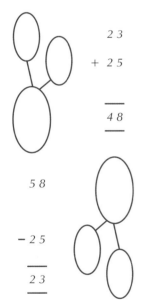

13.11 'Vertical' diagrams for addition and subtraction

selection of the numbers to use, rather than these being given by the teacher, because that might be interpreted as a request to calculate.

The generation of subtraction sentences through apparatus, diagrams and 'stories' can also be supplemented by the generation of number sentences by using the calculator. This is a context-free, meaningless way to arrive at the same numbers, and serves to emphasise that contexts are not necessary to decide the outcome (although that would of course be left implicit). The other advantage of calculators is that of speed and the consequent ease with which patterns can be created, which also help to enhance the child's growing understanding of subtraction in terms of the numbers that 'come up'.

Activities relating addition and subtraction

Emphasis in teaching should be on the relationship between addition and subtraction. Apparatus and models can reveal the inverse nature of the operations. In the number line, for example, addition goes 'up' where subtraction goes 'down' but otherwise the action is the same. With linking cubes or base 10 apparatus it is helpful to do work with the diagrams in Figure 13.10, making number sentences for addition and subtraction. In this case the inverse relationship is implied not at first by the numbers but by the diagrams – they are reflections of each other.

A further advantage of these diagrams is that, as the numbers are written to record the quantities in the circles below the circles to which they apply, they are in the correct arrangement of the number sentence – with only the words or symbols to insert. These diagrams also offer a painless way of showing children that the vertical presentation of addition and subtraction is 'just the same really', which has been known to trouble some children. By arranging the diagram at 90° (as in Figure 13.11), then writing the quantities down the side, the vertical calculation is shown.

Activities for subtraction by counting

Initially children's subtraction will be heavily based in counting. However, a developing awareness of the meaning of subtraction and the beginnings of numerical knowledge of subtraction facts should prompt other forms of mental calculation.

Subtraction within 10 is initially done by children putting all of the first number on the fingers, then counting off the second number, then counting what is left. For anything above ten the skill of counting back (see Module 3) can be used – that is, putting the first number 'in the head' and the second number on the fingers, and reciting backwards through the fingers to arrive at the answer. This method enables any subtraction to be calculated where the second number is 10 or less.

There are two alternative methods for extending the domain to include those where the difference is 10 or less, both of which require the additional skill of keeping track of how much is counted. For example, 23 – 19 can start at 23 and count back to 19 (rather than counting back 19 steps), with children keeping track of the number of steps, i.e. 4. Subtraction can also be done by counting on. To work out the answer to 23 – 19, start at 19 and count up to 23, keeping track of the number of steps taken.

In a way these two methods are parallel to the 'min' version of counting on, and can be taught readily to children. They are perhaps more in line with the 'difference' meaning of subtraction.

A sequence of development

The fact that mental methods for subtraction that rely wholly on counting are very limited can be illustrated by a sequence of development as increasing counting skills extend the range of subtractions which can be calculated using counting (see Table 13.2).

A sequence for using counting to subtract		
Counting stage	**Range of subtraction that can be calculated**	**Example**
Counting from 1	Subtraction within no more than 10	7 – 3 : hold up seven fingers and then put down three fingers
Counting on/back	Subtraction by no more than 10	15 – 8 : hold up eight fingers and then count back from fifteen 43 – 8 : hold up eight fingers. Start from 43 and count back. 29 – 11 : not enough fingers
Keeping track of how far counted	Subtraction with an outcome of no more than 10 (difference within 10)	15 – 8 : count up from eight to 15 (or down from 15 to 8), keeping track of how far 43 – 36 : count up from 36 to 43 (or down from 43 to 36), keeping track of how far 29 – 11 : not enough fingers
Counting in tens (with an ability to switch to ones when necessary)	Subtraction of numbers with a digit total no greater than 10 (e.g. 46 or 73)	53 – 34 : hold up three fingers and four fingers. Count down in tens from 53: 43 ... 33 ... 23. Switch to ones: 22 ... 21 ... 20 ... 19 75 – 38 : not enough fingers

Table 13.2

To do

Compare and contrast the sequence in Table 13.2 with that suggested in the FTM.

It is possible to see development in counting-based methods but, as with addition, there are always constraints based on the number of fingers that one can use. These constraints are absent when a number line, or base 10 apparatus, is available. Children can learn to use counting methods to subtract any numbers when such apparatus is there to help them, but this is not a productive avenue for development, as such equipment is not available outside the classroom. As in the final section of the table some children do learn to subtract larger numbers quite effectively using counting-based methods, by utilising an ability to count back in tens from any number, holding the quantity to be counted 'in their heads' rather than on their fingers. For example 83 – 47 may be answered as follows: 83 ... 73 ... 63 ... 53 ... 43 ... 42 ... 41 ... 40 ... 39 ... 38 ... 37 ... 36. This is, however, just one step away from a 'mental method' and most children who do this soon pass on to other non-counting-based approaches.

Activities for subtracting using non-counting methods

The standard written algorithms for subtraction, along with many mental methods for subtraction of larger numbers, need the child to be able to subtract mentally within 20 reasonably quickly. When working out 564 – 296 as its written form, for example, one part of the multi-step procedure involves subtracting 6 from 14, and in another part 9 from 15. If these are done by a counting process, children are likely to forget where they are in the overall procedure and go astray. The first and crucial step in learning to calculate subtraction properly is to become able to operate within 20 accurately and reasonably quickly. This is also helpful in extending their range of competence in mental methods (although in the case above they may indeed choose to operate differently, perhaps by adding 4 to each element and subtracting 300 from 568 – a mental 'equal additions' method!)

Subtraction within 20 using non-counting methods

Efficient subtraction occurs by inference based on knowledge. Initially the knowledge concerned is the addition knowledge described in Module 12. The first inference is that of subtraction facts in the same 'families'. In other words, children do not learn that 10 – 4 = 6; they learn that 6 + 4 = 10 and *infer* that 10 – 4 = 6. If this essential step is neglected only the high achievers in the class will make progress with subtraction, and their progress is based on having worked it out for themselves. To take all children to the standards of calculation in subtraction of which they are capable this fundamental inference must be taught, and reinforced over an extended period.

Inferences

The other inferences required for non-counting subtractions within 20 are those based on 'strategies' such as breaking numbers up into parts, and changing the elements of facts in principled ways, such as reducing both elements in a known subtraction by an equal amount to retain the same answer. There are:

- inferences based on adjustment from a known fact:

    '15 – 7 is 8 because 14 – 7 is 7 and 15 is one more'

- inferences based on making a parallel with a known fact:

    'for 15 – 7 add one to each is 16 – 8, which is 8'

- inferences based on breaking into parts and 'bridging' through 10:

    '15 – 7 is 5 down to 10 and a further 2 more is 8'.

These normally are not so well or widely done as inferences in equivalent addition facts, presumably because the subtraction facts on which they are based have themselves to be inferred.

A good context for the development of strategies is in group sessions in which the methods used by children are discussed by them, elaborated and symbolised by the teacher and tried out in an atmosphere of shared endeavour and exploration. The direct teaching of strategies also has its place, perhaps using a strategy diagram as in Figure 13.12.

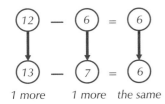

13.12 *Raising a strategy to the 'surface'*

189

Activities for subtracting over 20

For calculations with larger numbers there is a written procedure, based on the advantages of a place value system for numbers. Mental methods can also be extended to be effective with larger numbers.

Mental methods

The methods used for subtraction calculations of larger numbers mentally are parallel to those used for smaller numbers, although with the additional element in most cases of place value knowledge. They involve using knowledge and inference in strategies involving breaking numbers up into parts and dealing with the parts separately, and also working with numbers near to the numbers in the calculation which are easier to handle, and then making adjustments to arrive at the required answer. Again there is surprising diversity in children's methods.

Teaching mental strategies for subtraction

Some children calculate subtraction mentally by creating a mental image of a calculation and operating on it in the standard column by column fashion, mentally 'writing' answers and carry figures. Others use counting-based methods, some of which can be very effective. However, the mental methods of most children for subtraction involve inference from knowledge.

The most appropriate approach is to complement work on extending factual knowledge through patterns and games, and continued work on place value using base 10 apparatus, number lines and calculators, with opportunities to show and discuss the children's approaches to problems (with suggestions from the teacher when appropriate) – in other words an extension of the approach to teaching mental calculation of subtraction within 20.

Also it is reasonable, on occasion, to teach specific strategies, perhaps in connection with dealing with specific situations. For example one can teach the strategy of adjusting to halves, when the numbers are approximately half: seeing 52 – 27 as being close to 50 – 25; seeing 91 – 46 as being close to 90 – 45, etc. However, this approach has its limits because the number of possible calculations is too great, and all such strategies depend on knowledge which may or may not be present for the individual learner.

Written methods

Both decomposition and equal addition require that the number to be subtracted is placed below the number from which it is to be subtracted, with the 'columns' lined up on place value criteria. For subtraction with smaller numbers there is no point in a 'vertical' arrangement.

Column by column subtraction is straightforward enough as long as the digit at the bottom is smaller than the digit at the top. Difficulties with the subtraction procedure occur when the digit at the bottom is larger than the digit above it. Children do not find this procedure easy, as indicated by the range of errors which are made.

To do

Use base 10 materials to model decomposition, with a colleague acting as 'child'. For example, try 53 – 26; 136 – 63. As well as what you do with the apparatus, consider carefully what you would say, and how you would draw the child's attention to the various elements of the written procedure.

ROBERT'S METHOD

Robert, who was 7, was asked to work out 16 − 7. He did not do it mentally, but wrote it in a vertical format. This is what he wrote.

$$\begin{array}{r} \not{1}^{1}6 \\ -\quad 7 \\ \hline 9 \end{array}$$

Robert described what he did. '7 from 6 you can't do, so borrow a ten. 7 from 16 is 9'. Robert seemed unaware that he was now working with the same subtraction he had started with. How would you help Robert?

Success in teaching the standard written methods of subtraction comes from a greater investment of time, from the beginning, to attach meaning to the steps and elements of the procedure, so that the children are more likely to remember it. In the subtraction of 35 from 62, using decomposition, it is not just 'Cross out the six, and put a five, then write a one next to the two': 62 is *transformed* into 50 and 12, so as to have enough 'ones' to subtract 5. It is helpful to demonstrate why and how the written procedure operates by modelling it using base 10 apparatus. This approach is not to show the children how to work out the answer using apparatus, but to show what the marks on paper represent, and why they are made. It is essential therefore to have the written version 'unfolding' alongside the actions with the material.

Note that this can be done *either* with 53 made up using apparatus and 26 taken away from it ('There is not enough here to take 6 away') *or* with both 53 and 26 made up using the materials and a comparison made, corresponding with the two most common meanings of subtraction – reducing or diminishing a quantity on the one hand, and comparing or difference on the other. One can argue that the 'take away' meaning gives the clearer demonstration of the procedure, but if the child is doing a calculation to answer a difference problem it may be helpful to have a difference demonstration as well.

An example of demonstrating the subtraction algorithm by 'ghosting' the written changes can be found in Resnick and Ford (1981), also shown in Hughes (1986). You might compare what you did with this, and you may well feel that your approach is better, or at the very least that your use of language is more appropriate to your children.

To do

It is also possible to make the 'equal additions' procedure meaningful by demonstration. Demonstrate to a partner the 'equal additions' procedure for one or two subtraction problems, using base 10 materials.

To think about

Talk with some other adults about the language they remember from their schooling to refer to the subtraction algorithms, and make a list. Most of the metaphoric language arises in a futile attempt to make the procedure memorable, and not much of it is even half-way meaningful – nevertheless one has to say *something*. Which of the forms of language would you favour? What alternatives can you propose?

When making such demonstrations, or otherwise when talking to children about the written procedures, it is common for metaphors to be made in order to try to help the children make sense. Hence 'borrow' and 'pay back', 'one on the doorstep' and more.

The 'demonstration' approach requires children to practise the written procedure, and at this point it is *vital* that the apparatus is removed. If children have access to the apparatus they will learn a way to use it to get the answers; they will not 'ghost' the written algorithm. Although you will feel sympathy for them, and want to give them help, this should not involve giving them apparatus to answer subtraction problems. The value of the apparatus is to bring meaning to the procedure, not to enable children to calculate. An alternative approach would, in such circumstances, allow children to use the apparatus again until they felt confident to move back to using only written symbols.

Once children have reasonable mastery of a written method for subtraction, further practice should be given for subtraction calculations in a range of contexts, such as measurement-related subtractions, practical problems, games, parts of computer simulations and puzzles.

Informal methods

It is common to treat subtraction calculation just as a matter of learning the 'standard' algorithm and the knowledge that supports it (subtraction facts to 20 and place value facts), but time spent developing children's own 'made up' methods to work out answers (known as informal methods) can be very helpful.

To do

Design a game in which subtraction calculations are required – preferably one which can be played at different 'levels' of calculation demand.

Children's informal methods are usually a blend of mental methods, which they write down to help them to remember, and simple written calculations, the ones that they are comfortable with. For this reason they are sometimes known as 'hybrid' methods and sometimes 'idiosyncratic' methods.

IDIOSYNCRATIC SUBTRACTIONS

Here are three methods used by some 11 year old children to answer the problem 483 – 127.

400	80	$5\cancel{6}^{1}3$	
−100	−20	− 7	
300	60	5 6	356

127 + 3 = 130
130 + 70 = 200
200   283
356

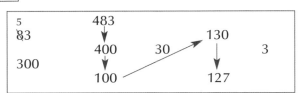

Analyse each method to decide what thinking was involved. How would you proceed with each child in order to make their method more efficient?

Working with children on their invented methods offers a springboard for developing mental work, and a reference point for making the standard method (or algorithm) meaningful. It is even plausible as a teaching style to start with each individual child's invented written method, and gradually to refine it to become the standard approach (echoing in the history of the individual the history of the mathematics).

Estimating and approximating

A further aspect of mental and informal methods is approximate calculation, or calculations through rounding. When faced with a problem such as 703 – 296 it is reasonable to argue that, as 703 is approximately 700 and 296 is approximately 300, the answer is approximately 400. It is further possible in this case to say that the answer is more than 400, as the larger number was rounded down and the smaller was rounded up. The next level of refinement is to conclude that the answer is between 400 and 420, as each element was rounded by less than 10 – and of course by this stage one is almost at the point of working out the exact answer.

A class activity

OBJECTIVE   To practise mental subtraction

ORGANISATION   Whole class

RESOURCES   Each child has two sets of number cards 0–9. The teacher has a large 100-number grid

ACTIVITY
- The teacher points to two numbers on the 100-number grid.
- Everyone calculates the difference and holds up two of their cards to show their answer.
- Children are selected to explain how they worked it out.

A group activity

OBJECTIVE   To work with difference

ORGANISATION   Groups of three or four

RESOURCES   Each group has four sets of 0 to 9 numbers cards

ACTIVITY
- One child, acting as dealer and player, shuffles all 40 cards and deals each of the players four cards.
- The dealer then challenges the players to use their four cards to make one of the following: the largest even difference, the smallest even difference, the largest odd difference, the smallest odd difference using two two-digit numbers.
- The game can be extended to three-digit and four-digit numbers – when each player will need six or eight cards.

193

Test your own knowledge: subtraction

1 Work out 371 – 195 mentally. Now try 4723– 2488. Now try 59 416 – 32 747. Try a six-digit subtraction. Check your answers by addition to the appropriate number.

2 Find as many solutions as you can, if they exist, for AB – BA = BC, where the same letter represents the same digit.

3 The subtraction 918 – 542 = 376, uses the digits 1–9 once and once only. There are at least seven more like this. Can you find some of them?

4 Use five 1s to make a subtraction with 100 as the answer.

5 How many different solutions can you find for ☐☐9 – ☐☐3 = 96

6 The number 27 reverses the order of the digits of the number 52 if you subtract the 27 from 52 (52 – 27 = 25). The number 27 acts as a reverser for five other two-digit numbers. Which are they? What is special about the six numbers? Can you find any other two-digit reversers?

7 In the following two subtractions the digits are reversed and the numbers reversed: 41 – 37 = 4 and 73 – 14 = 59. Find other pairs of numbers with a difference of 4, which, when their digits are reversed, have a difference of 59.

Review of key points ➤

➤ Learning about subtraction is a combination of understanding and knowledge

➤ In order for subtraction to be a useful skill it must be meaningful, in terms of what subtraction means, how it relates to real situations, and how the methods used to calculate answers are understood

➤ There are four different meanings for subtraction: splitting, reducing, comparing and change position up, as well as subtraction as the inverse of addition

➤ It is important that children are able to associate the language and symbols used in subtraction with the perceptions and actions they perform with materials and models

➤ Apparatus can be used to illustrate the meaning of subtraction and to demonstrate how subtraction algorithms work

➤ There is a danger that using apparatus inappropriately creates dependency and prevents learning

➤ Mental subtraction methods are based upon awareness of the place value system, knowledge of subtraction facts and inferences

Module 14   Learning to teach multiplication

Introduction

It is often assumed that children readily make the step from addition to multiplication as multiplication is viewed as a natural extension to addition. This expectation has an element of truth; however, when learning about multiplication children meet an unfamiliar set of number interpretations. Children are also misled by their early experiences in multiplication, which are mostly limited to whole numbers. The exposure only to whole-number situations suggests to children that multiplication always gives 'larger' answers, contrary to that which occurs when the numbers involved are fractions or decimals less than 1.

Multiplication in national curricula

Primary mathematics curricula devote considerable time in developing the concept and operation of multiplication. The following aspects appear prominently:

- understanding the operation of multiplication, including its commutative, associative and distributive properties
- using and applying multiplication, particularly in problem solving situations
- learning multiplication tables and facts to 10×10 for rapid recall
- developing a variety of mental methods with manageable numbers
- developing flexible, efficient and effective written methods
- understanding how to multiply by powers of 10
- understanding the ideas of product, multiple and factor.

Key terms

multiplication	a mathematical operation performed on two numbers, usually the numerical result of combining sets which contain the same number of objects, or by scaling a number by a factor
the '×' sign	'×' between two numbers, e.g. 3×6, indicates that one number is multiplied by the other. It is read as 'multiplied by' although often read as 'times' by children
multiplicand	the first number in a multiplication
multiplier	the second number in a multiplication
product	the numerical result of multiplication. Thus, 3 (multiplicand) $\times$ 6 (multiplier) $= 18$ (product)
multiple	the product of two numbers is also known as a multiple of both numbers. As 18 is the product of 3 and 6, 18 is a multiple of both 3 and 6
factor	the numbers in a multiplication are known as factors of the product. Thus, as $3 \times 6 = 18$, 3 and 6 are factors of 18

Key issues in multiplication

Related concepts and issues

Figure 14.1 provides an overview of the related concepts and issues which contribute to the development of the concept of multiplication.

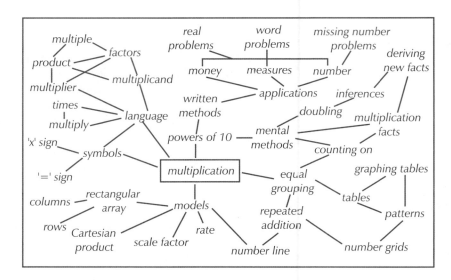

14.1 Concepts and issues associated with multiplication

Children learning about multiplication

It is natural for children to use their existing knowledge in new situations. They make sense of unfamiliar experiences involving multiplication by resorting to counting and addition. Often the numbers used in early multiplication tasks are relatively small and suggest to children that the process of counting is an appropriate method to find an answer, particularly when pictures are provided to help children understand the situation. Children are also encouraged to model a problem using materials such as counters or cubes, which themselves stimulate a counting response. An important target in teaching multiplication is to wean children from counting and adding to using multiplication when it is fitting to do so.

The concept of multiplication

The concept of multiplication is more than a quicker, but more complex, way of doing addition. Understanding multiplication demands a qualitative and meaningful modification in children's thinking from addition. Problem situations in which multiplication arises are different from addition situations as the action of joining, where appropriate, always involves equivalent sets that are of the same nature. When children use additive reasoning the numbers quantify what is in the sets and are not necessarily equivalent. Multiplicative reasoning is more complex in that the two sets are likely to be different in nature and cannot be physically joined to make any sense. Thus two ducks and three ducks when joined produce five ducks, but three bikes each with two wheels does not produce five bike-wheels!

In the multiplication situation with the three bikes there is a one-to-many correspondence or ratio between the set of bikes and the set of wheels, each bike has two wheels – a 1 to 2 correspondence. The 'two wheels' is a collective or composite unit, or grouping, with the number of bikes acting as a counter of the number of these units. The 1 to 2 correspondence is an invariant of the situation which is not present in additive reasoning. In multiplication the action of joining more bikes to the set of bikes is a replication of the 1 to 2 correspondence. Multiplication would no longer be appropriate if a bike having three wheels was put with the other bikes. When the replication is sustained the 1 to 2 ratio remains constant between the number of bikes and the number of wheels. This ratio is sometimes referred to as a scale factor, which is neither bikes nor wheels but a mathematical measure of the multiplicative situation. This measure in different ways is common to all six meanings of multiplication.

Meanings of multiplication

It is generally accepted that there are six different meanings of multiplication:

- equal grouping
- rectangular array
- number line
- Cartesian product
- scale factor or enlargement
- rate.

There is little agreement on the order in which the meanings or models should be introduced to children, although both Hervey (1966) and Brown (1981a) showed that the Cartesian product model is more difficult than those involving aspects of repeated addition. In practice, equal grouping is the model children first encounter in the classroom, as it is considered to be the natural extension of addition.

Equal grouping

Children's early experiences with multiplication involve the physical modelling of situations such as 'There are three vases. Each vase has two flowers. How many flowers are there altogether?' Children develop an awareness of this type of problem by putting out objects to match that described. In Figure 14.2a flowers have been equally grouped into 2s using vases to collect each group of two. Thus the three vases is the number of groups of two flowers, making six flowers in total. This model is often referred to as the 'repeated addition' model as children can find the total number of flowers by repeatedly adding the number in each vase.

(a)

6 groups of 2 with 1 over

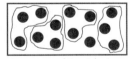

4 groups of 3 with 1 over

3 groups of 4 with 1 over

(b)

14.2 Repeated grouping

Only one level of abstraction is involved when children perform addition as each set, even when the two sets are equivalent, is perceived as comprising 'ones'. In contrast, multiplication requires understanding of the number of ones in each group and the number of groups, units of units. This idea of grouping or 'collective unit' is fundamental to multiplication. The emphasis in multiplication is mainly on equivalent sets and the number of such sets. These notions need to be carefully developed before the concept of multiplication is introduced. The action of grouping using a different size of group on the same (identical) set is an important prelude to the higher order thinking that multiplication demands. The identical sets in Figure 14.2b have been grouped using three different-sized units. When recorded in symbols we have $6(2) + 1 = 13$, $4(3) + 1 = 13$, and $3(4) + 1 = 13$. This leads to the equivalence of two mathematical statements or sentences such as $6(2) + 1 = 4(3) + 1$.

There exist many examples of collective units in real life that are helpful in developing the concept for multiplication purposes. Children have two arms, two legs, two eyes, two ears; there are three wheels on a trike, three legs on some types of stool; there are four wheels on a car, four legs on a dog; five fingers on a hand; six legs on a beetle; seven days in a week; eight legs on a spider. Such examples provide pictorial representations of a natural collective unit or grouping that has meaning for children as can nursery rhymes and finger plays.

Rectangular array

When objects are displayed in rows and columns a rectangular array is formed. The product of the number of rows and the number of columns is the number of objects in the array. In Figure 14.3a all three numbers (2, 3 and 6) in the multiplication $2 \times 3 = 6$ refer to cans, and in Figure 14.3b all the numbers (4, 5 and 20) refer to spots. This differs from grouping in Figure 14.2a where two types of objects were involved, vases and flowers.

Number track and number line

Jumps on stepping stones, number tracks and number lines (see Figure 14.4), is a popular method used by textbooks to model multiplication. In these models the first number refers to the number of jumps made, the second number is the size of every jump and the product is the total amount of the jumps.

Cartesian product

A Cartesian or cross product is formed when two sets of objects are combined to produce as many different pairs as possible. A typical Cartesian product problem involves the number of outfits that can be made combining two different-coloured pairs of shorts with three different-coloured shirts. In Figure 14.5 six lines (2 shorts by 3 shirts) are used to signify the possible pairings or outfits. The three numbers involved (2, 3 and 6) all refer to different ideas: 2 is the number of shorts, 3 the number of shirts and the product, 6, the number of outfits.

Scale factor

If Jenny has two chews and Robby has three times as many as Jenny,

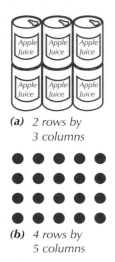

(a) 2 rows by
3 columns

(b) 4 rows by
5 columns

14.3 *Multiplication as rectangular arrays*

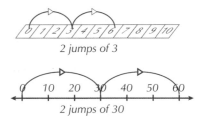

2 jumps of 3

2 jumps of 30

14.4 *Modelling multiplication on a number line*

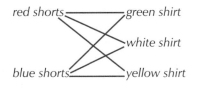

14.5 *Modelling multiplication as a cross product*

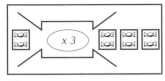

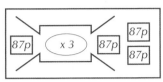

14.6 *Modelling multiplication as a scale factor*

To think about

How aware are you of the language you use? Discuss with colleagues the language each of you uses to say 7 × 9. What alternative ways are there of saying 7 × 9? Compile a list of the difficulties that each expression may cause children. In what ways does the language used reflect children's perceptions and actions when multiplying?

(a)   *three lots of four*

(b)   *four lots of three*

14.7 *3 × 4 or 4 × 3?*

To think about

Analyse some textbooks to find how they introduce multiplication language and symbolism. Are they consistent in their usage?

then he has six chews. This can be recorded as 3 × 2 chews = 6 chews. The '3 times' is a scale factor or 'enlargement' acting on the number of chews that Jenny has. In this example the answer is also a number of chews. A function machine is often used to illustrate the idea of enlargement (see Figure 14.6a). The input to the machine is 2 chews and the output is 3 lots of 2 chews, giving 6 chews.

Rate

The 'rate' model of multiplication is closely allied to the concept of ratio (see Module 7). It is, however, very much an everyday occurrence in shopping where the cost of an item may be stated in terms of a unit quantity. Thus a bar of chocolate may cost 87p and to find the cost of more than one bar a multiplier, given by the number of bars purchased, is used. Thus three bars cost 87p × 3 = 261p. A function machine (see Figure 14.6b) can also be used to support children's understanding of this type of multiplication.

Language and symbolism

Knowledge and understanding of the language and symbols associated with multiplication are crucial aspects of a child's ability to use and apply the operation successfully.

Each of the six models, outlined earlier, has its own peculiar language. Before the introduction of the multiplication sign children, both in everyday life and in the classroom, hear equivalent expressions such as three fours, three lots of four, three times four, three sets of four, three groups of four. These expressions are not perceived by children as being the same as four threes, four lots of three, four times three, four groups of three. The two sets of expressions are modelled diagrammatically in Figure 14.7.

The order of the number names in the expressions is particularly important. In Figure 14.7a 'three' comes first, describing the number of sets or groups; the 'four', coming second, refers to the number of mice in each set. Figure 14.7b sees the order of the number names reversed. Unfortunately, there are two other ways used to express the two different situations, both of which cause children difficulties. These are 'four three times' and 'three four times'. Which refers to which of the two situations?

It appears natural when notation is introduced to children that the order of the number names should be retained. This is the case if the sequence of development is as follows:

three lots of four → 3(4) → 3 × 4 → 3 multiplied by 4

Many textbooks do not adopt this 'obvious' order of development. Instead we find this apparently contradictory approach:

three lots of four → 3(4) → 4 × 3 → 4 multiplied by 3

Why does the order of the two numbers change from 3(4) to 4 × 3? It is mathematically correct to interpret 4 × 3 (4 multiplied by 3) as 4 three times (3 lots of 4), as it agrees with the function of the multiplier 3. Literally, this means that the multiplicand has an existence before the multiplier comes along to operate on it.

Multiplication by a power of 10

Multiplication of numbers greater than 10 by a single-digit number requires a knowledge of how to multiply by powers of 10, that is by 10, 100, 1000, ... Many errors in learning to multiply large numbers occur because of a lack of understanding of what happens to a number when it is multiplied by 10 or by other powers of 10. In Module 5 it was stressed that the popular rule for multiplying by 10, 'add a nought', is not only inappropriate but is the cause of future errors. The following explanation is one you may wish to use instead.

When a single-digit number is multiplied by 10 two important mathematical changes take place:

- the position of the digit moves from representing *ones* to representing *tens*
- the ones position vacated by the single digit is filled by a 0.

The changes are illustrated in Figure 14.8a. When a single-digit number is multiplied by 100 three important mathematical changes take place:

- the position of the digit moves from representing *ones* to representing *hundreds*
- the *ones* position vacated by the single digit is filled by a 0
- the empty *tens* position is filled by a 0.

The changes are illustrated in Figure 14.8b.

The relationship between a number and its products when multiplied by powers of 10 is an important feature of children's mental strategies. Knowledge of a multiplication fact combined with the associative law enables related facts to be derived based upon multiplying by a power of 10. For example, $2 \times 3 = 6$ leads to the following: $2 \times 30 = 2 \times 3 \times 10 = 60$, $20 \times 3 = 60$, $2 \times 300 = 600$, and so on.

Multiplication of decimals

Multiplication of a decimal by a whole number is frequently taught using the short multiplication algorithm with the decimal point being written in the answer box directly below its position in the multiplicand. This can create a mind set in children which then interferes with other algorithms that they might be taught when multiplying decimals. It is helpful if children are introduced to one algorithm that is applicable to multiplication of decimals, whatever the numbers involved. A prerequisite for understanding the following is division of a number by a power of 10.

An approximation of $4 \times 3 = 12$ would suggest that the answer 10.26 is in an acceptable region, but does not guarantee its accuracy.

A possible method of setting out the algorithm in a vertical format relating it to an equivalent 'whole number' algorithm is shown below.

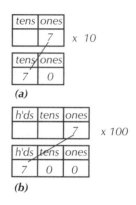

14.8 Multiplication by powers of 10

To think about

Describe the changes when a number is multiplied by 1000, 10000, ... Write a general statement to describe what happens when a number is multiplied by 10^n.

To do

Explain to a colleague how this example works.
$3.8 \times 2.7 = (38 \div 10) \times (27 \div 10) = (38 \times 27) \div 10 \div 10 = 1026 \div 10 \div 10 = 10.26$.
What would you do if a child wrote $(38 \times 27) \div 10 \div 10$ as $1026 \div 1$?

To do

Make up a decimal multiplication for yourself and write out the equivalent 'whole number' algorithm.

$$
\begin{array}{r}
3.8 \\
\times \ \underline{2.7}
\end{array}
\longrightarrow
\begin{array}{r}
38 \div 10 \\
\times \ \underline{27} \div 10 \\
266 \\
\underline{760} \\
\end{array}
$$

$$10.26 \longleftarrow \underline{1026} \div 100$$

Counting on

Counting begins with recitation of the counting sequence 1, 2, 3, 4, ..., 10. It progresses by counting on in steps of 2, 3, ..., 10, and later to other numbers such as 20, 50, 100, and 1000. The activity of counting on and back with a start number of 0 is a precursor to learning multiplication tables and facts. The importance of this kind of mental and oral activity cannot be over-estimated and it is recommended as daily practice in all primary classes.

Oral activities are frequently translated into written activities with sequences on number tracks, grids and lines, with children extending a sequence forward and backward, as well as writing in missing numbers. In this way children become familiar with products which they later meet in the multiplication tables.

Learning multiplication tables and facts

Most primary curricula require that children should know their multiplication facts up to 10×10. This requirement exceeds the demand that they should know the multiplication tables. If a child, when asked 'What is the answer to 8×9?', responds by saying an appropriate table he or she is not exhibiting knowledge of the multiplication fact $8 \times 9 = 72$. The FTM (National Numeracy Strategy 1999) says that 'numerate primary pupils' should 'know by heart all facts to 10×10.' The aim, therefore, should be for children to respond to a multiplication question up to 10×10 by recalling the answer directly from memory as well as knowing their tables. This implies that the teaching of tables is only a step towards developing the ability to rapidly recall any multiplication fact.

Multiplication tables up to 10×10 are easily extended to include multiples of 10. For example, because of the place value system it follows that, as $3 \times 2 = 6$, then $30 \times 2 = 60$, $300 \times 2 = 600$, and so on. Once children are confident with their tables they are in a position to 'say' the extended tables, such as $10 \times 2 = 20$, $20 \times 2 = 40$, $30 \times 2 = 60$, ..., $90 \times 2 = 180$, $100 \times 2 = 200$.

Building up tables

A crucial distinction needs to be made between what is known, for example, as the 'table of 3s' and the '3 times table' (Figure 14.9). The table of 3s collects together sets that have a cardinality of 3, whereas the 3 times table is about the total number in three sets. Some textbooks fail to establish the difference between the two equivalent ideas, table of 3s and 3 times table, often confusing the two.

There is no established order, based upon research evidence, for teaching the tables 0 to 10.

However, there is common agreement that the process of learning tables should begin with children building up a table using concrete apparatus, such as cubes or rods, moving on to pictorial representation before symbolising the two types of table and finally practising the tables both in written and oral forms (which may include repetition by 'chanting'). The example of the 2s is shown Figure 14.10.

To think about

Analyse the teachers' guide of a textbook series for suggestions of counting on and counting back activities.

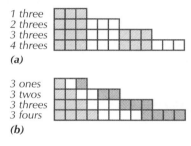

1 three
2 threes
3 threes
4 threes
(a)

3 ones
3 twos
3 threes
3 fours
(b)

14.9 Building up tables using squared paper

To think about

Analyse some textbook series to see if they make the distinction between the two types of table.

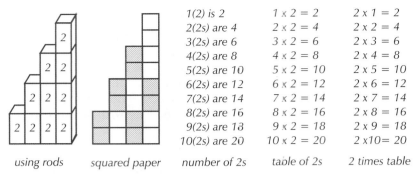

using rods	squared paper	number of 2s	table of 2s	2 times table
		1(2) is 2	1 x 2 = 2	2 x 1 = 2
		2(2s) are 4	2 x 2 = 4	2 x 2 = 4
		3(2s) are 6	3 x 2 = 6	2 x 3 = 6
		4(2s) are 8	4 x 2 = 8	2 x 4 = 8
		5(2s) are 10	5 x 2 = 10	2 x 5 = 10
		6(2s) are 12	6 x 2 = 12	2 x 6 = 12
		7(2s) are 14	7 x 2 = 14	2 x 7 = 14
		8(2s) are 16	8 x 2 = 16	2 x 8 = 16
		9(2s) are 18	9 x 2 = 18	2 x 9 = 18
		10(2s) are 20	10 x 2 = 20	2 x10= 20

14.10 *A variety of ways of representing collections of 2s*

Relationships between tables

Children seldom consciously observe the relationships that exist between the different tables. Most such relationships exist because of the distributive law of multiplication over addition. For example, the 5 times table can be formed by adding the 2 times and the 3 times tables as $2 + 3 = 5$. Hence, $6 \times 5 = 6 \times (2 + 3) = (6 \times 2) + (6 \times 3)$. In the case where a table number can be partitioned into the same two numbers the relationship is viewed as a doubling. This occurs when the 6 times table is derived from knowledge of the 3 times table, as shown in Table 14.1.

To do

Make a list of the different orders in which tables are introduced in different textbooks. Write a short paragraph on the order you would adopt, justifying your decision.

Relating the 3 times and 6 times tables

$3 \times 1 = 3$	double 3 = 6	$6 \times 1 = 6$
$3 \times 2 = 6$	double 6 = 12	$6 \times 2 = 12$
$3 \times 3 = 9$	double 9 = 18	$6 \times 3 = 18$
$3 \times 4 = 12$	double 12 = 24	$6 \times 4 = 24$

Table 14.1

If the distributive law of multiplication over subtraction is applied then the 9 times table can be quickly derived from the 10 times table minus the 1 times table, as in Table 14.2.

To do

Make a list of the advantages and disadvantages of a whole class chanting tables together. How could you organise a class to make chanting of tables efficient for rapid recall of facts?

Deriving the 9 times table from the 10 times table

$$9 \times 1 = 10 - 1 = 9$$
$$9 \times 2 = 20 - 2 = 18$$
$$9 \times 3 = 30 - 3 = 27$$
$$9 \times 4 = 40 - 4 = 36$$

Table 14.2

The 'higher' tables such as the 7s and the 9s are more likely to be taught later than the 'lower' tables such as the 2s and the 3s. This can lead to children practising the 'easier' tables more often than the more difficult ones. Teachers must guard against the danger of not practising sufficiently the 7, 8 and 9 times tables as they are the ones that require greater frequency of practice.

Multiplication facts

Multiplication facts exist independently of the tables. There are 121 facts to be learned from 0×0 to 10×10. This appears to be a formidable number, placing great demands on children's long-term memory for rapid recall of every fact. This assumes, however, that each fact is treated individually and unrelated to any other fact. Table 14.3 shows each fact with a category label A to G. These categories are described below. Many products fall into more than one category with categories not listed if a fact has already been shown as in a previous category.

A there are 21 facts involving 0, which are generalisable as $N \times 0 = 0 \times N = 0$

B there are 19 facts involving 1, which are generalisable as $N \times 1 = 1 \times N = N$

C there are 17 facts involving 2, which can be calculated using doubling as $N \times 2 = 2 \times N =$ double N

D there are 15 facts involving 10, which are generalisable as multiples of 10

E there are 13 facts involving 5, which are generalisable as $10 \times N$ or $N \times 10$ and halving

F there are 11 facts involving 9, which are generalisable as $(10 \times N) - N$, or $(N \times 10) - N$

G there are 5 facts that are square numbers i.e. $N \times N$.

Categorising multiplication facts

x	0	1	2	3	4	5	6	7	8	9	10
0	A	A	A	A	A	A	A	A	A	A	A
1	A	B	B	B	B	B	B	B	B	B	B
2	A	B	C	C	C	C	C	C	C	C	C
3	A	B	C	G		E				F	D
4	A	B	C		G	E				F	D
5	A	B	C	E	E	E	E	E	E	E	D
6	A	B	C			E	G			F	D
7	A	B	C			E		G		F	D
8	A	B	C			E			G	F	D
9	A	B	C	F	F	E	F	F	F	F	D
10	A	B	C	D	D	D	D	D	D	D	D

Table 14.3

To think about

Describe to a colleague at least two different ways of deriving each of the 20 missing products in Table 14.3 and explain the mathematical ideas you have used.

Twenty products are left which do not fit into any of the categories A–G. Using the commutative law the number to be learned can be halved to 10. These can be derived from close known products, or by doubling other known products.

The use of a few rules based upon the understanding of relationships, together with the derivation of facts from known facts, considerably decreases the memory demand of the multiplication facts for children. This cannot occur, however, unless opportunities are provided for children to explore, discuss, record, and explain the relationships between facts and to practise the learning of the 121 multiplication facts in relevant and meaningful contexts.

Patterns in multiplication tables

The structure of the number system is nowhere more apparent than in the patterns in multiplication tables. The value in children investigating patterns in different tables and describing and explaining the reasons for the patterns should not be underestimated in relation to the contribution such activities make towards children's understanding of mathematics (see Module 17). The patterns manifest themselves in three forms: through the use of apparatus, pictures and diagrams, and in the symbols themselves. We concentrate on diagrammatic and symbolic representations, considering:

- the 100-number grid
- patterns in the unit digits
- graphing tables
- multiples.

The 100-number grid

A 100-number grid is, perhaps, the most widely used method for representing pattern in tables and can be seen displayed on many primary classroom walls. Children's first experience of working with a 100-number grid occurs when they shade in number squares after counting on in a given number, say in 9s. Unfortunately, opportunities for children to develop their understanding of the mathematics behind the patterns on the 100 grid are often ignored. Figure 14.11 shows the pattern resulting from shading the products in the 9 times table.

To do

Make a poster of the different multiplication patterns on 100-number grids.

The right-to-left diagonal pattern always fascinates children. But why does the pattern have this 'shape'? That is the question that a teacher must ask and have the mathematical knowledge to provide an explanation that the children can understand. The 100 grid is constructed with 10 numbers in each row. Thus a movement downward from a number in a row to the number below in the next row is an 'add 10' movement. Similarly, a movement to the left is a 'subtract 1' movement. Combining an 'add 10' with an 'subtract 1' produces an 'add 9', which corresponds to an increase in 9 in each successive number in the 9 times table. This is equivalent to deriving the 9 times table from knowledge of the 10 times table (described earlier).

1	2	3	4	5	6	7	8	9	10
11	12	13	14	15	16	17	18	19	20
21	22	23	24	25	26	27	28	29	30
31	32	33	34	35	36	37	38	39	40
41	42	43	44	45	46	47	48	49	50
51	52	53	54	55	56	57	58	59	60
61	62	63	64	65	66	67	68	69	70
71	72	73	74	75	76	77	78	79	80
81	82	83	84	85	86	87	88	89	90
91	92	93	94	95	96	97	98	99	100

14.11 The 9 times table pattern on the 100-number grid

Patterns in the unit digits

Patterns exist in the unit digits of each of the tables and again the reasons for the patterns emphasise the structure of the number system. The pattern in the unit digits for the extended 3 times table are highlighted in Table 14.4.

To think about

The unit digits of the 3 times table numbers are cyclic in that the sequence of digits 3, 6, 9, 2, 5, 8, 1, 4, 7, 0 repeats itself. Will the sequence repeat itself forever if the table is extended? Can you prove it? All ten digits are used in the cycle. Why is this?

Pattern of the unit digits in the 3 times table																
3 times table	3	6	9	12	15	18	21	24	27	30	33	36	39	42	45	48	51
unit digits	3	6	9	2	5	8	1	4	7	0	3	6	9	2	5	8	1

Table 14.4

To do

Make a large poster for display in a classroom of the cyclic patterns of the unit digits in each of the tables 1 to 10. Write about the relationships between the different unit digit patterns and explain why they occur.

As the pattern is cyclic it can be represented on a circular number line producing an interesting visual pattern (see Figure 14.12). Young children construct the pattern in curve stitching activities using coloured thread.

Graphing tables

Each multiplication table, say the table of 3s, is a relationship between multiplicand (the number of 3s) and the product, where the multiplier (the number 3) is a constant. This relationship can be represented on a Cartesian graph. The tables from 1 to 10 are shown in Figure 14.13.

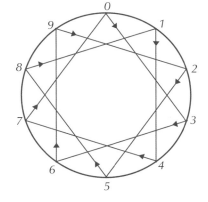

14.12 The unit digit pattern of the 3 times table

205

To do

Draw the graphs of the tables 1 to 10. How could you use the graphs to teach children to multiply fractions and decimals by whole numbers?

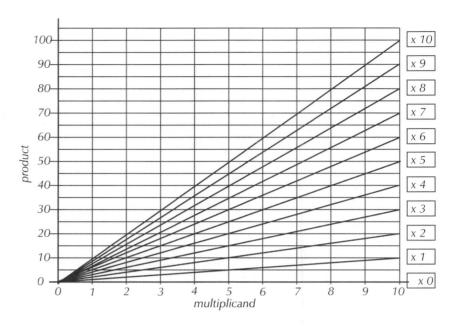

14.13 Graphs of the 0 to 10 times tables

Multiples

Every whole number is the product in at least one multiplication table. A listing of the tables to which each whole number 'belongs' provides another insight into the structure of the tables and highlights the nature of prime numbers. Space allows Table 14.5 to be shown only for the whole numbers to 10 and for tables up to 10. Thus, the number of times a multiple occurs in the tables is shown only for numbers up to 10. Extension, taking into account tables beyond 10 and numbers larger than 10, is left to the reader.

Products to be found in multiplication tables

Whole number	Table of										Number of times the product occurs
	1s	2s	3s	4s	5s	6s	7s	8s	9s	10s	
1	1 × 1										1
2	2 × 1	1 × 2									2
3	3 × 1		1 × 3								2
4	4 × 1	2 × 2		1 × 4							3
5	5 × 1				1 × 5						2
6	6 × 1	3 × 2	2 × 3			1 × 6					4
7	7 × 1						1 × 7				2
8	8 × 1	4 × 2		2 × 4				1 × 8			4
9	9 × 1		3 × 3						1 × 9		3
10	10 × 1	5 × 2			2 × 5					1 × 10	4

Table 14.5

To think about

Complete the 'number of times a product occurs' to 20. What is special about the products that are 2 times? What is special about the products that occur an odd number of times?

Numbers can be sorted into sets according to the tables to which they belong. This may be illustrated using Venn diagrams (Figure 14.14a), or Carroll (matrix) diagrams (Figure 14.14b).

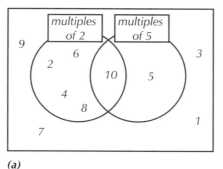

(a)   *(b)*

14.14 Sorting multiples

Mental methods of computation

National curricula place great emphasis on mental methods, including deriving new results from known facts. We have already considered how doubling can enable some table facts to be derived from other table facts.

MENTAL MULTIPLICATION

Threlfall and Frobisher (1998b) asked some primary school children to calculate mentally a series of multiplications. A 9 year old calculated 76 × 2, saying '70 times 2 is 140, then 6 times 2 is 12, making 152', making obvious use of the distributive law of multiplication over addition. Another 9 year old responded to 'What is 59 × 2?' by saying, '59 is nearly 60, so I added 60 and 60 which made 120, then I took away 2 to make 118.' This child transformed the problem to one which she could handle and then adjusted the answer. A similar approach was used by an 11 year old who, when asked for the answer to 0.96 × 2, said 'Two ones are 2. I then subtracted 0.04 twice to leave 1.92.' The ability of children to multiply mentally is not restricted to relatively small numbers. An 11-year-old boy when asked to multiply 75 by 80 said, 'I made them both into 80, giving 6400. I then took away five 80s, which is 400, so the answer is 6000.'

Ask a group of your colleagues to do the multiplications asked of the children. Make a list of the different strategies they use. What knowledge and understanding does each strategy use? How would you introduce children to such strategies?

It is apparent that children, even when they have not been taught methods to multiply mentally, are capable of doing so; they exhibit a knowledge and understanding of relationships in the number system that provide them with the tools necessary to multiply accurately in 'their heads'.

There are six important aspects of learning number that contribute to children performing mental multiplication successfully with understanding:

- knowledge of the 121 multiplication facts
- understanding of place value
- the ability to partition numbers in various ways
- knowledge of the distributive law of multiplication over addition and over subtraction
- knowledge of what happens when a number is multiplied by a multiple of 10
- the ability to double numbers.

However, having such ability, knowledge and understanding is insufficient as children need experience of combining two or more of them in various ways to develop a variety of strategies that they can call upon in response to different combinations of numbers in multiplication problems.

The reader is referred to the books by Threlfall and Frobisher (1998b) for a fuller account of potential multiplication strategies and approaches to teaching them.

Written methods

The stress on mental methods does not mean that written algorithms should not be taught. Indeed, national curricula make specific reference to the development of a variety of written methods for multiplication.

Every multiplication algorithm requires that children understand place value and are able to partition numbers. They also need knowledge of multiplying ones by ones, tens by ones and tens by tens. Without these prerequisites children are immediately at a disadvantage. One can see children, while attempting a long multiplication such as 46 × 27, having to find the answer to 6 × 7 using their fingers. Rapid recall of facts is essential for children to be able to have confidence in completing all the steps in an algorithm correctly and in the right order.

A diagrammatic approach

The different forms of multiplication algorithms require children to find 'partial products' which are then summed to find the total product. The methods are often known as partial product algorithms. The idea of partial products can be developed using a diagrammatic approach. It should be made clear, however, that this approach has a relationship to finding area of rectangles. Initially its introduction should involve the use of squared paper, making it possible for children to count and check their partial products. Figure 14.15a shows an early stage using squares, while Figure 14.15b illustrates how rectangles can be used to replace the counting of squares. Each stage of the development should be accompanied by an estimate of a product before performing calculations.

When the numbers become relatively large the use of squared paper becomes cumbersome – and should be unnecessary if the children understand the principles of partial products. When this occurs scale may be dropped and simple grids used as in Figure 14.15b.

Paper and pencil algorithms

It is essential that any written algorithm should be developed side by

To think about

Derive the answer to 35 × 19 in 'your head'. Which of the six aspects of learning number did you use? Find another way of doing the same multiplication.

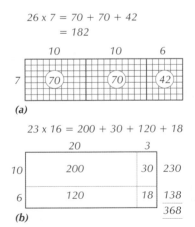

14.15 An approach to developing a multiplication algorithm

side with a diagrammatic representation before children use it independently of any pictorial support. The standard method with which you will be familiar is shown in Table 14.6, with the partial multiplications also shown. Adjacent to the standard algorithm is an 'area' method that relates very closely to the diagrammatic approach. The third method is very specialised and applies only to problems with numbers that lend themselves to doubling and halving.

Three algorithms for multiplying 36×27		
Standard algorithm	**'Area' algorithm**	**Doubling and halving algorithm**
$\begin{aligned} &\ \ 36 \\ &\underline{\times 27} \\ 30 \times 7 = &210 \\ 6 \times 7 = &42 \\ 30 \times 20 = &600 \\ 6 \times 20 = &\underline{120} \\ &\underline{972} \end{aligned}$	$\begin{array}{c\|ccc} \times & 30 & 6 & \\ \hline 20 & 600 & 120 & 720 \\ 7 & 210 & 42 & \underline{+252} \\ & & & 972 \end{array}$	$\begin{aligned} 36 \times\ \ 27 &= \\ 18 \times\ \ 54 &= \\ 9 \times 108 &= 900 + 72 \\ &= 972 \end{aligned}$

Table 14.6

To do

Place the six missing number problems in a predicted order of difficulty, giving reasons for your decisions. Compare what you have done with colleagues.

Missing number problems

There are six types of missing number multiplication problems as for the addition and subtraction. These are:

1 $a \times b = \square$

2 $a \times \square = c$

3 $\square \times b = c$

4 $\square = b \times c$

5 $a = b \times \square$

6 $a = \square \times c$

Word problems

Hendrickson (1986) categorised multiplication and division word problems. His four types of multiplication problems are described below.

Change problems

'Tina is given £2 every week for 6 weeks. How many pounds has she at the end of the 6 weeks?' This type of problem involves an initial set (£2), a change number (6 weeks), and a final set (the answer £12). Change problems are very frequently solved by some form of repeated addition.

Comparison problems

'Matthew has 2 computer games. He has 6 times as many music CDs.

How many music CDs does he have?' This type of problem has a referent set (2 computer games), a correspondence (6 times), and a comparison set (the number of CDs). The language of the problem as well as the context suggests that the appropriate operation is multiplication.

Selection problems

'Ricky makes pizzas with 2 kinds of salami and 3 kinds of cheese. How many different kinds of cheese and salami pizzas can he make?' This kind of problem requires multiplication to solve it unless every possible pizza is listed as a set of ordered pairs. The choice sets for each element are the set of salami and the set of cheeses, and the number of ordered pairs is the answer.

Rate problems

'A chew is 4p. Annabel buys 9 chews. How much do they cost her?' Rate problems involve two variables – 9 chews (the independent variable) and the total cost (the dependent variable) – and a rate of comparison between them, the cost (4p) of one chew.

It is important that children experience a variety of multiplication word problems in order to recognise when multiplication is the appropriate operation to perform. It does appear, however, that primary children prefer to use some form of repeated addition when solving change problems, rather than multiplication, even when the numbers are large. There is a strong case to be made for children concentrating on discussing together the appropriate operation for word problems without necessarily proceeding to solving the problem.

To think about

In what ways is this categorisation similar to the six meanings of multiplication?

Children and multiplication

Multiplication as repeated addition

Many children show understanding of the relationship between addition and multiplication, but this often does not extend to its symbolic representation.

SYMBOLISING REPEATED ADDITION

The authors asked 77 7–8-year-old children who had been recently introduced to multiplication to write in the missing number in:

$$17 + 17 + 17 + 17 + 17 = 5 \times \square$$

Only 19 children gave the correct answer and 20 children did not put any number in the box.

What do you think are the difficulties that caused so many children not to understand despite having been taught about multiplication? Devise a set of activities for this large group of children.

The difficulty of multiplication facts

The evidence suggests that multiplication facts are not equally difficult to learn for rapid recall and research continues to take place on the order of difficulty of the 100 facts.

THE MOST DIFFICULT

About 70 years ago, Norem and Knight (1930) conducted a study of the knowledge of 25 9–10-year-old American children of the multiplication facts from 0×0 to 9×9. They ranked the 100 facts in order of difficulty. The 'top ten' most difficult facts were 6×9, 7×8, 7×6, 8×6, 4×8, 4×9, 7×9, 7×7, 6×7, 4×7. In a later study of about 2000 children in Scotland, Murray (1939) found that, apart from 0×0, the most difficult facts were those which included a zero. When these were omitted the ten most difficult facts were 9×9, 8×9, 7×9, 7×8, 1×1, 7×7, 9×7, 8×8, 6×9, 6×8.

The knowledge of which facts children find most difficult to remember and quickly recall is an important pointer to those that require more practice than other, easier, facts. In both studies the predominance of the numbers 6, 7, 8 and 9 indicate where the problems occur. In general, there is a significant relationship between the size of the numbers and the difficulty children have in learning a fact. Why is this?

Campbell and Graham (1985) claim that the errors that children make when responding to multiplication facts which are 'highly systematic and very stable across samples' fall into three categories.

1 Table-related errors. These are mistakes children make when they give a correct answer to the wrong problem. Thus a child who gives 15 as the answer to 3×6 has given the answer to 3×5. The answers that are given in such circumstances are answers to neighbouring facts, usually where one of the numbers is the same.

2 Table-unrelated errors. These occur when the answer given is a number not to be found in the table of either of the numbers in the fact: $3 \times 6 = 17$ would be in this category.

3 Miscellaneous errors. This is a catch-all category for errors not belonging to the other two.

Campbell and Graham quote Norem's suggestion that 'children establish false associations during learning that weaken or interfere with the correct associations.' If this is correct it would indicate that teachers must be aware from an early stage of a child's learning of multiplication facts when and which errors occur and quickly take action to remedy the errors before a false association is established.

Common errors in pencil and paper multiplication

Misconception of the operation

Unfortunately it is not uncommon to see children treating multiplication as addition as in this example:

211

$$\begin{array}{r} 3\ 8\ 5 \\ \times \quad 1\ 6 \\ \hline 4\ 0\ 1 \end{array}$$

This may be carelessness, but may also be caused by lack of confidence in doing multiplication and resorting to performing an operation that they can do.

Incorrect setting down

It is essential when teaching long multiplication that ones are placed directly under ones, tens under tens, and so on. Children make mistakes when they fail to adhere to this practice. For example, 385×16 may be set down incorrectly as

$$\begin{array}{r} 3\ 8\ 5 \\ \times \quad 1\ 6 \\ \hline 3\ 8\ 5 \\ 2\ 3\ 1\ 0 \\ \hline 2\ 6\ 9\ 5 \end{array}$$

This can result in children multiplying by a 6 and a 1 as if they are both ones and not as 6 ones and 1 ten. Children may need to use squared paper to help them overcome this kind of mistake.

Table errors

When multiplying larger numbers children make errors in the multiplication facts that are required. This may be due to not knowing the facts, but may also be due to the extra demand of the problem. Asked for the fact independently a child could give the correct response, but might fail to do so when it is part of a larger multiplication.

Carrying errors

These are more apparent when children are taught short multiplication when it is necessary either to record a carry figure somewhere on the paper or to retain it in memory. There is no agreed position for a carry figure, and wherever it is put errors can occur due to its position. Here are three very common carrying errors:

$\begin{array}{r} 79 \\ \times \quad _56 \\ \hline 124 \end{array}$	$\begin{array}{r} 79 \\ \times \quad _56 \\ \hline 424 \end{array}$	$\begin{array}{r} 79 \\ \times \quad _56 \\ \hline 724 \end{array}$
The 5 which was carried has been added to the 7	The 5 which was carried has been forgotten	The 5 which was carried has been added to the 7 before multiplying by the 6

Errors with 0

When solving multiplications with large numbers involving a zero children, even though they have the correct knowledge of multiplication facts with zero, can write 736×0 as 736, confusing the calculation with the addition ($736 + 0 = 736$). This is mainly an error of carelessness, but should be pursued by asking the child to explain what he or she did.

Some ideas for teaching multiplication

Textbooks and multiplication

Textbooks are very conventional in their content and approach to the teaching of multiplication.

Activities with lattice multiplication

This remarkable Arabic method of multiplication, often known as Gelosia, is based upon products written in two squares with diagonals and an answer box along the bottom of the squares. Figure 14.16 shows how to multiply 49 by 36. The first number in the multiplication is written across the top of two squares, the second number downwards for two squares. The four separate products, $4 \times 3 = 12$, $9 \times 3 = 27$, $4 \times 6 = 24$ and $9 \times 6 = 54$, are written diagonally in the half-squares as tens and units. The digits are then added diagonally with carrying where appropriate.

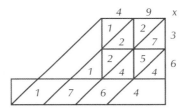

14.16 Multiplying 49 by 36 using a lattice approach

So that children do not waste time drawing the squares and the answer box you will find it helpful to provide them with ready-made diagrams. The importance of this method is the reason why it works. Give children the opportunity to discuss with each other why they think it works and to record their reasons in writing before some of them explain their thinking to the rest of the class.

A class activity

OBJECTIVE   To practise recall of multiplication facts

ORGANISATION   Whole class

RESOURCES
- Each child has a large 100-number grid and ten counters marked 1 to 10
- Teacher has a set of the 121 multiplication facts on cards, from which 10 are chosen as determined by the objective of the lesson

ACTIVITY
- The lesson is conducted in silence.
- Teacher holds up one of the multiplication cards.
- The children cover the answer on their number grid with counter 1.
- This is repeated for nine more cards and counters 2–10.
- At the end the answers are checked.

A group activity

OBJECTIVE   To match a rectangular array with its multiplication fact and the product

ORGANISATION   Small groups

RESOURCES   Each group has
- A set of 10 cards showing rectangular array of dots each of which represents a multiplication fact
- A set of matching 10 multiplication fact cards
- A set of matching 10 product cards

ACTIVITY
- The first child chooses any rectangular array.
- The next child in the group matches the array with the appropriate multiplication fact card.
- The third child matches the appropriate product card to the array and fact card.
- The activity continues until all ten sets have been made.
- When complete, the teacher checks the ten sets.

Test your own knowledge: multiplication

1   Find the missing numbers in these computations: **a** $7 + 8 + 9 = 3 \times \square$, **b** $24 + 26 + 28 = 3 \times \square$, **c** $15 + 16 + 17 + 18 + 19 = 5 \times \square$, **d** $200 + 400 + 600 + 800 + 1000 = 5 \times \square$

What is special about each computation? Describe a rule for working out such additions by multiplication.

2   Here are two sets of numbers. What is special about them?

Set A	0	1	2	3	4	5	6	7	8	9	10	11	12	13
Set B	1	2	4	8	16	32	64	128	256	512	1024	2048	4096	8192

a Find the answers to 4×16, 8×64. 64×128. Your answers should also be in Set B. The challenge is to find how you can add numbers in Set A to find the answers to multiplications in Set B.

b How can you use the numbers in Set A to find the answers to dividing numbers in Set B? Discuss with some colleagues the reason why it works.

3   The letters stand for digits. Find the missing digits.

```
      A 3              2 A
  ×     B          ×   B C
    5 C 1            2 C 0
                     2 D 2
                     E 2 2
```

4 Draw the graph of the –2 times table. Extend the graph to find the answer to –7.5 × –2

5 Construct a set of Napier's rods in the base 5 number system. Use your rods to multiply numbers in base 5

6 This 'square' has mystic properties. The product of the numbers in every row, every column and the two diagonals is the same. What are the missing numbers?

81		9
27	243	
	3	729

In what way are the numbers related to indices?

7 Each of the digits 2, 5, 8 and 9̇ has been used once only to make a three-digit by one-digit multiplication:

$$298 \times 5 = 1490$$

a Make all the three-digit by one-digit multiplications that are possible using each of the digits 2, 5, 8 and 9 once only. Which combination of digits produced the largest answer? Which combination produced the smallest answer?

b Repeat the activity with a different set of four digits.

c What is the rule for arranging any four digits as a three-digit by one-digit multiplication to form the largest answer?

d What is the rule for arranging any four digits as a three-digit by one-digit multiplication to form the smallest answer?

e What would the rules be if the multiplication was a two-digit by two-digit?

8 Investigate the patterns in the sum of the digits of table numbers.

Review of key points ➤ Learning of multiplication is a combination of knowledge, understanding and skills

➤ All six meanings of multiplication should be constantly experienced so that children develop an integrated concept of multiplication

➤ Development of an ability to use and apply multiplication should be an aim of every teacher and child

➤ An understanding of the language and symbolism associated with multiplication in all its forms are crucial to the learning of the concept

➤ Learning of multiplication facts for rapid recall is essential

➤ Exploration of pattern in multiplication tables and facts contributes to understanding both the concept and mathematics in general

➤ Knowledge of how to multiply by multiples of 10 is a prerequisite for efficient and effective mental and written calculations

➤ Children's individual mental and written methods should be shared by everyone

➤ Learning to multiply mentally and by written methods are skills that every child should attain

➤ Children should be given opportunities to discuss and work on and with a variety of real problems and word problems

Module 15   Learning to teach division

Introduction

Division is the last of the four 'rules' that children meet in primary school mathematics and is perceived by both teachers and children to be the most difficult to learn, particularly in relation to the standard algorithm, which teachers have problems in teaching and children find a daunting challenge. Yet all the evidence indicates that children come to school with a wide collection of strategies for solving division problems that are grounded in their understanding of the problem situations and relate closely to their existing concepts.

Division in national curricula

There are seven major objectives in teaching division in the primary school:

- understanding the concept and operation of division
- learning division facts for rapid recall, or derived from multiplication facts
- developing mental and non-calculator written methods through understanding
- using facts and methods to solve problems
- dividing decimal numbers by a whole number
- applying division in number, measurement and money
- understanding division as the inverse of multiplication.

Key terms

division a mathematical operation performed on two numbers, usually the numerical result of sharing a number of objects equally among a given number of sets, or by equally grouping a collection of objects into sub-sets

the '÷' sign represents the division operation and read as 'divided by', although children use a variety of other expressions, such as 'shared by'

dividend the first number in a division

divisor the second number in a division

quotient the result of a division. Thus, 12 (dividend) ÷ 3 (divisor) = 4 (quotient)

remainder the quantity left over when the whole number of times a divisor divides into a dividend is calculated. Thus, 13 (dividend) ÷ 4 (divisor) = 3 (partial quotient) + 1 (remainder)

divisible a number N is divisible by another number n when the quotient, $N \div n$, is a whole number. For example, 12 is divisible by 3 as 12 ÷ 3 is a whole number

factor a number n is a factor of another number N if it divides into it without a remainder. For example, 1, 2, 3, 4, 6 and 12 are all factors of 12

Key issues in division

Related concept and issues

Division is not a topic that should be taught unrelated to other areas of the primary mathematics curriculum. It is one of the many areas that are part of the cluster of topics that lie within multiplicative structures such as ratio, fractions and multiplication. Teachers should, therefore, be aware of the connections that division has with other issues and concepts. Figure 15.1 shows many of these connections.

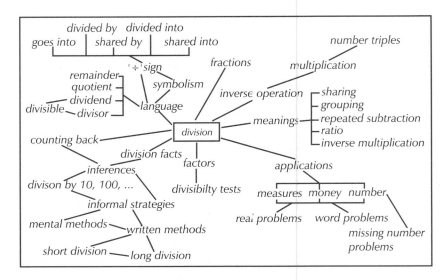

15.1 Concepts and issues associated with divisions

The concept of division

The development of the concept of division is known to take place over many years. Evidence tells us that many children leaving primary school still encounter difficulties with simple division facts, and many more are unable to use the long division algorithm efficiently and effectively. There is a strong case for extending the time that children are given for experiencing all kinds of division activities covering all the meanings of division before they are introduced to the formal symbolic representation. At present many teachers, encouraged by teachers' handbooks, provide children with division activities involving small numbers. This is understandable as large numbers of objects can cause manageability problems. However, this is a very limited view of how the division concept should be developed and restricts children's experiences considerably.

Meanings of division

There are five different meanings of division which you will meet as a teacher of primary mathematics:

- sharing
- grouping
- repeated subtraction
- ratio
- inverse of multiplication.

There is no agreed order in which the different meanings should be taught, if indeed a sequential order is deemed appropriate. The aim, whatever order and approach is used, is for children to develop an integrated meaning for the concept, enabling them to respond to any division situation with a recognition that the division operation will provide them with the solution.

Sharing

Sharing, also known as partition, partitive, dealing and distribution counting, strictly speaking should be called equal sharing, but this is taken as implicit in the use of the term – as it will be in the remainder of this module. The equality aspect of sharing is based upon the notion of 'fairness', which forms part of children's socialisation from the moment they are born and a concept which evidence suggests most children understand when starting school.

The question '12 sweets are shared equally between 4 children. How many sweets does each child get?' is an example of the sharing meaning of division (see Figure 15.2). Every sharing activity involves:

- a number of objects in a collection, the dividend is a given; 12 in the above example
- a number of sets into which the dividend is divided, the divisor is a given; 4 in the above example
- the number of objects in each set, the quotient is an unknown; 3 in the above example.

There are a number of important relationships that exist in any sharing activity with objects:

- the dividend is always larger than the divisor
- the divisor is always a whole number
- the quotient is always smaller than the dividend.

Unfortunately, there are considerable dangers for those children who only ever perceive division as sharing. Conceptual difficulties occur when a problem, such as 8 ÷ ½ occurs later in their learning.

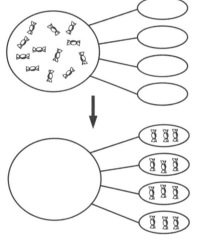

15.2 Sharing 12 sweets among 4 children

To think about

What are the difficulties that children may meet when faced with 8 ÷ ½ if they interpret the division sign to mean 'shared into'?

BISCUITS AND DOLLS

Davis and Pitkethly (1990) describe a very sophisticated strategy used by a pre-school girl in a sharing situation. The activity involved sharing 12 biscuits evenly between two dolls. Then Joey, a third doll, arrived and the child had to redistribute the biscuits so that they were shared evenly among the three dolls.

The girl gave two biscuits each to the two dolls, then two more, then one more and then one more. She was able to say that each doll had the same number of biscuits without stacking or counting them. 'When Joey arrived, she gave one biscuit to Joey and picked up all but one of the biscuits from in front of the other two dolls. She placed the ones she picked up in the middle and dealt out one at a time to the three dolls. She correctly counted four biscuits for each of the dolls and said that all three dolls had a fair share.'

What aspects of the girl's strategy do you find particularly interesting?

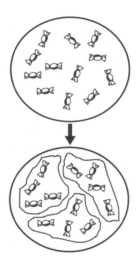

15.3 Grouping 12 sweets into sets of 4

To do

Write a series of story problems for children which satisfy the following:

a the divisor is a whole number and the quotient is a fraction
b the divisor is a fraction and the quotient is a fraction
c the divisor is a fraction and the quotient is a whole number.

The simplest sharing strategy places one object to each position or set, iteratively in a cyclic process, until all objects have been allocated. A more 'advanced' strategy uses a fixed number which is more than one in a cycle, but this number may vary from cycle to cycle.

Grouping

Grouping, sometimes known as measurement or quotition, considers how many times a given quantity can be made from a collection of objects. Strictly speaking grouping should be known as 'equal grouping'. Thus, 'How many bags of four sweets can be made from 12 sweets?' is an example of the grouping meaning of division (see Figure 15.3).

The activity involves

- a number of objects in a collection, the dividend is a given; 12 in the example
- a number of objects into which the dividend is grouped, the divisor is a given; 4 in the example
- the number of such groupings, the quotient is an unknown; 3 in the example.

The important relationships that exist in any grouping activity are:

- the dividend is always larger than the divisor
- the divisor does not have to be a whole number
- the quotient may be larger than the dividend.

In general, the concept of equal grouping with objects and the process used to bring it about appear very easy for most young children as they are able to move the objects to form groups or sets of the required number. However, when similar activities are asked in workbooks the demands are very different as the 'objects' are now immovable pictures perhaps presented in random positions.

DUCKS

In a survey, 55 children aged 5–6 years were asked to ring a set of ducks in groups of three. Just over a third of them were unable to do so correctly. Figure 15.4 shows four of the incorrect attempts.

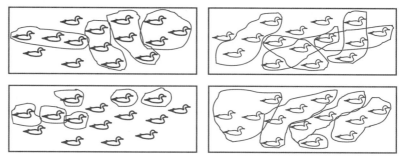

15.4 Children's attempts to group in 3s

Analyse each of the incorrect responses and record what you think each child's difficulties were when grouping in 3s. Compare your conjectures with those of colleagues.

Repeated subtraction

Just as multiplication can be viewed as repeated addition, division can be seen as repeated subtraction. Such a question may appear as 'How many times can 2 be taken away from 8?' With large numbers the appropriate process would be division. However, with small numbers subtraction is perhaps easier to perform. Indeed, the question does use the cue expression 'taken away', leading children to the repeated use of subtraction. Some children who are unable to keep track of the number of 2s draw a diagram which may have some or all of the properties shown in Figure 15.5.

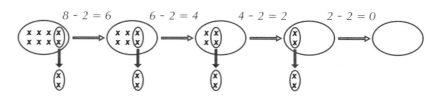

15.5 Repeatedly subtracting 2

It is not uncommon for children who have difficulty with the standard division algorithm resorting to some kind of repeated subtraction to find an answer. The diagram makes it apparent that counting back is a very useful skill for children to develop in order to answer questions having this meaning of division, and, when an integrated idea of division has been developed, to continue to use counting back, where appropriate, for some division problems.

Ratio

The problem 'Jill is 12 years old. Her sister is 3 years old. How many times older is Jill than her sister?' is an example of the ratio meaning of division. You will recognise that it has much in common with grouping and some educators would subsume this meaning under grouping. However, children seem to approach this type of problem very differently to grouping questions and frequently interpret 'how many times older' as 'how much older', giving 9 as the answer.

Inverse of multiplication

Knowledge of division as the inverse operation of multiplication is as important as knowing the similar relationship between addition and subtraction. Without this knowledge children have to learn the division facts independently of the multiplication facts, something which most find impossible to do.

Missing number division questions, such as, $36 \div \square = 9$, are answered more readily by asking 'What multiplied by 9 gives 36?', changing a division problem into a multiplication. In symbols this becomes

$36 \div \square = 9$ is equivalent to $\square \times 9 = 36$.

The inverse relationship of the two operations is much clearer in problems where a division (or multiplication) by a number is followed by multiplication (or division) by the same number, undoing the original division (multiplication) and thus leaving the original number unchanged. This can be expressed as $N \div n \times n = N$, or $N \times n \div n = N$, for all non-zero n.

> ### To do
>
> Write down the 7 'times' division table starting with $7 \div 7 = 1$, $14 \div 7 = 2$, and so on, to $70 \div 7 = 10$. Try learning the table. Ask a colleague to test you on the table with random questions.

UNDOING

A group of 68 8-year-old pupils were asked to find the answer to $78 \div 7 \times 7$. Only 22% gave the correct answer and 22% gave no answer. Most of the remaining answers appeared to be guesses, with 49 and 77 the most common errors.

The same group were asked to find the missing number in this problem:

$\square \div 9 \times 9 = 1000$

Only 10% were able to give the answer 1000. One child who gave 78 for the first problem wrote 9 for the second. Another child had 1000 correct but gave 14 as the first answer.

Prepare a lesson which aims to teach the inverse relationship between division and multipli-

Language and symbolism

There is little doubt that children can solve division problems before they have met the formality of division in the classroom and before encountering the division symbol. More and more evidence is being accumulated that suggests that children's difficulties with division mainly begin when they are introduced to division language and to the '÷' symbol.

Of the four number operations, division has the most language problems associated with it and the five common phrases used to say 8 ÷ 2 in words contribute to the problems. These are:

- 8 shared by 2
- 8 shared into 2s
- 8 divided by 2
- 8 divided into 2s
- How many 2s go into 8?

The origins of the phrases lie in their association with particular situations in which they make eminent sense. However, divorced from their associated contexts they take on meanings of their own which are frequently particular to individual children and may not be shared by teachers. Over a long period of time the phrases are used in classrooms in a variety of situations providing children with opportunities to integrate the different meanings of division with the five different phrases. Unfortunately, while some children realise that the procedures used to solve division problems, and the phrases used to express them, are interchangeable, many do not; these children become confused by the lack of compatibility in perceptions, actions and the language used in problem situations and their solutions.

Teachers need to become more aware of the language they use, particularly when teaching division. For example, you may hear teachers interchanging between the expressions '8 divided into 2', and '8 divided into 2s'. For children who have integrated the five meanings of division this causes few problems; for those who have not the different meanings of the two expressions leave children confused as to what teachers intend. '8 divided into 2' describes sharing, while '8 divided into 2s' denotes grouping. Understanding for such children is made even more difficult when the phrase '2s into 8 go ...' is also used.

Language and symbol difficulties are not confined to the early stages of learning division. When children are introduced to the formal setting out of division as

4 | 28

the dividend and divisor change places from the horizontal setting of 28 ÷ 4 and the division symbol is replaced by two connected lines which suggest, but do not say 'division'. Moreover the quotient is no longer written on the same line as the dividend and the divisor, it moves to the line above with rules as to where each digit should be written. Immediately difficulties emerge as what to say to children when using the formal layout. Once again there are a variety of expressions used by teachers, often more than one by the same teacher. The most common are '4s into 28', 'how many 4s in 28' and '4 divided into 28'.

Children's early learning about division

By the time children meet formal division in their lessons they are already familiar with the notion of symbols and the role they play in mathematics when operating on numbers. One would therefore think that children's learning would be that much easier than with the

To do

Conduct a survey of your colleagues on the language they use for the three problems 8 ÷ 2, 15763 ÷ 2037 and 6 ÷ ½. Make a record of the different language forms used. Make a similar survey of a class of 10–11 year olds. What differences and similarities are there? In what ways can the information help you to teach division better?

To do

Conduct another survey of your colleagues to find out the different expressions used for 28 ÷ 4 when written in the formal layout. How do they differ from what the same colleagues said when the divisions were presented horizontally?

223

operations that preceded division but the opposite is the case as many children struggle. This can be put down to the experiences that children are given in the classroom and the approach used. Although most teachers recognise how difficult children find division it is still the least liked of the four computational areas of the primary curriculum.

The evident difficulty and lack of enthusiasm for division may be due to a variety of reasons, the most significant of which are:

- the concern that teachers have about division may communicate itself to children
- some teachers lack confidence in teaching division as they themselves do not have a full and clear understanding of the division concept and its procedures
- division does not occur as frequently in children's everyday lives as the other three operations
- division is formalised too early in schools
- knowledge and strategies that children bring to the classroom are not built upon – or, even worse, are totally ignored.

Counting back

There is little doubt that counting back contributes to the development of some of the meanings of division and therefore should be developed as a skill from an early age. There is considerable doubt, however, that such counting back skills as children have are sufficiently related by teachers as possible ways of solving division problems where appropriate. Evidence of children's informal strategies indicates that they are very aware of the role that counting back and repeated subtraction can play when answering division word problems, but this does not appear to be developed by teachers into a conscious awareness where all children are able to deliberately select counting back or repeated subtraction as strategies.

Division by a multiple of 10

Dividing a multiple of 10 by a multiple of 10

Many errors in learning to divide large numbers occur because of lack of understanding of what happens to a number when it is divided by 10 or by other powers of 10. This learning begins with children dividing multiples of 10 by 10, such as $70 \div 10$, $800 \div 10$ or $260 \div 10$. Although it is important that children should become conscious of what happens to the digits in such division the analysis to consider this property should be delayed until children are successfully able to divide multiples of 10 by 10.

When a multiple of 10 is divided by 10, important mathematical changes take place:

- the digits, other than the zero in the ones position, move one place to the right
- the zero in the ones position disappears.

The changes are illustrated in Figure 15.6a and b.

MODULE 15 Learning to teach division

Draw a diagram to show what happens when a multiple of 100 is divided by 100. Describe the changes when a multiple of 10^n is divided by 10^n.

When a multiple of 100 is divided by 100 the important mathematical changes are

- the digits, other than the zero in the tens and ones positions, move two places to the right
- the zeros in the tens and ones position 'disappear'.

Division by a multiple of 10 with a decimal quotient

Learning how to divide multiples of 10 by 10 is the foundation for dividing any number by 10. There is, however, one significant change in that the result of dividing any number, other than a multiple of 10, by 10 is a decimal number. This is a major step for children and should be considered only when they are confident with the place value concepts associated with numbers to one decimal place. The 'rule' that digits move one place to the right still holds, but as there is no zero in the ones position the idea of it 'disappearing' is no longer relevant (see Figure 15.6c. The warning given in previous modules is here restated: *the decimal point does not move*.

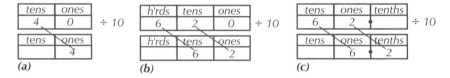

15.6 Dividing by 10

Learning division facts

There is no hard and fast rule about whether children should memorise division facts independently of multiplication facts. One view is that a stage is reached when, without the ability to rapidly recall a division fact, children's problem-solving abilities are handicapped to some degree. An alternative opinion is that to memorise division facts leads to memory overload; teaching them to relate division facts to multiplication facts not only releases memory load but also contributes to their understanding of the relationship between the two operations. Teachers who adopt the second view must ensure that their children have:

- a sound knowledge of multiplication facts for rapid recall
- a well established and working knowledge of the inverse operation relationship between multiplication and division
- an integrated understanding of the different meanings of division in order to use their understanding and knowledge of multiplication.

Remainders

The idea of remainders is unique to the mathematical operation of division. It is, however, one which many children meet in their sharing activities outside of school and have resolved in ways which do not necessarily match the mathematical notion of remainder.

The concept is not a difficult one for children to learn when using discrete objects and pictures. However, it is important to recognise that the mathematical notion of remainder as a whole number when related to division assumes that all possible sets of the divisor are made before a remainder is seen to be left. The more general idea of remainder is of a collection that is left over, irrespective of the number of sets of the divisor. That a remainder is a whole number of objects left over from the dividend (the original collection) is fundamental to the concept. Thus, only the division meanings of sharing, grouping and repeated subtraction have relevance to the concept of remainder.

The more general idea of remainder provides the setting for development of the mathematical concept, with children firstly making one grouping, or sharing one object out to each set, or subtracting one unit of the divisor from the dividend. This is followed by two, then three, and so on until it is not possible to repeat the process. Figure 15.7 illustrates the result of repeated groupings on the same dividend and recording each outcome. The final outcome should be recorded as the division 13 ÷ 3 = 4 remainder 1 and related to the expression 13 = 4(3) + 1.

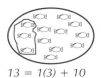 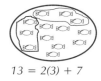

13 = 1(3) + 10   13 = 2(3) + 7   13 = 3(3) + 4   13 = 4(3) + 1

15.7 Repeatedly grouping in 3s with remainders

Mental methods

Mental division methods or strategies begin with knowledge of division facts that can be easily and quickly recalled or worked out, which are then combined with inferences based on:

- awareness of how the number system functions, including place value
- breaking numbers into parts and operating on the parts separately
- the derivation of new knowledge by changing the numbers in systematic ways
- knowledge of the distributive law of division over addition and subtraction when written, for example, as $72 \div 6 = (60 + 12) \div 6 = (60 \div 6) + (12 \div 6) = 10 + 2 = 12$
- knowledge of how to divide a number by multiples of 10.

Some children develop mental methods for division without having been taught them. Their methods are often sophisticated and based upon insightful understanding of how the number system works and its properties.

Written methods

There are two polarised schools of thought on the place of teaching

OWN METHODS

An 8-year-old was asked to share 140 equally between 2. The response was, '60 add 60 equals 120. 20 divided by 2 is 10. Add 60 and 10 gives 70.'

A 9 year old was asked to work out 195 divided by 2. The response was, '200 divided by 2 is 100. Take off 2½ leaves 97½.'

What knowledge and understanding did each child use? In what ways, if any, are the strategies related to the standard division algorithm?

Ask five of your colleagues to do two similar problems mentally and to describe their methods. Discuss their methods with them to see if they are conscious of why they work.

To do

Ask groups of 11-year-old children, teachers and colleagues for their views about long division. Make a list of the arguments for and against its place in the curriculum.

written division methods, short and long division as they are popularly known. One view holds that because technology is available long division should be left out of the primary curriculum. They support their position by pointing to the inordinate amount of time that is devoted to children learning how to perform what they claim are tedious and often irrelevant calculations. The opposite view recognises long division as being familiar to teachers and parents, and sees it having a place in the curriculum mainly on the basis of tradition. They support their position by claiming that technology is not always at hand when one needs to do long division; they claim it also has a place because it requires discipline to learn, which is intrinsically good for children to experience.

There is little doubt that most teachers are of the opinion that long division is an important stage in teaching, as they see it as the pinnacle of work in arithmetic in the primary school. It is essential, however, that the teaching of short and long division are based upon the informal strategies that children already possess.

Informal methods

Children's informal division methods develop before the formal teaching of division, and continue to be used by children who have little confidence in the algorithm they are taught.

Murray *et al.* (1991) describe seven different informal strategies that 7–10-year-old children used when solving division word problems.

Direct representation
Responding to the problem 'Divide 18 cookies among three children' Leane and Conrad represented the problem by drawing 'children'. Leane divided the cookies one at a time to each child and Conrad gave two at a time to each child.

Numerical accelerated dealing
In this strategy children draw iconic representations of the children which may be only dots. Yolande, when asked to divide 24 balloons

15.8 A child's strategy for sharing 24 balloons among four children

among 4 children, drew the children and wrote numbers under them as she shared out the balloons, firstly in 5s and then another 1 to each child as in Figure 15.8 writing the total, 6, beneath the 5 and 1.

It appears that children use estimation to decide how many to deal out on each round. Murray *et al.* (1991) found children using two types of estimation, repeated estimation or trial and error, and estimate and adjust. These are illustrated for the division 70 ÷ 5.

- repeated estimation:

70 ÷ 5						
try	10	10	10	10	10	(too low)
try	15	15	15	15	15	(too high)
try	14	14	14	14	14	(just right)

- estimate and adjust:

70 ÷ 5						
try	10	10	10	10	10	(too low)
adjust	4	4	4	4	4	

Subtraction

Murray *et al.* (1991) describe three 'different conceptualizations (for) subtraction as a method of division'.

- Estimation: for 81 ÷ 3 Emmerentia (grade 3) used this approach:

  $80 - 20 - 20 - 20 \rightarrow 20 - 6 - 6 - 6 \rightarrow 2 + 1 \rightarrow 3 - 1 - 1 - 1 \rightarrow 0$
  $81 \div 3 = 27$

- Subtracting the number of objects dealt out in each round: this strategy was used by Estelle (grade 1) for 18 ÷ 3:

  $18 - 3 = 15 \rightarrow 15 - 3 = 12 \rightarrow 12 - 3 = 9 \rightarrow 9 - 3 = 6 \rightarrow 6 - 3 = 3 \rightarrow 3 - 3 = 0$

- Repeatedly subtracting the divisor: Antoinette (grade 3) used this approach to solve the problem of the number of buses needed for 350 children when a bus holds 70 children:

  $350 - 70 \rightarrow 280 - 70 \rightarrow 210 - 70 \rightarrow 140 - 140 \rightarrow 0$
  $350 \div 70 = 5$

Double counting

Double counting uses repeated addition until the total reaches the given dividend. For example, 15 ÷ 3 would be solved by either writing 3 + 3 + 3 + 3 + 3 and then counting the number of 3s, or by saying 3, 6, 9, 12, 15 and making a tally, written or mental, of the number of 3s counted.

Addition

Stephen (grade 2) answered the question 'Divide 18 sweets among three children' by trial and error estimation using addition of repeated numbers. He wrote 4 + 4 = 8 and rejected this, replacing it with 5 + 5, which was finally replaced by 18 = 6 + 6 +6.

Multiplication

The use of multiplication is a formalisation of the strategies which have gone before. Thus, Etian (grade 3), when solving 83 ÷ 13, wrote

$13 + 13 \rightarrow 26 + 13 \rightarrow 39 \times 2 \rightarrow 78$ and
$1 + 1 + 1 + 1 + 1 + 1 \rightarrow 6$ rem 5,

moving from addition to representing the repeated addition as multiplication.

Decomposition of the dividend into multiples of the divisor
Murray *et al.* (1991) state that 'this method indicates the ability of a student to reconceptualise a number as the sum of multiples of iterable units, and is by far the most common strategy among the more experienced students.' Botha (grade 3) for $53 \div 3$, wrote

$53 \rightarrow 50 + 3 \rightarrow 30 + 21 + 2$, which is $10 + 7 + 0 = 17$ rem 2.

To think about

Use each of the informal strategies described to divide 29 by 4. What knowledge, skills and processes did you use for each strategy? Compare your analysis with your colleagues. In what ways has the experience of using different strategies helped you understand more about dividing?

To do

Make a list of the mathematical and cognitive demands that short division makes of children.

To think about

Discuss with your colleagues the arguments for and against the inclusion of short division in the primary mathematics curriculum.

Paper and pencil algorithms

Short division
Here are two formats of 'short' division, which differ mainly in the placing of the quotient.

$$5 \overline{)3\,4\,{}^4 7}$$
$$6\,9 \text{ rem. } 2$$

$$\overset{69 \text{ rem. } 2}{5 \overline{)3\,4\,{}^4 7}}$$

There are a number of major distinctions between short and long division:

- short division is set out on one horizontal line and the answer is placed either below or above the dividend, depending on the format (as opposed to long division where it is always written above the dividend)
- the divisor in short division is usually a single digit, long division being retained for larger divisors
- the 'remainders' in short division are carried to the next place on the right as superscripts, not written as the result of subtractions as in long division.

The consequences of the above are that short division, which appears on the surface to be a simpler way of dividing, places a greater demand on children operating mentally than long division. Children also are placed in the position of having to decide between the two types.

Long division
The long division algorithm requires that both the dividend and the divisor are broken down (decomposed), resulting in the process of dividing occurring several times in a sequence of steps. The quotient is the addition of a number of sub-quotients.

The standard method for long division is not unique in decomposing large dividends into smaller parts to operate on them; many mental strategies in all four operations require this skill. One significant difference of the written algorithm for long division from the other three operations is its start on the left-hand side of the dividend – that is, with the largest place value position and not with the position furthest right.

At no time during the whole process is the original dividend divided by

229

To do

Use the long division algorithm to find the answer to 3947 ÷ 29. Make a note of every perception and thought that you make as well as the actions you perform. Compare your list with those made by some of your colleagues.

To think about

Discuss with a colleague how you would help children make the transition from the repeated subtraction method to the standard algorithm.

To do

In what way does Method C differ from Method B? Write down everything you would say to a class of children when teaching them the long division algorithm. Compare your list with those of colleagues. Analyse what you have written to find out any assumptions or omissions you make, or where your expressions are not sufficiently clear or explicit about what is happening and why it is done.

To think about

Which of the methods do you favour? What are the pros and cons for each method?

the divisor. The operation takes place on a sequence of one-digit or two-digit numbers which are the result of remainders from the previous division. Children find the string of numbers that are divided perceptually and cognitively difficult to relate to the original dividend because that which the divisor is divided into continually changes into different units.

The two methods described below are suggested in the FTM (National Numeracy Strategy 1999). The division is $977 \div 36$.

- Method A: Using multiples of the divisor

$$
\begin{array}{r}
977 \\
- \ 360 \quad (10 \times 36) \\
\hline
617 \\
- \ 360 \quad (10 \times 36) \\
\hline
257 \\
- \ 180 \quad (5 \times 36) \\
\hline
77 \\
- \ 72 \quad (2 \times 36) \\
\end{array}
$$

Answer: 27 rem. 5

- Method B: Using the standard algorithm:

$$
\begin{array}{r}
27 \text{ rem. } 5 \\
36\overline{)977} \\
- \ 720 \quad (20 \times 36) \\
\hline
257 \\
- \ 252 \quad (7 \times 36) \\
\hline
5
\end{array}
$$

Answer: $27\frac{5}{36}$

- The FTM suggests another possible form of standard algorithm, as shown below.

Method C:

$$
\begin{array}{r}
27 \\
36\overline{)977} \\
- \ 72 \\
\hline
257 \\
- \ 252 \\
\hline
5
\end{array}
$$

Method B goes some way to helping children understand what is happening by including the value of each product, using a subtraction sign to show that a remainder is sought and by showing each product as the product of the divisor and each sub-quotient. However, it refrains from showing that each remainder is divided by the original divisor, as shown below.

$$
\begin{array}{r}
27 \\
36\overline{)977} \\
720 \\
\hline
36\overline{)257} \\
252 \\
\hline
5
\end{array}
$$

Missing number problems

There are six types of missing number division problems. These are:

1 $a \div b = \square$

2 $a \div \square = c$

3 $\square \div b = c$

4 $\square = b \div c$

5 $a = b \div \square$

6 $a = \square \div c$

Word problems

Categories of word problems

Hendrickson (1986) categorised multiplication and division word problems. His four types of division problems, which are relevant to primary children, are the same as for multiplication as the two operations are part of the more general concept of multiplicative relations.

Change problems

Change 1: 'Anna has 15 chews. She gives 3 chews to each of her friends. How many of her friends get chews?' This grouping problem involves an initial (larger) set (15 chews), a final (smaller) known set size (3 chews), with the change number (5 friends), to be found. Change problems of the grouping type are frequently solved by some form of repeated subtraction.

Change 2: 'Gareth has 15 marbles that he gives to his 3 friends. How many marbles will each get if they all get the same number?' This sharing problem involves an initial (larger) set (15 marbles) and a known change number (3 friends), with the size of the final set (5 marbles) to be found. Change problems of the sharing type are initially solved by a sharing process.

Comparison problems

Compare 1: 'Bruce has 15 pence. He has 3 times as much as Bronwyn has. How much does Bronwyn have?' This type of ratio division problem has a comparison set (15 pence), with a many-to-one correspondence (3 times) and a referent set, the number of pence (5 pence). The language of the problem as well as the context misleadingly suggests that the appropriate operation is multiplication.

Compare 2: 'Ricky has 3 football cards and Debbie has 15 football cards. Debbie has how many times as many cards as Ricky?' This type of ratio division problem has a comparison set (3 cards) and a referent set (15) with a question about the many-to-one correspondence (5 times). The language of the problem as well as the context misleadingly suggests that the appropriate operation is multiplication.

Selection problems

'James has 15 different rugby kits of shirts and shorts. He has 3 different shirts. How many different kinds of shorts does he have?' This kind of

To think about

What are the relationships between Hendrickson's categories and the five meanings of division?

To do

Here are seven problems for you to solve. Check your answers with some colleagues. What was it about each question that determined the way you wrote the answer?

1 30 senior citizens go by car to Hastings. Each car holds 4 passengers. How many cars are needed?

2 30 apples are divided fairly among 4 children. How many apples will each child get?

3 A 30 cm strip of paper is cut into 4 cm lengths. How many such pieces will there be?

4 A family go for a 30 km walk. They divide the walk into 4 equal stages. What is the length of each stage?

5 A gardener plants 30 roses in rows of 4 bushes per row. How many rows does he plant?

6 A rectangular room is 30 m². The width of the room is 4 m. How long is the room?

7 Raj is 4 years old. His father is 30 years old. How many times older is Raj's father than Raj?

problem requires division to solve it unless every possible kit is listed as a set of ordered pairs. The number in one choice set and the number of pairs (kits) are given and the number in the other choice set has to be found.

Rate problems

'A sprinter runs 100 metres in 10 seconds. What is his average speed in metres per second?' Rate problems involve two variables, 100 metres (the independent variable) and 10 seconds (the dependent variable), and a rate of comparison between them (the average speed) has to be found.

Word problems and remainders

Over the last few years increasing emphasis has been placed on division word problems which involve children in operating on the resulting remainder in the division answer in order to give a sensible response to the problem. Such an operation may require a rounding up or down of the quotient, dependent on the nature of the problem situation. In other problems the 'remainder' may be written as a fraction or a decimal.

Factors of a number

The rectangular array approach to finding factors relates division to multiplication. For example, to find the factors of 12, children are given either linking cubes or squared paper. They then try to make filled 'rectangles' with their 12 cubes or rectangles of 12 squares on their paper. They repeat the activity, making other rectangles with 12 cubes or squares. These are shown in Figure 15.9a, with the number of rows and the number of columns representing factors of 12. There are repeats as 1 (row) × 12 (columns) is equivalent to 12 (rows) × 1 (column), so three rectangles can be eliminated, leaving the factors of 12 as 1 and 12, 2 and 6, and 3 and 4. These are collected to give the set 1, 2, 3, 4, 6 and 12.

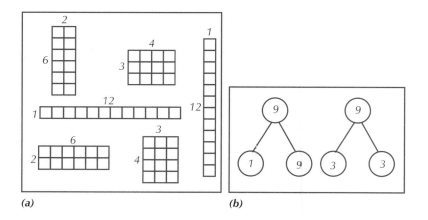

(a)   *(b)*

15.9 Two approaches for finding factors

An alternative approach which demands knowledge of the inverse of multiplication meaning of division is the one-level factor tree. Figure 15.9b shows the two factor trees for the number 9. In each case 9 has been split into two numbers which, when multiplied, give 9. The set of factors of 9 are therefore 1, 3 and 9, as 3 is not repeated.

Divisibility tests

Not all primary mathematics textbooks include activities which consider how to decide whether a number is exactly divisible by another number. The 'rules' for making such decisions are known as divisibility tests. The FTM requires that pupils should be taught to 'recognise and know some tests of divisibility.'

Relating division and multiplication

Both the sharing and grouping meanings of division provide opportunities for children to explore with objects and diagrams the inverse operation relationship between division and multiplication.

The division process of equal sharing is reversed by the multiplication process of equal grouping; the sets formed after division are grouped back in the original set, as illustrated in Figure 15.10.

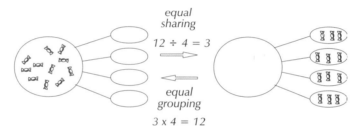

equal sharing
$12 \div 4 = 3$
equal grouping
$3 \times 4 = 12$

15.10 Relating division and multiplication

Children and division

The non-commutativity of division

Many primary school children fail to appreciate that addition and multiplication are commutative, but that subtraction and division are not. This is partly due to them experiencing the commutativity of addition first and generalising the property to the other operations as they meet them.

DOES 36 ÷ 4 = 4 ÷ 36?

Some 10-year-old pupils were asked 'Does $36 \div 4$ have the same answer as $4 \div 36$?', and to explain why. 51% said yes, 30% said no, with 9% giving no response. These are some typical responses:

'Yes it has to be because they are the same sums like $5 + 2 = 7$ and $2 + 5 = 7$'
'No, because you can't divide 4 by 36 because its value is smaller'
'No, because you can't divide 4 by 36 because 4 is a smaller number'

How could you make children aware of the non-commutativity of division when they may not understand fractions?

Difficulty and errors in division facts

Murray (1939) tested over 700 Primary 3 children in Scotland on 90 division facts associated with dividing by the numbers 1–9. The ten facts having the highest difficulty ranking were, in order of decreasing difficulty, $1 \div 1$, $81 \div 9$, $6 \div 6$, $2 \div 2$, $63 \div 9$, $54 \div 9$, $5 \div 5$, $8 \div 8$, $9 \div 9$, $56 \div 8$.

Zero errors

Although this type of error does not occur as often as it does with multiplication facts it is still one that children who have little understanding of the concept of zero frequently make. For example, they write or say $0 \div 3 = 3$. This error becomes particularly important when children meet the division of zero in a short or long division problem, such as $8064 \div 4$, giving the answer as 2416 or 216.

Confusing the operation

Children on some occasions perform an incorrect operation other than division when faced with a question such as $56 \div 8$. This may be due to carelessness or haste to respond quickly and consequently misreading the division sign. The category of divisions of the type $N \div N$ appear to be particularly prone to this, with children giving zero as the answer.

Errors involving the number 1

Some children write or say that, for example, $9 \div 1 = 1$. It would appear that there are insufficient classroom activities for young children involving sharing or grouping where the divisor is equal to 1. This is to some degree understandable as to ask a child how many groups of 1 can be made from 8 objects appears trivial, as to a lesser extent does saying, 'How many apples will 1 child get if there are 8 apples to share equally among the child?' More work needs to be done by teachers establishing the pattern that emerges when considering $N \div 1$ for different values of N.

Reversals

The first type of reversal is caused by children reading a division from right to left. For example, $24 \div 7$ is read in reverse order as 'How many 7s go into 42?'. In this case the answer given is 6.

A second type of reversal occurs when children interchange one of the digits of the dividend for the divisor. An example will illustrate this: the answer to $18 \div 6$ is given as 2 because $18 \div 6$ is read as $16 \div 8$.

Using a standard algorithm

The common errors when children use a standard algorithm tend to fall into four categories:

- errors associated with basic number facts of all four of the operations
- errors arising from the remainders at various stages
- errors due to zeros at some part of the procedure
- errors because of a lack of understanding of the concept of division and the process of dividing.

To do

Analyse a textbook series to see how frequently the ten most difficult facts in Murray's study are asked relative to other division facts.

168 ÷ 7

Here are the responses from four 10-year-olds to the division 168 ÷ 7 set out in the long division format.

$$
\begin{array}{r} 144 \\ \hline 7\,\big)\,16^28 \end{array}
\qquad
\begin{array}{r} 023 \\ \hline 7\,\big)\,16^28 \end{array}
\qquad
\begin{array}{r} 712 \\ \hline 7\,\big)\,168 \end{array}
\qquad
\begin{array}{r} 23 \\ \hline 7\,\big)\,1^16^28 \end{array}
$$

Here are the responses from three 11-year-olds to the division 859 ÷ 27 set out in the long division format.

$$
\begin{array}{r} 30 \\ \hline 27\,\big)\,859 \end{array}
\qquad
\begin{array}{r} 27 \\ 54 \\ 81 \end{array}
\qquad
\begin{array}{r} 32\ r\ 5 \\ \hline 27\,\big)\,8^85^59 \end{array}
\qquad
\begin{array}{r} 1\,2\,2.7 \\ 4\,2\,9.5 \\ \hline 27\,\big)\,8^15^19 \\ 5\,5\,2.2 \end{array}
$$

What are the errors, if any, that each child makes?

Some ideas for teaching division

Textbooks and division

As with multiplication, textbooks are very conventional in their approach to the teaching of division, although there is great variation in content.

A class activity

OBJECTIVE To estimate the size of a quotient relative to 1

ORGANISATION Whole class

RESOURCES Teacher has a large number of divisions on cards with answers less than 1, equal to 1 and more than 1

ACTIVITY
- Teacher holds up a division card.
- Children respond by saying whether the answer is less than, equal to or more than 1
- They must also explain how they know.
- The activity can be extended to word problems presented orally.

A group activity

OBJECTIVE	To practise grouping with remainder
ORGANISATION	Small groups
RESOURCES	Each group has a set of objects

ACTIVITY

- A number of objects, say 17, is counted out by each child.
- The children proceed to group the objects in 2s, then 3s, 4s, 5s and so on, recording each grouping as a division with partial quotient and remainder in a table.

Test your own knowledge: division

1   Write realistic word problems which could be solved by dividing 51 by 4 and which have the following answers: $12\frac{3}{4}$, 13, 12

2   Use a calculator to find $598\,473\,947$ divided by $98\,762$. Use the decimal part of the answer to find the whole number remainder to the division. Check your answer by multiplication and addition.

3   Without working out the separate parts find the quotient and the remainder in these two examples:

   a $(6 \times 147 + 1) \div 6$

   b $(6 \times 147 + 1) \div 2$

4   Find what the missing numbers could be. How many solutions are there?

   $$\boxed{\,\,} \div \boxed{9} = 9 \text{ rem. } 9$$

5   Does 24 divide exactly into 42^{72}? Explain how you know to a colleague.

6   Divide $3^3 \times 5^2 \times 7$ by 15. What is the quotient and the remainder?

7   Given that $2726 \div 58 = 4$ find the products of:

   a $272.6 \div 58$

   b $2.726 \div 58$

   c $0.2726 \div 58$

   d $27.26 \div 5.8$

8   Investigate all the factors of numbers from 1 to 100

   a What is special about numbers with 2 factors?

   b What is special about numbers with 3 factors?

   c What sort of numbers have an odd number of factors?

9   **a** How many factors has the product of 2×3?

   b How many factors has the product of $2 \times 3 \times 5$?

c How many factors has the product of $2 \times 3 \times 5 \times 7$?

d Generalise for the number of factors that the product of the first n prime numbers has.

Review of key points ➤ Division is seen by teachers and children to be the most difficult of the four operations to learn

➤ Children should experience all five meanings of division in activities which cover a wide range of small and large numbers

➤ It is essential that children develop an integrated meaning for division

➤ Children bring to school an extensive variety of successful experiences of division situations

➤ Informal division strategies that many children possess can be the basis for successful whole class lessons

➤ The variety of informal and formal language used to express the symbolic representation of a division can be confusing for learners

➤ The development of mental division methods is an essential aim of a primary mathematics curriculum

➤ There is much debate about the need for children to learn the long division algorithm

➤ Children should develop the skills to solve real problems and word problems which extend over the five meanings of division

---

Part 3

Module 16   Learning to teach pre-algebra: an overview

Introduction

The well researched difficulties secondary children have with learning algebra have given impetus to the study of what is now referred to as pre-algebra and consideration of the appropriate age for introducing children to pre-algebraic ideas. Because of the close relationship between number and algebra there is a strong case to be made for children in primary years experiencing pre-algebraic concepts.

Relationships between number and algebra in national curricula

Most primary curricula fail to mention the development of the relationships between number and algebra or pre-algebra in particular. The following should be considered as pre-algebra in the primary years. More detail will be found in Modules 17–21.

- observing, predicting, explaining and generalising patterns in words and letters
- exploring and using relations, mappings and functions
- exploring, interpreting and constructing diagrammatic representations of numerical information
- expressing functions and their graphs in words and in letters
- constructing, interpreting and solving simple equations and formulae
- reasoning algebraically
- solving problems using algebraic concepts and skills.

Key terms

variable	a representation for an 'object', usually a letter, which can take any value from a given set of values
coefficient	the number which is part of the product of a number and a variable
relation	an association that connects two numbers
relationship	exists between two quantities, when a change in one (the independent variable) may cause a change in the other (the dependent variable)
mapping	a relationship between members of two sets of variables
function	assigns to each independent variable one, and only one, dependent variable

equation   two quantities form an equation when related by an equals sign; an equation may be a true or a false statement; an equation does not necessarily contain a variable

formula   an equation which has two or more variables can be said to be a formula

Key issues in pre-algebra

Related concepts and issues

The roots of pre-algebra lie in the common elements of the number and algebra systems. The connections between these two systems provide the areas of pre-algebra. This development and the connections are shown in Figure 16.1.

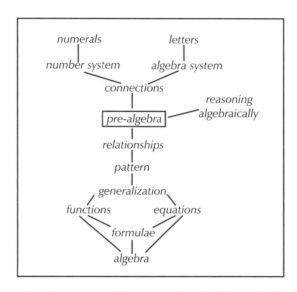

16.1 Concepts and issues associated with pre-algebra

Relationship between number and algebra

Why do so many children find algebra difficult after success with arithmetic? It could be that most of primary mathematics is related visually to concrete or diagrammatic models of situations, an approach which is explored in Modules 1–9. Algebra, not having an obviously visual nature, does not appear to lend itself easily to such an approach, although Modules 17–21 show how this is possible.

On the surface the difference between algebra and number, as perceived by children and primary teachers, is the use of letters rather than numerals. The difference, however, is in the generality of algebra as opposed to the particularity of arithmetic: it is in this that its power lies. The similarity is the behaviour of numbers and letters in the two systems with similar structures. It is the idea of generality, and the similar behaviour of numbers and letters, on which the teaching of pre-algebra should concentrate whenever opportunities arise.

239

It is often claimed that algebra is a generalisation of arithmetic in that 'all it does' is replace numbers with letters. This view has been a dominant influence in the approach to teaching mathematics in secondary schools for many years: it has had little success with most children. For an improvement in children's achievement in algebra we must look beyond such a simplistic relationship by unpacking what the claim means and by teasing out the connections between arithmetic and algebra.

If arithmetic and algebra are treated as two separate topics the connections between them, other than numbers becoming letters, are unlikely to be apparent to children. The connections can be categorised as:

- relationships between numbers, which can be expressed as general statements
- the finding of missing numbers, or unknowns, in equalities and identities
- working with functions and formulae at every opportunity, expressing them in words and with letters.

These three connections are explored in detail in the coming modules.

What is pre-algebra?

There is no agreed definition of what pre-algebra is, or what it should be about. In this book we view pre-algebra as the development of concepts, ideas and skills that are common to arithmetic and algebra, but which can be used solely in the field of number. Their use will raise questions about relationships and possible generalisations. Relationships and the establishment and recording of general statements about numbers have their foundations in pattern. We devote Module 17 to the teaching of pattern as a possible route into algebra.

What is algebra?

Although we have continued to refer to algebra no definition has been provided. This is partly because so many different definitions can be found, but also because the time was not appropriate to introduce a formal definition. Put simply, algebra is the study of a mathematical system of generalised computations involving unknowns, called variables, and knowns, called numbers. All systems have rules or laws associated with them and algebra is no different.

Laws of algebra

The set of rules, or laws, to which algebra conforms are derived as a generalisation of the properties of number systems (see Module 11) on the basis of many examples of number relationships. For example, $3 + 2 = 2 + 3$ gives rise to the commutative property of addition, which can be written as $a + b = b + a$, for all numbers a and b. As algebra deals with unknowns, represented by letters, the relationships between the unknowns (the letters) are stated as rules; expressions made up of letters must obey such rules. This, unfortunately, is what children perceive the learning of algebra to be, 'a set of rules to be learnt and performed on letters'. The pre-algebraic laws which you may recognise (and which are provided solely for your information) are:

1 The commutative law of addition: $a + b = b + a$

2 The commutative law of multiplication: $a \times b = b \times a$, written by convention as $ab = ba$

3 The associative law of addition: $a + (b + c) = (a + b) + c$

4 The associative law of multiplication: $a \times (b \times c) = (a \times b) \times c$, written as $a(bc) = (ab)c$

5 The distributive law of multiplication over addition: $a \times (b + c) = (a \times b) + (a \times c)$, written as $a(b + c) = ab + ac$

6 Existence of 0, the identity element in addition: $a + 0 = a$

7 Additive inverses: for each a there exists $(-a)$ such that $a + (-a) = 0$, the identity

8 Existence of 1, the identity element in multiplication: $a \times 1 = a$

9 Multiplicative inverse: for each non-zero a there exists $1/a$ such that $a \times 1/a = 1$, the identity.

It is difficult for those who have experienced success with these rules, and found the manipulation of letters to have some inherent satisfaction, to appreciate the anxiety which they cause many learners. The aim of introducing pre-algebraic notions to children, thus bridging the cognitive gap between number and algebra, is to eliminate such problems for future learners.

Symbol conventions

There are three conventions associated with the writing of algebraic expressions which are the cause of many misconceptions and errors in the learning of algebra.

Omission of the multiplication sign
When writing a product of numbers for the first time the multiplication sign is essential. For example, the omission of the '$\times$' sign for $3 \times 2 = 6$ would end with $32 = 6$. However, in algebra it is the convention to write $a \times b$ as ab. You will also find $a \times b$ written with a 'dot', $a.b$, instead of the '$\times$' sign. This is inappropriate to use with numbers as 3×2 would then be written as 3.2, which could be read and interpreted as 3 point 2.

Coefficient precedes the variable in a product
As the commutative law holds $N \times 2$ is written not as $N2$ but, by convention, as $2N$.

Omission of the coefficient when its value is 1
When the coefficient in a product is equal to 1, by convention it is omitted in the product. For example, $1N$ is written as N.

Logo and spreadsheets

Logo is a computer language which allows pupils experience of the important mathematical process of generalisation, and can provide a friendly environment for the introduction of symbolism. For example, pupils who have had experience of drawing several different-sized squares using Logo may notice that only the length of the square is varying in their commands. A comparison of the Logo commands for three squares, for example REPEAT 4[FD 50 LT 90], REPEAT 4[FD 80

LT 90] and REPEAT 4[FD 20 LT 90], may help pupils to appreciate the introduction of the variable:LENGTH in the general procedure

TO SQUARE:LENGTH
REPEAT 4[FD:LENGTH LT 90]
END

To do

Find a book that teaches you Logo.

Research by Sutherland (1989) suggests that pupils who are experienced in the use of Logo accept that a variable in Logo represents a range of numbers and are not unhappy about using single letter names like L or X instead of words like LENGTH. They even accept expressions like $X+5$ in the context of Logo. The crucial question is whether such acceptance of Logo will help pupils' algebraic understanding. This may depend on the nature and extent of the Logo experience.

Spreadsheets, using a computer, have also been found to help pupils towards algebraic understanding (Healy and Sutherland, 1991). Number patterns can easily be explored and generalised. For example, to generate the multiples of 3 the number 3 could be typed in the cell A1 and the formula $=A1+3$ entered in A2. This formula could then be dragged down the A column as far as required. Any sequence of numbers with a constant difference can be generated in a similar way to give practice in pattern spotting. The more difficult task of spotting the general term of a sequence, or relating each number to the order of the number can be encouraged with games like 'Guess my rule'. A cell could be allocated for the input number and a simple formula based on this cell entered in the chosen output cell. Pupils take turns typing in an input number while the class guess the rule from the output number (see Module 18). The spreadsheet also allows pupils to test out mathematical relationships without having to work out the formal spreadsheet language. Using the mouse (or arrow keys and Enter) the relationship between cells can be indicated physically and then seen algebraically on the screen in terms of the cell names. Thus 'the spreadsheet environment can be thought of as some sort of intermediary between natural language and formal algebra' (Sutherland, 1990).

To do

Learn how to use spreadsheets.

Test your own knowledge: pre-algebra

1 a Add any two odd numbers. Is their sum divisible by 2? Repeat with other pairs of odd numbers. Write a general statement about the sum of two odd numbers.

   b Prove that the sum of any two odd numbers is divisible by 2

2 a Multiply any two even numbers. Is their product divisible by 4? Repeat with other pairs of even numbers. Write a general statement about the product of two even numbers.

   b Prove that the product of any two even numbers is divisible by 4

3 a Choose any four-digit number. Reverse it. Show that the difference between your number and its reversal is a multiple of 9. Repeat this with some more four-digit numbers.

   b Write a general statement about the difference of a four-digit number and its reversal.

    c Prove that $abcd - dcba$ is a multiple of 9. You may wish to use your knowledge of the expanded notation for place value to help you.

4 Find four values for N that make $1/N - 1/(N + 1)$ equal to $1/N(N + 1)$. Compare your solutions with those of your colleagues. What conclusion can you draw from what you have found out?

5   **a** Find three consecutive numbers whose product is the value of $2^3 - 2$

    b Find three consecutive numbers whose product is the value of $3^3 - 3$

    c Find three consecutive numbers whose product is the value of $4^3 - 4$

    d Write a general statement about the product of three consecutive numbers and the value of $N^3 - N$.

Review of key points

➤ Many secondary children have difficulties learning algebra

➤ There is a strong case for introducing pre-algebraic ideas into the primary curriculum

➤ Pre-algebra comprises the concepts, ideas and skills which are common to arithmetic and algebra while continuing to work with them in the field of number

➤ The observation of and explanation for pattern in number is one of the most important aspects of pre-algebra

➤ The systems of number and algebra behave in similar, but not identical, ways

➤ Generalisations, functions, equations and formulae are topics which connect number and algebra

➤ Logo and spreadsheets may be a way of introducing children to algebraic ideas

---

Module 17　Learning to teach pattern

Introduction

Pattern permeates the whole of mathematics. Many mathematicians have referred to the origins of mathematics in the study of patterns. For example Sawyer (1955) claimed that 'Mathematics is the classification and study of all possible patterns', suggesting that whenever pattern exists mathematics can be developed from it. Such claims about the close association of pattern and mathematics are reflected in the work we are expected to do with children in school. Through pattern activities children not only make more sense of mathematics but also make more sense of the world. Ultimately, the patterns children find and study can lead to powerful ideas such as generalisation and algebraic formulae. Thus pattern is perhaps not so much a topic to be taught, as a critical strand for much of the mathematics curriculum.

Pattern in national curricula

National curricula reflect the view that pattern is not a topic to be studied in its own right, but an intrinsic part of mathematics that can be found in most aspects of the subject. The major references to pattern are:

- copying, continuing and devising repeating patterns
- developing ideas of regularity and sequencing
- number sequences, including sequences of odd and even numbers
- patterns in addition, subtraction, multiplication and division
- patterns within and among multiplication tables
- explaining patterns and using them to make predictions
- interpreting and generalising patterns, and expressing generalisations in words and letters
- explaining patterns used in mental methods
- patterns of square and triangular numbers
- exploring prime numbers.

Key terms

pattern　order, regularity, repetition and symmetry in and between mathematical 'objects', which include symbols

structure　the result of relationships arising from the construction of mathematical systems; manifests through pattern

sequence　a set of mathematical 'objects' ordered according to some rule, often called a number pattern when the 'objects' are numbers

repeating pattern	a sequence that repeats itself every given number of terms; the given number is known as the period of the pattern	
prime number	a whole number which has only 1 and itself as factors	
square number	a number which is the result of multiplying a whole number by itself	
triangle number	a number which is the sum of consecutive numbers starting at 1	

Key issues in pattern

What is pattern?

In mathematics we mostly use the word 'pattern' in relation to a search for order or structure, and so regularity, repetition and symmetry are often present. Thus, even when we complete the very elementary task of tabulating numbers in a 1 to 100 grid, as in Figure 17.1, we can see a structure involving patterns based simply on the way digits are repeated. This is one of the earliest ways in which formal mathematics reveals patterns to children; those same patterns also contribute to the learning process. The fact that there is a simple structure makes it easier for children to grasp how numbers are constructed, and how they continue.

1	2	3	4	5	6	7	8	9	10
11	12	13	14	15	16	17	18	19	20
21	22	23	24	25	26	27	28	29	30
31	32	33	34	35	36	37	38	39	40
41	42	43	44	45	46	47	48	49	50
51	52	53	54	55	56	57	58	59	60
61	62	63	64	65	66	67	68	69	70
71	72	73	74	75	76	77	78	79	80
81	82	83	84	85	86	87	88	89	90
91	92	93	94	95	96	97	98	99	100

17.1 The 100-number grid

Early concepts of pattern

It is important that teachers know why pattern is such an important strand in mathematics, and where it might lead. But for children, and therefore also for teachers, the early work is usually very much simpler. The beginnings, perhaps, lie in play activities such as arranging toys or other objects, in lines, squares or other arrays, or in using a variety of colours to construct an 'attractive' picture. National curricula have formalised this early work through reference to copying, continuing, describing and/or devising patterns or sequences. Figure 17.2 shows two linking cube activity cards which have been used successfully with young children, who make the patterns using cubes and then extend them in both directions. There are many opportunities for number work when children have made such patterns.

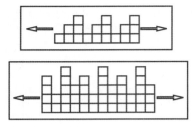

17.2 Activity cards for linking cube sequences

To do

Make a list of some number questions you could ask children about the patterns in Figure 17.2.

An aim of such activities is to produce numerical data. When such data has been recorded it becomes appropriate to look for what we would call pattern or structure. The search for pattern and structure is made easier through such '-ing' activities as sorting into categories, re-arranging in particular orders, predicting new elements of a list (perhaps using repeating elements), and extending. On the basis of such work, together with a growing feeling for what the possible regularities or rules for analysis and extension might be, and a developing understanding of the familiar operations of arithmetic ($+, -, \times, \div$), awareness of the range of what might be counted as a pattern will emerge. All of this takes time in the early years, throughout which period it might not be sensible for teachers to expect children to understand what is meant by the word 'pattern' in mathematics, but to just experience its existence and its appeal.

Related concepts and issues

Once the concept of pattern is more firmly established, work with numbers and number sequences becomes an essential and frequent element within primary mathematics lessons. Explorations based on addition facts, place value, multiplication tables, and classifications like odd and even run through much of the middle primary years. In this period, there are hosts of relevant and helpful activities in which children can engage to develop mathematical understanding. The map in Figure 17.3 illustrates this. The map also reveals possible further extensions, like functions and graphs,

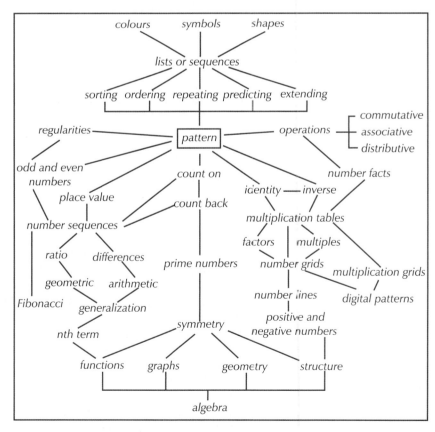

17.3 Concepts and issues associated with patterns

which form a smaller part of primary mathematics. But pattern leads ever onwards, and the map indicates links with more general, broad areas such as the study of structure, and with geometry. The ultimate summing up of where pattern leads is algebra.

A route to algebra

One justification for the emphasis on pattern in national curricula is the belief that pattern provides a helpful route into algebra. Many children find algebra inaccessible, and experience frustration in their attempts to master the mathematics. Algebra is essential to mathematics, and teachers cannot avoid exploring it with children in primary classes. Using patterns in no way solves all the teaching problems associated with algebra, but patterns offer a relatively painless way of justifying and developing the use of letters.

Number sequences

When children in the early years of primary school learn to count on and count back in steps of 1, 2, 3 and so on, they are creating the basis for study of pattern and sequences. This is continued when they investigate patterns in the products of multiplication tables (see Module 14). Sequences studied in their own right develop deeper insight into such structures. For example, given a simple sequence of numbers which incorporates patterns

3, 5, 7, 9, 11, 13, 15, 17, 19, 21, ...

it is possible to look for a way of analysing and describing how the patterns develop. Children may not see in the sequence the patterns that we think are so obvious. For example, many children will say 'The numbers are all odd', or 'The numbers get bigger'. The most obvious property to us may be that the numbers increase steadily, and the difference between consecutive numbers is always 2. Thus, the number 2 is very significant in the analysis. Having decided that the 'terms' increase consistently by 2, we now need to know why they start with 3, and not perhaps with 1 (which would have given us the 'odd numbers'), or any other number. An algebraic way to approach this would be to list the terms alongside their 'position'. In other words, the first term should be placed alongside 1, the second alongside 2, and so on, giving us Table 17.1. Children should then be encouraged to look for a functional relationship between the matching pairs of numbers in the two rows – in other words, what rule determines how we can obtain all of the term numbers from their corresponding position numbers: 3 from 1, 5 from 2, 7 from 3, and so on?

Odd numbers and their position in the sequence										
Position	1	2	3	4	5	6	7	8	9	10	...
Term	3	5	7	9	11	13	15	17	19	21	...

Table 17.1

Earlier work on 'I think of a number' problems can provide the experience and knowledge to enable children to see that each term number is 'twice the position number add 1'. Such a description in

To do

Consider the sequence 3, 5, 7, 9, 11, 13, 15, 17, 19, 21, 23, 25, 27, 29, ... from a child's perspective. What patterns do you think they might see in the sequence other than the 'increase by 2' pattern? Present the sequence to some children and ask them to tell you any patterns that they can see.

words might be considered a helpful step on the road to '2 × position number + 1', and then to using '*n*' to stand for the position number, and thus '$2n + 1$' to represent this '*n*th' term. Mathematically, $2n + 1$ is the value of the general term, represented by '*t*', for the given sequence, and we can see how the 2 (which we identified early on as being very significant) is reflected in the 'formula' $t = 2n + 1$. We may then use this formula to find any further term, for example the 17th term in the sequence would be $t_{17} = 2 \times 17 + 1 = 35$. What is more, we have introduced the use of a letter as a variable, and have therefore made a preliminary step into algebra. Of course, any letter could be used here, and much subsequent mathematics is based on using and graphing functions such as $x \rightarrow 2x + 1$, or $y = 2x + 1$ (see Module 18), where x and y are commonly used rather than n and t

Much of the work on pattern in primary textbooks revolves around the use of number sequences. However, not all number sequences are of the same structure as these. The example in the previous section has a constant difference of 2, and there are many sequences with a constant difference, for example the odd numbers:

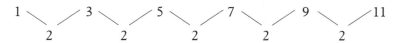

the even numbers:

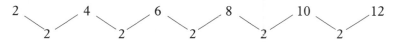

and many more, such as:

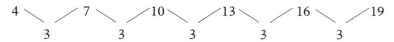

and

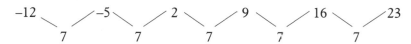

To think about

Find the 'general term' for each of the examples above. Work with a colleague to make up more constant difference sequences and test each other on finding the general term in each case. Explain to each other any quick ways of obtaining the formula.

Such constant difference sequences are sometimes called 'arithmetic progressions'. Note that the word 'sequence' is going to be used a great deal in this module, as the mathematical term for a list of numbers like those above. Sometimes you will find the word 'series' used in books but, strictly speaking, a series in mathematics is not the same thing as a sequence, because a series should involve sums of numbers, and so the word 'series' will not be used in this module.

Polygonal numbers

Square numbers

Number sequences with a very different structure arise when we investigate 'polygonal numbers'. The most obvious example is the 'square numbers' ($1 = 1^2$, $4 = 2^2$, $9 = 3^2$, $16 = 4^2$, and so on), which crop up very frequently in the study of mathematics, and which are fundamental in many important results like area formulae and Pythagoras' theorem. Figure 17.4 depicts diagrammatically the first five square numbers based on dots. It should not be necessary to tabulate these against their position numbers to assert that the formula is $t = n^2$.

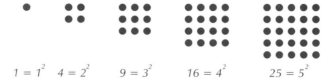

$1 = 1^2$ $4 = 2^2$ $9 = 3^2$ $16 = 4^2$ $25 = 5^2$

17.4 A representation of the square number sequence

The first interesting property about polygonal numbers arises when we investigate differences of square numbers.

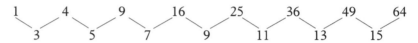

The differences with polygonal numbers are not constant. In fact, they are the odd numbers. We could, however, include the 'second differences' in our table, as well as the 'first differences', as in Table 17.2. Here, not surprisingly, we find that the second differences are always 2. It is characteristic of rules or formulas involving n^2 that the first differences increase as an arithmetic progression, and it is the second differences which are constant. One further consequence is that we can use our analysis of the structure of the sequence to continue it. Every second difference is 2, so each new first difference is the next odd number, so we can add successive odd numbers to provide more terms: $64 + 17 = 81, 81 + 19 = 100, 100 + 21 = 121, 121 + 23 = 144$, and so on.

First and second differences in the square number sequence														
Square numbers	1		4		9		16		25		36		49	64
First differences		3		5		7		9		11		13		15
Second differences			2		2		2		2		2		2	

Table 17.2

Triangle numbers

Another set of simple polygons is the triangles, and the triangle or triangular numbers form another sequence which occurs frequently in mathematics. Figure 17.5 shows how the sequence of triangle numbers is built to form the dots of successively larger triangles. This sequence is shown in Table 17.3. Here, we can see that the second difference is always 1, the first differences are the counting numbers from 2 upwards, so the next numbers in the sequence are $28 + 8 = 36, 36 + 9 = 45, 45 + 10 = 55$, and so on.

249

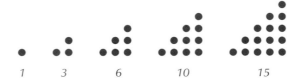

17.5 A representation of the triangle number sequence

To think about

The difficult question is, what is the algebraic rule or formula for the general term of the triangle numbers? This is left as a task for the reader though the answer will be found later in this module.

First and second differences in the triangle number sequence							
Triangle numbers 1		3		6		10	

Triangle numbers   1   3   6   10   15   21   28
First differences   2   3   4   5   6   7
Second differences   1   1   1   1   1

Table 17.3

To think about

The cubic numbers (1, 8, 27, 64, 125, ...) are based on using unit cubes to make successively bigger cubes. Investigate the cubic numbers, their differences and the rule or formula for the general term.

There are many more sets of polygonal numbers, based on pentagons, hexagons, and so on, and indeed there are polyhedral numbers too, based on solids such as the tetrahedron and the cube. It is not appropriate to take up any more space on such sequences here, though the cubic numbers are worthy of private investigation.

Prime numbers

Prime numbers are important in mathematics in many ways, for example as the basis of factorisation. Unfortunately, no-one has ever discovered a satisfactory pattern which leads to a formula for calculating the value of any prime number. One important investigation for primary children involves finding all the primes up to 100, by striking out in the 1–100 grid every number which has a factor other than 1 and itself – that is, numbers which have at least three factors. Thus, all even numbers greater than 2 are struck out because they have the factor 2 and possibly others; together with all additional numbers which are multiples of 3 (9, 15, 21, 27, 33, 39, 45, 51, 57, 63, 69, 75, 81, 87, 93, 99), all additional multiples of 5 (25, 35, 55, 65, 85, 95), and all additional multiples of 7 (49, 77, 91). The result of this investigation is illustrated in the 1–100 square in Figure 17.6, and it leaves us with the prime numbers:

2, 3, 5, 7, 11, 13, 17, 19, 23, 29, 31, 37, 41, 43, 47, 53, 59, 61, 67, 71, 73, 79, 83, 89, 97

To do

In the process of striking out all multiples, why is it only necessary to strike out the multiples of 2, 3, 5 and 7? What multiples is it only necessary to strike out on a 1–200 grid, a 1–300 grid, and so on? Write a general statement that describes what multiples it is only necessary to strike out on a 1-*n* grid.

Primes should be investigated as the first important example of a sequence which might be expected to have a pattern, but does not.

Fibonacci numbers

Another well known sequence is the Fibonacci numbers:

1, 1, 2, 3, 5, 8, 13, 21, 34, 55, 89, 144, 233, ...

X	2	3	X	5	X	7	X	X	X
11	X	13	X	X	X	17	X	19	X
X	X	23	X	X	X	X	X	29	X
31	X	X	X	X	X	37	X	X	X
41	X	43	X	X	X	47	X	X	X
X	X	53	X	X	X	X	X	59	X
61	X	X	X	X	X	67	X	X	X
71	X	73	X	X	X	X	X	79	X
X	X	83	X	X	X	X	X	89	X
X	X	X	X	X	X	97	X	X	X

17.6 Prime numbers on the 100-number grid

The rule which defines this sequence in words is 'each new number is the sum of the previous two numbers'. There is no formula for the general term of the kind which emerged from earlier sequences considered in this module. The original sequence defined by Fibonacci in the twelfth century began with the numbers 1, 1, as here, though it is possible to define other similar sequences starting with any two numbers of your choice.

Constant ratio sequences

The first sequences in this module had a constant difference property. Another important kind of sequence grows not with a constant difference but with a constant ratio. Modules 8 and 11 draw attention to the distinction between additive relationships and multiplicative relationships, with the latter being at the heart of ideas of ratio and proportion. Not surprisingly, sequences with a constant ratio grow on a multiplicative basis, for example:

2, 4, 8, 16, 32, 64, 128, 256, ...

Here, each new term is twice the previous, and if we tabulate position against term, as in Table 17.4, it should help us to see that the formula is $t = 2^n$ (see Module 10). Investigating differences does not really help us to analyse such constant ratio sequences (why not?). It should be clear from this, and from the Fibonacci sequence, that finding differences is of limited use in the exploration of sequences in general, and children need to be encouraged to investigate sequences in other ways. Successive terms here grow in magnitude very quickly, and the numbers can soon become very large indeed. However, Module 5 makes it clear that this would not be the case if decimals were to be involved, in other words when n is small. Table 17.5 shows how the terms grow (to 3 decimal places) when the constant ratio is 1.05.

Powers of 2 and their position in the sequence									
Position	1	2	3	4	5	6	7	8	...	n
Term	2	4	8	16	32	64	128	256	...	t
	2^1	2^2	2^3	2^4	2^5	2^6	2^7	2^8	...	2^n

Table 17.4

A geometric sequence with a constant ratio of 1.05									
n	0	1	2	3	4	5	6	7	8
t	1000	1.050	1.103	1.158	1.216	1.276	1.340	1.407	1.477

Table 17.5

Such 'geometric progressions' are usually considered to be more difficult than the constant difference sequences, and therefore play a much smaller part in school mathematics before advanced courses in mathematics. Nevertheless, they are very important in the world. Table 17.5 provides the basis of compound interest calculations at 5%. Thus, if £1000 were to be invested and left to gain compound interest at 5%, the sum (principal) would grow annually as in Table 17.6.

Compound interest calculated annually at 5%									
End of year	0	1	2	3	4	5	6	7	8
Principal (to nearest £)	1000	1050	1103	1158	1216	1276	1340	1407	1477

Table 17.6

Another important sequence with constant ratio 10 provides the structure of our place value system (see Modules 4 and 5):

..., 0.001, 0.01, 0.1, 1, 10, 100, 1000, ...

Functions and graphs

Two other large areas of study in mathematics are functions and graphs, and these grow naturally out of the study of number patterns, as may already be clear (see Modules 18 and 19). The first number sequence studied in this module is shown in Table 17.7. Translating the vertical number pairs (1, 3), (2, 5), (3, 7), etc., into co-ordinates, this data may be represented graphically and the pattern displayed pictorially. Constant difference sequences such as that in Table 17.7 produce straight line (linear) graphs. This extension to work on number patterns is further developed in Modules 18 and 19.

To think about

Use the tables in the section on constant difference sequences to investigate the graphs obtained. Now investigate tables in other sections to investigate the shapes of graphs obtained.

Searching for the relationship between an odd number and its position in the sequence										
n	1	2	3	4	5	6	7	8	9	...
t	3	5	7	9	11	13	15	17	19	...

Table 17.7

Structure

'Structure' is a word used for the collection of regularities and symmetries which we find in mathematics, particularly when considering the outcomes of operations in mathematics. At primary school, most children generally only meet the four elementary operations ($+, -, \times, \div$), but these four are sufficient to give rise not only to the '-tivity' properties – commutativity, associativity and distributivity – but also to concepts such as identity (0 for $+$, 1 for $\times$) and inverse (see Module 11).

Children and pattern

Pre-school progress

Young children's 'play' activities incorporate a wide range of materials, including beads, pegs, tiles, blocks, construction kits, drawing and painting equipment – and indeed anything movable that might be available. Sometimes, it is clear that what they make possesses characteristics of what teachers might call 'pattern', such as symmetry, repetition and other forms of regularity. There is little, if any, official guidance for teachers about what activities these children ought to be engaged in, and what progress ought to be expected. SCAA (1996) appears to suggest a curriculum which allows no creativity, rather one of simply recognising and copying patterns. On the other hand, HMI (1989) places considerable emphasis on children being allowed to explore, create and continue their own patterns. The importance of encouraging creativity in all spheres of human interest, however, suggests that a curriculum which incorporates the encouragement of creativity is better than one which does not.

PATTERN PLAY

A research project by Gura (1992) detected a tendency for children to fall into three categories when working with blocks. Some children primarily seemed interested in patterns, others used their blocks as story props, and others used their blocks in both ways. These results suggest that the 'dramatists' need to be guided into more varied ways of working with blocks and other such materials. Athey (1990) has shown how pre-school children impose their own structure onto a wide variety of play materials. A detailed study by Garrick (see Garrick *et al.*, 1999) tracked the progress of children from 3½ to 4½ years of age, using pegs, beads and mosaic tiles, focusing on patterning by colour and by position. It seems that significant development takes place in children's spatial structuring of materials in this year. The suggestion from this study is that it seems more important for teachers to encourage self-initiated work, and for the children to share their products with others, including the teacher, rather than risk them becoming constrained by models imposed by an adult.

There is very limited evidence related to the perception of pattern in pre-school children and only a little more with those in early years' classes.

PATTERN PERCEPTION

Rawson (1993) conducted an interesting study with children who were mostly aged 5–6, and who were expected to sort a collection of objects into 'pattern' and 'not pattern'. Rawson commented particularly on how difficult it is for young children to verbalise the observations on which they make their decisions. The 3½–4½-year-old children referred to above (Garrick *et al.*, 1999) were also asked to select, with reasons for choice, a favourite necklace from those worn by teddy bears. It seemed that only a minority of the children used characteristics of colour organisation as a criterion for choice. Many just liked a particular teddy bear!

The implication from all the evidence available is that the recognition of pattern is not as easy for young children as might be thought by adults, and therefore that copying and continuing might present quite difficult challenges, once again suggesting that talk based on children's own pattern-making activities is particularly important.

Repeating patterns

Linear repeating patterns (for example ■, ▲, ▲, ■, ▲, ▲, ...) receive some emphasis in curriculum recommendations. Threlfall (1999) suggests two purposes for repeating pattern work:

- that it is useful as a basis for subsequent work in number and measurement. In other words, the repeating pattern work might not be essential but, having done it, it can be exploited in a number of ways
- that repeating patterns provide valuable pre-algebra experiences.

The main issue here is how children react to working with such sequences, and Threlfall (1999) has suggested two strands to development:

- one is, not surprisingly, increasing complexity of pattern
- the other is concerned with how the child perceives the patterns, and thus perhaps this strand involves a major developmental threshold.

A repeating pattern may be perceived either in the form of a chant (for example, 'red green yellow yellow red green yellow yellow') or in terms of what is repeated (for example 'one red one green two yellows'). The suggestion is that the chanting approach does not necessarily imply an understanding of what is repeated. Only when children can be said to understand the rule of construction in a more sophisticated way can they answer questions like 'What colour would be the thirteenth in the list?' and 'In a list of the first twenty-five elements, how many would be red?'

Generally, younger primary school children are expected to work with repeating patterns more than are older children. This may be due to teachers of children in the later primary years assuming that such work has been done in the earlier years and, perhaps, adopting the attitude that it is inappropriate, 'too babyish', for older children There are dangers here, because it is the younger children who may not have reached the stage of fully understanding the unit of repeat. Both Phillips (1969) and Wood (1988) have suggested that many younger primary children (5–7 years), and some older, are limited in how they can think about repeating patterns. Phillips also reminds us that children can sometimes seem to be operating with a strategy when they are not, and in this case that might mean that repeating pattern work is ineffective. If developmental factors are at play here, the solution is to ensure that children have the opportunity to continue with repeated pattern work into the later primary years.

PATTERN CONTINUATION

Several 7–8-year-old children were given the repeating pattern In Figure 17.7 and asked 'If the pattern continues, what would be the 25th shape?'. They were also requested to explain how they worked it out. As the answer had only two possibilities it is not surprising that the vast majority gave the correct answer, 'square'. Here are a selection of children's explanations:

'I worked it out by counting in twos and it ended up in a square.'
'I used lines and circles (these were drawn on the sheet) and counted.'
'Because I knew that the square was an odd number.'
'I counted two squares and two circles.'

What knowledge and understanding does it appear that each child has about the repeating pattern? What processes and inferences did each child use to find the answer?

17.7 A repeating pattern of squares and circles

Odd and even numbers

The partitioning of whole numbers into odd and even is referred to by most national curricula, and appears to be an expected early development of pattern. But how do children understand this classification? What enables them to decide whether a number is odd or even, and can they apply their rules consistently and reliably? It should be clear to readers that the 100 grid in Figure 17.1 reveals the odd and even numbers very simply, in its alternate columns. One active approach is to count objects into pairs, so that the distinction is between situations in which there is or is not one single object left at the end. An example of a pictorial approach is illustrated in Figure 17.8.

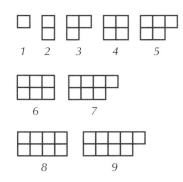

17.8 A pictorial representation of odd and even numbers

Such approaches, and many other possibilities, may be helpful, but there is evidence that children still cannot reliably classify larger numbers as even or odd. In other words, the pattern rules which they have built up in their minds through all the activities in which they have been engaged are not adequate for dealing with larger numbers.

For numbers like 17, 46, 81, 129 and 2374, it should be clear to readers that it is necessary to focus only on the final digit, but children appear to be frequently influenced by other digits in such larger numbers. A survey across the entire age range of nearly 500 primary school children and from a variety of schools has provided detailed information about this phenomenon in relation to two-digit numbers. The percentages of correct responses for Year 6 children are shown in Table 17.8. Naturally, the performance of children in younger age groups was inferior to that summed up in the table. The information and implications arising from this evidence are too many and too varied to include here, and readers are referred to Frobisher (1999). Suffice to say that we cannot assume that children in any age group have a thorough understanding of odd and even numbers, and work involving this classification must continue throughout the primary years.

To think about

Choose some of the two-digit numbers in Table 17.8 that have less than a 70% success rate. Try to explain children's reasoning which resulted in the incorrect response. Discuss your ideas with colleagues.

Percentage of correct identification of a number whether even or odd

		Unit digit									
		0	1	2	3	4	5	6	7	8	9
Tens digit	0	47	84	84	83	84	86	86	87	86	91
	1	84	82	82	82	78	84	79	85	76	85
	2	86	47	88	71	86	69	84	69	81	69
	3	71	80	72	81	70	81	74	86	68	80
	4	87	68	82	69	79	70	83	75	86	76
	5	74	85	69	86	71	76	70	81	66	84
	6	79	79	83	65	80	67	82	75	82	71
	7	67	84	67	84	71	80	68	82	64	85
	8	84	69	84	67	83	62	87	72	84	66
	9	67	88	68	82	62	78	69	86	68	85

Table 17.8

Number facts

An adequate and acceptable level of numeracy requires knowledge of number facts as a basis (see Modules 12 to 15). The question is how children should be helped to build up the necessary knowledge:

- through rote exercises such as recitation
- through exposure in meaningful contexts
- through recognition and use of pattern
- a combination of approaches?

In the short term, it can seem as if rote learning enables more facts to be remembered more quickly. What occurs over a period of time, however, is the phenomenon known as 'interference', in which errors occur by accidental association with other similar knowledge. For example, even adults frequently give 54 as the answer to 7×8, when in fact it is the answer to 6×9. If facts have been learned by rote, it seems there is an unavoidable need to continue rehearsing known facts (and for children this has to occur alongside the attempts to acquire more and more new facts). But if facts are learned through the automatisation of inferential derivation strategies, there is a logic onto which pupils can fall back for confirmation. The issues discussed here are considered more fully by Threlfall and Frobisher (1999). The use of inference has been discussed in all four of the operations modules, mainly in relation to mental methods with relatively small numbers. But are children able to use knowledge of addition with small numbers to infer from patterns answers to questions with larger numbers?

PATTERN INFERENCE

Seventy-six 7–8-year-old children were asked to continue the pattern in these additions:

$$3 + 9 = 12$$
$$30 + 90 = \square$$
$$300 + 900 = \square$$

A third of the children gave no answers, or were incorrect for both questions. Only three children gave an incorrect first answer, but wrote 1200 for the second addition, suggesting that they had calculated the answers not inferred them. 34% gave correct answers to both questions. The interesting responses were from those who gave 120 as the answer to the first addition and then a related, but incorrect, answer to 300 + 900. The most frequent response was 1020 given by 7 children, nearly 1 in 10. Many of the other answers used a 1, a 2 and one or more 0s. These were some such responses: 1220, 10020, 100020, 1120, 12000.

Discuss with some colleagues the responses described above. What do you think it suggests about children's use of pattern to infer answers to additions when large numbers are involved?

Number patterns

There is no doubt that activities based on number sequences form an important element of primary school mathematics. However, it is important to know how successful children are in dealing with the variety of different tasks, and how much of the approach to algebra discussed earlier in this module it is reasonable to attempt in the primary school. The issue of number sequences as a viable approach to algebra has been researched extensively.

NUMBER SEQUENCES

In the summary of research published by the APU (undated, p. 416), and based on the ability of 11 and 15-year-old pupils to continue the sequences (1) 1, 2, 4, 8, ..., (2) 1, 3, 6, 10, ..., (3) 1, 4, 9, 16, ..., (4) 1, 1, 2, 3, 5, ..., we find that 'Finding terms in number patterns gets progressively more difficult the further the terms are from those given in the question. More pupils can continue a pattern than can explain it. Number pattern rules are described by a large proportion of pupils in relation to differences between terms. Generally, oral explanations of rules ... are given by more pupils than can write an explanation.'

One particularly significant finding is that related to differencing, because earlier discussion within this module has already attempted to make it clear that differencing is only helpful in certain kinds of sequence. It is abundantly clear from this and from a variety of other studies, for example that of Orton and Orton (1996), that many pupils use differencing indiscriminately, as if it is the only method available and as if it is bound to work in all circumstances.

GENERALISATION METHODS

In a study by Stacey (1989), involving pupils aged 9–11, and in which terms like the 20th were demanded in a variety of constant difference sequences, several more elaborate unsuitable methods were identified. These same inadequate methods were also used by older pupils, including those involved in studies by Stacey (1989) and by Orton and Orton (1996).

The first was the use of counting on, which could be used only when sequences were based on pictures. The second, called here the Difference Product method, occurs when students used the difference and multiplied this by the term number – thus in the sequence 1, 4, 7, 10, ... the 20th term would be $3 \times 20 = 60$. The third, called here the Short Cut method, is based on the assumption that, for example, the 20th term would be $5 \times$ the 4th term, that is $5 \times 10 = 50$, in the sequence used as an illustration. Using the general term $t_n = 3n - 2$, we can see that the correct 20th term for this sequence is 58.

The critical question is, when do children become capable of establishing and using this general term, or even any reliable informal method of finding and applying a general term? In general only a small minority of 11-year-old children are currently able to use a general term to calculate other terms like the 20th or the 100th. Sequences based on polygonal numbers, and other sequences in which it is the second difference which is constant, are even more difficult. Research evidence of children's performance on number sequences is discussed more fully by Orton (1999).

Some ideas for teaching pattern

To do

Analyse at least two textbook series and compare their content, order and approach toward the development and use of pattern.

Textbooks and pattern

Few textbook series view pattern as anything other than another topic in the primary curriculum. Many give scant consideration to its role even as a topic and you may find that it does not appear at all in some series, nor in the curriculum of your school.

Pattern in teaching mathematics

It is essential in any approach to teaching mathematics through pattern that children are actively involved in as many stages of the process as possible. Figure 17.9 shows a model of the important stages in the process.

The teacher's role in this process is not a passive one, but requires that they constantly ask questions which draw children's attention to relationships and properties that they might otherwise not observe. They should also sense when the time is appropriate to bring the class together to talk about issues which have arisen with individual children, seeking clarification, opinions and explanations.

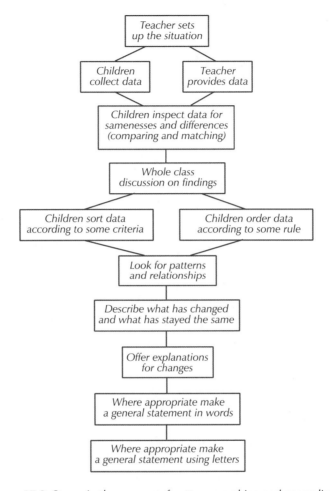

17.9 Stages in the process of pattern searching and generalisation

Activities with addition

In moving from counting to other methods of adding, children begin to base their thinking on 'ties'. Thus, it is important to help children to develop an appreciation of the patterns of ties, through such means as linking cubes, then number rods such as Cuisenaire, and finally more symbolic representations. This approach is illustrated in Figure 17.10. Here, as so very often in mathematics, pattern arises from the numbers but is best illustrated pictorially, More details of a teaching programme within which this appeal to pattern might occur are included in Threlfall and Frobisher (1999).

It is important that children then develop knowledge of the combinations and partitions relating to particular numbers. An example of

259

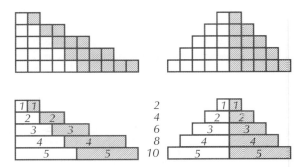

17.10 Visual and symbolic patterns in 'ties'

this is shown in Figure 17.11a, which focuses on 'the story of 10', though the same can be done for other numbers. This 'story of 10' may then be used as a way of extending to larger numbers, as in Figure 17.11b. There are similar activities with apparatus which explore the patterns in the other three number operations.

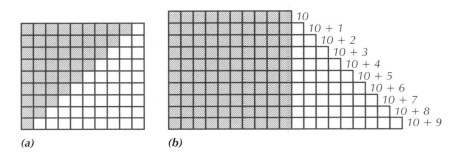

(a)   *(b)*

17.11 The 'story of 10' and an extension

Activities with the 100 number grid

Either version of the 100 number grid (0–99 or 1–100) may be used to illustrate patterns, including patterns of multiples. The activity of finding the prime numbers, discussed earlier (and sometimes known as the Sieve of Eratosthenes), is in a sense the climax of this simple search for patterns. Shading multiples of any number reveals a pattern, but some patterns are more appealing than others (see Module 14). Shading multiples of 9 allows a focus on the fact that there is an important extra numerical pattern here, namely that the digits in any multiple of 9 add up to 9 (note that 99 requires digit pairs to be added twice). Shading multiples of 8 and then, on the same hundred square, multiples of 4, and then multiples of 2, reveals important connections. The same can be done for 6 and 3, 6 and 2, 9 and 3, and 10 and 5. Each revealed pattern allows a focus on the characteristics of the numbers which are shaded, and on those which are not shaded, which can form the beginnings of an analysis of the important concept of divisibility (see Module 15).

Activities with multiplication tables

All written versions of multiplication tables necessarily record the number patterns involved (see Module 14). However, the more advanced version in Table 17.9 incorporates all multiplication tables and reveals patterns in unusual ways. Here the numbers 1–12 are recorded along axes as if they were for a graph, and then products are recorded within the box. Children can then explore and comment on where particular numbers occur, and some children will notice that there is a visual pattern to where, for example, the number 12 occurs. In fact, the reason for using products up to 12 × 12 is to obtain some numbers which crop up six times. Other products, like 6, 8 and 9, occur fewer times, but still the same kind of pattern is revealed. The patterns involve symmetry, of course, which in itself arises from commutativity, and hence we can see how an activity based only on multiplication tables can open the door to the kinds of studies of structure discussed earlier. Colouring all the boxes containing 24, or 12, or whatever, highlights the products, reinforces knowledge of products, and surreptitiously also introduces a kind of graph, a hyperbola, which is important to many children in subsequent secondary school mathematics (see Module 14).

Incorporating multiplication tables into one table

12	12	24	36	48	60	72	84	96	108	120	132	144
11	11	22	33	44	55	66	77	88	99	110	121	132
10	10	20	30	40	50	60	70	80	90	100	110	120
9	9	18	27	36	45	54	63	72	81	90	99	108
8	8	16	24	32	40	48	56	64	72	80	88	96
7	7	14	21	28	35	42	49	56	63	70	77	84
6	6	12	18	24	30	36	42	48	54	60	66	72
5	5	10	15	20	25	30	35	40	45	50	55	60
4	4	8	12	16	20	24	28	32	36	40	44	48
3	3	6	9	12	15	18	21	24	27	30	33	36
2	2	4	6	8	10	12	14	16	18	20	22	24
1	1	2	3	4	5	6	7	8	9	10	11	12
X	1	2	3	4	5	6	7	8	9	10	11	12

Table 17.9

Activities with square numbers

The patterns in the square numbers, revealed by studying first and second differences, have already been discussed, and the general term, $t = n^2$, is obvious. One important additional pattern to emphasise here is the connection between the odd numbers and the square numbers:

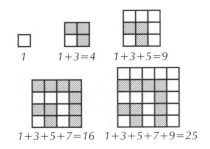

$$1 = 1$$
$$4 = 1 + 3$$
$$9 = 1 + 3 + 5$$
$$16 = 1 + 3 + 5 + 7$$
$$25 = 1 + 3 + 5 + 7 + 9$$

17.12 The sum of consecutive odd numbers starting at 1 is a square number

and so on. This may be illustrated pictorially, as in Figure 17.12 A valuable practical activity is to cut out L-shapes representing 3, 5, 7, 9, etc., and fit them together to make larger and larger square numbers.

Activities with triangle numbers

Triangle numbers and counting numbers

The triangle numbers form a deceptively simple sequence. Here, the connection is with the counting numbers:

$$1 = 1$$
$$3 = 1 + 2$$
$$6 = 1 + 2 + 3$$
$$10 = 1 + 2 + 3 + 4$$
$$15 = 1 + 2 + 3 + 4 + 5$$

and so on. What could be easier? Children are given number strips, each representing a counting number. The triangle numbers are then constructed as the sum of the counting numbers starting at 1, as illustrated in Figure 17.13. Some children may be able to write a general statement in words about the pattern they notice.

Triangle numbers and square numbers

Triangle numbers are closely related to square numbers. To investigate the relationship children need two sets of the first five, say, triangle numbers, including 1, on card as in Figure 17.13. Children are challenged to use their triangle numbers to make squares. The result is shown in Figure 17.14, with $T(1) + T(2) = 2 \times 2$, $T(2) + T(3) = 3 \times 3$, $T(3) + T(4) = 4 \times 4$, and so on. Again some children may be able to write a general statement in words about the pattern they notice.

The number 36 is both a triangle number and a square number. Are there other whole numbers with this property? High attainers can investigate this question. A computer program or spreadsheet might help.

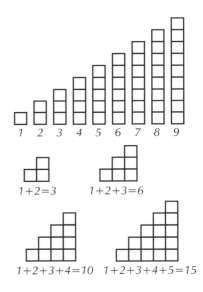

17.13 The sum of consecutive counting numbers starting at 1 is a triangle number

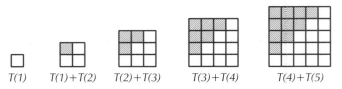

17.14 The sum of two consecutive triangle numbers is a square number

Making rectangles with triangle numbers

Two of the same triangle number can be put together to make a rectangle. This may not in itself be a particularly challenging activity, but it leads to an interesting relationship. To investigate the relationship

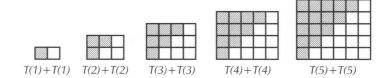

$T(1)+T(1)$ $\quad$ $T(2)+T(2)$ $\quad$ $T(3)+T(3)$ $\quad$ $T(4)+T(4)$ $\quad$ $T(5)+T(5)$

17.15 Twice a triangle number is a rectangle number

children need two sets of the first five, say, triangle numbers, including 1, on card as in Figure 17.13. Children are challenged to use their triangle numbers to make rectangles. The result is shown in Figure 17.15, with T(1) + T(1) = 1 × 2, T(2) + T(2) = 2 × 3, T(3) + T(3) = 3 × 4, and so on. Table 17.10 lists the relationships in order enabling the general statement $T(N) + T(N) = N \times (N + 1)$ to be inductively reasoned. This can be simplified to $2T(N) = N(N + 1)$.

Twice a triangle number is a rectangle number
$T(1) + T(1) = 1 \times 2$
$T(2) + T(2) = 2 \times 3$
$T(3) + T(3) = 3 \times 4$
$T(4) + T(4) = 4 \times 5$
$T(5) + T(5) = 5 \times 6$

Table 17.10

The simplified general statement leads to the conclusion that

$$T(N) = \frac{N(N + 1)}{2}$$

giving a formula with which to calculate the value of any triangle number.

A class activity

OBJECTIVE   To explore patterns in addition

ORGANISATION   Whole class

RESOURCES   Teacher has two large addition grids as shown in Figure 17.16, but with no numbers at the start

ACTIVITY
- Teacher writes in the same number, say 5, in each of the answer boxes.
- Children are asked for two numbers whose sum is 5

| 4 | + | 1 | = | 5 |

| 2 | + | 3 | = | 5 |

| 5 | + | 0 | = | 5 |

| 3 | + | 2 | = | 5 |

| 0 | + | 5 | = | 5 |

| 1 | + | 4 | = | 5 |

(a)

| 5 | + | 0 | = | 5 |

| 4 | + | 1 | = | 5 |

| 3 | + | 2 | = | 5 |

| 2 | + | 3 | = | 5 |

| 1 | + | 4 | = | 5 |

| 0 | + | 5 | = | 5 |

(b)

17.16 Addition grids for pattern searching

- A child comes out and writes the numbers, if correct, in the boxes.
- The activity is repeated until all additions are exhausted, as in Figure 17.16a.
- Children are asked to look for patterns.
- The additions are ordered by the children as shown in Figure 17.16b.
- Discussion takes place on the reasons for the patterns, what changes, what stays the same and why.

A group activity

OBJECTIVE   To sort and order subtractions

ORGANISATION   Small groups

RESOURCES   Each group has a set of subtraction cards with single-digit answers 1, 2 and 3, for example $9 - 8 = 1$, $8 - 7 = 1$, ... $9 - 7 = 2$, $8 - 6 = 2$, ..., $9 - 6 = 3$, $8 - 5 = 3$, $7 - 4 = 3$, ...

ACTIVITY   The children sort and later order the subtraction cards in various ways, always describing the patterns they see and why they work.

Test your own knowledge: pattern

1   What is the generalised formula relating two successive triangle numbers and a square number?

2   What is the generalised formula relating two of the same triangle number and a rectangle number?

3   Investigate pentagonal numbers.

4   **a** Find the answers to each of these and continue the pattern as far as it will go:

$$11 \div (1 + 1) =$$
$$22 \div (2 + 2) =$$
$$33 \div (3 + 3) =$$
$$44 \div (4 + 4) =$$
$$55 \div (5 + 5) =$$

b Explain why the pattern works. Write a proof using the letter N to represent a digit.

c Investigate what happens for three-digit numbers with the digit repeated, e.g. $111 \div (1 + 1 + 1)$, and so on.

d Extend the pattern to 4-, 5-, 6-, ...-digit numbers with the digits repeated.

5 13 is a prime number. Place a 1 after the 13 to make 131. Is this a prime? Find all the other two-digit numbers which have this property. What happens if you place a 2 after a two-digit prime? What happens if you place a 3 after a two-digit prime? Continue the investigation for other digits placed after a prime.

6 The numbers 44, 272, 3 768 673 are all palindromic numbers. Describe what is special about palindromic numbers. How many are there between 0 and 99, 100 and 199, 200 and 299, ...? Investigate more about palindromic numbers.

7 The number 16 is a square number. If we insert 15 in the middle (between the 1 and 6) we get the number 1156, which is also a square number (use your calculator to test this). Repeat to produce 111 556. Is this a square number? Continue to insert 15 in the middle of each square number formed. Is every new number a square number?

8 Does this pattern continue for ever?

$$1 \times 9 = 10 - 1$$
$$2 \times 9 = 20 - 2$$
$$3 \times 9 = 30 - 3$$
$$4 \times 9 = 40 - 4$$

Explain why. Explain why the pattern works.

9 Does this pattern continue for ever?

$$(1 \times 9) + 2 = 11$$
$$(12 \times 9) + 3 = 111$$
$$(123 \times 9) + 4 = 1111$$

Explain why. Explain why the pattern works.

10 Use a calculator to investigate patterns in recurring decimal equivalents of unit fractions with prime denominators.

Review of key points

➤ Pattern is all around in mathematics

➤ Perceiving, understanding, and using patterns form important elements of learning mathematics

➤ Pattern work begins with colouring and with constructions involving shapes

➤ Children should be encouraged to be creative and to discuss their patterns with others

➤ Odd numbers and even numbers are patterns which are experienced relatively early, but many children experience difficulties recognising the odd or even nature of larger numbers

➤ Children's growing grasp of addition, subtraction, multiplication and division may be greatly helped by drawing attention to and building on patterns

➤ Tables, grids, hundred squares, and other systematic means of recording all form useful devices which enlighten pattern studies and emphasise structure

➤ Number sequences are very important because they form the basis on which many mathematical topics will be developed later

➤ To learn mathematics through pattern children should always attempt to describe a pattern and explain why a pattern 'works'

➤ Children should be encouraged to express generalisations of patterns in words. Some high attainers may be able to use letters

➤ Pattern studies form one valuable route into algebra

Module 18   Learning to teach functions

Introduction

Functions rank with numbers and sets as fundamental concepts of mathematics – and, perhaps more importantly, are part of every child's life. The aim that every child should be 'numerate' demands that we should provide children with the means to think functionally and with the ability to interpret situations they may meet in which functions are used.

Functions in national curricula

Very few national primary mathematics curricula contain explicit references to functions, leaving their study to later years. However, there is implicit reference to functions in other concepts included in curricula, such as relationships and mappings. You are likely to find the following related ideas in a primary curriculum:

- exploring, using and explaining relationships
- interpreting, generalising and using mappings
- plotting co-ordinates
- recognising relationships between co-ordinates on a graph
- using number machines.

Key terms

variable	see Module 16
relationship	see Module 16
mapping	see Module 16
function	assigns to each value of the independent variable one, and only one, value of the dependent variable
domain	the set of all possible values of the independent variable of a function
range	the set of all possible values of the dependent variable of a function
rule	operates on each member of a domain to produce its **image** in the range; name sometimes given to function

---

Key issues in functions

Related concepts and issues

Function is an algebraic concept, with strong links to number, with number patterns providing an excellent source for both early and later

267

functional thinking. As functions provide a thread running through the curriculum it is impossible to show all the related concepts and issues in one diagram: thus Figure 18.1 shows only the most important.

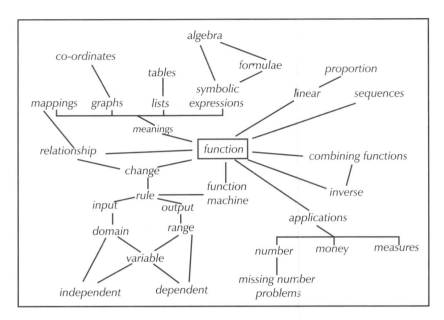

18.1   Concepts and issues associated with functions

Concept of function

At an intuitive level a function is a relationship between quantities. As such, it is has no physical characteristics and cannot be felt, moved or seen. This is true of all concepts, yet many of those that children meet in primary mathematics have representations modelled by physical entities.

Children's experience of functionality is of two kinds:

- situations in which one variable is given and the other is usually unknown, it having to be calculated according to some rule. For example, when children buy football cards the rule may be '10 cards for 20p'. The children know how many cards they want and calculate how much money they need

- situations where the two variables are patently obvious, but with no apparent rule. For example, children 'know' that as they count the numbers get bigger; they believe that the older they get, the taller they will get; the more they attend school, the more they will learn!

These are all perceptions of functional relationships between two variables, one which comes first (the independent variable) and the other (the dependent variable). To understand such functional relationships children need to:

- have knowledge of the variables
- know how the variables relate to each other, that is the rule
- understand the situation in which the variables are embedded.

Most functions that children meet in the primary curriculum are likely to be 'linear' in that they have a direct proportional relationship between two variables; for example, the value of each odd number in terms of its position in the odd number sequence (see Module 17), and the conversion of centimetres to inches.

Functional relationships may depend on several variables. For example, the income generated from a theatre performance may simply depend on the number of tickets sold. This would be income as a function of the one variable, tickets sold. However, the income is more likely to depend on the number of tickets sold at various prices. Income is now a function of several variables. The area of a rectangle is a function of two variables, its length and its breadth.

To think about

What are the everyday uses of the word 'function'? How could you harness these to introduce the idea of mathematical function to primary children?

Meanings of function

There are four different ways in which children meet functions in the mathematical sense. Functions are really understood only when an integrated meaning is established such that children can not only move freely from one to the other but are also able to choose the particular one that is appropriate to the situation and to the problem. The four meanings are:

- mapping diagrams
- lists
- graphs
- symbolic representations.

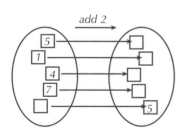

18.2 The 'add 2' mapping

Mapping diagrams

Functions are often viewed as mappings between sets. Mappings are used from an early age for practising operations on numbers (as shown in Figure 18.2), where children work out the missing numbers. In this example missing numbers 'appear' in both sets, requiring children to have some understanding of 'undoing' a rule, in this case, the inverse of 'add 2' which is 'subtract 2'.

The set of input numbers is known as the *domain* of the function. The set of output numbers, the *images* of the input numbers, is known as the *range*. The idea of input and output numbers relates to the use of function machines discussed later.

Lists

A list or table of input numbers shown as corresponding to output numbers is also taken as a function. Although strictly speaking the

A function as a listing of inputs and outputs

Halve and add 3.5	
Input	Output
1	4
2	4.5
3	5
4	5.5
5	6

Table 18.1

function is the listing, it is usual for the rule to be explicitly stated, as in Table 18.1.

Each input and its corresponding output form an ordered pair. If the set of ordered pairs is collected from the list then we have (1, 4), (2, 4.5), (3, 5), (4, 5.5,), (5, 6), ...; this set may also be taken to define the function.

Graphs

Most graphs that primary children construct and interpret are manifestations of functions. A graph provides a visual representation of the data and the relationship that exists between each pair of co-ordinates, the ordered pairs. A thorough discussion of co-ordinate graphs as functions can be found in Module 19.

Symbolic representations

Symbolic representations of functions take many forms, only some of which are appropriate for primary children. You may meet some of these at some time in your teaching career. Each of the following represents the function 'add 2'.

- $\square \xrightarrow{\text{add 2}} \square$, or $\square \xrightarrow{+2} \square + 2$
- $\square \to \square + 2$, or $f(\square) = \square + 2$
- $x \to x + 2$, or $f(x) = x + 2$, or $y = x + 2$

Models of functions

Concrete materials

Coloured tiles, counters, number rods and base 10 apparatus all lend themselves to activities which illustrate what happens when a function is applied to a quantity.

To think about

Discuss with a colleague the assumptions that each representation makes and the cognitive demands of working with each one. Which do you think are appropriate for primary children and how could you introduce them to children?

MAKING SHAPES

Neil was making shapes with grey and white cubes. His teacher encouraged him to surround white cubes with grey borders to make patterns. Figure 18.3 shows five shapes that Neil made.

Neil's teacher suggested that he counted the number of white and grey cubes in each shape and make a table of his data. He made Table 18.2, but failed to order the data. When this was pointed out to him he produced Table 18.3. Ordering of data is an important process in the search for patterns and relationships.

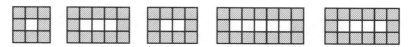

18.3 Neil's shapes

Number of white cubes	Number of grey cubes
1	8
4	14
2	10
3	12
5	16

Table 18.2

Number of white cubes	Number of grey cubes
1	8
2	10
3	12
4	14
5	15

Table 18.3

When asked to describe any patterns Neil talked about the number of white cubes going up in 1s and the grey cubes going up in 2s. To draw Neil's attention to the functional relationship between the number of white and grey cubes his teacher drew a function machine as in Figure 18.4 and asked him what rule the machine would use to find the number of grey cubes if he knew how many white cubes were in the bag. After 'playing' with numbers for a while he responded by saying, 'Double and add 6.'

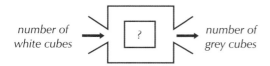

number of white cubes → [?] → *number of grey cubes*

18.4 A function machine representation

Function machines

A function machine was shown in Figure 18.4. They have also been used in previous modules as models of operations (see Modules 12 to 15). There are four major uses for function machines:

To do

Work with a small group of colleagues. One of you acts as the machine and needs to work out, say, 10 inputs and outputs for a given rule which only the machine knows. The machine tells the group an input and its corresponding output. The group have to guess the rule. If on the first occasion this is not achieved then another input–output is given until a person 'guesses' the rule. It is advisable to make the unknown rules relatively easy when first doing the activity.

As a group discuss the strategies that each of you used. Compare their efficiency and effectiveness.

To think about

Look at as many textbook series as you can to find out any language and symbolism which you feel is indicative of functions or functional thinking. Is it apparent that the writer of the books was aware of this? In what ways does the language and symbolism assist children's development of the function concept?

- to practise number skills
- to create and work with number patterns
- to use the processes of guessing and predicting
- to provide opportunities for generalising rules in words and symbols.

In textbooks you will find a variety of pictures and diagrams of function machines used to illustrate the function process. Whatever the picture or diagram, they have three aspects in common:

- an 'opening' for inputting an object, usually a number
- a rule for operating on or transforming the input
- an 'opening' for outputting an object, usually a number.

Activities with function machines and numbers usually give children two of the three aspects and ask them to find the third. When the input and rule are given the objective is to practise calculations. The most challenging activities are those where inputs and their corresponding outputs are given and the rule has to be found. Recognising and recording the constant relationship between input and corresponding output numbers is the act of generalisation.

Language and symbols

Words such as functions, mapping, domain, image, range, and so on, are strange to most children. The introduction of such language should be delayed until it is apparent that children have developed a sound understanding of the formal aspects of function. Little is lost – in fact much is gained – if everyday expressions, such as starter set (domain) and finishing set (range), are used.

Although there is some evidence that 'boxes' used to represent a missing number can be confusing for a minority of children, the difficulties created by the use of letters to represent numbers far outweigh the difficulties of using boxes.

Inverse function

The function machine is an excellent device for considering the concept of inverse function. This may be viewed in three different ways:

- using the same machine backwards; that is, in reverse
- two separate machines which do the 'opposite, as in Figure 18.5a
- two machines, one followed by the other, so that the eventual output is the same as the original input, as in Figure 18.5b.

In Figures 18.5a and b it does not follow, of course, that the rule for the second machine is the inverse of the rule of the first machine when only one pair of input–output numbers is given. More than one pair is necessary in order for children to inductively reason that the rule is the inverse function.

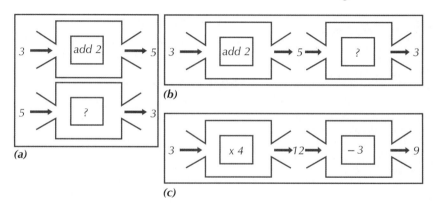

18.5 Combining function machines and inverse functions

Combining functions

Primary children can explore what happens when two function machines are combined, as they were with the above inverse machines. Combining functions means to operate with one function on its input and then to follow this by operating with the second function on the output from the first. This is illustrated in Figure 18.5c with '×4' as the first function operating on 3, giving an output of 12. The second function, '−3', then operates on the 12, producing a final output of the combined functions of 9. You will often find this recorded as

$$3 \xrightarrow{\times 4} 12 \xrightarrow{-3} 9.$$

The combination of function machines allows children to investigate whether the order of the two machines, or functions, makes a difference to the output for any given input. The question is, 'Are functions, in general, commutative?' (see Module 20)

Functions and formulae

A formula is equivalent to a function of one or more independent variables. For example, the circumference of a circle is a function of the diameter in that as the diameter changes so does the circumference; they are related by the formula $C = \pi d$, where C is the length of the circumference and d is the length of the diameter. The area of a rectangle is a function of two variables, the length and the breadth, and can be expressed as $A = l \times b$.

Children and functions

Learning about functions

Function is an important but difficult concept. There are aspects of the concept which can usefully be learned in the primary school as the functional relationships children have experienced outside the classroom provide the basis for a more formal approach, but only if its development is spread over many years of schooling. The development of formal functional ideas goes hand in hand with the development of other algebraic concepts and skills and cannot be treated in isolation.

273

To think about

Consider the topics in a primary mathematics curriculum and record where it may be possible and apt to draw children's attention to the functions which are part of the learning of the topic. Select two topics and expand on how you might do this.

To do

With a colleague make a list of the content and order of how function machines could be used in a textbook series.

Early experiences

Many of the activities young children perform at school are functional in nature. Only two are considered here.

Coats and coat pegs

When children put their coats on pegs with their name or picture on they are performing a functional activity.

Number names and symbols

When a numeral card is held up and children respond by saying its name they are operating a one-to-one functional relationship in that every numeral has one, and only one, name. The rule for matching numeral to name is determined purely by convention.

Some ideas for teaching functions

Textbooks and functions

Most textbooks fail to explicitly develop the concept of function, although it is implicit in many other areas of primary mathematics.

A class activity

OBJECTIVE
To practise calculation skills

ORGANISATION
Whole class

RESOURCES
- A function machine made from a large box, attractively decorated, together with a collection of at least five different function cards such as 'add 2', 'subtract 4', or more complex functions, such as '× 4 + 2', that can be attached to the front of the function machine

- A set of number cards for each child and a set for each operator
- You may also wish the function machine operator to have a list of outputs for any input within the domain in use. This speeds up the activity

ACTIVITY
- One child acts as the function machine operator at the front of the class.
- The operator chooses a function card which is attached to the front of the machine.
- Teacher chooses a child to put an input number into the machine.
- The rest of the class calculate the output and raise the appropriate number card.
- The operator then outputs the correct number, which is shown to the class.
- The activity is repeated for other input numbers.
- Children take turns as operators with different rules.

A group activity

OBJECTIVE	To collect and record information about children in the class
ORGANISATION	Small groups
RESOURCES	Large sheets on which the information can be recorded and displayed

ACTIVITY

- Each group collects information and constructs a mapping diagram of names of children of the whole class about one of the following:

  1 day of week of birthday this year

  2 ways children go home from school

  3 how many members in their family

  4 how many pets they have

  5 month of their birthday.

- Each group finds different ways of representing the information.

Test your own knowledge: functions

1 Name the variables and the functional relationships in:

a a footballer kicking a ball into the air

b water from a tap running into a bowl

c a light bulb as it is switched on and off.

2 What is the functional relationship between a diameter of a regular hexagon and the length of its side? How can this be expressed as a formula?

3 How many variables is the perimeter of a rectangle a function of? What are they? Write the perimeter as a functional relationship and a formula.

4 Write down as many variables as you can that determine the total cost of running a car each year.

5 Write down four different functions that produce an output of 7 for an input of 2

6 Find two different functions that for inputs of 3 and 7 give outputs of 1 and 4 respectively.

7 What is the inverse function of: **a** $f(x) = x + 3$, **b** $g(x) = 4x - 2$

8 The two functions $f(x) = x + 3$ and $g(x) = 4x - 2$ have the same output for some input. What is this input?

9 The two functions $f(x) = x + 3$ and $g(x) = 4x - 2$ are combined in the order f followed by g. What is the result of the combination written as a single function? What single function is equivalent to g followed by f?

Review of key points ➤ The development of the concept of function should be an aim of every primary mathematics curriculum

➤ Children constantly experience functions and their effects in their everyday lives

➤ Function is a fundamental concept of mathematics

➤ Although not explicitly stated in many curricula, functions provide a thread which weaves through many topics in the primary curriculum

➤ Functions can be expressed in terms of relationships, mappings and co-ordinates

➤ Children bring to their formal learning of functions a wide collection of informal experiences

➤ Missing number problems can lead to the study of pattern and functions

➤ To develop an integrated understanding of the concept of function children should have a variety of experiences of the four meanings of function

Module 19 Learning to teach diagrammatic representations

Introduction

Diagrammatic representations of numerical data are used to portray mappings and functions, in such a way as to bring to the surface that which might otherwise be hidden in a symbolic representation of the data. They are also used to specify locations, the most well known of which is the Cartesian co-ordinate system.

Diagrammatic representations in national curricula

A fundamental requirement of most primary curricula is that children should develop a variety of means of communicating mathematical information. They achieve this by:

- knowing a variety of ways of representing numerical data diagrammatically
- drawing and interpreting various mapping diagrams
- constructing Cartesian axes and plotting points to specify locations
- drawing and working with graphs of functions
- expressing 'rules' of function graphs in words and symbols.

Key terms

relation an association that connects two numbers

ordered pair a pair of numbers where the order in which they are written is important

co-ordinates an ordered pair or triple of numbers used to denote position

axes the reference lines of a system for denoting position

origin the point from which positions of all other points are measured

---

Key issues

Related concepts and issues

When numbers are under consideration the possibility of a diagram being used should be at the forefront of the mind of the user. The list of related concepts and issues could, therefore, include the whole of the number work in a primary curriculum. In one map this is not possible; Figure 19.1 shows only the most important of the related concepts and issues.

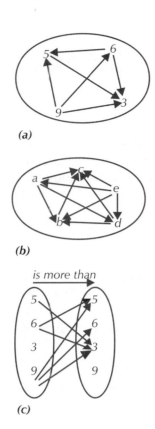

(a)

(b)

is more than

(c)

19.2 The 'more than' relation

To do

Diagrams like this contain a wealth of information. How is it possible to use the lines and arrowheads to decide which is the largest number in the set? Or the smallest number in the set? The letters in Figure 19.2b represent numbers. Write them in order of size, largest first. Explain to a colleague how you worked it out.

Make a list of other relations using small numbers that could be taught to 6-year-olds, and for which mapping diagrams could help children's understanding of the relations.

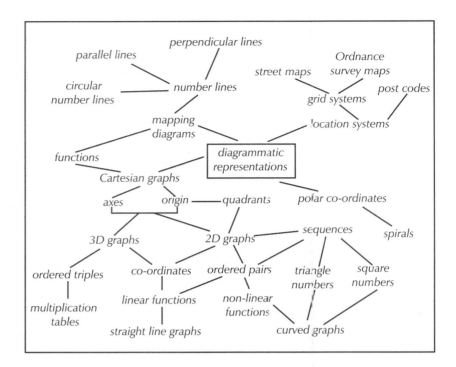

19.1 Concepts and issues associated with diagrammatic representation

Mapping diagrams

Mapping diagrams fall into two kinds:

- diagrams which relate members within a set
- diagrams which relate members between two sets.

Relations within a set

An early relation which young children are able to work with is 'is more than'. For two numbers this is written as, for example, 5 is more than 3. Such an approach considers 5 only in relation to 3. If there are more than two numbers a set enclosure is appropriate, with the relation 'is more than' shown between pairs of numbers by a line and an arrowhead indicating the direction of the relation (Figure 19.2a).

Mappings between sets

A mapping between two sets is one of the meanings given to the function concept (see Module 18). Another purpose of a mapping diagram is to illustrate relations. The information in Figure 19.2a can be shown representing the set of numbers as a domain and a range, as in Figure 19.2c.

A pair of parallel number lines

Teachers should not limit children's experiences of diagrammatic representations to those they 'know' are appropriate to particular circumstances. Children should be given opportunities to decide for themselves, with reasoned justification, why some representations are better than others. In this way they are developing as mathematical thinkers.

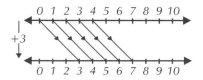

19.3 The 'add 3' mapping

Parallel number lines are very useful representations that provide insight into mappings and functions. They can be used with success in the primary school. Figure 19.3 illustrates part of the 'add 3' function.

There are many opportunities in representations for exploring pattern and structure leading to increased understanding of functions that it would be a mistake for teachers not to look further with primary children at what the representations have to offer from a wider mathematical perspective.

Perpendicular number lines
Functions can be represented using number lines at right angles to each other. Figure 19.4a illustrates the function 'subtract 2' using number lines at right angles.

Figure 19.4b represents the function 'subtract the number from 10'. Children find this a particularly fascinating diagram as it produces an 'envelope' of a parabola with the straight lines acting as tangents to an unseen curve. You will often find children constructing this diagram and others similar to it as part of what is commonly known as 'curve stitching', but with no mathematical purpose. We hope you will not fall into the same trap.

To think about

Work with a colleague to compare and contrast the similarities and differences of the 'add 3' and the 'add 5' functions represented on parallel number lines. What are the mathematical reasons for the similarities and differences? What would the graphs of the 'subtract 3' and 'subtract 5' functions look like? How can this help with the teaching of inverse operations?

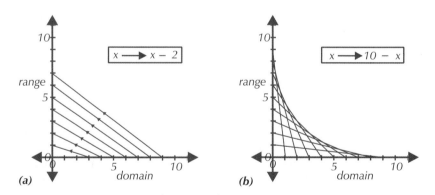

19.4 Two function diagrams using lines at right angles

A circular number line
When the domain and range of a function are the same a circular number line can be used to represent both. As the number of points positioned on the circumference of a circle will be finite, more than one number is mapped to each point. In Figure 19.5 there are 36 points around the circumference and, as the numbers start at 0, the number 36 is also mapped to the 0 position, 37 to the 1 position, and so on. Figure 19.5 represents the 'doubling' function, $1 \to 2$, $2 \to 4$, $3 \to 6$, $4 \to 8$, and so on. The heart-shaped envelope in called a cardioid. The idea can be extended to consider the functions $x \to 3x$, $x \to 4x$, and so on.

To do

Use two perpendicular number lines to draw the function $x \to 10 - x$, for positive and negative values of x.

279

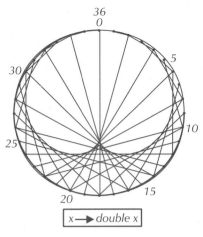

19.5 The doubling function on a circular number line

Location systems

Post codes are an everyday example of a location system. The ones of most concern to us are those based upon a grid. A grid system enables the position of a region, or more usually an area, to be defined. An example of a grid system is street maps. To find a particular street or road we look it up in the index, which refers the reader to a page on which there is a map, and also to a square on that map, say B3 (see Figure 19.6). The reader is left to search in the labelled square to find the place in question. The squares are usually numbered from left/right and lettered up/down, although the example shown in The National Numeracy Strategy (1999) Framework for 7–8 year olds reverses this approach. Road maps and guides to town centres use a similar system. Squares are chosen for regions because the units of distance are all to a given scale.

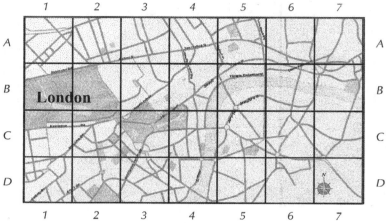

19.6 A street map using location symbols

It is customary in such grids to give the label of each square with the letter first followed by the number, say B3. However, the labels in each direction use different symbols so there is no possible confusion and 3B means the same as B3. It is, however, advisable to use the order of across followed by up/down from the very start.

Co-ordinate systems

In co-ordinate systems the position of a point is labelled, not a region. The point is labelled by means of numbers, not letters and numbers. Thus, the point (3, 4) must not be confused with the point (4, 3). The order of the numbers which are the parts of the label matters and is an agreed convention which must be adhered to.

Longitude and latitude

Longitude and latitude is the system used in atlases and on Ordnance Survey maps. Longitude comes first and is marked across the top and bottom of the page from left to right. Latitude comes second and is marked on both left and right hand sides of the page moving upwards. On the globe, longitude is measured in degrees east or west of the Greenwich Meridian, which represents zero degrees of longitude. The labels for longitude are usually placed along the equator. Latitude is

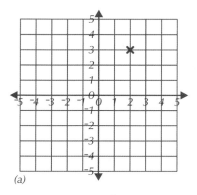

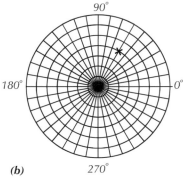

(a)

(b)

19.7 Cartesian and polar co-ordinate systems

measured in degrees north or south of the equator, and the equator represents zero degrees of latitude.

Cartesian co-ordinates

Two-dimensional Cartesian co-ordinates
The most commonly used system of labelling and identifying a point in two dimensions is the Cartesian system (see Figure 19.7a). In a two-dimensional system it is usual to have two perpendicular lines through a fixed point called the origin. The lines are marked off at fixed units left to right from the origin, and bottom to top starting at the origin. The zero on each line is at the origin. By convention the distance across is always given first, followed by the distance up or down. The point (2, 3) is shown in Figure 19.7a by a cross.

It is usual to start teaching co-ordinates using only the first quadrant, extending to the negative parts of the axes and hence all four quadrants, by age 10–11.

Three-dimensional Cartesian co-ordinates
Three co-ordinates are required to position a point in three-dimensional (3D) space (see Figure 19.8a). The combined 1–10 multiplication tables can be graphed using a 3D Cartesian system. Centicubes, 1 cm linking cubes, are useful for building up a 3D graph of smaller tables. An alternative approach uses a 10×10 pegboard as the x–y plane. The third axis, the z axis, is represented by a vertical stick at the corner where the x and y axes meet. An appropriate scale for the z axis is 5 mm for 1 unit. Each product (that is, the answer to a multiplication fact) is represented by the top of a vertical straw at the position in the x–y plane given by the two numbers in the product. For example, the fact $4 \times 5 = 20$ has a straw placed at (4, 5) in the x–y plane, the straw being 20 units high. Figure 19.8b is a partly completed drawing of the activity. The authors have found this activity to be highly successful with a class of mixed-ability 9–10 year olds.

To do

Work with some colleagues to build the three-dimensional representation of the multiplication tables as described. What patterns do you notice? Make a record of your observations and compare them with those of other groups.

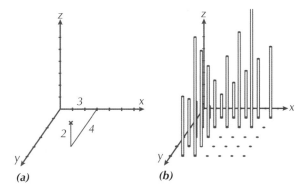

(a)   (b)

19.8 A three-dimensional system and its use with multiplication tables

Two-dimensional polar co-ordinates
In this system there is a fixed point from which is drawn a straight line, the 0° or base line (see Figure 19.7b). The position of any point is described in relation to how far it is along the base line and how much the line must turn anticlockwise to go through the point. Thus, a point whose

281

co-ordinates are (4, 60) is 4 units along the line and 60° anticlockwise around from the base line. The base line acts as the 'axis' for both the measurement of the straight-line distance and the angular displacement.

As polar co-ordinates require understanding of angles it is likely that only high attainers will be able to work with polar graphs. For those children that can the construction of spirals using polar graph paper is an interesting, challenging and worthwhile activity.

Cartesian graphs of functions

The set of ordered pairs which represent a function can be plotted on a two-dimensional Cartesian system to explore any visual patterns that may arise. The simplest of these which are appropriate for older primary children are $x \rightarrow x, x \rightarrow 2x, x \rightarrow 3x$, and so on. In effect the functions and their graphs are the multiplication tables. This relationship should be brought to the children's attention as many secondary children appear unaware of the relationship between, for example, $x \rightarrow 2x$ $(y = 2x)$ and the 2 times table (see Module 14).

There are many linear functions whose straight-line graphs are appropriate for primary children, such as converting money from one currency to another, and converting temperatures in Celsius to Fahrenheit. Many patterns in the form of sequences of numbers or shapes also produce linear functions and graphs (see Module 17).

> ### To think about
>
> The plotting of whole number ordered pairs leaves gaps between each point. The important questions are 'Can the points be joined up with a straight line?' and ' Do the intervening points have a meaning?' How would you help children understand the answers to these two questions?

Children and diagrammatic representations

The errors children make when using Cartesian co-ordinates are mainly due to not remembering the conventions.

- Children will sometimes forget that the x co-ordinate always comes first in any pair. This leads to the plotted point having the reverse of the co-ordinates which were given to be plotted: e.g. what was given as (5, 3) is plotted as (3, 5)
- Plotting points when the scale on one or both of the axes is not the width of one square on the graph paper to one unit on the axes
- Associating Cartesian co-ordinates with a region, not a point. Repeated association of the word 'point' with a pair of co-ordinates can help. It is good practice to say 'plot the point (3, 4)' rather than 'plot (3, 4)'.

Some ideas for teaching diagrammatic representations

Textbooks and diagrammatic representations

> ### To think about
>
> Analyse two textbook series contrasting the approach of the writers in the way they use diagrammatic representations of numerical relationships. What omissions are noticeable?

A look through a textbook series will immediately provide you with the approach of the writer(s) in relation to how diagrammatic representation is used:

- to illustrate mappings and functions
- to develop further mathematical ideas arising from their representations.

Generally, textbooks spend some time on the former without developing the latter.

A class activity

OBJECTIVE   To introduce co-ordinates

ORGANISATION   Whole class with children seated in chairs in rows and columns

RESOURCES   Co-ordinate cards to match the position of each child relative to two walls

ACTIVITY
- The whole class are questioned about how they could give instructions for someone to walk from the classroom door to any child in the room using only the co-ordinates in the correct order.
- Give instructions, such as, 'Stand up if your first co-ordinate is a 3'.
- The class discuss the relationship between the visual patterns of the children standing and the instruction.

A group activity

OBJECTIVE   To practise recognition of co-ordinates using the well known Battleship game

ORGANISATION   Pairs

RESOURCES   Two pegboards and six pegs for each child, two each of three colours to represent two submarines, two destroyers and two battleships

ACTIVITY
- Axes need to be drawn on the pegboards.
- Each child places the six pegs on the pegboard.
- Each child takes it in turn to call out co-ordinates to their opponent.
- A hit or a miss is acknowledged – a hit results in the sinking of the vessel (the peg is removed) and full details of the vessel given.
- The winner is the one to sink all the opponent's vessels first.

Test your own knowledge: diagrammatic representation

1   Using two parallel number lines draw the representation of the function $x \rightarrow 10 - x$. Repeat the activity for $x \rightarrow 12 - x$, $x \rightarrow 14 - x$, and so on, using the same pair of lines. Describe to a colleague what you notice.

2   Use a circular number line as the domain, and a straight number line as the range, to draw a representation of the function $x \rightarrow 2x$ ($y = 2x$)

3   Plot the corners of the square whose co-ordinates are O (0, 0), A (2, 0), B (2, 2), and C (0, 2). For each of the following transformations, plot the image and write down any relationship which you observe between the co-ordinate of the original square and its image:

283

    a reflection in the x axis

    b reflection in the y axis

    c rotation of 90° anticlockwise about O

    d rotation of 180° anticlockwise about O

    e rotation of 270° anticlockwise about O

    f reflection in the line $y = x$

    g reflection in the line $y = -x$

4 Graph the following functions on the same axes for values of x from –3 to 3:

    a $y = 3x$

    b $y = 3x + 2$

    c $y = 3x - 2$

    d $y = -3x$

    e $y = -3x + 2$

    f $y = -3x - 2$

What relationships do you notice between the graphs and between their algebraic representations?

5 Graph the following functions on the same axes for values of x from –4 to 4:

    a $y = x^2$

    b $y = x^2 + 2$

    c $y = -x^2$

    d $y = -x^2 + 2$

What relationships do you notice between the graphs and between their algebraic representations?

6 Use polar graph paper to plot these points: (1, 10), (2, 20), (3, 30), ... Is the relationship between the co-ordinates linear? What kind of graph did you plot?

Review of key points ➤ Children should experience different forms of diagrammatic representation to illustrate relationships

➤ Co-ordinates refer to points, not to areas or regions

➤ Introductory activities which in fact are grid systems rather than co-ordinate systems may cause some difficulties for children, but both systems need to be understood

➤ Conventions such as 'the x co-ordinate comes first, the y co-ordinate second' must be adhered to

➤ When plotting points which are obtained from a relationship it may or may not make sense to join up the points with a straight or curved line, and the intervening points may not have a meaning

➤ Diagrams and Cartesian graphs provide a pictorial way of looking at relations and functions

➤ Linear relationships can help to show the connections between algebra and geometry

➤ It is possible for primary children to work with and understand three-dimensional graphs

Module 20　Learning to teach early algebra

Introduction

Many secondary children encounter difficulties with the fundamental ideas of algebra and in learning the skills of algebraic manipulation. It is argued that one reason lies in primary children having little teaching of pre-algebraic ideas that prepare the groundwork for more formal study. This module considers a range of such ideas within the ability of many primary children. It does not set out to show how to teach children to manipulate symbols according to a set of rules, but seeks to describe contexts and situations which help children to understand what algebra is about.

Early algebra and national curricula

The vast majority of primary mathematics curricula make no specific reference to pre-algebra, nor to early ideas in algebra. There are, however, references to topics that contribute to the development of algebra, some of which have already been listed in other modules. The major ones are:

- describing the general term of a sequence
- finding missing numbers in statements where symbols are used
- understanding and using function machines
- beginning to understand that a letter can stand for an unknown number
- understanding and using simple formulae
- interpreting, generalising and using mappings
- expressing mappings in words and then in letters as symbols.

Key terms

expressions	combinations of symbols, numerical and letters
equality	two arithmetical or algebraic 'quantities' are equal when they have the same value
the '=' sign	the sign that relates two 'quantities' that are equal in value
identity	two 'quantities' are said to be identical when they are equal for all values of the variable
the '≡' sign	the sign that relates two 'quantities' that are identical

---

Unfortunately, it is common practice to use the '=' sign when relating an identity rather than the correct '≡' sign. This makes it important that teachers are conscious of the difference between identities and equations and that they help children to recognise the difference.

Key issues in early algebra

Related concepts and issues

Number concepts and operations provide the basic blocks on which algebra is built. However, these are too many and varied to be included in a map of related issues and concepts. Figure 20.1 shows connections between major topics which contribute to the development of later work in algebra, and the important processes which are a fundamental part of its study.

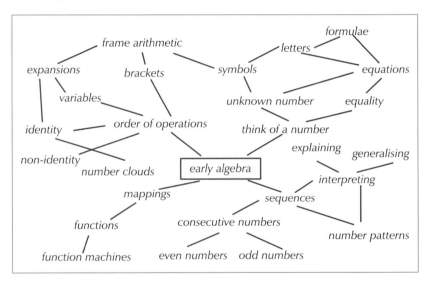

20.1 Concepts and issues associated with early algebra

Frame arithmetic and identities

Frame arithmetic involves the use of 'boxes' or 'frames' in which numbers can be written. However, it extends beyond missing numbers to considering 'algebraic' identities and non-identities. An example of this is when young children, who have just learnt about addition, try to find the missing numbers in the arithmetical identity $2 + \square = 1 + \square + 1$. Much later this leads to investigating the algebraic identity $2(N + 1) = 2N + 2$ written as $2 \times (\square + 1) = (2 \times \square) + 2$. Most primary children are capable of finding numbers which, if written in the frames, would make two expressions equal, or not equal. A challenge is to find a number that makes the two expressions in Table 20.1a unequal, and to find a number that makes the expressions in Table 20.1b equal. When children conclude that no such numbers exist they should attempt to explain why.

Testing the equality of expressions

(a)

□	2 × (□ + 1)	(2 × □) + 2	equal
1	4	4	yes
2	6	6	yes
3	8	8	yes
4	10	10	yes
5	12	12	yes
6	14	14	yes

(b)

□	2 × (□ + 3)	(2 × □) + 5	equal
1	8	7	no
2	10	9	no
3	12	11	no
4	14	13	no
5	16	15	no
6	18	17	no

Table 20.1

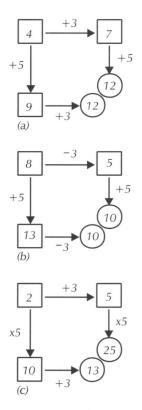

20.2 A move from known to unknown numbers

Order of number operations

Interchanging order

Many expressions in algebra involve more than one operation, and the order in which the operations are applied to an 'unknown' may be commutative, in the sense that changing their order does not change the value of the expression for any given value of the 'unknown'. Consideration of the order of applying two number operations can begin as soon as children are able to add simple numbers.

Steward (1996) describes how this idea can be explored using diagrams. Figure 20.2 shows three such diagrams which use different combinations of the four operations with specific starter numbers.

Children should record the data they collect when testing the order of a pair of operations. This may be done in a table with different starter numbers. For Figure 20.2c this would be $2 + 3 \times 5 = 25$ and $2 \times 5 + 3 = 13$. Discussing the two expressions and comparing the order of the operations gives rise to the need for brackets to avoid confusion as to which operation is performed first. The expressions are more meaningful for children when written as $(2 + 3) \times 5 = 25$ and $(2 \times 5) + 3 = 13$.

Note that there exists an 'order of precedence', which states the order in which operations should be performed in a multi-operation expression making the use of brackets, in some cases, superfluous. BODMAS is often used with children to enable them to remember that the order of operations is **b**rackets, **o**f, **d**ivision, **m**ultiplication, **a**ddition and finally **s**ubtraction.

Relationships between outcomes

Consider the two expressions $5(N + 3)$ and $5N + 3$, where the operations are +3 and × 5. The expression $5(N + 3)$ is equivalent to $5N + 15$. The numerical difference between this and $5N + 3$ is 12. Thus, whatever the value of N, the value of the two expressions always differs by 12. Try this with a number of different values of N. When the constant difference is 0 between two expressions, whatever the value of N, then the operations are commutative.

Consecutive numbers

Little attempt is made in many primary curricula to develop the idea of consecutive numbers, yet this simple notion is full of potential for many numerical investigations, and for a way into algebra.

Counting numbers

The sequence of counting numbers provides children with their first introduction to consecutive numbers. The two numbers 3 and 4 are consecutive in that 4 follows immediately after 3, and 3 comes immediately before 4. More importantly, each member of a set of consecutive counting numbers is 1 more than its predecessor. Thus, if N is a whole number, N and $N + 1$ are two consecutive whole numbers, and N, $N + 1$, $N + 2$ are three consecutive whole numbers. Continuing this pattern we have that N, $N + 1$, $N + 2$, $N + 3$, $N + 4$, and so on, are consecutive whole numbers.

Also, each member of a set of consecutive whole numbers is 1 less than its successor. Thus, $N - 1$ and N are two consecutive numbers. This extends to ..., $N - 4$, $N - 3$, $N - 2$, $N - 1$ and N, which are also consecutive numbers. Combining the two consecutive sequences enables the set of consecutive counting numbers to be written as

$$..., N - 4, N - 3, N - 2, N - 1, N, N + 1, N + 2, N + 3, N + 4, ...$$

Constant difference sequences

The counting sequence of whole numbers is a special case of a constant difference sequence having a difference of 1 between each successive, or consecutive, member of the sequence. Two particular sequences considered in Module 17 were the consecutive even numbers and the consecutive odd numbers, each of which has a constant difference of 2. Both can be written using the same general sequence ..., $N - 8$, $N - 6$, $N - 4$, $N - 2$, N, $N + 2$, $N + 4$, $N + 6$, $N + 8$, ..., the even sequence arising when N is chosen to be even and the odd sequence when N is chosen to be odd.

Number clouds

Sawyer (1964) describes how 'cloud' diagrams may be used to introduce:

- the concept of a variable whole number
- ways of combining such variables
- their symbolic representations.

Whole numbers can be represented as a collection of linear dots: 4 and 5 are shown as examples in Figure 20.3a. If the 'numbers' are on strips of card they can be added and subtracted (finding the difference), as in Figure 20.3b. These activities are the kind that you may see early years' children working with. The move to algebra begins when all but part of the two end dots are covered with a 'cloud' in order to hide the actual number of dots, thus enabling symbols, say N and M, to be introduced to 'stand for', or represent, unknown numbers as in Figure 20.3c. Different unknown numbers should not be represented by the same letter. Consequently the need to use more than one letter arises.

To think about

Use BODMAS to calculate the answer to $\frac{1}{2}$ of $(2 + 8) \times 18 - 6 \div 3$, without using a calculator. Then try it with different calculators. Discuss your conclusions with some colleagues, explaining what you think is happening.

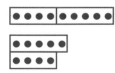

To do

Use the generalised sequence ..., $N - 4$, $N - 3$, $N - 2$, $N - 1$, N, $N + 1$, $N + 2$, $N + 3$, $N + 4$, ... to write nine consecutive numbers when $N = 1000$, 10000, 100000, 1000000.

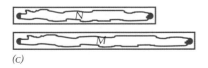

(a)

(b)

(c)

20.3 Combining known and unknown numbers

Just as children record the putting end-to-end of 4 and 5 as 4 + 5, the putting end-to-end of the unknown numbers N and M is recorded as $N + M$, and the difference of N and M as $M - N$ (as M is 'seen' to be larger).

The addition of 1 to an unknown number N is achieved by placing a 1 card on the end of the number N – as in Figure 20.4, which also illustrates $N + 4$, $N + N$, and $2 \times N$, which is written by convention as $2N$. Discussion is needed with children to establish that $N + N$ and $2 \times N$ are equivalent; that is, they have the same value for all values of N. $N + N = 2N$ is an identity.

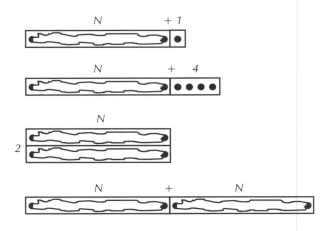

20.4 Combining knowns and unknowns

Most primary children need the assistance of cards, as above, which represent known or unknown numbers in:

- developing understanding of the concepts involved
- operating with the numbers
- ways of expressing them symbolically
- having some understanding of the difference between 'equality' and 'identity'.

Family names

Sawyer (1964) also describes how the number card idea can be extended by considering the families of odd and even numbers. He suggests that a typical member of each family could be represented as in Figure 20.5a and b, with $2N$ and $2N + 1$ representing an even and an odd number, respectively.

With various sizes of unknown even and odd numbers many activities can be undertaken which explore what family of numbers the sum of two or more even or odd numbers belongs to. Figure 20.5c shows that the sum of two odd numbers has the shape of an even number. The addition of even and odd numbers was summarised in Table 17.8. Many older primary children are able construct their own general numbers for $3N$, $3N + 1$ and $3N + 2$ on cards and then investigate the sums of members of the three different families.

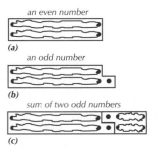

20.5 Unknown numbers which are even or odd

To think about

Here is one for you
to try:
- think of a number
- add 3
- double your answer
- subtract 2
- halve the number you now
  have
- subtract the number you
  first thought of
- your answer is 2
Why does it work?

Number tricks

There are many number 'tricks' that you can use with children, and later encourage them to try to create. The easiest tricks to use as pre-algebra activities are usually based upon the principle that, whatever number is initially thought of, the final answer, after a sequence of calculations, is the same. Number tricks are only a motivation; the objective is to determine why the trick works.

Encourage children to reason why such tricks work and, if possible, to develop a diagrammatic or symbolic way of explaining them.

IMAGES

Figure 20.6 shows how a 10-year-old girl explained why she thought the above trick worked using a rectangle as an image to represent her number. This is only a short step from placing an *N* in the rectangle, and then dropping the rectangle altogether.

- *think of a number*
- *add 3*
- *double your answer*
- *subtract 2*
- *halve the number you now have*
- *subtract the number you first thought of*
- *you are left with **2***

20.6 A child's way of explaining a 'think of a number' problem

Generalising number patterns

An approach to writing the *n*th term of a sequence, firstly in words and then in symbols, was discussed in Module 17. Here we look at how number patterns involving operations can lead to algebraic identities. Here is a simple one to start with:

line 1: $2 \times 1 = (2 \times 2) - 2$
line 2: $2 \times 2 = (2 \times 3) - 2$
line 3: $2 \times 3 = (2 \times 4) - 2$
line 4: $2 \times 4 = (2 \times 5) - 2$
line 5: $2 \times 5 = (2 \times 6) - 2$
line 6: $2 \times 6 = (2 \times 7) - 2$

The activity involves:

- writing the number pattern for all to see

- together, checking that the left-hand side *does* equal the right-hand side for each line

- asking children to describe any patterns they notice within and between expressions, concentrating on what stays the same and what changes

- asking children to write down the next two or three lines in the pattern
- discussing how they were able to continue the pattern
- discussing the relationships between the line number and other numbers in each line
- challenging the children to write down what line 100 will look like
- discussing as a class the different ways of finding line 100
- introducing the notion of line N and relating each number in each line to N, ending with the identity: $2 \times N = 2 \times (N + 1) - 2$
- trying some values of N to test the identity
- discussing how one side of the identity can be transformed to look like the other side.

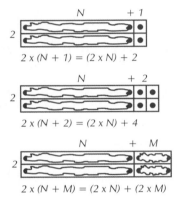

$2 \times (N + 1) = (2 \times N) + 2$

$2 \times (N + 2) = (2 \times N) + 4$

$2 \times (N + M) = (2 \times N) + (2 \times M)$

20.7 Diagrams representing algebraic expressions

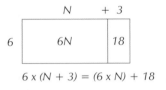

$6 \times (N + 3) = (6 \times N) + 18$

20.8 A simplified way of representing an algebraic expression

Diagrammatic representation

A diagrammatic approach to expansions of algebraic expressions leading to identities uses Sawyer clouds and mirrors the modelling of long multiplication in Module 14. The idea is based upon representing multiplication using 'rectangular' regions. This was anticipated in the representation of $2 \times N$ in Figure 20.4. Two lots of $N + 1$, that is $2 \times (N + 1)$ as in Figure 20.7, is a relatively short step to make, extending to $2 \times (N + 2)$, $2 \times (N + 3)$, ..., and finally $2 \times (N + M)$. The Sawyer clouds can, after a suitable time, be replaced with 'general' rectangles as in Figure 20.8.

Function machines

The combining of function machines was introduced in Module 18. It is an excellent way of considering how a change in the order of two functions may change the eventual output for the same input. Figure 20.9 shows the two functions $x \rightarrow 2x$ and $x \rightarrow x + 3$ using a frame to represent the input, combined in two ways.

The lists in Table 20.2 show the outputs for a variety of inputs for each of the combined machines. These should be compared so that the common difference between the two outputs for the same input is observed and the reason for it discussed.

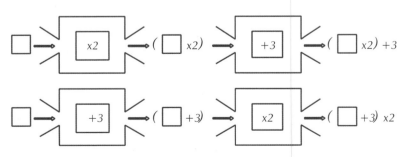

20.9 The effect of changing the order of operations

You may have noticed the similarity of this approach to that of the order of two operations approach. How are they alike? In what ways do they differ? What would be gained by children experiencing both approaches?

Inputs and outputs for the two expressions in Figure 20.9			
(a) $\square \rightarrow (\square \times 2) + 3$		(b) $\square \rightarrow (\square + 3) \times 2$	
Input	Output	Input	Output
1	5	1	8
2	7	2	10
3	9	3	13
4	11	4	14
5	13	5	16
6	15	6	18

Table 20.2

Children and early algebra

Research into children's difficulties and misconceptions in algebra has concentrated on secondary children, as for many years little algebra, including what is claimed to be pre-algebra, has been taught to children younger than 11.

The equals sign

Children appear to give different interpretations to the equals sign in arithmetic and algebra. Primary children tend to view the sign as either an indication to do something, or the result of something having happened. This contrasts with the way it is necessary to understand the equals sign in algebra as a relation between two 'quantities'. To illustrate this point here is an arithmetic problem: 'Jenny is given £5 as a present. She buys a magazine for £1.50 and has £7.50 left in her purse. How much money did Jenny have to start with?' In solving this problem many primary children and some secondary children, will frequently write $7.50 + 1.50 = 9 - 5 = 4$. The equals sign is viewed, here, as saying 'gives' in a left to right direction.

Confusion with letters

Primary children's experience of using letters in their learning of mathematics is usually restricted to abbreviations for measures, such as 3 m meaning 3 metres, or in a formula, such as $A = l \times b$. Thus, a child's first reaction to the use of a letter representing a number may be to relate it to an abbreviation. You will have noticed in this module that, where possible, the letter N has been used, it being both an abbreviation for the word 'number' and representing a number.

Discontinuities between arithmetic and algebra

Although many mathematics educators claim that algebra is a natural extension of arithmetic, children bring to algebra conceptions, knowledge and skills that are not directly transferable from arithmetic. There are a number of adjustments, revisions and enlargements that children have to make to their intuitive approach to solving arithmetic problems in order to handle the more formal structures of algebra. This is due to primary children seldom being required to make the arithmetical procedures they use open and explicit as getting the correct answer dominates their learning of mathematics. From an early stage of experiencing number operations primary children should be taught to be aware, for example, that $2 + 3$, $9 - 4$ and 5 are equivalent and therefore interchangeable whenever appropriate and necessary. Children who do not appreciate the significance of the concept of equivalence between arithmetical expressions are unlikely to understand, for example, that $N + 2$ is equivalent to a number when N represents a number.

Conventions

There are three conventions in algebra that do not occur in arithmetic which children have to learn (see Module 16). The major one which concerns primary children is the omission of the '$\times$' sign between a number and a letter, such as $2 \times N$ written as $2N$. Some children, when introduced to this convention, are then doubly confused as they expect to see N written as $1N$.

Some ideas for teaching early algebra

To think about

For many years primary mathematics textbooks contained few, if any, activities that could be classified as algebra or pre-algebra. Analyse two of the most recent primary series to see what aspects of pre-algebra are included.

Textbooks and early algebra

The lack of explicit reference to algebra in primary textbooks does not mean that related ideas are not to be found. What it does suggest is that authors may not have consciously provided pre-algebra activities.

A class activity

OBJECTIVE To calculate values of simple expressions written with frames for numbers

ORGANISATION Whole class

RESOURCES Teacher has:

- a set of 10 algebraic expression cards, such as $(2 \times \square) + 3$, and
- a set of ten number cards 1–10

ACTIVITY

- The two sets are placed side by side at the front of the class in a random order.
- The teacher holds up one card from each set.
- The children calculate the value of the expression for the given number.
- The activity is repeated for the remaining cards.

A group activity

OBJECTIVE   To use frames to represent the same number in a sequence

ORGANISATION   Small group

RESOURCES   None

ACTIVITY

- Teacher writes on chalkboard or OHP the sequence:

  $\Box - 3, \Box - 2, \Box - 1, \Box, \Box + 1, \Box + 2, \Box + 3$

- Children are asked for a number greater than 10 to put in the first frame. Each group works together to find out the value of the first term.
- They are then asked for the values of the other terms in a random order for the same number in the frames.
- The teacher writes the sequence on the board as the values are given.
- The sequence is then searched for patterns.
- The activity is repeated for other 'frame' numbers.

Test your own knowledge: early algebra

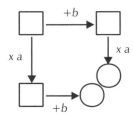

20.10 Using letters to represent operations

1   The diagram in Figure 20.10 uses letters to represent numbers.

a Prove that, whatever the input number, the two outputs differ by the product of *b* and 1 less than *a*, that is $b(a - 1)$. For what value of *a* are the two operations commutative, whatever the value of *b*?

b Find the difference between the two outputs when any two operations are combined in different orders. For what values of *a* or *b*, if any, are the two operations commutative?

2   **a** What kind of number is the sum of the two consecutive numbers *N*, $N + 1$?

b What kind of number is the sum of the three consecutive numbers $N - 1, N, N + 1$?

c What kind of number is the sum of the four consecutive numbers $N - 1, N, N + 1, N + 2$?

d What kind of number is the sum of *k* consecutive numbers?

3   Here are two number patterns:

line 1: $(3 \times 4) - (1 \times 5) = 7$ line 1: $3 \times 1 = (4 \times 1) - 1$

line 2: $(4 \times 5) - (2 \times 6) = 8$ line 2: $5 \times 3 = (4 \times 4) - 1$

line 3: $(5 \times 6) - (3 \times 7) = 9$ line 3: $7 \times 5 = (4 \times 9) - 1$

line 4: $(6 \times 7) - (4 \times 8) = 10$ line 4: $9 \times 7 = (4 \times 16) - 1$

For each pattern:

a Check the equality of each line.

    b Work out the generalised identity for line N

    c Test the accuracy of your identity for $N = 10, 100, 1000$

    d Show that the two sides of the identity are equivalent.

4 When N is even then $N - 2$, N and $N + 2$ are three consecutive even numbers.

    a Prove that the sum of three consecutive even numbers is divisible by 6

    b Prove that the sum of five consecutive even numbers is divisible by 10

    c Prove that the sum of seven consecutive even numbers is divisible by 14

    d Prove that the sum of $2k + 1$ consecutive even numbers is divisible by $2(2k + 1)$

5 **a** Draw a rectangular diagrammatic representation of $(N + 1)(N + 1)$ to show that it is identical to $N^2 + 2N + 1$

    b Repeat the activity for $(N + 2)(N + 2)$, $(N + 3)(N + 3)$, and $(N + 4)(N + 4)$. Generalise to show to show that $(N + k)(N + k) = N^2 + 2kN + k^2$

6 **a** Draw a rectangular diagrammatic representation of $(N + 1)(N - 1)$ to show that it is identical to $N^2 - 1$

    b Repeat the activity for $(N + 2)(N - 2)$, $(N + 3)(N - 3)$, and $(N + 4)(N - 4)$

    c Generalise to show to show that $(N + k)(N - k) = N^2 - k^2$

Review of key points ➤ Few primary textbooks consciously include early algebra activities

      ➤ In schools algebra is usually taught as a generalisation of arithmetic

      ➤ There are significant discontinuities between arithmetic and algebra that have to be overcome by learners

      ➤ Frame arithmetic uses frames or boxes instead of letters to represent variables or unknown numbers

      ➤ Simple identities can be used to introduce primary children to the idea of variable, brackets and expansions

      ➤ Diagrammatic representation of algebraic expressions is a possible introduction to the use of letters for numbers

---

Module 21   Learning to teach equations

Introduction

Equations are omnipresent in mathematics. The processes of modelling and finding the solution to real problems require creation and solving of equations at all stages of children's development. As soon as children begin to ask 'How many more do I need?' they are concerned with an equation, with an unknown the value of which they seek to find.

Equations in national curricula

There is much variation in the content of primary mathematics curricula in relation to equations. You can expect your national curricula to incorporate all, some, or none of the following:

- constructing, expressing and using simple formulae expressed in words, then in symbols
- understanding that a letter can stand for an unknown number
- developing and solving linear equations arising from problems
- solving simple inequations.

Key terms

the '=' sign	the sign that relates two expressions that are equal in value
equation	two expressions form an equation when related by an equals sign; an equation may be a true or a false statement; an equation does not necessarily contain a variable
solving an equation	to solve an equation means to find a value or values of the variable that makes the equation true
equivalent equation	two equations are equivalent if they have the same solution
formula	an equation which has two or more variables can be said to be a formula

---

Key issues in equations

Related concepts and issues

Figure 21.1 shows some of the connections between the many concepts and issues that children will have experienced in their learning before encountering equations. It also indicates the different names that are given to the variable in an equation and how these are names attached to symbols, be they frame or letter.

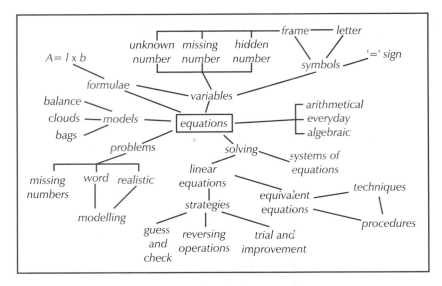

21.1 Concepts and issues associated with equations

Why equations in the primary years?

With a move in mathematics curricula away from a fixed and narrow focus on procedural techniques to a greater prominence of conceptual understanding, the study of equations in the primary years should be given serious consideration. Further reasons for having equations in the primary mathematics curricula are:

- opportunities abound for missing number problems that are within the ability of most primary children

- the use of a frame or box for a variable makes ideas associated with equations much easier to understand than the same equations with letters

- leaving the introduction of equations to the secondary years invites the prospect of failure.

Meanings of equation

The '=' symbol

Most primary children view the '=' sign (read as 'is equal to' or 'equals') as an instruction to do something to the numbers on the left-hand side to obtain an answer which they then write on the right-hand side of the sign: they also perceive the role of the sign as separating the problem from the answer. These are very limited meanings and cause children concern when they try to reconcile them with arithmetical statements such as $6 = 4 + \square$. They are further confused when they are introduced to equivalent arithmetical statements such as $2 + 3 = 4 + 1$, where there appears to be no request, nor a place, for an answer. One suggestion that may overcome some of the problems associated with the sign is, from its introduction, to be read as 'has the same value as', which provides children with a literal interpretation which the word 'equals' does not.

What is '□' or '*x*' in an equation?

In your reading you may find equations subsumed under the name of mathematical sentences which also include inequations, such as $3 + N < 5$. You are also likely to find that equations and inequations use either a frame (or box) or a letter to represent the variable. Whatever is used, children and teachers have their own meanings which they attach to the symbol. Here are some of the names you will hear children and teachers using:

- a hidden number
- a missing number
- the unknown number
- the variable.

Everyday equations

When the word equation is used there is a tendency to think immediately of algebra. The reason for this lies in teachers leaving any reference to equations to secondary schooling when its first appearance occurs in courses in algebra. As Skemp (1971) makes clear, everyday statements such as 'Today is Sunday', 'The team I support is Liverpool', and 'The number before 6 is 5' are equations as 'is' could be replaced by the '=' symbol. Thus, early ideas of non-mathematical equations are embedded in children's everyday language experience and may be used to extend children's understanding to arithmetical and algebraic equations.

Arithmetical equations

Although few teachers and children view the statement '4 = four' as an equation, it is an example of how the equality relation is used when children match a numeral to its name. Similarly, arithmetical statements such as $3 + 2 = 5$ are unlikely to be referred to by teachers as equations. This is unfortunate, as this is exactly what $3 + 2 = 5$ is; an equation that relates the numbers 3, 2 and 5. If, perhaps, teachers were to introduce the notion of, and the word for, equation from an early age then children may more readily accept that $5 = 3 + 2$ is also an equation, and not ' the wrong way round' as some children say.

A mathematical statement may be true or false. For example, the statement $3 + 4 = 6$ is false, but nevertheless is an equation as an equals sign is used to relate quantities.

Algebraic equations

Some claim that when an equation contains a variable we move from arithmetic to algebra, whatever symbol is used to represent the variable. Thus, $3 + \square = 5$ is considered to be an equation and is part of the study of algebra. Others consider the equation to be algebraic when a letter is used, for example $3 + N = 5$.

It is not possible to say whether the equation $3 + N = 5$ is true or false as N may take many different values depending on its domain. When $N = 4$ the equation becomes $3 + 4 = 5$, which is obviously a false statement. When children are asked to solve an equation implicit in the

To think about

Discuss with your colleagues the thinking that lies behind each of the names given to the variables in an equation and the action(s) that each suggests.

To do

Conduct a survey of some friends who are not in the teaching profession to ascertain their view on the place of $3 + \square = 5$ and $3 + N = 5$ in arithmetic or algebra. Do the same with colleagues. How do their opinions differ, if at all? Does the distinction matter? Why?

299

To do

Which category contains identities? Which category contains non-identities? Write an algebraic equation for each of the above categories. Explain your equations and their solutions to a colleague.

question is the requirement that the value chosen for the variable must make the statement true: this is what is meant by 'solve the equation'. The value or values of the variable that makes the equation a true statement is called the solution or solutions of the equation.

Algebraic equations can be categorised according to the number of solutions they have in the following way:

- equations which have a finite number of solutions
- equations which have an infinity of solutions
- equations for which there are no solutions.

Equivalent algebraic equations

The teaching of equations in secondary schools tends to lay stress on the procedural steps for solving equations, without giving sufficient prominence to the intrinsic concepts underlying equivalent equations. Most mathematics educators would argue that the procedural skills necessary to solve equations have no place in the teaching of equations in the primary school. Thus, the emphasis should be on the ideas associated with equivalent equations.

The elegance of equivalent algebraic equations lies in each having the same solution. A complex equation can be transformed into an equivalent, but much simpler, equation for which the solution is 'obvious'. The example below shows how this works.

$$\frac{2(N + 7)}{9} = 8$$

is transformed into

$$2(N + 7) = 72 \text{ (how?)}$$

which becomes

$$(N + 7) = 36 \text{ (how?)}$$

and finally

$$N = 29 \text{ (how?)}$$

If we check the solution of the final equation by substituting $N = 29$ in the original equation we have

$$\frac{2(29 + 7)}{9} = \frac{2 \times 36}{9} = \frac{72}{9} = 8$$

21.2 Equivalent equations for a realistic problem

Although the idea of equivalent equations seems to be a difficult concept it appears that primary children are able to move from one equation to an equivalent equation when the original equation is set in a context which children understand, and to which they are able to relate (Van Reeuwijk, 1995). Consider, for example, the problem set out in Figure 21.2. Here, older primary children have little difficulty interpreting the diagram as the cost of three packets of cornflakes is £3.60 and that the question is asking for an equivalent equation, that is the cost of one packet. In algebraic symbolism the question may be written as, 'Given that $3P = £3.60$, what is the value of P?'

To think about

In what ways could the context and presentation of an equation help or hinder children's ability to answer successfully?

Rules for producing equivalent equations

There are four basic rules, any one of which applied to an equation transforms it into an equivalent equation having the same solution. The rules are:

- add the same number to both sides of the equation
- subtract the same number from both sides of the equation
- multiply both sides of the equation by the same number
- divide both sides of the equation by the same number as long as the number is not 0.

The four rules apply whether 'the same number' is a particular number, say 8, or the variable in the equation. For example, $3 = 2/x$ is equivalent to $3x = 2$, provided $x \neq 0$. Why is this?

Models for equations

Equation balance

Fundamental to the concept of equation is the search for equality of the quantities on the two sides of the equals sign; the two sides, in effect, balance. It is this notion of balance which has resulted in an approach to equations based on diagrams of a balance and 'weights'. The idea is an extension of the number balance which was introduced to model addition in Module 12 and is illustrated in Figure 21.3.

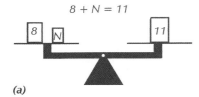

$8 + N = 11$

(a)

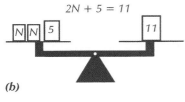

$2N + 5 = 11$

(b)

21.3 Using a balance to represent an equation

'Clouds' as unknowns

In Module 20 the idea of clouds was used to represent an unknown number. The idea can be extended to introduce equations with whole number solutions, as illustrated in Figure 21.4.

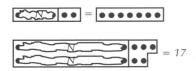

$= 17$

21.4 Using 'clouds' to represent an equation

'Bags' as unknowns

Sawyer (1964) suggested the idea of a 'bag' to represent an unknown which, when drawn in a particular way, may eventually be replaced by an 'x' as a shortened form of the drawing. Consider, for example, the simple word problem 'Martha has some biscuits. Ricky has twice as many biscuits as Martha. Altogether they have 27 biscuits. How many biscuits does each child have?' This may be translated into pictures by suggesting to children that Martha's biscuits are collected together in a bag and that Ricky's collection of biscuits will be two bags, each having the same number of biscuits as Martha's. The translation is shown in Figure 21.5a, with the final equation in Figure 21.5b.

To think about

What are the pros and cons of the 'balance' and the 'cloud approaches?

To think about

What assumptions are made in this approach and what possible misconceptions might children develop?

(a)   *(b)*

21.5 Translating a problem into symbols

Primary children are able to develop their own skills for solving equations presented in picture form divorced from a word problem. Teachers who use this method should ask children to provide a story which translates the equation back into a 'real' problem, thus giving relevance to the equation.

Systems of equations

Both Sawyer (1964) and van Reeuwijk (1995) suggest the introduction of equations to children through a system of equations rather than using a single linear equation. Sawyer claims that '... simultaneous equations represent a problem for which algebra – or the disguised algebra of picture drawing – is a natural method.' Linear equations involve one variable, two simultaneous equations incorporate two variables (as in the example in Figure 21.6 – quoted by van Reeuwijk – where the variables are the cost of a hat and the cost of a pair of glasses).

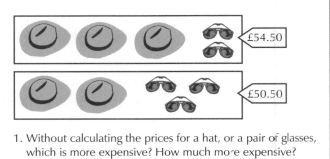

1. Without calculating the prices for a hat, or a pair of glasses, which is more expensive? How much more expensive?

2. Use the two pictures to make a new combination of glasses and hats, and write down the cost of this new combination.

3. Make a combination of only hats or only glasses and find its price.

4. What is the price of one hat? And of one pair of glasses?

21.6 A realistic problem involving two simultaneous equations

Strategies for solving equations

As the aim of teaching equations in the primary school is to develop conceptual understanding of equations, as opposed to techniques and skills, children should be provided with opportunities to discover their own strategies for solving linear equations. These can be categorised as:

- guess and check
- trial and improvement
- reversing operations.

Guess and check

'Guess and check' is perhaps the most primitive of strategies. It is natural at the early stages of learning about equations for children to make a guess at the value of the unknown number and check its validity by working out one or both sides of the equation to test for equality. The strategy remains at a rudimentary level when children continue to randomly guess. There are dangers in allowing children to continue using this unsophisticated approach as they quickly become discouraged if they fail to alight by chance on the correct solution. The intervention of the teacher is essential before this stage is reached, drawing children's attention to how they can use one guess to inform their next guess.

To do

Use a 'guess and check' strategy to solve the equation $N^2 - 3N = 78$.

Trial and improvement

'Trial and improvement' involves children in reasoning that one or more guesses provides them with information which can help them make a 'better' next guess. For example, if 8 is guessed as the value of N in $2N + 5 = 17$ then on checking, the 'equality' becomes $21 = 17$. This suggests that the guess was too large and, perhaps, a smaller guess of 1 might be better. This gives $7 = 17$ for the equality, suggesting that the guess is now too small. Combining the two pieces of information we can conclude that the next guess should be between 1 and 8, and nearer to 8 than to 1. Why is this?

Reversing operations

Figure 21.4b illustrated the equation $2N + 5 = 17$ using the cloud representation of an unknown. This lends itself to children visually removing 5 dots from each side, reversing the addition, and then sharing the remaining 12 dots between each unknown, reversing the multiplication by 2. With simple numbers children perform the reversing of operations mentally as they do when such equations are presented orally in the form of 'I am thinking of a number. I double it and then add 5. The answer is 17. What is my number?' For most primary children this level of operating is an achievement which lays the foundation for using the reversing operations strategy when equations are taught in a more formal manner in secondary school.

Equations as formulae

It is a surprise to most teachers that formulae are equations, as they state an equality relationship between two or more variables. For most primary children their only experience of algebra, other than with missing numbers, is when they are introduced to formulae. The area of a rectangle, $A = l \times b$, is usually the first and only formula that most children meet. Some may move on to considering the perimeter of rectangles, $P = 2(l + b)$, with only a few being taught the circle formulae, $d = 2r$, $C = 2\pi r$ and $A = \pi r^2$.

The primary curriculum, however, has many opportunities for introducing children to the idea of formulae besides the conventional ones given above. For example, a T-shirt may cost £6; then a relationship exists between the number of T-shirts bought and the total cost which can be expressed as a formula. The letters used in the formula are open for children to decide. In the T-shirt example it might well be decided to let T be the number of T-shirts and C the cost in pounds, in which case the formula is $C = 6T$.

To think about

Look through your national primary mathematics curriculum to see where it might be possible to introduce equations or formulae.

Children and equations

Errors and misconceptions

As it has not been fashionable to teach equations in the primary school little is known about the errors and misconceptions that such children make. The following, however, offer guidance to teachers in primary schools as to the approach to be avoided, and suggest possible ways forward:

- many children cannot see the need for formal methods when solving simple equations
- children resist using formal methods to solve equations, preferring instead their own intuitive methods which have proved successful in the past
- children's perception of learning a collection of procedures to solve a variety of equations rather than interpreting what the solutions mean invites the formation of negative attitudes
- for many children the relationship between a procedure and checking the solution in the equation is seldom developed.

Van Reeuwijk (1995), working with 10–11-year-old children on setting equations in realistic situations, concluded:

- when solving equations children are more creative and function at a higher cognitive level than expected
- when children are given the opportunity to decide which strategy is the most appropriate to solve an equation and which they have the most confidence in, the better they perform.

Performance

SOLVING EQUATIONS

The APU (1980) looked at the performance of a large group of 11-year-old children in primary education when answering a variety of questions related to equations. Table 21.1 lists the questions and the facilities the children found in solving them.

The simple equations using frames to represent unknowns were answered very well, showing that equations, when presented in a form that children understand, are not beyond the ability of most primary children. Questions M3 and M4 required children to operate on an equation to produce an equivalent equation. These were answered less well than the straightforward equations, perhaps because they contained letters. This is partly confirmed in that about 80% of children answered a similar question correctly when it was expressed verbally. Substituting values in an equation or formula, as in M5, was very badly answered.

Some ideas for teaching equations

To think about

Look at as many primary textbook series as you have time for to see the coverage given to the different aspects of equations which have been discussed in this module.

Textbooks and equations

Very little work on equations is to be found in primary textbooks, apart from missing number problems using frames or boxes and the formula for the area of a rectangle.

Performance of 11-year-old pupils on questions related to equations		
	Question	**Facility (%)**
M1:	Find which number ☐ stands for $12 - ☐ = 8$	88
M2:	Find which number ☐ stands for $51 + ☐ = 90$	75
M3:	n stands for a number $n + 4 = 21$ so $n + 5 = ☐$	63
M4:	B stands for a number $B - 9 = 21$ so $B - 10 = ☐$	51
M5:	Fill in the missing values of M in this table according to the equation $M + N = 4$	19

N	0	1	2	3	4
M	4				

Table 21.1

A class activity

OBJECTIVE   To solve oral equations

ORGANISATION   Whole class

RESOURCES   None

ACTIVITY
Teacher reads out equations of the form, 'I am thinking of a number. I add seven. My answer is 16. What number was I thinking of?'. Children respond verbally.

A group activity

OBJECTIVE   To find equations which have the same solution – that is, equivalent equations

ORGANISATION   Small groups

RESOURCES   Each group has four sets of equivalent equations with each equation on a separate card; each set being equivalent equations that result from solving a complex equation. For example, one set could contain the equations $2(3x + 7) = 50$; $3x + 7 = 25$; $3x = 18$; $x = 6$

ACTIVITY

- All the cards are mixed and placed face up.
- Each group sorts the cards into sets having the same solution.
- They order the cards and describe the operations or transformations that have been performed on each equation to produce the next in the order.
- One child from each group describes to the rest of the class one of the sorts and explains why the equations are equivalent.

Test your own knowledge: equation

1   Each of the bags in Figure 21.7 contains the same number of sweets. How many sweets are there in each bag? Explain to a colleague how you worked it out.

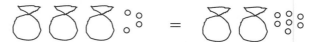

21.7 How many sweets are in each bag?

2   Table 21.2 shows the number of items bought at a bakery and the total cost on three occasions. How much is a tart, a bun, a cake?

Tarts	Buns	Cakes	Cost
2	7	1	£1.89
4	5	2	£2.61
1	4	2	£2.21

Table 21.2

3   For a party Alice's mum makes twice as many ham sandwiches as salad sandwiches. The 21 children each eat 3 ham and 1 salad sandwich. Alice's mum and dad together eat 9 ham and 9 salad sandwiches. Half of what is left is given to the dog. The rest, 4 ham and 5 salad sandwiches, are eaten for supper. How many ham and salad sandwiches were made?

4   Haroon thinks of a number. He adds 7, divides by 2, subtracts 1 and multiplies by 3. His answer is 51. What number did Haroon think of?

5   In what way is the equation $N^2 + 2N + 1 = 121$ related to our place value system? Can you find another solution of the equation?

6   Solve the simultaneous equations $J + F = 50$ and $F - J = 30$. The solutions are the ages of John and his father. Devise a word problem for the equations using the ages of John and his father.

7   Using the information in question 6 to find how old John will be when he is half as old as his father.

8   In 1990 Harry was 25 and his cousin was 45. In what year is Harry's cousin twice as old as Harry?

9   Write four different equations that have the solution $N = 7$. Why are your

equations equivalent? What operations do you need to perform on each equation to transform them into each other?

10 Use trial and improvement to find a solution to $x^2 + x^3 = 100$ to two decimal places. You may find a calculator helpful.

Review of key points
➤ The formal teaching of equations with emphasis on procedures has no role in the primary mathematics curriculum

➤ There is a place for equations in the primary curriculum when the stress is on the conceptual development of equations, presented in a realistic context and in an understandable way

➤ Misconceptions associated with the meaning and interpretation of the equals sign can hinder children's understanding of equations

➤ Teachers and children use different names for the variable in an equation

➤ The use of a frame or box for the variable appears to have more meaning for primary children than a letter

➤ Equations begin as statements in everyday life, continue as arithmetical statements and finally become algebraic statements, any of which may be true or false

➤ It is implicitly understood that when solving an equation the search is for a value of the variable that makes the equation true

➤ Understanding the concept of equivalent algebraic equations is the basis for developing procedures for solving equations in the secondary school

➤ The use of different models for the teaching of equations contributes to primary children's conceptual understanding of equations

➤ There are three strategies which primary children use when solving equations, 'guess and check', 'trial and improvement', and 'reversing operations'

➤ Formulae are equations involving two or more variables

Useful books on teaching mathematics in the primary school

Anghileri, J. (1995) *Children's Mathematical Thinking in the Primary Years*. London: Cassell.

Askew, M. (1998) *Teaching Primary Mathematics*. London: Hodder & Stoughton.

Askew, M. and Wiliam, D. (1995) *Recent Research in Mathematics Education 5–16*. London: HMSO.

Association of Teachers of Mathematics (1967) *Notes on Mathematics in Primary Schools*. London: Cambridge University Press.

Atkinson, A. (1992) *Mathematics with Reason: The Emergent Approach to Primary Maths*. London: Hodder and Stoughton.

Ball, G. (1990) *Talking and Learning*. Oxford: Blackwell.

Biggs, E.E. and MacLean, J.R. (1969) *Freedom to Learn*. Ontario: Addison-Wesley.

Borasi, R. (1996) *Reconceiving Mathematics Instruction: A Focus on Errors*. Norwood, NJ: Ablex Pub. Corp.

Brown, T. (1988) *Coordinating Mathematics Across the Primary Classroom*. London: The Falmer Press.

Burton, L. (1994) *Children Learning Mathematics: Patterns and Relationships*. Hemel Hempstead: Simon & Schuster.

Clarke, S. and Atkinson, S. (1996) *Tracking Significant Achievement in Primary Mathematics*. London: Hodder & Stoughton.

Clemson, W. and Clemson, D. (1994) *Mathematics in the Early Years*. London: Routledge.

Clemson, W. and Clemson, D. (1996) *Maths in Colour*. Cheltenham: Stanley Thornes.

Cockburn, A. D. (1988) *Teaching Mathematics with Insight: The Identification, Diagnosis and Remediation of Young Children's Mathematical Errors*. Basingstoke: The Falmer Press.

Cockcroft, W.H. (1982) *Mathematics Counts*. London: HMSO.

Comer, T. (1996) *Opportunities for Mathematics in the Primary School*. Stoke-on-Trent: Trentham Books.

Davis, A. and Petit, D. (1994) *Developing Understanding in Primary Mathematics*. London: The Falmer Press.

Deboys, M. and Pitt, E. (1980) *Lines of Development in Primary Mathematics*. Blackstaff: Belfast.

Dickson, L., Brown, M. and Gibson, O. (1984) *Children Learning Mathematics: A Teacher's Guide to Recent Research*. Eastbourne: Holt, Rinehart & Winston.

Downes, L.W. and Paling, D. (1958) *The Teaching of Arithmetic in Primary Schools*. Oxford: Oxford University Press.

Duncan, A. (1992) *What Primary Teachers Should Know About Maths*. London: Hodder & Stoughton.

Early Childhood Education Group (1997) *Learning Mathematics in the Nursery: Desirable Approaches*. London: BEAM.

Fielker, D. (1997) *Extending Mathematical Ability Through Whole Class Teaching*. London: Hodder & Stoughton.

Glenn, J.A. and Sturgess, D.A. (1977) *Towards Mathematics*. Huddersfield: Schofield and Sims.

Hart, K.M. (ed.) (1981) *Children's Understanding of Mathematics: 11–16*. London: Murray.

Haylock, D. (1995) *Mathematics Explained for Primary Teachers*. London: Chapman.

Haylock, D. and Cockburn, A. (1997) *Understanding Mathematics in the Lower Primary Years*. London: Chapman.

Hopkins, C., Gifford, S. and Pepperell, S. (eds) (1996) *Mathematics in the Primary School*. London: Fulton.

Hughes, M. (1986) *Children and Number: Difficulties in Learning Mathematics*. Oxford: Basil Blackwell.

Jennings, S. and Dunne, R. (1997) *QTS Mathematics for Primary Teachers: An Audit and Self-Study Guide*. London: Letts Educational.

Jennings, S. and Dunne, R. (1998) *QTS Teaching Mathematics in Primary Schools: A Handbook of Lesson Plans*, Knowledge and Teaching Methods. London: Letts Educational.

Lewis, A. (1996) *Discovering mathematics with 4- to 7-year olds*. London: Hodder & Stoughton.

Liebeck, P. (1984) *How Children Learn Mathematics*. Harmondsworth: Penguin Books.

Merttens, R. (ed.) (1977) *Teaching Numeracy: Maths in the Primary Classroom*. Leamington Spa: Scholastic.

Montague-Smith, A. (1997) *Mathematics in Nursery Education*. London: Fulton.

Nunes, T. and Bryant, P. (1996) *Children Doing Mathematics*. Oxford: Blackwell.

Open University (1998) *Passport to Mathematics*. Milton Keynes: Open University Press.

Orton, A. (1992) *Learning Mathematics: Issues, Theory and Classroom*

Practice. London: Cassell.

Orton, A. (ed.) (1999) *Pattern in the Teaching and Learning of Mathematics*. London: Cassell.

Orton, A. and Frobisher, L. (1996) *Insights into Teaching Mathematics*. London: Cassell.

Paling, D. (1982) *Teaching Mathematics in Primary Schools*. Oxford: Oxford University Press.

Pound, L. (1999) *Supporting Mathematical Development in the Early Years*. Buckingham: Open University Press.

Qualifications and Curriculum Authority (1999) *Standards in Mathematics: Exemplification of Key Learning Objectives from Reception to Year 6*. London: Department for Education and Employment.

Schools Council (1964) *Mathematics in Primary Schools*. London: HMSO.

Shuard, H., Walsh, A., Goodwin, J. and Worcester, V. (1991) *PrIME Calculators, Children and Mathematics*. Hemel Hempstead: Simon & Schuster for the National Curriculum Council.

Skemp, R.R. (1989) *Mathematics in the Primary School*. London: Routledge.

Straker, A. (1993) *Talking Points in Mathematics*. Cambridge: Cambridge University Press.

Suggate, J., Davis, A. and Goulding, M. (1998) *Mathematical Knowledge for Primary Teachers*. London: Fulton.

Thyer, D. and Maggs, J. (1991) *Teaching Mathematics to Young Children*. London: Cassell.

Thompson, I. (1997) *Teaching and Learning Early Number*. Buckingham: Open University Press.

Van Lehn, K. (1990) *Mind Bugs: The Origins of Procedural Misconceptions*. London: MIT Press.

Williams, E. and Shuard, H. (1994) *Primary Mathematics Today*, 4th edition. Harlow: Longman.

Bibliography

Anghileri, J. (1997) Uses of counting in multiplication and division. In I. Thompson (ed.) *Teaching & Learning Early Number*. Buckingham: Open University Press.

Askew, M. (1998) *Teaching Primary Mathematics*. London: Hodder and Stoughton.

Askew, M., Brown, M., Rhodes, V., Wiliam, D. and Johnson, D. (1997) *Effective Teachers of Numeracy*. London: King's College, University of London.

Assessment of Performance Unit (1980) *Mathematical Development: Primary Survey Report No. 1*. London: HMSO.

Assessment of Performance Unit (undated) *A Review of Monitoring in Mathematics 1978 to 1982, Part 1*. London: HMSO.

Athey, C. (1990) *Extending Thought in Young Children*. London: Paul Chapman.

Aubrey, C. (1997) Children's early learning of number in school and out. In I. Thompson (ed.) *Teaching & Learning Early Number*. Buckingham: Open University Press.

Bednarz, N. and Janvier, B. (1979) The understanding of place-value (numeration). In *3rd International Conference for the Psychology of Mathematics Education*. Warwick: Warwick University Press.

Bednarz, N. and Janvier, B. (1982) The understanding of numeration. *Educational Studies in Mathematics*, **13**(1), 33–57.

Burningham, J. (1992) *The Shopping Basket*. London: Random House.

Branford, B. (1908) *A Study of Mathematical Education*. Oxford: The Clarendon Press.

Brown, M. (1981a) Number operations. In K. Hart (ed.) *Children's Understanding of Mathematics: 11–16*. London: Murray.

Brown, M. (1981b) Place value and decimals. In K. Hart (ed.) *Children's Understanding of Mathematics: 11–16*. London: Murray.

Campbell, J.I. and Graham, D.J. (1985) Mental multiplication skill: structure, process and acquisition. *Canadian Journal of Psychology*, **39**(2), 338–366.

Çemen, P.B. (1993) Adding and subtracting integers on the number line. *Arithmetic Teacher*, **March**, 388–389.

Clemson, D. and Clemson, W. (1994) *Mathematics in the Early Years*. London: Routledge.

Cockcroft, W. H. (1982) *Mathematics Counts*. London: HMSO.

Davis, G.E. and Pitkethly, A. (1990) Cognitive aspects of sharing. *Journal of Research in Mathematics Education*, **21**(2), 145–153.

Department for Education/Welsh Office (1995) *Mathematics in the National Curriculum*. London: HMSO.

Dickson, L., Brown, M. and Gibson, O. (1984) *Children Learning Mathematics*. Eastbourne: Holt, Rinehart & Winston for The Schools Council.

Donaldson, M. (1978) *Children's Minds*. London: Fontana Press.

Duffin, J. (1997) The role of calculators. In I. Thompson (ed.) *Teaching & Learning Early Number*. Buckingham: Open University Press.

Figueras, O. (1989) Two different views of fractions: Fractionating and operating. In G.Vergnaud, J. Rogalski and M. Artigue (eds) *Proceedings of the XIII Conference for the Psychology of Mathematics Education*. Paris: CNRS.

Frobisher, L. (1999) Primary school children's knowledge of odd and even numbers. In A. Orton (ed.) *Pattern in the Teaching and Learning of Mathematics*. London: Cassell.

Fuson K.C. and Hall J.W. (1983) The acquisition of early number word meanings. In H.P. Ginsburg (ed.) *The Development of Mathematical Thinking*. New York: Academic Press.

Galton, M. and Simon, B. (1980) *Progress and Performance in the Primary School*. London: Routledge.

Garrick, R., Threlfall, J. and Orton, A. (1999) Pattern in the nursery. In A. Orton (ed.) *Pattern in the Teaching and Learning of Mathematics*. London: Cassell.

Gelman R. and Gallistel C.R. (1978) *The Child's Understanding of Number*. Harvard: Harvard University Press.

Ginsburg, H. (1977) *Children's Arithmetic: The Learning Process*. New York: Van Nostrand.

Ginsburg, H.P. and Baron, J. (1993) Cognition: young children's construction of mathematics. In R.J. Jensen (ed.) *Early Childhood Mathematics*. New York: Macmillan.

Gura, P. (1992) *Exploring Learning: Young Children and Block Play*. London: Paul Chapman.

Hart, K. (1981) Ratio and proportion. In K.M. Hart (ed.) *Children's Understanding of Mathematics: 11–16*. London: Murray.

Healy, L. and Sutherland, R. (1991) *Exploring Mathematics with Spreadsheets*. Hemel Hempstead: Simon and Schuster.

Hendrickson, A.D. (1986) Verbal multiplication and division problems: Some difficulties and some solutions. *Arithmetic Teacher*, **April**, 26–33.

HMI (1989) *Aspects of Primary Education: The Teaching and Learning of Mathematics*. London: HMSO.

Hervey, M. (1966) Children's responses to two types of multiplication problems. *Arithmetic Teacher*, **33**, 288–291.

Horril, P.J.F. (ed.) (1986) *Maths A–Z*. Harlow: Longman.

Hughes, M. (1986) *Children and Number*. Oxford: Blackwell.

Jones, G.A., Thornton, C.A., Putt, I.J., Hill, K.M., Mogill, A.T., Rich, B.S. and Van Zoest, L.R. (1996) Multidigit number sense: a framework for instruction. *Journal for Research in Mathematics Education*, **27**(3), 310-336.

Karplus, R., Karplus, E., Formisano, M. and Paulsen, A-C. (1977) A survey of proportional reasoning and control of variables in seven countries. *Journal of Research in Science Teaching*, **13**, 411–417.

Kieren, T.E. (1988) Personal knowledge of rational numbers – Its intuitive and formal development. In J. Hiebert and M. Behrs (eds) *Number Concepts and Operations in the Middle Grades*. Reston, VA: NCTM, Erlbaum.

Kouba, V.L., Carpenter, T.P. and Swafford, J.O. (1989) Number operations. In M.M. Lindquist (ed.) *Results from the Fourth*

Mathematics Assessment of Educational Progress. Reston, VA: NCTM.

Larcombe, A. (1985) *Mathematical Learning Difficulties in the Secondary School*. Milton Keynes: Open University Press.

Leeds City Council Department of Education (1997) *A Framework for Entry Assessment*. Leeds: Leeds City Council.

Liebeck, P. (1990) Scores and forfeits – an intuitive model for integer arithmetic. *Educational Studies in Mathematics*, **21**, 221–239.

Mack, N.K. (1990) Learning fractions with understanding: Building on informal knowledge. *Journal of Research in Mathematics Education*, **21**(1), 16–33.

Malpas, A.J. (1975) Subtraction of negative numbers in the second year: anatomy of a failure. *Mathematics in School*, **July**, 3–5.

Mathematical Association (1970) *Primary Mathematics: A Further Report*. London: Bell.

Matthew, G. (1967) *Nuffield Mathematics Project: I Do, and I Understand*. London: W & R Chambers.

Meadows, S. (1986) *Understanding Child Development*. London: Unwin Hyman.

Moore, I. (1991) *Six Dinner Sid*. Hemel Hempstead: Simon and Schuster.

Müller, D. (1979) Perceptual reasoning and proportion. *Mathematics Teaching*, **87**, 20–22.

Munn, P. (1994) The early development of literacy and numeracy skills. *European Early Childhood Education Research Journal*, **2**(1), 5–19.

Murray, H., Olivier, A. and Human, P. (1991) Young children's division strategies. In F. Furinghetti (ed.) *Proceedings of the 15th International Conference for the Psychology of Mathematics*. Assisi, Italy: Universita di Genova.

Murray, J. (1939) The relative difficulty of the basic number facts. In *Scottish Council for Research in Education Studies in Education. Vol 1*. London: University of London Press.

National Numeracy Strategy (1999) *The Framework for Teaching Mathematics*. London: HMSO.

Neuman, D. (1991) Early conceptions of fractions: a phenomenographic approach. In E. Furinghetti (ed.) *Proceedings of the 15th Conference for the Psychology of Mathematics Education*. Assisi, Italy: Universita di Genova.

Noelting, G. (1980) The development of proportional reasoning and the ratio concept. *Educational Studies in Mathematics*, **11**, 217–253 and 331–363.

Norem, G.B. and Knight, F.B. (1930) The learning of the one hundred multiplication combinations. In *The 29th Year-book of the National Society for the Study of Education: Report on the Society's Committee on Arithmetic*. Bloomington, IL: Public School Publishing Co.

Nunes, T. and Bryant, P. (1996) *Children Doing Mathematics*. Oxford: Blackwell.

Ohlsson, S. and Bee, N. (1991) Intra-individual differences in fractions arithmetic. In E. Furinghetti (ed.) *Proceedings of the 15th Conference for the Psychology of Mathematics Education*. Assisi, Italy: Universita di Genova.

Orton, A. (1992) *Learning Mathematics: Issues, Theory and Classroom Practice*. London: Cassell.

Orton, A. (1999) *Pattern in the Teaching and Learning of Mathematics*. London: Cassell.

Orton, J. and Orton, A. (1996) Making sense of children's patterning. In L. Puig and A. Gutiérrez (eds) *Proceedings of the 20th International Conference for the Psychology of Mathematics Education*. Valencia: Universitat de València.

Peck, D.M. and Jencks, S.M. (1981) Conceptual issues in the teaching and learning of fractions. *Journal for Research in Mathematics Education*, **12**(5), 339–348.

Phillips, J.R. (1969) *The Origins of Intellect: Piaget's Theory*. San Francisco: W.H. Freeman.

Qualifications and Curriculum Authority (1999) *Teaching Mental Strategies: Guidance for Teachers at Key Stages 1 and 2*. London: Department for Education and Employment.

Rawson, B. (1993) Searching for pattern. *Education 3–13*, **21**(3), 26–33.

Rees, R. and Barr, G. (1984) *Diagnosis and Prescription in the Classroom: Some Common Maths Problems*. London: Harper & Row.

Resnick L.B. and Ford W.W. (1981) *The Psychology of Mathematics for Instruction*. Hillsdale, NJ: Erlbaum.

Resnick, L.B., Nesher, P., Leonard, F., Magone, M., Omanson, S. and Peled, I. (1989) Conceptual bases or arithmetic errors: the case of decimal fractions. *Journal for Research in Mathematics Education*, **20**(1), 8–27.

Sawyer, W.W. (1955) *Prelude to Mathematics*. Harmondsworth: Penguin Books.

Sawyer, W.W. (1964) *Vision in Elementary Mathematics*. Harmondsworth: Penguin Books.

School Curriculum and Assessment Authority (1995) *Report on the 1995 Key Stage 2 Tests and Tasks in English, Mathematics and Science*. London: SCAA.

School Curriculum and Assessment Authority (1996a) *Nursery Education: Desirable Outcomes for Children's Learning on Entering Compulsory Education*. London: SCAA.

School Curriculum and Assessment Authority (1996b) *Report on the 1996 Key Stage 2 Tests and Tasks in English, Mathematics and Science*. London: SCAA.

School Curriculum and Assessment Authority (1997) *Looking at Children's Learning*. London: SCAA.

Scottish Office Education Department (1991) *Curriculum and Assessment in Scotland, National Guidelines: Mathematics 5–14*. Edinburgh: Scottish Office.

Sewell, B. (1981) *Use of Mathematics by Adults in Daily Life*. Leicester: The Advisory Council for Adult and Continuing Education.

Skemp. R.R. (1971) *The Psychology of Learning Mathematics*. Harmondsworth: Penguin Books.

Skemp, R.R. (1976) Relational understanding and instrumental understanding, *Mathematics Teaching*, **77**, 20–26.

Stacey, K. (1989) Finding and using patterns in linear generalising problems. *Educational Studies in Mathematics*, **20**, 147–164.

Steward, D. (1996) 3 Tasks. *Mathematics in Schools*, **25**(2), 14–17.

Stewart, I. (1975) *Concepts of Modern Mathematics*, Harmondsworth: Penguin Books.

Streefland, L. (1984) Search for the roots of ratio: some thoughts on the long term learning process. *Educational Studies in Mathematics*, **15**, 327-348.

Sutherland, R. (1989) Providing a computer-based framework for algebra thinking. *Educational Studies in Mathematics*, **20**, 317–344.

Sutherland, R. (1990) The potential of computer-based environments. In P. Dowling and R. Noss (eds) *Mathematics versus the National Curriculum*. Basingstoke: The Falmer Press.

Thompson, I. (ed.) (1997) *Teaching and Learning Early Number*. Buckingham: Open University Press.

Threlfall, J. (1996) The role of practical apparatus in the teaching and learning of arithmetic. *Educational Review*, **48**(1), 3–12.

Threlfall, J. (1999) Repeating patterns in the early primary years. In A. Orton (ed.) *Pattern in the Teaching and Learning of Mathematics*. London: Cassell.

Threlfall, J. and Frobisher, L. (1998a) *Starting Mental Maths Strategies*. Oxford: Heinemann.

Threlfall, J. and Frobisher, L. (1998b) *Teaching Mental Maths Strategies, Books 3 to 6*. Oxford: Heinemann.

Threlfall, J. and Frobisher, L. (1999) Patterns in processing and learning addition facts. In A. Orton (ed.) *Pattern in the Teaching and Learning of Mathematics*. London: Cassell.

Thyer, D. and Maggs, J. (1971) *Teaching Mathematics to Young Children*. Eastbourne: Holt, Rinehart & Winston.

van Reeuwijk, M. (1995) Students' knowledge of algebra. In L. Meira and D. Carraher (eds) *Proceedings of the 19th International Conference for the Psychology of Mathematics Education*. Recife: Universidade Federal de Pernambuco.

Van Lehn, K. (1990) *Mind Bugs: The Origins of Procedural Misconceptions*. London: MIT Press.

Vergnaud, G. (1983) Multiplicative structures. In R. Lesh and M. Landau (eds) *Acquisition of Mathematics Concepts and Processes*. London: Academic Press.

Ward, M. (1979) *Mathematics and the 10-year-old*. London: Evans.

Watanabe, T. (1994) Children's notion of units and mathematical knowledge. In J.P. da Ponte and J.F. Matos (eds) *Proceedings of the 18th Conference for the Psychology of Mathematics Education*. Vol. 4, 361–368. Lisbon: University of Lisbon.

Wood, D. (1988) *How Children Think and Learn*. Oxford: Blackwell.

Index